Patrick Kevin Foley

American Authors

Patrick Kevin Foley

American Authors

ISBN/EAN: 9783337389451

Printed in Europe, USA, Canada, Australia, Japan

Cover: Foto ©ninafisch / pixelio.de

More available books at **www.hansebooks.com**

AMERICAN AUTHORS

1795–1895

A BIBLIOGRAPHY OF FIRST AND NOTABLE EDITIONS
CHRONOLOGICALLY ARRANGED WITH NOTES

BY P. K. FOLEY

WITH AN INTRODUCTION BY
WALTER LEON SAWYER

BOSTON
PRINTED FOR SUBSCRIBERS
1897

Five Hundred Copies, Octavo.

No. 64

COPYRIGHT 1897 BY P. K. FOLEY

OF CERTAIN BOOKS—AND MEN.

When the wind was east and a sullen sky lowered upon a sodden street, seven students slept and dreamed. In his dream each visited a bookshop and from an ignoble resting-place drew a bundle of pamphlets. There was an Amherst catalogue in the collection, and there was also a speech by Daniel Webster. An Old Farmer's Almanac neighbored a sermon by the Reverend Shear Jashub Baalam on The Iniquity of Unitarianism and A List of Lighthouses and Fog-Signals in the United States. Next came the Annual Report of the New York Central Railroad for 1882: and under it were six copies of "Tamerlane, by a Bostonian," which the enraptured dreamer bought for five cents apiece.

This is the Tamerlane mythus, read by the light of reason. In the accepted version, the collector—there was but one, and he was awake,—sneered unfeelingly and put the pamphlets back: but any book-hunter who has had experience of Special Providences, (as all have) will find this quite too incredible for fable, even. And since Special Providences are matter of record, and since, moreover, no man can—or durst—name the collector who did this thing, knowledge must revise the tale and science must explain it. Seven collectors dreamed; the dream was so vivid that it lingered in memory as the apotheosis of a familiar story; by telepathy the story was transferred to the dreamers' sympathetic acquaintance —say, seven hundred. Each man recalls it, in one or other reading, so often as he does or does not overlook a bargain. At the full of the moon and in the midsummer silly season it gets into the newspapers.

In all seriousness, it is safe to discredit—on general principles —any narrative which fails to recognize the sweet little cherub that sits up aloft keeping watch for the luck of the collector. Sooner or later, whether the book flaunts in a window or hides in a garret, the man to whom it belongs is irresistibly drawn to it. Such an one would intuitively divine that the inconspicuous volume lettered "Il Pesceballo" enshrined the words of Lowell; that the "Incidental Poems" of Robert Dinsmoor, Rustic Bard, was the medium of Whittier's first appearance in book form; that the unlovely earthern jar offered at auction in a Maine village (and knocked down, by the way, at ten cents), contained an impossible razor *and* "Fanshawe." Thanks to this blessed principle, or force, or power,—which perhaps it were impious to seek to define—the book-lover may dabble in odd volumes, even. His personal cherub successfully solicited a Boston man to buy the second volume of Matthew Arnold's "Poems" in the edition of 1869,—an unregarded trifle in a dealer's odds and ends. News of the purchase came to a fellow in the gentle art; and presently the Bostonian received from him the first volume in the same edition, which had been picked up at auction in another city. The Philistine will say that this is improbable: and so it is: but it is true: and equally true is the correlative that, as the fly-leaves showed, these two volumes originally belonged to the same man, and met in the hands of another disciple after Heaven knows what wandering and mischance!

All this of course suggests the axiom that a prize may offer anywhere and at any moment. In the catalogue of a New England public library, "My Summer in a Garden" is classified as "Agriculture"; and under the general title, "Medicine," and the subtitle, "Pathology: Diseases," the unconscious humorist who perpetrated the book has listed Defoe's "Journal of the Plague in London." At first glance, the connection between first editions and a certain Connecticut town is not half so apparent as the silken thread of fancy that attaches Mr. Warner to the farming interest. Yet in that Connecticut town a man I love discovered Lowell's own copy of the Birmingham Address, a very treasure-house of corrections and notes in autograph,—and bore it away for twenty-five cents! I might add that in the same place, on another occasion, my friend found "The Rose and the Ring," blushing, as it were, in its original pink boards—blushing, perhaps, for that it occupied a fifteen-cent counter. But such reminiscences are distracting; and they are useless: for the Connecticut bookseller is dead, and no more bargains linger in an unlikely place to refresh the spirit of the collector who goes that way.

I pause here to drop a tear for the bookseller. Peace to his ashes! He was not wholly of them who sell books as butchers sell mutton, by the pound, the bones with the meat; but he had been; and though from the commercial point of view it seems a sad thing that he should die before he learned the value of his stock, there is warning for others in the circumstance that as he became sophisticated his health failed. Doubtless it would be easy to demonstrate that to buy at five cents and sell for twenty-five is the only rule of conduct calculated to preserve a dealer in body and mind. There was notably one man in the circle of my professional acquaintance who prospered by this means. Yet he has fallen. Injudicious patrons have offered him of the fruit of the tree of knowledge, and he has eaten. His former principle of business now applies to none save drygoods editions—which he sells to the gentlemen who boast that they "buy books for the contents." I foresaw the end, when he began to prattle of "firsts." Soon he became curious in bindings. Next he was aware of the extra-illustrator and re-revised his price-list in a commendable endeavor to make the punishment fit the crime; but now he finds that the collector of book-plates must also be reckoned with: and in the attempt to adjust his tariff to the needs or caprices of five several classes of purchasers, he ages visibly.

When under one's very eyes a worthy tradesman undergoes this process of degeneration, one sighs for the days of the Crofts sale, when original quarto editions of Shakespeare's plays fetched from one to eleven shillings apiece; or one wishes that he might at least have attended the Elliot Woodward auction, in 1869, and bought "A Year's Life" for twenty-five cents. (Mr. Foote's copy realised thirty-three dollars.) Always it seems that the time has been when black swans and pink pearls were less rare than they are at present, when robins nested in January, and when the bookworm lifted up his voice in song under the poor man's window. Some day. under pressure of this conviction, I think I shall take to the road. Your true Yankee never destroys anything but his neighbor's vices. He will not throw away a book. There are early Poes and Hawthornes, not to speak of Freneaus and Mathers, stuffed in barrels, stored in barn-chambers, in any of the older villages, waiting the advent of the collector who shall be brave enough to set up a peddler's cart. Dares any affirm that that man will not buy a Bay Psalm Book with a tin teapot?

I grant that the hero of such a quest may fall victim to the superstition that every printed thing is worthy—a form of dementia to which the collector who rigidly restricts himself to a specialty is perhaps peculiarly liable. But if he survives he will bring back —not the spoil of the land alone, but—enthralling memories of natives who carry the aforesaid superstition to its logical ultimate, that a volume long preserved must be very valuable. These figure at stated intervals in the suburban correspondence of almost any newspaper as owners of "a book printed more than three hundred years ago," *ergo*, worth a deal of money. For my own part, I have great joy of the citizens of Grangerville who achieve distinction at so cheap a rate. They are amply fellowed in innocent fatuity: but, while other amiable idiots become enlightened and cease to be diverting, the proud possessor of a worthless black-letter is a well-spring of delight, he and his children's children, to the latest generation. The average man can not rebuke his folly: he has not the documents. The collector will not: for in a state of society where, the more charming the catalogue, the more destructive is the subsequent bill, an inexpensive pleasure is a thing sedulously to be maintained.

It is not impossible (there are degrees in folly!) that from this admission some would draw the inference that a book-lover deprecates his outlay. I hasten therefore to approve that noble saying of Erasmus: *Statimque ut pecuniam accepero, Græcos primum auctores, deinde vestes emam.* In this sign we conquer. "And *afterwards* some clothes" expresses, I am sure, the feeling of every true collector. One may inadvertently acquire books that are no books, one may be seduced by "bargains" that future experience disavows, and then one may seek a safe place and indulge in the language that Erasmus doubtless employed under similar conditions. But the man who regrets or apologizes for making the right choice between a new coat and a faultless first is no more worthy to be called collector. Indeed I question whether he who does not persistently and joyously buy books he cannot afford is entitled to all the honor attaching to that name.

Here one might enlarge upon those pleasures of the chase which are revealed to the impecunious alone. Yet the millionaire is a man and a brother; and I could find it in my heart to wish he might experience the emotions that an auction stirs in *us*. (Observe I do not say we attend auctions: rather forego the richest entertainment earth affords—that provided by the woman-who-wants-to-bid—than openly countenance the damnable heresy that law-reports and medical treatises and volumes of sermons are books!) Figure to yourself the collector, removed from obtrusive rivalries and the sordid eloquence of the auctioneer, sitting down with his catalogue to choose the lots he must have and the others that he would like to have. Fancy his earnest questionings whether a certain classic may not at this time respond to a modest bid; whether the "nine volumes" so ambiguously described include first editions; whether in a given instance it will be wiser to say "no limit" or to let the temptation pass and trust a Special Providence at some future time to be made manifest? Picture the debate between bargains and bankruptcy, the occasional conflicts of conscience and inclination, the dreams of what books may come! And finally try to do justice to the resolute and happy heroism that mails a list of bids which may obliterate a month's salary! The man who had a standing order for the Kelmscott Press publications as issued knows naught of these tragic joys. To him who would make trial of a new sensation, all sensations, they are cheap at any price.

It will be quite safe, however, to leave the praise of poverty to the rich, those ardent champions of inexpensive virtues. Only let me confess, before we depart the subject, that discretion fixes a limit to my solicitude for my fellow poor. Since I do not affect omniscience, I decline to decide, even for their benefit, the rival claim of auctioneer and bookseller to the chief place in their regard. And though I have known a judicious smile to reduce the price of a book one-half, I shall not advise them how to encounter the enemy—whether in the trustfulness that (may) win forbearance or in the calm superiority that (may) inspire apologetic awe. Yet surely it is well to warn all and sundry that, while a trick of countenance may sometimes serve one's turn, enduring success in collecting rests upon other foundations, that these are in a measure commercial, and that a book-merchant of whatsoever class may contribute to establish them. Of course a student of catalogues looks to share the reproach of Magliabecchi, that he was a learned man among booksellers and a bookseller among learned men: but perhaps this is not quite so terrible as it sounds. There are booksellers and booksellers, and again there are learned men and—persons who join their titles to their signatures. If it seemed worth while, it would be interesting to contrast a score of book-hunters with an equal number of gentlemen more or less learned, who condemn their pursuit: but we have the courage of our convictions, and we are already vain enough. Let us pass to consider how we may add to our faith knowledge.

And first a word concerning Mr. Foley's experience. When I began to know him, years ago, he was just passing out of the scrapbook stage. At this period one is able to appreciate, willing to collect, almost anything: he cuts up catalogues and toilsomely constructs long lists of books that God permitted to be created and advertised, but never suffers to be sold. It is the young collector's apprenticeship to genuine enthusiasm. If he boggles at the scrapbooks, be sure he will never go further. My friend survived the test. As he gave over the ambition to own a duplicate of every book in the Congressional Library, he began to long for intimate knowledge of a few books, say eight or ten thousand. Then he condensed the scrapbooks into a little volume that, whether for additions or corrections, has accompanied him ever since. It has been my happiness to watch its expansion into this volume. Public and society libraries, dealers' pricelists and private collections have, in the course of the process, suggested details, and to the friends who have been most helpful Mr. Foley will make his own acknowledgment. It is my duty to bear testimony to the untiring zeal and prodigious patience that have carried on a work with which I am proud to be—ever so remotely—associated.

The present enterprise aside, I am sure that Mr. Foley would second me in urging the reader to treasure the suggestion of a home-made, strictly personal, pocket bibliography—a compend of titles, dates, identifying features, and average prices. One may be ever so conversant with authorities, but find at the critical moment that he has forgotten some all-important detail. A portable memorandum will tend then and always to disburden the memory, sustain the purse, and solace the soul. And be it remembered that one's cherub will not strive against willful ignorance and that the Special Providences which may bless the lame seldom accrue to the benefit of the lazy!

Since much of this may seem assured and peremptory, it is time to confess that I have no collection : only a bookcase. I have not even a copy of that "unique" Whittier title, the "Narrative of James Williams," which, once announced, has begun to repeat itself with distressing frequency, as "unique" titles sometimes do —one happy man in Boston exhuming two copies from his anti-slavery collection. Yet since it is permitted to love the things one does not own and to glorify the deeds one can not imitate, I do not apologize for yielding to the temptation to gossip. If opportunity served I would like to speak of, for instance, the rare books that—like the works of Thomas Taylor, the Platonist,—are found in every catalogue. So I might tell how Mrs. Browning bought for her son first editions of Shelley and Keats, and recommend her example to American mothers who may in like manner entertain Robert Brownings unawares. Using the euphemism of the delightful William James, (who wrote, in 1817, of "Military *Occurrences* . . . . between Great Britain and the United States") I could mention those bibliographies which sagacious booksellers might catalogue under the heading, "Facetiæ." Indeed, one who writes of books finds many matters pregnant with eloquent discourse: yet since to some I may seem to have yielded our position, I must turn to right myself, and so make end.

Yet, on second thought, what to the lover of books matters the world's opinion? If he be true man, the lust of possession has never blinded him to worth or worthlessness ; rarity has not become synonymous with value ; things have not usurped the place of qualities. True, he has had his defeats and his successes, like other men,—his little hour of triumph, his days of bitterness and his nights of humiliation. Fortune has frowned on him, perhaps. Friends have misinterpreted his kindest purpose. Often he has failed in his duty to himself, in which, if one rightly perceives it, resides the sum of duties. But, God be thanked, there are friends who have patience and who do not misunderstand, voices that rise above the turmoil audibly to console and strengthen! God be thanked that, though he sin and suffer, he may have fellowship with them that aspire, and the transmitted hope that he may win to their heights and, whether here or otherwhere in the material universe, dwell in the spirit in their clear sunlight!

Thus, by these devious ways, we return to our—dreams? Shall we say the brightest concerns that day when every Horace shall have his Mæcenas and every Dibdin, his Spencer? Not so whilst we seriously consider our books, arch-enemies of frivolity and low aims. *Æsop, Saadi, Cervantes, Regnard, have been taken by corsairs, left for dead, sold for slaves, and know the realities of human life.*

WALTER LEON SAWYER.

Boston, March 1, 1897.

PREFATORY NOTE.

The assumed requirements of the collector, and others likely to feel interest in such a compilation as the present — and these requirements constitute the compiler's law — seeming rather to be served by a reliable reference handbook than by an elaborate essay in bibliography, the lines upon which it has been compiled will be readily apparent. It will also be understood why its scope is limited to the authors of the century indicated, 1795–1895, — the principal creators of American literature: the writings of Jonathan Edwards, the Mathers, and others of ante-revolutionary days, more reasonably demanding classification as "Americana" or "Divinity."

The preceding paragraph will explain why authors whose works are almost wholly of a scientific, political or religious character are omitted, and why occasional pamphlets of similar nature are included only when the literary standing of the author demanded reference to every production. The same rule has been applied to works with which the authors represented were editorially connected.

As an important step towards securing accuracy and fulness of detail the lists prepared of their writings have been submitted to the living authors included, for their approval, and any additions which they might suggest. All have courteously and cordially responded, with very few exceptions, — and of these last no writings are likely to exist save such as are duly chronicled on the publishers' bulletins.

Contributions to magazines, annuals and other serials are not quoted separately, unless, as in the case of Dr. Holmes, the articles, or many of them, have never been reprinted. Reports of commemorative exercises, celebrations, or similar occasions, containing addresses, poems, etc., by eminent authors, and each of itself complete, receive separate mention, as also do notable reprints which experience proves to be more eagerly sought after than the original issues. The Aldrich numbers of the "Vest Pocket" series, not to mention several less recent reprints, very forcibly confirm this assertion.

Whilst it may be urged that the titles of works not wholly the production of the authors to whom they are credited, assume rather formidable proportions, recent experiences prove the Aldrich collector ready to pay a higher price for "Jubilee Days" than for "Poems, by T. B. A."; that the Emerson collector desires the "Sermon at the Ordination of Rev. Chandler Robbins, by Rev. Henry Ware," as eagerly as he does the "Essays" of 1841; that the Holmes collector hungers for "Songs of the Class of 1829," especially the little pamphlet of 1854, as intensely as for "The Harbinger"; that the Lowell worshipper "hunts" assiduously for "Memorial: R. G. S.," and reports of various celebrations, and the Whittierite dreams himself the possessor of the Kenoza Lake pamphlet, or "Incidental Poems of the Rustic Bard." Such examples, and they are only a few of many, make it apparent that in extension of lists the collector will more readily condone sins of commission than those of omission.

In most cases the titles have been copied from the title page; where the work was not accessible the most approved authority was followed. The works of many of the authors included, more especially Cooper and Irving, were published simultaneously in New York and London, and sometimes with alteration of date and title; in such instances it is thought best to quote the American issue, as that most esteemed by collectors.

Believing the author best qualified to decide upon the title of his work, alteration or abbreviation of the original is avoided, unless uniformity and practicability suggested prefixing to the title the designation "edited," or "translated"; or where such titles as "Narrative of Arthur Gordon Pym, etc.," made abbreviation seem advisable. In such exceptions the condensation is indicated by "leaders," and the reading retained is such as not to obscure identification of title.

In details as to size, date and place of publication, etc., the methods observed in compiling the higher class of modern catalogues commend themselves as most comprehensive and effective for the collector's purpose, and are accordingly adopted. Where place or date of publication is omitted from title page, such additions appear in brackets, thereby rendering unnecessary the repetition of "n. p.; n. d.," etc. Other additions by the compiler will also appear in brackets, or in the form of notes appended to certain titles.

When a work is credited to an author and his (or her) connection therewith is not indicated on the title page, to facilitate identification such work is included in the alphabetically arranged lists of anonymous and pseudonymous titles, even though the author's name should appear in the index or appended to his contribution. With the same view a title is termed anonymous where the title page is so, even if the work be copyrighted by the author, or his name, initials or pseudonym appear in connection with the introduction, notes, or elsewhere. Any work including two or more authors is credited to the author whose contribution occupies first place in arrangement or importance; in all cases of collaboration cross-references indicate the authors represented and remove the necessity of crediting such work to each. A few titles which do not appear in their proper arrangement, owing to errors in transcription and other causes, are appended at the end of the volume.

The points here dwelt upon will, it is hoped, prove explanatory of the lines followed. There remains for the compiler only to express his gratitude to those who have aided him, one of whom, the late beloved Professor Child, of Harvard University, who supplied, and at much personal inconvenience, extensive and important data, has passed beyond the reach of such acknowledgments. Thanks are due, and are hereby tendered, to the several authors and publishers who with unfailing courtesy and kindness answered the demands made upon them, this more especially so in the case of Messrs. Houghton, Mifflin & Co., whose connection with so many notable authors greatly enlarged their proportion of the enquiries; to Charles F. Libbie, Esq., of Boston, whose valuable bibliographical library was generously placed at the compiler's service; to Miss Louise Imogen Guiney, of Auburndale, who kindly supplied from her collection the titles of otherwise inaccessible works of Thomas William Parsons, and to Dr. R. M. Bucke, of London, Ontario, to whom is almost wholly due the credit for the list of Walt Whitman's writings.

P. K. F.

AMERICAN AUTHORS.

ABBEY, HENRY. 1842—

    May Dreams. 12mo. New York, 1862.

    Ralph and other Poems. 16mo. Rondout, N. Y., 1866.

    Stories in Verse. 16mo. New York, 1869.

    Ballads of Good Deeds, and other Verse. 16mo. New York, 1872.

ERRATA.

Page 2, line 32; for 1829, read 1892.
" 4, " 11; " 1870, " 1869.
" 12, " 10; " v., 1853, read v., 1852.
" 14, " 20; " 1882, " 1812.
" 61, " 13; " 12mo., " 8vo.
" 98, " 1; " Frederick, Harold, read Frederic, Harold.
" 129, " 4; " 1876 read 1877.
" 135, " 39; " Sage " Saxe.
Pages 148 and 149; for Hutton, Lawrence, read Hutton, Laurence.
Page 151, line 42, omit iv.
" " " 44, read iv., v., vi., vii.
" 175, " 15; for Italienne, read Italiani.
" 179, " 13; " 1877, read 1876.
" 201, " 31; omit Anonymous.
" 254, " 27; for New York, 1836, read Hartford, 1835.
" 291, " 5; " 1848, read 1849.

(Edited.) Chapters from Jane Austen. 16mo. Boston [1888].

(Edited.) Rhymes, Selections and Phrases. 12mo. Boston [1889].

Dear Old Story-Tellers. Portrait. 12mo. Boston [1889].

(Edited.) The Poets' Year. Oblong 8vo. Boston [1890].

(Edited.) Lyrics of the Hudson, by H. N. Powers. 16mo. Boston [1891].

The Story of Jane Austen's Life. Portrait. 16mo. Chicago, 1891.

The Presumption of Sex: and other Papers. 16mo. Boston, 1892.

AKERS, ELIZABETH [CHASE]. 1832—

Forest Buds from the Woods of Maine. By Florence Percy. 16mo. Boston, 1856.

Poems. 24mo. Boston, 1866.

The Silver Bridge and other Poems. 16mo. Boston, 1886.

Queen Catherine's Rose. 16mo. Dublin and London, 1886.

Two Saints. A Tribute to the Memory of Henry Bergh. . . (Privately printed.) 12mo. 1886.

[Anonymous.] The Triangular Society: Leaves from the Life of a Portland Family. 12mo. Portland, 1886.

The High-Top Sweeting and other Poems. 12mo. New York, 1891.

ALBEE, JOHN. 1833—

St. Aspenquid of Agamenticus. An Indian Legend. (Privately printed.) 12mo. Portsmouth, N. H., 1879.

Literary Art: a Conversation between a Poet, a Painter, and a Philosopher. 16mo. New York, 1881.

Newcastle; Historic and Picturesque. Illustrations. 12mo. Boston, 1884.

Prose Idyls. 12mo. Boston, 1829.

ALCOTT, AMOS BRONSON. 1799-1888.

    Observations on the Principles and Methods of Infant Instruction. 8vo. Boston, 1830.

    The Doctrine and Discipline of Human Culture. 12mo. Boston, 1836.

    The Story without an End. Translated from the German . . . by Sarah Austin; with a Preface, and Key to the Emblems, by A. B. Alcott. Illustrations. 16mo. Boston, 1836.

    Conversations with Children on the Gospels. 2 volumes, 12mo. Boston, 1836-37.

    [Anonymous.] Emerson. Portrait. (Privately printed.) Square 16mo. Cambridge, 1865.

    Tablets. 16mo. Boston, 1868.

    Concord Days. 12mo. Boston, 1872.

    Table Talk. Heliotype title. 16mo. Boston, 1877.

    New Connecticut. An Autobiographical Poem. (Privately printed; 200 copies.) 16mo. Boston, 1881.

    Sonnets and Canzonets. 16mo. Boston, 1882.
        ***The same. With autograph, and photographic portraits. (50 copies.) 16mo. Boston, 1882.

    Ralph Waldo Emerson: an Estimate of his Character and Genius; in Prose and Verse. Portrait and illustrations. 12mo. Boston, 1882.

    New Connecticut: an Autobiographical Poem. Portrait. 16mo. Boston, 1886.

ALCOTT, LOUISA MAY. 1831-1888.

    Flower Fables. Illustrations. 12mo. Boston, 1855.
        ***Republished as Little Lulu's Library. Boston, 1885.

    Hospital-Sketches. 16mo. Boston, 1863.

    Moods. Illustrations. 12mo. Boston, 1864.

    On Picket Duty, and other Tales. 12mo. New York, 1864.

    The Rose Family. 16mo. Boston, 1864.

Morning Glories and other Tales. 12mo. New York, 1867.

Aunt Kip. 8vo. Boston, 1868.

Proverb Stories. 8vo. Boston, 1868.

Psyche's Art. 8vo. Boston, 1868.

Nelly's Hospital. 8vo. [Washington, 1868.]

Little Women; or, Meg, Jo, Beth and Amy. Illustrations. 2 volumes, 16mo. Boston, 1868–69.

Kitty's Class-Day at Harvard. Square 16mo. Boston, 1868.

Concord Sketches. Twelve Photographs from Drawings. By Mary Alcott, with Text by L. M. Alcott. Small 4to. Boston, 1870.

An Old-fashioned Girl. Illustrations. 16mo. Boston, 1870.

Little Men: Life at Plumfield with Jo's Boys. Illustrations. 16mo. Boston, 1871.

Aunt Jo's Scrap-Bag. 6 volumes, 16mo. Boston, 1871–79.

Work. Illustrations. 16mo. Boston, 1873.

Eight Cousins; or, the Aunt-Hill. Illustrations. 16mo. Boston, 1875.

Silver Pitchers, and Independence, a Centennial Love-Story. 16mo. Boston, 1876.

Rose in Bloom: a Sequel to Eight Cousins. Illustrations. 16mo. Boston, 1876.

[Anonymous.] A Modern Mephistopheles. 16mo. Boston, 1877.

Under the Lilacs. Illustrations. 16mo. Boston [1878].

Meadow Blossoms. Illustrations. 4to. New York [1879].

Water-Cresses. Illustrations. 4to. New York [1879].

Sparkles for Bright Eyes. Illustrations. 4to. New York [1879].

Jack and Jill. Illustrations. 16mo. Boston, 1880.

Spinning-Wheel Stories. 16mo. Boston, 1884.

Jo's Boys, and how they turned out : a Sequel to Little Men. 16mo. Boston, 1886.

A Garland for Girls. 16mo. Boston, 1887.

Life, Letters and Journals. Edited by Edna D. Cheney. Portraits and illustrations. 12mo. Boston, 1889.

Comic Tragedies : written by Jo and Meg and acted by the Little Women. Portrait and illustrations. 12mo. Boston, 1893.

***See also THOREAU, H. D.

ALDEN, WILLIAM LIVINGSTON. 1837—

Domestic Explosives and other Sixth Column Fancies. (From The New York Times.) 12mo. New York, 1877.
***An unauthorized edition of Domestic Explosives was published as The Comic Liar, New York, 1882.

Shooting Stars, as observed from the Sixth Column of The Times. Illustrations. 16mo. New York, 1879.

The Canoe and the Flying Proa. 32mo. New York, 1878.

The Moral Pirates. Illustrations. 16mo. New York, 1880.

Christopher Columbus, the First American Citizen. 16mo. New York, 1881.

The Cruise of the Ghost. Illustrations. 16mo. New York, 1882.

The Cruise of the Canoe Club. Illustrations. 16mo. New York, 1883.

The Adventures of Jimmy Brown. Illustrations. 16mo. New York, 1885.

A New Robinson Crusoe. Illustrations. 16mo. New York, 1888.

The Loss of the Swansea. Illustrations. 16mo. Boston [1889].

Trying to find Europe. Illustrations. 16mo. London, 1890.

A Lost Soul. 12mo. London, 1892.

Told by the Colonel. 12mo. New York [1892].

ALDRICH, ANN REEVE. 1866-1892.

> The Rose of Flame and other Poems of Love. 16mo. New York, 1889.
>
> The Feet of Love. Portrait and Illustrations. 12mo. New York, 1890.
>
> Songs about Life, Love, and Death. 16mo. New York, 1892.

ALDRICH, THOMAS BAILEY. 1836—

> The Bells. A Collection of Chimes. By T. B. A. 12mo. New York, 1855.
>
> Daisy's Necklace and what came of it. (A Literary Episode.) 12mo. New York, 1857.
>
> The Course of True Love never did run Smooth. 12mo. New York, 1858.
>
> The Ballad of Babie Bell and other Poems. 12mo. New York, 1859.
>
> Pampinea and other Poems. 16mo. New York, 1861.
>
> Out of his Head, a Romance. 12mo. New York, 1862.
>
> Poems by Thomas Bailey Aldrich. Portrait. 24mo. New York, 1863.
>
> The Poems of Thomas Bailey Aldrich. 24mo. Boston, 1865.
>> *₊* Of the poems comprising this edition, nine (including Friar Jerome's Beautiful Book), pp. 11-97, are now first collected, also At the Morgue, p. 146, and seven of the eight sonnets, pp. 233-240. The omission of the word "been," which should end third line, first stanza, p. 102, indicates the earlier issues of the edition.
>
> Père Antoine's Date-Palm. (Privately Printed.) Small 4to. Boston, 1866.
>
> Pansie's Wish. Small 4to. Boston, 1867.
>
> The Story of a Bad Boy. Illustrations. 12mo. Boston, 1870.
>
> Jubilee Days. An Illustrated Daily Record of the Humorous Features of the World's Peace Jubilee. [16 numbers, June 17-July 4, 1872.] 4to. Boston, 1872.
>> *₊* Edited, anonymously, by T. B. Aldrich and W. D. Howells, who, with E. P. Whipple, were the principal contributors.

Marjorie Daw and other People. 12mo. Boston, 1873.

Prudence Palfrey. Frontispiece. 12mo. Boston, 1874.

Cloth of Gold and other Poems. 16mo. Boston, 1874.

Flower and Thorn. Later Poems. 16mo. Boston, 1877.

Miss Mehetabel's Son [and Père Antoine's Date-Palm]. Illustrations. 32mo. Boston, 1877.

A Midnight Fantasy, and The Little Violinist. Illustrations. 32mo. Boston, 1877.

A Rivermouth Romance. Illustrations. 32mo. Boston, 1877.

The Queen of Sheba. 12mo. Boston, 1877.

Babie Bell. Illustrations. Square 12mo. Boston, 1878.

The Story of a Cat. Translated from the French of Emile de la Bédolliere. Illustrations. 12mo. Boston, 1879.

The Stillwater Tragedy. 12mo. Boston, 1880.

The Little Violinist. Reprinted with the Author's Permission and sold at the Fair of the Massachusetts Society for the Prevention of Cruelty to Children. Square 12mo. [Cambridge,] 1880.

Friar Jerome's Beautiful Book, and other Poems. 16mo. Boston, 1881.

XXXVI Lyrics and XII Sonnets. 16mo. Boston, 1881.
  *₀*The two preceding volumes consist of selections from Cloth of Gold, and Flower and Thorn.

Poems. Illustrated by the Paint and Clay Club. Portrait on steel, and 28 illustrations. 8vo. Boston, 1882.
  *₀*Also 6 copies printed on Japan paper for presentation by the author. 8vo. Boston, 1882.

From Ponkapog to Pesth. 12mo. Boston, 1883.

Mercedes and Later Lyrics. Small 8vo. Boston, 1884.

Poems. Household Edition [newly revised]. Portrait. 12mo. Boston, 1885.

(With M. O. W. Oliphant.) The Second Son. A Novel. 12mo. Boston, 1888.

Wyndham Towers. Small 8vo. Boston, 1890.

The Sisters' Tragedy, with other Poems, Lyrical and Dramatic. Small 8vo. Boston, 1891.

An Old Town by the Sea. 16mo. Boston, 1893.

Two Bites at a Cherry, with other Tales. 16mo. Boston, 1894.

Mercedes. A Tragedy . . . As produced at Palmer's Theatre. 12mo. Boston, 1894.

Unguarded Gates and other Poems. 12mo. Boston, 1895.
*₊*Of this work 50 copies were issued wholly uncut, with paper labels. 12mo. Boston, 1895.

The Story of a Bad Boy. With New Preface. Illustrations by A. B. Frost. 12mo. Boston, 1895.
*₊*See also BRYANT, W. C.; HOLMES, O. W.; SILL, EDWARD R.; STEDMAN, E. C.

ALLEN, JAMES LANE . . .

Flute and Violin, and other Kentucky Tales and Romances. 12mo. New York, 1891.

The Blue-Grass Region of Kentucky, and other Kentucky Articles. Illustrations. 8vo. New York, 1892.

John Gray: a Kentucky Tale of the Olden Time. Portrait. 12mo. Philadelphia, 1893.

A Kentucky Cardinal. Illustrations. Square 16mo. New York, 1895.

ALLSTON, WASHINGTON. 1779–1843.

The Sylphs of the Seasons, with other Poems. 12mo. London, 1813.
*₊*Also 16mo. Boston, 1813.

[Anonymous.] Monaldi: a Tale. 12mo. Boston, 1841.

Lectures on Art and Poems. Edited by R. H. Dana, Jr. 12mo. Boston, 1850.

Outlines and Sketches. Engraved by I. and S. W. Cheney. Oblong 4to. Boston, 1850.

Life and Letters, by Jared D. Flagg. Full-Page Reproductions of Allston's Paintings. Square 8vo. New York, 1892.

APPLETON, THOMAS GOLD. 1812-1884.

    Faded Leaves. [By] T. G. A. Frontispiece. Small 4to. Boston. 1872.

    A Sheaf of Papers. By T. G. A. 16mo. Boston, 1874.

    A Nile Journal. Illustrations. 12mo. Boston, 1876.

    Syrian Sunshine. Frontispiece. 16mo. Boston, 1877.

    [Anonymous.] Boston Museum of the Fine Arts. A Companion to the Catalogue. 16mo. Boston, 1877.

    Windfalls. 16mo. Boston, 1878.

    Chequer Work. Illustrations. 16mo. Boston, 1879.

    Life and Letters. Prepared by Susan Hale. Portrait. 12mo. New York, 1885.

ARNOLD, GEORGE. 1834-1865.

    Drift: a Sea-Shore Idyl, and other Poems. [Edited, with a memoir, by William Winter.] Portrait. 16mo. Boston, 1866.

    Poems Grave and Gay. [Edited by William Winter.] 16mo. Boston, 1867.

    Poems [complete edition]; edited, with Biographical Sketch, by William Winter. Portrait. 12mo. Boston, 1871.

AUSTIN, JANE GOODWIN. 1831-1894.

    Fairy Dreams, or Wanderings in Elf-Land. Square 16mo. Boston, 1860.

    [Anonymous.] Dora Darling: the Daughter of the Regiment. Engraved title. 16mo. Boston, 1865.

    Outpost: a Novel. 16mo. Boston, 1866.

    Cipher: a Novel. Illustrations. 8vo. New York, 1869.

    The Shadow of Moloch Mountain. Illustrations. 8vo. New York, 1870.

    Moonfolk: a True Account of the Home of the Fairy Tales. Illustrations. 8vo. New York, 1874.

[Anonymous.] Mrs. Beauchamp Brown. 16mo. Boston, 1880.

[Anonymous.] A Nameless Nobleman. 16mo. Boston, 1881.

[Anonymous.] The Desmond Hundred. 16mo. Boston, 1882.

Nantucket Scraps; or the Experiences of an Off-Islander, in Season and out of Season. 16mo. Boston, 1882.

Standish of Standish: a Story of the Pilgrims. 12mo. Boston, 1889.

Doctor Le Baron and his Daughter: a Story of the Old Colony. 12mo. Boston, 1890.

Betty Alden. The First-Born Daughter of the Pilgrims. 12mo. Boston, 1891.

David Alden's Daughter and other Stories of Colonial Times. 12mo. Boston, 1892.

BALLOU, MATURIN MURRAY. 1820—

Biography of Rev. Hosea Ballou. 12mo. Boston, 1852.

History of Cuba, or Notes of a Traveller in the Tropics. Illustrations. 12mo. Boston, 1854.

Miralda, or the Justice of Tacoma. A Drama... 12mo. New York [1858].

Fanny Campbell, the Female Pirate Captain. A Tale of the Revolution. By Lieut. Murray. 16mo. New York [1860].

Treasury of Thought, forming an Encyclopædia of Quotations from Ancient and Modern Authors. 8vo. Boston, 1871.

Pearls of Thought. 16mo. Boston, 1881.

(Edited.) Notable Thoughts about Women. A Literary Mosaic. 12mo. Boston, 1882.

Due West, or Around the World in Ten Months. 12mo. Boston, 1884.

Due South; or, Cuba, Past and Present. 12mo. Boston, 1885.

(Edited.) Edge-Tools of speech. 8vo. Boston, 1886.

Under the Southern Cross. Travels in Australia, Tasmania, New Zealand, Samoa and other Pacific Islands. 12mo. Boston, 1887.

Due North, or Glimpses of Scandinavia and Russia. 12mo. Boston, 1887.

Genius in Sunshine and Shadow. 12mo. Boston, 1887.

Footprints of Travel; or, Journeyings in Many Lands. 12mo. Boston, 1888.

The New Eldorado. A Summer Journey to Alaska. 12mo. Boston, 1889.

Aztec Land. 12mo. Boston, 1890.

Equatorial America. Descriptive of a Visit to St. Thomas, Martinique and the Principal Capitals of South America. 12mo. Boston, 1892.

The Story of Malta. 12mo. Boston, 1893.

The Pearl of India. 12mo. Boston, 1894.

BANCROFT, GEORGE. 1800–1892.

Poems. 12mo. Cambridge, 1823.

Prospectus of a School to be established at Round Hill, Northampton, Mass. By George Bancroft and Joseph Green Cogswell. 8vo. [Cambridge, 1823.]

Greek Grammar, by Philip Carl Buttman, abridged [by George Bancroft]. Folded plate. 16mo. Paris, 1824.

(Translated.) Reflections on the Politics of Ancient Greece, by A. H. L. Heeren. 8vo. Boston, 1824.

(Edited.) The Latin Reader, from the Fifth German Edition, by Frederick Jacobs. 16mo. Northampton, 1825.

De Vita Excellentium Imperatorum of Cornelius Nepos; from the 3d Edition of J. H. Bremi. Edited, with English Notes [by George Bancroft]. 12mo. Boston, 1826.

An Oration delivered on the Fourth of July, 1826, at Northampton, Mass. 8vo. Northampton, 1826.

(Translated.) A History of the Political Systems of Europe, by A. H. L. Heeren. 2 volumes, 8vo. Northampton, 1829.

Review of the Report of the Committee of Ways and Means; and of the Message of the President of the United States Relative to the United States Bank. 8vo. Philadelphia, 1831.

History of the United States. Portraits, maps and illustrations. 10 volumes, 8vo. Boston, 1834-75.
  _{*} i., 1834; ii., 1837; iii., 1840; iv., 1852; v., 1853; vi., 1854; vii., 1858; viii., 1860; ix., 1866; x., 1875.
  *_{*}*The same. Large paper. (50 copies.) 10 volumes, royal 8vo. 1861-75.

Oration delivered before the Democracy of Springfield and Neighboring Towns, July 4, 1836. 8vo. Springfield, 1836.

Address at Hartford, before the Delegates of the Democratic Convention of the Young Men of Connecticut, Feb. 18, 1840. 8vo. [Hartford, 1840.]

History of the Colonization of the United States. Abridged by the Author. [Not republished.] Maps and plates. 2 volumes, 16mo. Boston, 1841.

Monument to the Memory of Andrew Jackson. By B. M. Dusenbury. [Eulogy by George Bancroft, Washington, June 27, 1845, pp. 33-51.] 8vo. Nashua, 1846.

The Semi-Centennial Celebration of the New York Historical Society, Nov. 20, 1854. [Oration by George Bancroft, The Necessity, the Reality, and the Promise of the Progress of the Human Race, pp. 5-37, and speech by W. C. Bryant, pp. 69-70.] 8vo. New York, 1854.

Miscellanies. 8vo. New York, 1855.

The Life of F. W. von Steuben, by Frederick Kapp. With an Introduction by George Bancroft. Portrait. 12mo. New York, 1859.

Letter on the Exchange of Prisoners during the American War of Independence. 8vo. [New York, 1862.]

Oration on the 22d of February, 1862. To which is added Washington's Farewell Address. [Comprising] No. 29, Pulpit and Rostrum. 12mo. New York, April 15th, 1862.

Mr. Bancroft and his Boston Critics. 8vo. [New York, 1862.]

The League for the Union. Speeches by George Bancroft and James Milliken. 8vo. Philadelphia, 1863.

Life of Edward Livingston, by C. H. Hunt. With Introduction by George Bancroft. 8vo. New York, 1864.
*⁎*The same. Large paper. (100 copies.) 2 portraits on India paper. 4to. New York, 1864.

Oration . . . . April 25, 1865, at the Funeral Obsequies of Abraham Lincoln. Pulpit and Rostrum, Nos. 34 and 35. Portrait. 12mo. New York, 1865.

Memorial Address on the Life and Character of Abraham Lincoln. Portrait. 8vo. Washington, 1866.
*⁎*The same, with nine additional pages. Large paper. (50 copies.) 4to. Washington, 1866.

Life of Philip II. of Spain, by Charles Gayarre. With Introductory Letter by George Bancroft. 8vo. New York, 1866.

Joseph Reed: a Historical Essay. Portrait. 8vo. New York, 1867.

History of the Formation of the Constitution of the United States. 2 volumes, 8vo. New York, 1882.

History of the United States; with the Author's Latest Revisions. 6 volumes, 8vo. New York, 1884–86.

A Plea for the Constitution of the United States, wounded in the House of its Guardians. 32mo. New York, 1886.

Martin Van Buren to the End of his Public Career. 8vo. New York, 1889.
*⁎*See also BRYANT, W. C.; and IRVING, W.

BANGS, JOHN KENDRICK. 1862—

[Anonymous.] Roger Camerden, a Strange Story. 16mo. New York, 1886.

(With S. W. Van Schaik.) The Lorgnette. Illustrations. Square 16mo. New York, 1886.

Katherine, a Travesty. (Privately printed.) 16mo. [New York] 1888.

Mephistopheles: a Profanation. (Privately printed.) 16mo. New York, 1888.

(With Frank D. Sherman.) New Waggings of Old Tales. By Two Wags. Illustrations. 16mo. Boston, 1888.

Tiddledywink Tales. Illustrations. 12mo. New York, 1891.

In Camp with a Tin Soldier. Illustrations. 12mo. New York, 1892.

The Tiddledywinks' Poetry-book. Illustrations. Oblong 12mo. New York, 1892.

Coffee and Repartee. Illustrations. 32mo. New York, 1893.

Half Hours with Jimmieboy. Illustrations. 12mo. New York, 1893.

Toppleton's Client; or, a Spirit in Exile. 12mo. London, 1893.

Three Weeks in Politics. Illustrations. 32mo. New York, 1894.

The Water Ghost. Illustrations. 16mo. New York. 1894.

The Idiot. Illustrations. 16mo. New York, 1895.

Mr. Bonaparte of Corsica. 16mo. New York, 1895.

BARLOW, JOEL. 1755-1882.

The Prospect of Peace: a Poetical Composition, delivered in Yale College, July 23, 1778. 12mo. New York, 1778.

[Anonymous.] An Elegy on the Late Honorable Titus Hosmer, Esq.; One of the Counsellors of the State of Connecticut. 16mo. Hartford, 1780.

[Anonymous.] Poem spoken at the Public Commencement at Yale College, New Haven, Sept. 11, 1781. 8vo. Hartford [1781].

A Translation of Sundry Psalms, which were omitted in Dr. Watts' Version; to which is added a Number of Hymns. 12mo. Hartford, 1785.

The Vision of Columbus; a Poem in Nine Books. 8vo. Hartford, 1787.

An Oration delivered at the North Church in Hartford, at the Meeting of the Connecticut Society of the Cincinnati, July 4, 1787. 4to. Hartford [1787].

The Conspiracy of Kings: a Poem addressed to the Inhabitants of Europe, from another Quarter of the World. 8vo. Paris, 1792.
  *₊*The same. 8vo. Newburyport, 1793.

Advice to the Privileged Orders in the Several States of Europe, resulting from the Necessity and Propriety of a General Revolution in the Principle of Government. Parts 1 and 2. 8vo. Paris, 1792–93.
  *₊*The same. London, 1792–93; New York, 1792–94.

A Letter to the National Convention, on the Defects in the Constitution of 1791. To which is added The Conspiracy of Kings: a Poem. 8vo. New York [1793].

The Vision of Columbus; a Poem in Nine Books. The Fifth Edition, corrected. To which is added The Conspiracy of Kings: a Poem. 8vo. Paris, 1793.

A Letter addressed to the People of Piedmont. Translated from the French by the Author. 12mo. New York, 1795.

"The Hasty Pudding," a Poem in Three Cantos. Written at Chambery in Savoy, January, 1793. 8vo. New York, 1796.

Political Writings. A New Edition, corrected. 12mo. New York, 1796.

[Anonymous.] The Second Warning; or Strictures on the Speech of John Adams, President of the United States, at the Opening of Congress in November Last. 8vo. Paris, 1798.

Letters to his Fellow-Citizens of the United States (i.) on the System of Policy hitherto pursued by their Government, and (ii.) on Certain Political Measures proposed to their Consideration. 8vo. [Paris, 1799.]
  *₊*The same. 8vo. London, 1800; 8vo. Philadelphia, 1801.

A Second Letter to his Fellow-Citizens of the United States. . . 8vo. New York, 1801.

Two Letters to the Citizens of the United States, and One to General Washington . . . . on our Political and Commercial Relations. 12mo. New Haven, 1806.

[Anonymous.] Prospectus of a National Institution to be established in the United States. 8vo. Washington, 1806.

The Columbiad: a Poem. Portrait and 11 plates. 4to. Philadelphia, 1807.

Letter to Henry Gregoire in Reply to his Letter on the Columbiad. 8vo. Washington, 1809.

The Columbiad. With Last Corrections of the Author. 4 plates. Royal 8vo. Paris, 1813.

The Vision of Columbus. With Explanatory Notes. From a revised Edition of the Author. 16mo. New York, 1814.

Life and Letters, with Extracts from his Works, and hitherto unpublished Poems, by Charles B. Todd. Portrait. 8vo. New York, 1886.

BARTLETT, JOHN. 1820 —

A Collection of Familiar Quotations, with Complete Indices of Authors and Subjects. 12mo. Cambridge, 1855.

A New Method of Chess Notation. 12mo. Cambridge, 1857.

Familiar Quotations: being an Attempt to trace to their Sources, Passages and Phrases in Common Use. 16mo. Boston, 1868.
  ***The same. Large paper. (100 copies.) Small 8vo. Boston, 1868.

The Shakespeare Phrase-Book. Square 12mo. Boston, 1881.

Catalogue of Books on Angling, including Icthyology, Pisciculture, Fisheries and Fishing Laws. Square 8vo. Boston, 1882.

[Anonymous.] Choice Thoughts from Shakespeare. 8vo. London, 1886.

A|New and Complete Concordance or Verbal Index to Words, Phrases, and Passages in the Dramatic Works of Shakespeare, with a Supplementary Concordance to the Poems. 4to. New York, 1894.

BARTLETT, JOHN RUSSELL. 1805-1886.

The Progress of Ethnology: An Account of Recent Archæological, Philological and Geographical Researches in Various parts of the Globe tending to elucidate the Physical History of Man. 8vo. New York, 1847.

Dictionary of Americanisms. A Glossary of Words and Phrases, usually regarded as Peculiar to the United States. 8vo. New York, 1848.
  ***The same. Large paper. (10 copies.) Royal 8vo. New York, 1848.

Reminiscences of Albert Gallatin. 8vo. New York, 1849.

Personal Narrative of Explorations and Incidents in Texas, New-Mexico, California and Chihuahua. Map and illustrations. 2 volumes, 8vo. New York, 1854.

The Literature of the Rebellion. A Catalogue of Books and Pamphlets relative to the Civil War. . . . (250 copies.) 8vo. Boston, 1866.
  ***The same. Large paper. (60 copies.) Royal 8vo. Boston, 1866.

Memoirs of Rhode Island Officers . . . . during the Great Rebellion. Plate and 34 portraits. 4to. Providence, 1867.
  ***Mr. Bartlett also compiled a bibliography of Rhode Island (8vo., and royal 8vo., 1864), and edited several works treating on Rhode Island local history.

BATES, ARLO. 1850 —

[Anonymous.] Patty's Perversities. 16mo. Boston, 1881.

F. Seymour Haden and Engraving. (Privately printed.) Square 16mo. Boston, 1882.

[Anonymous.] Mr. Jacobs: a Tale of the Drummer, the Reporter and the Prestidigitateur. 32mo. Boston, 1883.

The Pagans. 16mo. New York, 1884.

A Wheel of Fire. 12mo. New York, 1885.

Berries of the Brier. 16mo. Boston, 1886.

(Edited.) Old Salem, by Eleanor Putnam. 16mo. Boston, 1886.
  ***The same. Large paper. (20 copies.) 8vo. Boston, 1886.

Sonnets in Shadow. 16mo. Boston, 1887.

A Lad's Love. 16mo. Boston, 1887.

(With Eleanor Putnam.) Prince Vance. The Story of a Prince with a Court in his Box. Illustrations. Square 12mo. Boston, 1888.

The Philistines. 12mo. Boston, 1889.

Albrecht. 16mo. Boston, 1890.

A Book o' Nine Tales. 16mo. Boston, 1891.

The Poet and his Self. 16mo. Boston, 1891.

Told in the Gate. 12mo. Boston, 1892.

In the Bundle of Time. 16mo. Boston, 1893.

Poem: The Torch-Bearers: delivered at the Centennial Celebration of the Incorporation of Bowdoin College, June 28, 1894. 8vo. Boston, 1894.

BELLAMY, EDWARD. 1850 —

Six to One: A Nantucket Idyl. Square 16mo. New York, 1878.

Dr. Heidenhoff's Process. 16mo. New York, 1879.

Miss Ludington's Sister. A Romance of Immortality. 16mo. Boston, 1884.

Looking Backward. 2000–1887. 12mo. Boston, 1888.

BENJAMIN, PARK. 1809–1864.

A Poem on the Meditation of Nature, spoken Sept. 26th, 1832. . . . 8vo. Hartford, 1832.

(Edited.) The New World: a Weekly Family Journal of Popular Literature, Science, Art and News. Illustrations. 8 volumes, 4to. New York, 1841–44.

Poetry: a Satire, pronounced before the Mercantile Library Association, at its 22d Anniversary. 8vo. New York, 1842.

Infatuation: a Poem spoken before the Mercantile Library Association of Boston, Oct. 9, 1844. 8vo. Boston, 1844.

The Book of British Ballads. Edited by S. C. Hall. With Preliminary Remarks to each Ballad, and an Introduction by Park Benjamin. 8vo. New York, 1844.

Wayside Flowers: a Collection of Poems. By Mrs. M. St. Leon Loud. [With preface, pp. v.–viii., by Park Benjamin.] Portrait. 12mo. Boston, 1851.

*.*See also HOLMES, O. W.

BENJAMIN, SAMUEL GREENE WHEELER. 1837 —

    Constantinople, The Isle of Pearls, and other Poems. 16mo. Boston, 1860.

    Ode on the Death of Abraham Lincoln. 12mo. Boston, 1865.

    The Turk and the Greek, or Creeds, Races, Society and Scenery, in Turkey, Greece, and the Isles of Greece. 12mo. New York, 1867.

    Tom Roper: a Story of Travel. Illustrations. 16mo. Philadelphia, 1868.

    The Choice of Paris. A Romance of the Troad. 12mo. New York, 1870.

    (Translated, anonymously.) Advice of a Father to a Son, imitated from the Latin of Muretus, by N. Francois. 8vo. Albany, 1871.

    What is Art? or, Art Theories and Methods concisely stated. 8vo. Boston, 1877.

    Contemporary Art in Europe. Illustrations. Royal 8vo. New York, 1877.

    The Atlantic Islands as Resorts of Health and Pleasure. Illustrations [by the author and others]. 8vo. New York, 1878.

    The Multitudinous Seas. Illustrations. 16mo. New York, 1879.

    Our American Artists. Illustrations. 2 volumes, 4to. Boston [1879–81].

    The World's Paradises; or, Sketches of Life, Scenery, and Climate in Noted Sanitaria. 16mo. New York, 1880.

    Art in America. A Critical and Historical Sketch. Illustrations. Square 8vo. New York, 1880.

    Troy: its Legend, History and Literature, with a Sketch of the Topography of the Troad, in the Light of Recent Investigations. 16mo. New York, 1880.

    A Group of Etchers. 20 full-page etchings. (500 copies.) Folio. New York, 1882.

    The Cruise of the Alice May, in the Gulf of St. Lawrence and Adjoining Waters. Illustrations. 8vo. New York, 1884.

    Persia and the Persians. Portrait and illustrations [by the author and others]. Square 8vo. Boston, 1887.

    The Story of Persia. Illustrations. 12mo. New York, 1887.

    Sea Spray; or, Facts and Fancies of a Yachtsman. 16mo. New York, 1888.

BIRD, ROBERT MONTGOMERY. 1803-1854.

    [Anonymous.] Calavar; or, the Knight of the Conquest: a Romance of Mexico. 2 volumes, 12mo. Philadelphia, 1834.

    The Infidel; or, the Fall of Mexico: a Romance. [A sequel to Calavar.] 2 volumes, 12mo. Philadelphia, 1835.

    [Anonymous.] The Hawks of Hawk Hollow. A Tradition of Pennsylvania. 2 volumes, 12mo. Philadelphia, 1835.

    [Anonymous.] Sheppard Lee. 2 volumes, 12mo. Philadelphia, 1836.

    Nick of the Woods; or, Jibbenainosay. A Tale of Kentucky. 2 volumes, 12mo. Philadelphia, 1837.

    [Anonymous.] Peter Pilgrim: or, a Rambler's Recollections. 2 volumes, 12mo. Philadelphia, 1838.

    The Adventures of Robin Day. 2 volumes, 12mo. Philadelphia, 1839.

BISHOP, WILLIAM HENRY. 1847 —

    Detmold. 18mo. Boston, 1879.

    Old Mexico and her Lost Provinces: a Journey to Mexico, South California, and Arizona. Illustrations. 12mo. New York, 1883.

    The House of a Merchant Prince: a Novel of New York. 12mo. Boston, 1883.

    Choy Susan and other Stories. 12mo. Boston, 1885.

    Fish and Men in the Maine Islands. Illustrations. 16mo. New York, 1885.

The Golden Justice. 12mo. Boston, 1887.

The Brown Stone Boy and other Queer People. 12mo. New York [1888].

[Anonymous.] Sergeant Von, or a Long Chase. 12mo. New York [1889].

The Yellow Snake: a Story of Treasure. 12mo. New York [1891].

(Translated.) The Faience Violin, by Champfleury [Jules Fleury]. 12mo. New York, 1893.

A Pound of Cure. A Story of Monte Carlo. 16mo. New York, 1894.

Writing to Rosina. Illustrations. 16mo. New York, 1894.

The Garden of Eden, U. S. A., a very Probable Story. 12mo. Chicago, 1895.

BLOEDE, GERTRUDE (STUART STERNE). 1845—

Poems. 4to. New York, 1874.

Angelo. A Poem. 18mo. Boston, 1878.

Giorgio and other Poems. 16mo. Boston, 1881.

Beyond the Shadow and other Poems. Square 16mo. Boston, 1888.

Piero da Castiglione. 18mo. Boston, 1890.

The Story of Two Lives. 12mo. New York, 1891.

BOKER, GEORGE HENRY. 1823-1890.

The Lesson of Life and other Poems. 12mo. Philadelphia, 1847.

Calaynos: a Tragedy. Square 12mo. Philadelphia, 1848.

Anne Boleyn: a Tragedy. 12mo. Philadelphia, 1850.

The Podesta's Daughter and other Poems. 16mo. Philadelphia, 1852.

Plays and Poems. 2 volumes, 12mo. Boston, 1856.

The Second Louisiana. May 27, 1863. Broadside.

Poems of the War. 12mo. Boston, 1864.

Our Heroic Themes: a Poem read .... Harvard University, July 20th, 1865. 16mo. Boston, 1865.

[Anonymous.] Tardy George. '(Privately printed; 60 copies.) 4to. New York, 1865.

[Anonymous.] How McClellan took Manassas. (Privately printed; 50 copies.) 4to. New York, 1865.

Konigsmark, The Legend of the Hounds and other Poems. 12mo. Philadelphia, 1869.

The Book of the Dead. 12mo. Philadelphia, 1882.
*,*See also TAYLOR, BAYARD.

BOLLES, FRANK. 1856-1894.

(With E. L. Baylies and E. M. Parker.) A Collection of Important English Statutes, showing the Principal Changes in the Law of Property; together with some other Enactments of Common Reference. 4to. Cambridge, 1880.
*,*Other editions, two at least, were brought out by Mr. Bolles alone.

Harvard University. A Brief Statement of what Harvard University is, how it may be entered, and how its Degrees may be obtained. 8vo. Cambridge [1891].

Land of the Lingering Snow. Chronicles of a Stroller in New England from January to June. 16mo. Boston, 1891.

At the North of Bearcamp Water. Chronicles of a Stroller in New England from July to December. 16mo. Boston, 1893.

Students' Expenses. A Collection of Letters from Undergraduates, Graduates and Professional School Students. Describing in Detail their Necessary Expenses at Harvard University. With an Introduction. 8vo. Cambridge, 1893.

From Blomidon to Smoky, and other Papers. 16mo. Boston, 1894.

Chocorua's Tenants. Illustrations. 16mo. Boston, 1895.

BOYESEN, HJALMAR HJORTH. 1848-1895.

Gunnar. A Tale of Norse Life. 18mo. Boston, 1874.

A Norseman's Pilgrimage. 12mo. New York, 1875.

Tales from Two Hemispheres. 18mo. Boston, 1876.

Falconberg: a Novel. Illustrations. 12mo. New York, 1878.

Goethe and Schiller. Their Lives and Works; with a Commentary on Faust. 12mo. New York, 1878.

Queen Titania. 12mo. New York, 1881.

Ilka on the Hill-Top and other Tales. 12mo. New York, 1881.

Idyls of Norway and other Poems. 16mo. New York, 1882.

[Anonymous.] A Daughter of the Philistines. 16mo. Boston, 1883.

The Story of Norway. Illustrations. 12mo. New York, 1886.

The Modern Vikings: Stories of Life and Sport in the Northland. Illustrations. 12mo. New York, 1887.

Vagabond Tales. 12mo. Boston, 1889.

The Light of her Countenance. 12mo. New York, 1889.

Against Heavy Odds, and A Fearless Trio. Illustrations. 12mo. New York, 1890.

The Mammon of Unrighteousness. 12mo. New York, 1891.

Essays on German Literature. 12mo. New York, 1892.

The Golden Calf. 12mo. Meadville, 1892.

Boyhood in Norway. Illustrations. 12mo. New York, 1892.

Social Strugglers. 12mo. New York, 1893.

A Commentary on the Writings of Henrik Ibsen. 12mo. New York, 1894.

Literary and Social Silhouettes. Portrait. 16mo. New York, 1894.

Norseland Tales. Illustrations. 12mo. New York, 1894.

Essays on Scandinavian Literature. 12mo. New York, 1895.

BRAINARD, JOHN GARDINER CALKINS. 1796–1828.

Occasional Pieces of Poetry. 12mo. New York, 1825.

The Literary Remains of John G. C. Brainard. With a Sketch of his Life [pp. 7-36]. By John G. Whittier. 12mo. Hartford [1832].

Poems. A New and Authentic Collection, with an Original Memoir of his Life [by J. G. Whittier]. Portrait. 16mo. Hartford, 1842.

BRIGGS, CHARLES FREDERICK. 1804-1877.

Harry Franco: A Tale of the Great Panic. 2 volumes, 12mo. New York, 1837.

Bankrupt Stories. By Harry Franco. Illustrations. 8vo. New York, 1843.

The Haunted Merchant. 12mo. New York, 1843.

Working a Passage, or Life in a Liner. 12mo. New York, 1844.

The Trippings of Tom Pepper: an Autobiography. 8vo. New York, 1844.

(With others, anonymously.) Seaweeds from the Shores of Nantucket. 12mo. Boston, 1853.

(Edited, with G. P. Putnam, anonymously.) Homes of American Authors; comprising Anecdotical, Personal and Descriptive Sketches. By Various Writers [W. C. Bryant, G. W. Curtis and others]. Portraits and illustrations. 8vo. New York, 1853.

(With Augustus Maverick.) The Story of the Telegraph and the History of the Atlantic Cable. Portrait and illustrations. 12mo. New York, 1858.
 *˳*See also POE, EDGAR A.

BRISTED, CHARLES ASTOR (CARL BENSON). 1820-1874.

A Letter to the Hon. Horace Mann: being a Reply to Certain Attacks on Stephen Girard, and John Jacob Astor, in a Work entitled Thoughts for a Young Man. 18mo. New York, 1850.

The Upper Ten Thousand: Sketches of American Society. By A New Yorker. 12mo. London, 1852.

Five Years in an English University. 2 volumes, 12mo. New York, 1852.

Pieces of A Broken-Down Critic picked up by Himself. 8vo. New York, 1858.
 *˳*The same. 4 volumes. 8vo. Baden-Baden, 1858-59.

The Cowards' Convention. 8vo. New York [1862].

A Few Words of Warning to New Yorkers on the Consequence of a Railroad in Fifth Avenue. 8vo. New York, 1863.

No Surrender. 12mo. [New York, 1863.]

A Letter to Dr. Henry Halford Jones, Editor of The Wintertown Democrat [Josiah G. Holland, of The Springfield Republican], concerning his Habit of giving Advice to Everybody and his Qualifications for the Task. 8vo. New York, 1864.

The Interference Theory of Government. 16mo. New York, 1867.

Fancy Signatures. 8vo. [New York, 1869.]

On the Pronunciation of Languages; practically considered with Reference to Teaching. 8vo. New York, 1870.

Anacreontics. Engraved title. (Privately printed.) Small 4to. New York, 1872.

BROOKS, CHARLES TIMOTHY. 1813-1883.

A Poem pronounced before the Phi Beta Kappa Society, at Cambridge. . . . 8vo. Boston, 1845.

Aquidneck: a Poem. . . . with other Commemorative Pieces. 16mo. Providence, 1848.

Slovenly Peter. 8vo. New York, 1849.

[Anonymous.] The Controversy touching the Old Stone Mill. . . . Newport, R. I. With Remarks, Introductory and Conclusive. 12mo. Newport, 1851.

Songs of Field and Flood. 12mo. Boston, 1853.

Roman Rhymes: being Winter Work for a Summer Fair. 12mo. Cambridge, 1869.

William Ellery Channing: a Centennial Memory. Portrait and illustrations. 12mo. Boston, 1880.

Poems, Original and Translated: selected and edited by W. P. Andrews. With a Memoir by C. W. Wendte. 12mo. Boston, 1885.

*.*Mr. Brooks also published several translations from the German (including the works of Richter), for a complete list of which see appendix to the 1885 edition of Poems, pp. 231-235; see also HOWE, JULIA WARD.

BROOKS, MARIA. 1795-1845.

    Judith, Esther, and other Poems. By A Lover of the Fine Arts. 16mo. Boston, 1820.

    Zóphiël [first canto] and other Poems. 18mo. Boston, 1825.

    Zóphiël; or the Bride of Seven [and other poems]. By Maria del Occidente. 16mo. London and Boston, 1833.
        *.*Reprinted, for the benefit of the Polish exiles, 16mo. Boston, 1834.

    Idomen; or the Vale of Yumuri. (Privately printed.) 12mo. New York, 1843.
        *.*A new edition of Mrs. Brooks' poems, edited, with memoir, by Mrs. Z. B. Gustafson, and containing poems previously uncollected, was published, 12mo. Boston, 1879.

BROUGHAM, JOHN. 1814-1880.

    A Basket of Chips. Illustrations. 12mo. New York, 1855.

    The Bunsby Papers. Illustrations. 12mo. New York, 1856.

    Life in New York. 12mo. New York, 1856.

    Irish Echoes. Illustrations. 12mo. New York, 1856.

    Humorous Stories. 12mo. New York, 1857.

    Poem [The Age of Gold] : delivered before the Theta Delta Chi Society, . . . April 29th, 1857. 8vo. New York, 1857.

    (Edited, with John Elderkin.) Lotus Leaves. Original Stories, Essays and Poems. [By John Hay, Mark Twain, Brougham and others.] Square 8vo. Boston, 1875.

    Life, Stories and Poems. Edited [with memoir] by William Winter. Portraits, facsimiles and illustrations. 12mo. Boston, 1881.
        *.*Brougham was also the author of numerous plays — they numbered one hundred and fourteen in 1857 — almost all of which appeared in French's American Drama series. A collective edition (edited by R. S. Mackenzie) was announced in 1857, but was never completed.

BROWN, CHARLES BROCKDEN. 1771–1810.

    Alcuin: a Dialogue on the Rights of Women. 16mo. New York, 1797.

    [Anonymous.] Wieland; or, the Transformation. An American Tale. 16mo. New York, 1798.

    Ormond; or, the Secret Witness. 16mo. New York, 1799.

    [Anonymous.] Arthur Mervyn; or, Memoirs of the Year 1793. 2 volumes, 12mo. Philadelphia, 1799.

    Arthur Mervyn. Second Part. 12mo. New York, 1800.

    Edgar Huntley; or, the Memoirs of a Sleepwalker; with Cicero, a Fragment. 3 volumes, 12mo. Philadelphia, 1801.

    Clara Howard. 16mo. Philadelphia, 1801.

    [Anonymous.] Address to the Government of the United States, on the Cession of Louisiana. 8vo. [Philadelphia] 1803.
        *₀*The same. A new edition, revised. 8vo. Philadelphia, 1803.

    The Literary Magazine and American Register. [Edited by C. B. Brown, who was also the principal contributor.] 8 volumes, 8vo. Philadelphia, 1803–1807.

    Jane Talbot: a Novel. Plate. 16mo. Philadelphia, 1804.

    A View of the Soil and Climate of the United States of America; with Supplementary Remarks upon Florida, on the French Colonies of the Mississippi and Ohio and in Canada; by the Comte de Volney. Translated, with Occasional Remarks, by C. B. Brown. Maps and plates. 12mo. Philadelphia, 1804.

    Valerian, a Narrative Poem. . . . by John Blair Linn. [With memoir of the author by C. B. Brown.] 4to. Philadelphia, 1805.

    The British Treaty. 8vo. [Philadelphia, 1807.]

    The British Treaty with America; with an Appendix of State Papers which are now First published. 8vo. London, 1808.

[Anonymous.] An Address to the Congress of the United States on the Utility and Justice of Restrictions upon Foreign Commerce. With Reflections on Foreign Trade in General and the Future Prospects of America. 8vo. Philadelphia, 1809.

Beauties of Tom Brown; by C. H. Wilson. Edited, with biography of the author, by C. B. Brown. 12mo. London, 1810.

**See also DUNLAP, WILLIAM.

BROWNE, CHARLES FARRAR (ARTEMUS WARD). 1834-1867.

Artemus Ward: his Book. Illustrations. 12mo. New York, 1862.

Artemus Ward: his Travels. Illustrations. 12mo. New York, 1865.

Betsey Jane Ward: hur Book of Goaks. Illustrations. 12mo. New York [1866]. [Ascribed to Browne.]

Artemus Ward in London, and other Papers. Illustrations. 12mo. New York, 1867.

Artemus Ward's Panorama. As exhibited at the Egyptian Hall, London. Edited by his Executors, T. W. Robertson and E. P. Hingston. Illustrations. 12mo. New York, 1869.

Complete Works. With Memoir by E. P. Hingston. Portraits, facsimiles and illustrations. Small 8vo. London [1869].

Sandwiches. Illustrations. 8vo. New York, 1870.

BROWNELL, HENRY HOWARD. 1820-1872.

Poems. 12mo. New York, 1847.

The People's Book of Ancient and Modern History. 8vo. Hartford, 1851.

The Discoverers, Pioneers and Settlers of North and South America, from the Earliest Period to the Present Time. . . . 8vo. Boston, and Cincinnati, 1853.

Ephemeron. A Poem. 12mo. New York, 1853.

The People's Book of American History. 2 volumes, 8vo. Hartford, 1854.

Lyrics of a Day; or Newspaper Poetry. By A Volunteer in the U. S. Service. 12mo. New York, 1864.

War-Lyrics and other Poems. 12mo. Boston, 1866.

Poems [complete edition]. 12mo. New York, 1867.

Gulf-Weed. [A poem.] Third Annual Reunion of the Society of the Army and Navy of the Gulf, Newport, July 7th, 1871. Broadside. [Newport, 1871.]

BRYAN, DANIEL. . . .

The Mountain Muse: comprising The Adventures of Daniel Boone, and The Power of Virtuous and Refined Beauty. 12mo. Harrisonburg, Va., 1813.

The Day of Gratitude; Poems occasioned by the Recent Visit of Lafayette to the United States. 8vo. Philadelphia, 1826.

The Appeal for Suffering Genius [R. S. Coffin, The Boston Bard]: a Poem. 8vo. Washington, 1826.

Thoughts on Education and its Connexion with Morals: a Poem. 8vo. Richmond, 1830.

BRYANT, WILLIAM CULLEN. 1794-1878.

The Embargo; or, Sketches of the Times; Satire. By A Youth of Thirteen. 12mo. Boston, 1808.

The Embargo; or Sketches of the Times. A Satire. The Second Edition, corrected and enlarged, together with The Spanish Revolution and other Poems. 12mo. Boston, 1809.

Poems. 8vo. Cambridge, 1821.

(Edited, with R. C. Sands, anonymously.) The Atlantic Magazine. 8vo. New York, 1824.

(Edited, with R. C. Sands, anonymously.) The New York Review and Athenæum Magazine. 2 volumes, 8vo. New York, 1825-26.

[Anonymous.] Miscellaneous Poems selected from The United States Literary Gazette. 18mo. Boston, 1826.
***Of the poems twenty-three are by W. C. Bryant and fourteen by H. W. Longfellow.

(Edited, anonymously.) The United States Review and Literary Gazette. [October, 1826-September, 1827.] 2 volumes, 8vo. Boston and New York, 1826-27.

[Anonymous.] The Talisman, for 1828, 1829, 1830. Plates. 3 volumes, 18mo. New York, 1827, 1828, 1829.

*₊*Conducted by W. C. Bryant (who contributed fifteen poems and thirteen prose sketches), G. C. Verplanck, and R. C. Sands.

The American Landscape. Engraved from Original and Accurate Drawings; with Historical .... Illustrations [by W. C. Bryant]. 4to. New York, 1830.

Poems [including many now first collected]. 12mo. New York, 1832.
*₊*Part of the edition was issued with Boston imprint, 1832.

Tales of the Glauber Spa. By Several American Authors. 2 volumes, 12mo. New York, 1832.
*₊*Edited by Bryant, who also contributed the introduction, vol. i., pp. 5-19, and the tales, The Skeleton's Cave, and Medfield, vol. i., pp. 193-276. The remaining tales were Child Roeliff's Pilgrimage, and Selim, by J. K. Paulding; Le Bossu, by Catherine Sedgwick; Mr. Green, and Boyuca, by R. C. Sands, and The Block-House, by W. Leggett.

Poems. [Third edition, enlarged.] 12mo. Boston, 1834.

Poems. [Newly revised, with additions.] Vignette. 12mo. New York, 1836.
*₊*Of the copies bearing this date some are designated "third edition" and copyrighted 1836, whilst the copies designated "fourth edition" are copyrighted 1835.

The Jubilee of the Constitution, a Discourse delivered .... New York .... 30th of April, 1839; being the 50th Anniversary of the Inauguration of George Washington as President of the United States. ... By John Quincy Adams. [Together with a report of the Celebration, including ode by Bryant, p. 124, and ode by Grenville Mellen, pp. 135-136.] Frontispiece. 8vo. New York, 1839.

(Edited.) Selections from the American Poets. 18mo. New York, 1840.

Popular Considerations on Homœopathia. 8vo. New York [1841].

The Fountain and other Poems. 12mo. New York, 1842.

An Address to the People of the United States, in Behalf of the American Copyright Club, adopted at New York, Oct. 18, 1843. 8vo. New York, 1843.

The White-Footed Deer and other Poems. 12mo. New York, 1844.

Poems. Portrait and illustrations. 8vo. Philadelphia, 1847.

A Funeral Oration, occasioned by the Death of Thomas Cole, delivered before the National Academy of Design. . . . 8vo. New York, 1848.

Letters of a Traveller in Europe and America. 12mo. New York, 1850.

The Picturesque Souvenir. Letters of a Traveller; or Notes of Things seen in Europe and America. Illustrations. Square 8vo. New York, 1851.

A Memorial of James Fenimore Cooper. [Consisting of discourse by Bryant, pp. 39-74, and tributes by Bancroft, Irving. Melville, Emerson, Hawthorne, Prescott, Simms, Longfellow, and others.] Portrait. 8vo. New York, 1852.

Poems. Collected and arranged by the Author [with corrections, and poems not included in previous editions]. 2 volumes, 12mo. New York, 1854.

Poems. [With introduction not published elsewhere.] 12mo. Dessau, 1854.

Celebration of the 200th Anniversary of the Town of Bridgewater, June 3, 1856. [Hymn, by Bryant, pp. 18-19.] Illustrations. 8vo. Boston, 1856.

Letters of a Traveller. Second Series. 12mo. New York, 1859.

Gifts of Genius: a Miscellany of Prose and Poetry by American Authors [including Longfellow, Lowell, Holmes, Aldrich, and Morris]. With a Preface [and contributions] by W. C. Bryant. 12mo. New York, 1859.

Celebration of the 200th Anniversary of the Settlement of Hadley, Mass., June 8, 1859. . . . [Ode by Bryant, pp. 70-71.] 8vo. Northampton, 1859.

A Discourse on the Life, Character and Genius of Washington Irving, delivered . . . . April 3, 1860. 12mo. New York, 1860.

A Forest Hymn. Illustrations. Square 8vo. New York [1860].

Poems [newly revised]. 24mo. New York, 1862.

Only Once. Original Papers, by Various Contributors [including Bryant, Lowell, Whittier and Bayard Taylor]. Published for the Benefit of the New York Infirmary for Women and Children. Portraits. 4to. New York [1862].

Thirty Poems. 12mo. New York, 1864.

A Year in China, and a Narrative of Capture and Imprisonment when Homeward Bound, on Board the Rebel Pirate Florida. By Mrs. H. Dwight Williams. With Introductory Notes by William Cullen Bryant. 12mo. New York, 1864.

Voices of Nature. Illustrations. Square 16mo. New York, 1865.

Obsequies of Abraham Lincoln, in the City of New York, under the Auspices of the Common Council. By David Valentine. [Oration by George Bancroft, pp. 163-175, and Funeral Ode, by Bryant, p. 191.] Portrait and illustrations. Royal 8vo. New York, 1866.

Dinner to Señor Matias Romero, Envoy Extraordinary and Minister Plenipotentiary from Mexico, 29 March, 1866. [Address by Bryant, pp. 26-28.] 4to. New York, 1866.

A History of the Celebration of Robert Burns' 110th Natal Day, at the Metropolitan Hotel. New York. [Address by Bryant, pp. 31-33.] 8vo. Jersey City, 1869.

Some Notices of the Life and Writings of Fitz-Greene Halleck. (Privately printed.) 8vo. New York, 1869.

Hymns. (Privately printed.) 12mo. [New York, 1869.]

Letters from the East. 12mo. New York, 1869.

Discourse on the Life and Character of Giulian C. Verplanck. 8vo. New York, 1870.

(Translated.) The Iliad of Homer. 2 volumes, royal 8vo. Boston, 1870.

(Translated.) The Odyssey of Homer. 2 volumes, royal 8vo. Boston, 1871.

The Song of the Sower. Illustrations. Square 8vo. New York, 1871.

(Edited.) A Library of Poetry and Song. Portrait. 8vo. New York, 1871.

Poems. [Newly revised, with additions.] Square 16mo. New York, 1871.

The Gospel in the Trades. By Alexander Clark. With an Introduction by W. C. Bryant. 8vo. Philadelphia, 1871.

(Edited.) Picturesque America; or, the Land we live in. A Delineation by Pen and Pencil of . . . . . . our Country. Illustrations. 2 volumes (or 48 parts), royal 4to. New York, 1871-74.

The Story of the Fountain. Illustrations. Square 8vo. New York, 1872.

The Little People of the Snow. Illustrations. Square 8vo. New York, 1873.

Orations and Addresses. 12mo. New York, 1873.

A Memorial of the Inauguration of Ward's Statue of Shakespeare in the Central Park. [With address by Bryant and poems by R. H. Stoddard, Bayard Taylor, John Brougham and others.] Illustrations. (Privately printed; 40 copies.) 8vo. New York, 1873.

Among the Trees. Illustrations. Square 8vo. New York, 1874.

(With Sidney Howard Gay.) A Popular History of the United States, from the First Discovery of the Western Hemisphere by the Northmen, to the End of the Civil War. Preceded by a Sketch of the Pre-Historic Period and the Age of the Mound Builders. Portraits and illustrations. 4 volumes (or 51 parts), 8vo. New York, 1876-81.

To William Cullen Bryant at Eighty Years, from his Friends and Countrymen. [Addresses by Bryant, pp. 21-24, and 43-45.] Frontispiece. 8vo. New York, 1876.

Poems [including many now first collected]. Collected and arranged by the Author. Portrait and illustrations. Square 8vo. New York [1876].

Studies in Bryant: a Text-Book. By Joseph Alden. With an Introduction [pp. 5-10] by W. C. Bryant. 16mo. New York, 1876.

A Happy New Year. Carriers' Address, 1877. [The Flood of Years.]. 8vo. [New York, 1876.]
 *.*Also issued with illustrations. 8vo. New York, 1877.

Tribute to W. C. Bryant, by R. C. Waterston, at the Meeting of the Massachusetts Historical Society, June 13, 1878. With an Appendix [including Bryant's last address, at the unveiling of the bust of Mazzini, pp. 47-51]. 8vo. Boston, 1878.

A New Library of Poetry and Song. Newly revised and edited with Introduction [by Bryant] and Memoir [by R. H. Stoddard]. Portraits and illustrations. 2 volumes (or 21 parts,—the final part consisting of memoir), 4to. New York, 1878.

Poetical Works. Household Edition. 12mo. New York, 1879.

Thoughts on Religious Life, by Joseph Alden. With an Introduction [pp. 7-12] by W. C. Bryant. Square 16mo. New York, 1879.

Biography, with Extracts from his Private Correspondence [and juvenile and other poems now first published]. By Parke Godwin. Portraits. 2 volumes, square 8vo. New York, 1883.

Poetical Works. Edited by Parke Godwin. Portraits. 2 volumes, square 8vo. New York, 1883.

Complete Prose Writings. Edited by Parke Godwin. Portraits. 2 volumes, square 8vo. New York, 1884.

Complete Works of Shakespeare. Edited by W. C. Bryant, assisted by E. A. Duycinck. Illustrations. 3 volumes, 4to. New York, 1886.

***See also BANCROFT, G.; BRIGGS, C. F.; DANA, R. H.; HOLMES, O. W.; PAULDING, J. K.; and WARNER, C. D.

BUNNER, HENRY CUYLER. 1855-1896.

A Woman of Honor. 16mo. Boston, 1883.

Airs from Arcady and Elsewhere. 16mo. New York, 1884.
***The same. Large paper (36 copies for private distribution). 8vo. New York, 1884.

The Midge. 12mo. New York, 1886.

The Story of a New York House. Illustrations. 12mo. New York, 1887.

(With others.) A Portfolio of Players. Illustrations. 4to. New York, 1888.
***The same, with proof impressions of the illustrations. 4to. New York, 1888.

Short Sixes. Stories to be read while the Candle burns. Illustrations. 16mo. New York, 1891.

Zadoc Pine and other Stories. 12mo. New York, 1891.

The Runaway Browns. Illustrations. 12mo. New York, 1892.

Rowen. "Second-Crop" Songs. 12mo. New York, 1892.

Made in France: French Tales re told with a U. S. Twist. Illustrations. 12mo. New York, 1893.

A Selection of [56] Cartoons from Puck, by Joseph Keppler, with Text and Introduction by H. C. Bunner. (300 copies.) 4to. New York, 1893.

More Short Sixes. Illustrations. 12mo. New York, 1895.
***See also MATTHEWS, BRANDER.

BURDETTE, ROBERT JONES. 1844 —

The Rise and Fall of the Mustache and other "Hawk-Eyetems." Illustrations. 12mo. Burlington, Iowa, 1877.

Hawkeyes. 12mo. New York, 1879.

William Penn, 1644-1718. 16mo. New York, 1882.

Innach Garden and other Comic Sketches. 12mo. New York, 1886.

BURLEIGH, WILLIAM HENRY. 1812-1871.

Poems. 12mo. Philadelphia, 1841.

Our Country: its Dangers and its Destiny: a Desultory Poem. . . . 12mo. Allegheny, Pa., 1841.

The Republican Pocket Pistol. Facts, Opinions, and Arguments for Freedom. 2 parts, 8vo. New York, 1860.

The Rum Fiend. 12mo. New York, 1871.

Poems. With a Sketch of his Life, by Celia Burleigh. Portrait. 12mo. New York, 1871.

BURNETT, FRANCES HODGSON. 1849 —

That Lass o' Lowrie's. Illustrations. 12mo. New York, 1877.

Theo. 12mo. Philadelphia [1877].

Dorothy. 12mo. Philadelphia, 1877.
₀ Republished as Vagabondia, Boston, 1883.

Kathleen. A Love Story. 12mo. Philadelphia, 1877.

Surly Tim and other Stories. 12mo. New York, 1877.

Our Neighbour Opposite. 12mo. London, 1878.

Lindsay's Luck. 16mo. New York, 1878.

Quiet Life. Square 16mo. Philadelphia [1878].

Miss Crespigny. Square 16mo. Philadelphia [1878].

Pretty Polly Pemberton. Square 16mo. Philadelphia [1878].

Haworth's. Illustrations. 12mo. New York, 1879.

Natalie and other Stories. 12mo. London, 1879.

The Tide on the Moaning Bar. 12mo. London, 1879.

Jarl's Daughter and other Stories. 12mo. Philadelphia [1879].

Louisiana. 12mo. New York, 1880.

A Fair Barbarian. 16mo. Boston, 1881.

Through One Administration. 12mo. Boston, 1883.

Little Lord Fauntleroy. Illustrations. 8vo. New York, 1886.

Sara Crewe; or, what happened at Miss Minchin's. Illustrations. 8vo. New York, 1888.

Editha's Burglar. A Story for Children. Illustrations. Square 12mo. Boston, 1888.

Miss Defarge [also Brueton's Bayou, by John Habberton]. 12mo. Philadelphia, 1888.

The Pretty Sister of José. Illustrations. 12mo. New York, 1889.

Little Saint Elizabeth and other Stories. Illustrations. 8vo. New York, 1890.

Giovanni and the other: Children who have made Stories. 8vo. New York, 1892.

The Drury Lane Boys' Club. 32mo. Washington, 1892.

The One I knew the Best of all: a Memory of the Mind of a Child. Illustrations. 12mo. New York, 1893.

Piccino and other Child Stories. Illustrations. 8vo. New York, 1894.

Two Little Pilgrims' Progress: a Story of the City Beautiful. 8vo. New York, 1895.

BURROUGHS, JOHN. 1837 —

Notes on Walt Whitman as Poet and Person. 16mo. New York, 1867.
*.*The same. Second edition, with additions. 12mo. New York, 1871.

Wake – Robin. 16mo. New York, 1871.

Winter Sunshine. 16mo. New York, 1875.

Birds and Poets with other Papers. 16mo. Boston, 1877.

Wake – Robin. Second Edition, corrected [with additional chapter on the blue-bird]. 16mo. New York, 1877.

Locusts and Wild Honey. 16mo. Boston, 1879.

Pepacton. 16mo. Boston, 1881.

Essays from the Critic. By John Burroughs, E. C. Stedman, Walt Whitman, R. H. Stoddard . . . and others. 12mo. Boston, 1882.

Fresh Fields. 16mo. Boston, 1884.

Signs and Seasons. 16mo. Boston, 1886.

Indoor Studies. 16mo. Boston, 1889.

Riverby. 16mo. Boston, 1894.

Works. Etched frontispieces and engraved title-pages. 9 volumes, 12mo. Boston, 1895.

The Natural History of Selborne, by Gilbert White. With an Introduction by John Burroughs. Illustrations. 2 volumes, 12mo. New York, 1895.

BUTLER, WILLIAM ALLEN. 1825—

    Barnum's Parnassus; being Confidential Disclosures of the Prize Committee on the Jenny Lind Song. 12mo. New York, 1850.

    [Anonymous.] Nothing to wear: an Episode of City Life. Illustrations. 16mo. New York, 1857.

    Two Millions. Illustrations. 16mo. New York, 1858.

    Martin Van Buren: Lawyer, Statesman and Man. 16mo. New York, 1862.

    [Anonymous.] Memorial of Charles H. Marshall. Portrait. 8vo. New York, 1867.

    Poems. 16mo. Boston, 1871.

    Lawyer and Client; their Relations, Rights and Duties. 16mo. New York, 1871.

    [Anonymous.] Mrs. Limber's Raffle, or a Church Fair and its Victims. 16mo. New York, 1877.

    Domesticus. A Tale of the Imperial City. 12mo. New York, 1886.

    The Revision of the Statutes of the State of New York, and the Revisers. An Address . . . . . January 22, 1889. Portraits. Square 8vo. New York, 1889.

    Oberammergau, 1890. Illustrations. 4to. New York, 1891.

        *₀*See also TAYLOR, BAYARD.

BYNNER, EDWIN LASSETTER. 1842–1893.

    [Anonymous.] Nimport. 16mo. Boston, 1877.

    Tritons. A Novel. 16mo. Boston, 1878.

    [Anonymous.] Damen's Ghost. 16mo. Boston, 1881.

    Penelope's Suitors. 24mo. Boston, 1887.

    Agnes Surriage: a Romance of Colonial Massachusetts. 12mo. Boston, 1887.

    (With Lucretia P. Hale.) An Uncloseted Skeleton. 12mo. Boston, 1888.

The Begum's Daughter. Illustrations. 12mo. Boston, 1890.

The Chase of the Meteor and other Stories. Illustrations 12mo. Boston, 1891.

Zachary Phips. 12mo. Boston, 1892.

CABLE, GEORGE WASHINGTON. 1844 —

Old Creole Days. 12mo. New York, 1879.

The Grandissimes. 12mo. New York, 1880.

Madame Delphine. Square 12mo. New York, 1881.

Dr. Sevier. 12mo. New York, 1884.

The Creoles of Louisiana. Illustrations. 8vo. New York, 1884.

The Silent South [also, The Freedman's Case in Equity and Convict Lease System]. Portrait. 16mo. New York, 1885.

Bonaventure. 12mo. New York, 1888.

The Negro Question. 8vo. New York, 1888.

Strange True Stories of Louisiana. Illustrations. 12mo. New York, 1889.

The Southern Struggle for Pure Government. 8vo. Boston. 1890.

[Anonymous.] A Memory of Roswell Smith. Portrait. (Privately printed.) 8vo. [New York, 1892.]

The Busy Man's Bible, and how to study and teach it. 16mo. Meadville, Pa., 1893.

John March, Southerner. 12mo. New York, 1894.

CALVERT, GEORGE HENRY. 1803-1889.

Illustrations of Phrenology, being a Selection of Articles from the Edinburgh Phrenological Journal, etc. 26 illustrations. 12mo. Baltimore, 1832.

A Volume from the Life of Herbert Barclay. 12mo. Baltimore, 1835.

Lecture on German Literature. 12mo. Baltimore, 1836.

(Translated.) Don Carlos: a Dramatic Poem by Schiller. 12mo. Baltimore, 1836.

Count Julian: a Tragedy. 12mo. Baltimore, 1840.

Cabiro. Cantos I and II. 12mo. Baltimore, 1840.

(Translated.) Correspondence between Schiller and Goethe, from 1794 to 1805. 12mo. New York, 1845.

Scenes and Thoughts in Europe. By An American. 12mo. New York, 1846.

Poems. 12mo. Boston, 1847.

Scenes and Thoughts in Europe. Second Series. 12mo. New York, 1852.

Oration on the Fortieth Anniversary of the Battle of Lake Erie . . . . . Newport, September 10, 1853. 8vo. Cambridge, 1853.

Comedies. 12mo. Boston, 1856.

Introduction to Social Science. A Discourse. 12mo. New York, 1856.

[Anonymous.] Joan of Arc: a Poem. In Four Books. (Privately printed.) Riverside Press. [Cambridge,] 1860.

Travels in Europe: its People and Scenery. Frontispiece. 12mo. Boston, 1860.

Anyta and other Poems. 16mo. Boston, 1863.

The Gentleman. 16mo. Boston, 1863.

Arnold and André: an Historical Drama. 16mo. Boston, 1864.

Cabiro: a Poem. Part 2. [Cantos III, IV.] 16mo. Boston, 1864.

First Years in Europe. 12mo. Boston, 1866.

Some of the Thoughts of Joseph Joubert. With a Biographical Notice. 12mo. Boston, 1867.

Ellen: a Poem. 12mo. New York, 1869.

Goethe. His Life and Work: an Essay. 12mo. Boston, 1872.

The Maid of Orleans: an Historical Study. 12mo. New York, 1874.

Brief Essays and Brevities. 12mo. Boston, 1874.

Essays Æsthetical. 12mo. Boston, 1875.

The Life of Rubens. Portrait. 12mo. Boston, 1876.

A Nation's Birth and Other National Poems. 12mo. Boston, 1876.

Charlotte von Stein. Portrait and plate. 12mo. Boston, 1877.

Wordsworth: a Biographic Æsthetic Study. Portrait. 16mo. Boston, 1878.

Shakespeare: a Biographic Æsthetic Study. Portrait. 16mo. Boston, 1879.

Coleridge, Shelley, Goethe. Biographic Æsthetic Studies. 16mo. Boston [1880].

Life, Death, and other Poems. Square 16mo. Boston [1882].

Angeline: a Poem. Square 24mo. Boston [1883].

Brangonar: a Tragedy. Square 16mo. Boston [1883].

Mirabeau: an Historical Drama. 16mo. Boston [1883].

Sybil: a Poem. Square 16mo. Boston [1883].

Three Score and other Poems. Square 16mo. Boston, [1883].

The Nazarene: a Poem. Square 16mo. Boston [1883.]

CARLETON, WILLIAM. 1845 —

Poems. 12mo. Chicago, 1871.

Farm Ballads. Illustrations. Square 8vo. New York, 1873.

Farm Legends. Illustrations. Square 8vo. New York, 1876.

Young Folks' Centennial Rhymes. Illustrations. 12mo. New York, 1876.

Farm Festivals. Illustrations. Square 8vo. New York, 1881.

City Ballads. Illustrations. Square 8vo. New York, 1885.

City Legends. Illustrations. Square 8vo. New York, 1889.

City Festivals. Illustrations. Square 8vo. New York, 1892.

Rhymes of our Planet. Portrait and illustrations. 12mo. New York, 1895.

CARPENTER, HENRY BERNARD. 1839-1890.

American Character and Influence. Oration . . . . . Boston, July 4, 1883. 8vo. Boston, 1883.

The Old Beacon. A Poem. Square 16mo. Boston, 1884.

Liber Amoris: being the Book of Love of Brother Aurelius. 12mo. Boston, 1887.

A Poet's Last Songs. With Introduction by James Jeffrey Roche. Portrait. 12mo. Boston, 1891.

CARRUTHERS, WILLIAM A. 1800-1850.

The Kentuckian in New York. By a Virginian. 2 volumes, 12mo. New York, 1834.

The Cavaliers of Virginia, or the Recluse of Jamestown, an Historical Romance of the Old Dominion. 2 volumes, 12mo. New York, 1834.

The Knights of the Horse-Shoe; a Traditionary Tale of the Cocked Hat Gentry of the Old Dominion. 8vo. Wetumpka, Alabama, 1845.

CARY, ALICE. 1820-1871.

Poems, by Alice and Phœbe Carey. 12mo. Philadelphia, 1850.

Clovernook; or Recollections of our Neighborhood in the West. Frontispiece and vignette title. 12mo. New York, 1852.

Hagar; a Story of To-Day. 12mo. New York, 1852.

Lyra, and other Poems. 12mo. New York, 1852.

Clovernook. Second Series. 12mo. Boston, 1853.

Clovernook Children. Illustrations. 12mo. Boston, 1855.

Poems. 12mo. Boston, 1855.

Holywood. 12mo. Boston, 1855.

Married, not Mated; or how they lived at Woodside and Throckmorton Hall. 12mo. New York, 1856.

The Josephine Gallery. Edited by Alice and Phœbe Cary. Portraits. Square 8vo. New York, 1859.

Pictures of Country Life. 12mo. New York, 1859.

Ballads, Lyrics and Hymns. Portrait. 12mo. New York, 1866.

The Bishop's Son. 12mo. New York, 1867.

Snow-Berries. A Book for Young Folks. Illustrations. Square 16mo. Boston, 1867.

A Lover's Diary. Illustrations. Square 16mo. Boston, 1868.

From Year to Year: a Token of Remembrance. Edited by Alice and Phœbe Cary. Illustrations. 12mo. New York [1869].

Last Poems of Alice and Phœbe Cary. Edited by Mary Clemmer. 12mo. New York, 1873.

Ballads for Little Folk. By Alice and Phœbe Cary. Edited by Mary Clemmer. Illustrations. Small 4to. New York, 1873.

Poetical Works of Alice and Phœbe Cary. 4 volumes, 12mo. New York, 1874.

A Memorial of Alice and Phœbe Cary, with some of their Later Poems. Edited by Mary Clemmer. Portraits. 12mo. New York, 1875.

(With Phœbe Cary.) Early and Late Poems. 12mo. Boston, 1887.

*₀*On the title-pages of the earlier works of the Cary sisters, the name was spelled Carey, but after a few issues the "e" was omitted.

CARY, PHŒBE. 1825–1871.

    Poems and Parodies. 12mo. Boston, 1854.

    Poems of Faith, Hope and Love. 12mo. New York, 1868.
    _{*} See also CARY, ALICE.

CATHERWOOD, MARY HARTWELL. 1847 —

    A Woman in Armor. By Mary Hartwell. 12mo. New York, 1875.

    Craque-o'-Doom. Illustrations. 12mo. Philadelphia, 1881.

    Rocky Fort. Illustrations. 12mo. Boston, 1882.

    Old Caravan Days. Illustrations. 12mo. Boston, 1884.

    The Secrets at Roseladies. Illustrations. 12mo. Boston, 1888.

    The Romance of Dollard. With a Preface by Francis Parkman. Illustrations. 12mo. New York [1889].

    The Story of Tonty. Illustrations. 12mo. Chicago, 1890.

    The Lady of Fort St. John. 12mo. Boston, 1891.

    Old Kaskaskia. 12mo. Boston, 1893.

    The White Islander. 12mo. New York, 1893.

    The Chase of Saint Castin, and other Stories of the French in the New World. 12mo. Boston, 1894.

CAWEIN, MADISON JULIUS. 1865 —

    Blooms of the Berry. 12mo. Louisville, 1887.

    The Triumph of Music and other Lyrics. 12mo. Louisville, 1888.

    Accolon of Gaul, with other Poems. 8vo. Louisville, 1889.

    Lyrics and Idyls. (400 copies.) 12mo. Louisville, 1890.

    Days and Dreams. 12mo. New York, 1891.

    Moods and Memories. (250 copies.) 16mo. New York, 1892.

    Red Leaves and Roses. 16mo. New York, 1893.

Poems of Nature and Love. (250 copies.) 16mo. New York, 1893.

Intimations of the Beautiful and other Poems. (350 copies.) 12mo. New York, 1894.

The White Snake and other Poems, translated from the German into the Original Metre. (100 copies.) 12mo. Louisville, 1895.

CHANNING, WILLIAM ELLERY. 1818 —

Poems. 16mo. Boston, 1843.

Poems. Second Series. 16mo. Boston, 1847.

Conversations in Rome; between an Artist, a Catholic, and a Critic. 16mo. Boston, 1847.

The Woodman and other Poems. 16mo. Boston, 1849.

Near Home. [Concord, Mass.] 16mo. Boston, 1858.

The Burial of John Brown. 8vo. [Boston, 1860.]

The Wanderer. A Colloquial Poem [with preface, pp.v.-viii., by R. W. Emerson]. 12mo. Boston, 1871.

Thoreau: the Poet Naturalist. With Memorial Verses [by R. W. Emerson, not published elsewhere, and others]. 12mo. Boston, 1873.

Memoir of John Brown, ... by F. B. Sanborn. With Memorial Verses by W. E. Channing. Illustrations. 8vo. Concord, 1878.

Eliot. A Poem. 32mo. Boston, 1885.

John Brown, and the Heroes of Harper's Ferry. A Poem. 32mo. Boston, 1886.

***See also THOREAU, H. D.

CHENEY, JOHN VANCE. 1848 —

The Old Doctor. A Romance of Queer Village. 12mo. New York, 1881.

Thistle Drift. 16mo. New York, 1887.

Wood Blooms. 16mo. New York, 1888.

The Golden Guess: Essays on Poetry and the Poets. 12mo. Boston, 1892.

Wood Notes Wild. Notations of Bird Music; by Simon Pease Cheney. Edited, with Appendix, Notes, Bibliography, and Index, by J. V. Cheney. 12mo. Boston, 1892.

Ninette, a Redwoods Idyll. 8vo. San Francisco, 1894.

Queen Helen and other Poems. (150 copies.) 12mo. Chicago, 1895.

CHILD, FRANCIS JAMES. 1825-1896.

Four Old Plays. Three Interludes: Thersites, Jack Jugler, and Heywood's Pardoner and Frere: and Jocasta, a Tragedy by Gascoigne and Kinwelmarsh; with Introduction and Notes [by Francis J. Child]. 8vo. Cambridge, 1848.

(Edited.) The Poetical Works of Edmund Spenser . . . with Notes, Original and Selected. Portrait. 5 volumes, 12mo. Boston, 1855.

(Edited.) English and Scottish Ballads. 8 volumes, 16mo. Boston, 1857-59
　*.*The same. Large paper. 8 volumes, 12mo. Boston, 1860.

(Edited.) An Elementary English Grammar, by Robert Gordon Latham. With Appendix by D. R. Goodwin. 16mo. Boston, 1861.

Observations on the language of Chaucer's Canterbury Tales. [In] Memoirs of the American Academy of Arts and Sciences. New Series, vol. viii. 4to. Cambridge, 1862.

[Compiled, anonymously.] War-Songs for Freemen. Dedicated to the Army of the United States. With Appropriate Music. 16mo. Boston, 1862.

[Edited, anonymously.] Poems of Religious Sorrow, Comfort, Counsel and Aspiration. 12mo. New York, 1863.

Observations on the Language of Gower's Confessio Amantis. [In] Memoirs of the American Academy of Arts and Sciences. Vol. ix. 4to. Boston, 1864.
　*.*Also published, separately, 4to. Boston, 1868.

Bishop Percy's Folio Manuscript. Ballads and Romances. Edited by John W. Hales and Frederick J. Furnival, assisted by [F. J.] Child [and others]. Vols. i.-iii. 8vo. London, 1867-68.

[With others.] Is William Claflin a Hard Money Man? Broadside. [Boston, 1876.]

The English and Scottish Ballads. Edition de luxe. (1,000 copies). 10 parts, 4to. Boston [1882-97].
***This is an entirely new work, and has no dependence upon the earlier collection.

The Epic Songs of Russia, by Isabel F. Hapgood, with an Introductory Note by F. J. Child. 8vo. London, 1885.

(Edited.) The Child of Bristowe : a Legend of the Fourteenth Century. 8vo. Cambridge, 1886.

(Edited.) Stories from the Persian. Abdûlla of Khorassan ; Ahmed the Cobbler. 12mo. Cambridge [1887.]
***See also, LOWELL, JAMES R.

CHILD, LYDIA MARIA. 1802-1880.

Hobomok. A Tale of Early Times. By An American. 12mo. Boston, 1824.

The Rebels, or Boston before the Revolution. 12mo. Boston, 1825.
***Republished, with the author's revisions, 12mo. Boston, 1850.

The First Settlers of New England : or, the Conquest of the Pequods, Narragansets, and Pokanokets. . . . By A Lady of Massachusetts. Frontispiece. 16mo. Boston, 1829.

The Frugal Housewife. 12mo. Boston, 1829.

The Coronal. A Collection of Miscellaneous Pieces written at Various Times. Frontispiece. 18mo. Boston, 1831.

The Mother's Book. 12mo. Boston, 1831.

The Girls' Own Book. 12mo. Boston, 1832.

The Biographies of Lady Russell and Madame Guyon. Portrait. 16mo. Boston, 1832.

The Biographies of Madame de Staël and Madame Roland. Portrait. 16mo. Boston, 1832.

Biographies of Good Wives. Frontispiece. 16mo. Boston, 1833.
***The three preceding volumes comprised the series entitled The Ladies' Family Library.

An Appeal in Favor of that Class of Americans called Africans. Frontispiece. 12mo. Boston, 1833.

(Edited.) The Oasis. [Anti-Slavery contributions by the editor, J. G. Whittier, Elizabeth Whittier and others.] 16mo. Boston, 1834.

The History of the Condition of Women in Various Ages and Nations. 2 volumes, 16mo. Boston, 1835.

Authentic Narratives of American Slavery. 12mo. Newburyport, 1835.
***The same. Second edition, enlarged. 12mo. Newburyport, 1836.

The Evils of Slavery and the Curse of Slavery. 12mo. Newburyport, 1836.

An Anti-Slavery Catechism. 12mo. Newburyport, 1836.

Philothea, a Romance. 12mo. Boston, 1836.

The Family Nurse. 12mo. Boston, 1837.

The Anti-Slavery Almanac. 16mo. New York, 1843.

Letters from New York. 2 volumes, 12mo. New York, 1843–45.

Flowers for Children. 3 volumes, 12mo. New York, 1844–46.

Fact and Fiction. 12mo. New York, 1847.

Sketches from Life. 2 volumes, 12mo. Philadelphia, 1850.

Isaac T. Hopper: a True Life. Portrait. 12mo. Boston, 1853.

The Progress of Religious Ideas through Successive Ages. 3 volumes, 12mo. New York, 1855.

New Flowers for Children. 12mo. New York, 1855.

Autumnal Leaves: Tales and Sketches in Prose and Rhyme. 12mo. New York, 1857.

The Patriarchal Institution described by Members of its own Family. 12mo. New York, 1860.

The Right Way the Safe Way proved by Emancipation in the British West Indies and Elsewhere. 12mo. New York, 1860.

Correspondence between Lydia M. Child and Governor Wise and Mrs. Mason, of Virginia. 12mo. Boston, 1860.

The Duty of Disobedience to the Fugitive Slave Act. An Appeal to the Legislature of Massachusetts. 12mo. Boston, 1860.

Looking towards Sunset. From Sources Old and New, Original and Selected. 12mo. Boston, 1865.

The Freedman's Book. 12mo. Boston, 1865.

A Romance of the Republic. 12mo. Boston, 1867.

(Edited.) Rainbows for Children. 16mo. Boston, 1867.

An Appeal for the Indians. 12mo. New York [1868].

Stories for Young Folks. 5 volumes, 18mo. Boston, 1869-70.

(Edited.) Aspirations of the World. A Chain of Opals. 16mo. Boston, 1878.

Letters, with an Introduction [pp. v.-xxv., and poem, Within the Gate, pp. 269-271] by John G. Whittier, and an Appendix by Wendell Phillips. Portrait. 12mo. Boston, 1883.

CHIVERS, THOMAS HOLLEY. 1807-1858.

Conrad and Eudora; or, the Death of Alonzo. A Threnody. 16mo. Philadelphia, 1834.

Nacoochee; or, the Beautiful Star, with other Poems. 12mo. New York, 1837.

The Lost Pleiad, and other Poems. 8vo. New York, 1845.

Eonchs of Ruby. A Gift of Love. 8vo. New York, 1851.

Virginalia ; or, Songs of my Summer Nights. A Gift of Love for the Beautiful. 12mo. Philadelphia, 1853.

Memoralia ; or, Phials of Amber full of the Tears of Love. 12mo. Philadelphia, 1853.

A Gift of the Beautiful. 12mo. Philadelphia, 1853.

Atlanta ; or, the True Blessed Island of Poesy. . . . 8vo. Macon, Ga., 1855.

The Sons of Usna ; a Tragic Apotheosis in Five Acts. 12mo. Philadelphia, 1858.

CLARKE, McDONALD. 1798-1842.

A Review of the Eve of Eternity, and other Poems. 8vo. New York, 1822.

The Elixir of Moonshine ; being a Collection of Prose and Poetry by the Mad Poet. 18mo. Gotham, A. M. 5822. [New York, 1822.]

The Gossip ; or, a Laugh with the Ladies, a Grin with the Gentlemen, and Burlesque on Byron ; a Sentimental Satire with other Poems. 18mo. New York, 1823.

Sketches. 18mo. New York, 1826.

Afara ; or, the Belles of Broadway. 4 parts, 8vo. New York, 1829.

Death in Disguise ; a Temperance Poem. 18mo. Boston, 1833.

Poems. Portrait. 12mo. New York, 1836.

A Cross and a Coronet. 12mo. New York, 1841.

CLEMENS, SAMUEL LANGHORNE (MARK TWAIN). 1835 —

The Celebrated Jumping Frog of Calaveras County, and other Sketches. Edited by John Paul. 16mo. New York, 1867.

The Innocents Abroad ; or, the New Pilgrims' Progress. Illustrations. 8vo. Hartford, 1869.

Mark Twain's (Burlesque) Autobiography and First Romance. Illustrations. 12mo. New York [1871].

Mark Twain's Memoranda. From The Galaxy. 8vo. Toronto. 1871.

Roughing It. Illustrations. 8vo. Hartford, 1872.

Sketches, New and Old. Illustrations. Square 8vo. Hartford, 1873.

The Innocents at Home [and A Burlesque Autobiography]. 16mo. London [1873].

(With Charles D. Warner.) The Gilded Age. Illustrations. 8vo. Hartford, 1874.
 *₀*The same. 3 volumes, small 8vo. London, 1874.

Number One. Mark Twain's Sketches. Illustrations. 8vo. New York [1874].

Mark Twain's Sketches, New and Old. Now First published in Complete Form. Illustrations. Square 8vo. Hartford, 1875.

The Adventures of Tom Sawyer. Illustrations. Square 8vo. Hartford, 1876.

Old Times on the Mississippi. 12mo. Toronto, 1876.

A True Story, and The Recent Carnival of Crime. Illustrations. 32mo. Boston, 1877.

Punch, Brothers, Punch ! and other Sketches. Square 16mo. New York [1878].

A Tramp Abroad. Portrait and illustrations. 8vo. Hartford, 1880.

The Prince and the Pauper : a Tale for Young People of all Ages. Illustrations. 8vo. Boston, 1882.

The Stolen White Elephant. 12mo. Boston, 1882.

Life on the Mississippi. Illustrations. 8vo. Boston, 1883.

The Adventures of Huckleberry Finn, Tom Sawyer's Comrade. 16mo. London, 1884.
 *₀*The same. Illustrations. 8vo. New York, 1885.

Mark Twain's Library of Humor. Illustrations. 8vo. New York, 1888.

A Connecticut Yankee at King Arthur's Court. Illustrations. Square 8vo. New York, 1889.

Merry Tales. 12mo. New York, 1892.

The American Claimant. Illustrations. 8vo. New York, 1892.

The £1,000,000 Bank Note, and other New Sketches. Frontispiece. 12mo. New York, 1893.

Tom Sawyer Abroad. Illustrations. 8vo. New York, 1894.

The Tragedy of Pudd'nhead Wilson, and the Comedy, Those Extraordinary Twins. Portrait and illustrations. 8vo. Hartford, 1894.

*.*See also HOWELLS, W. D.

COFFIN, ROBERT STEVENSON. 1797-1857.

The Printer, and several other Poems. 12mo. Boston, 1817.

Miscellaneous Poems of The Boston Bard. Plate. 18mo. Philadelphia, 1818.

Poems. By The Boston Bard. 24mo. New York, 1823.

The Life of The Boston Bard. Written by Himself. 12mo. Mt. Pleasant, N. Y., 1825.

Oriental Harp. Poems of The Boston Bard. 8vo. Providence, 1826.

The Boston Bard to the Citizens of Boston. 8vo. Boston, 1826.

Epistle to Joseph T. Buckingham, Esq. 8vo. Boston, 1826.

The Eleventh Hour, or Confessions of a Consumptive. 12mo. Boston, 1827.

CONWAY, MONCURE DANIEL. 1832 —

(Edited.) The Collegian. A Monthly Magazine. 8vo. Dickinson College, Carlisle, Pa., 1850(?)

Free Schools in Virginia. . . . 12mo. Fredericksburg, Va., 1850.

A Discourse on the Life and Character of Chief Justice William Cranch. 8vo. Washington, 1855.

Pharisaism and Fasting. A Discourse. 8vo. Washington, 1855.

The True and the False in Prevalent Theories of Divine Dispensation. . . . 8vo. Washington and Boston. 1855.

The Old and the New: a Sermon containing the History of the First Unitarian Church in Washington. 8vo. Washington, 1855.

The One Path; or the Duties of North and South. 8vo. [Washington, 1856.]
***An anti-slavery discourse, Jan. 26, 1856, which led to the expulsion of the author from the pulpit of the Unitarian church in Washington.

Spiritual Liberty. Discourse, Feb. 17, 1856. 12mo. [Washington, 1856.]

Virtue vs. Defeat. A Discourse, Nov. 9th, 1856 [after presidential election]. 8vo. Cincinnati, 1856.

The Theatre. [Discourse in defence of the drama.] 8vo. Cincinnati, 1857.

Tracts for To-Day. 12mo. Cincinnati, 1858.

East and West, an Inaugural Discourse. . . . 8vo. Cincinnati, 1859.

The Natural History of the Devil. 12mo. Albany, 1859.

Thomas Paine: a Celebration [of his 123d birthday]. . . . Cincinnati, Jan. 29, 1860. 8vo. Cincinnati, 1860.
***This discourse was described by Moreau as the first word favorable to Paine ever uttered from a pulpit.

(Edited.) The Dial. A Monthly Magazine. . . . 8vo. Cincinnati, 1860.

The Rejected Stone: or Insurrection vs. Resurrection in America. By A Native of Virginia. 12mo. Boston, 1861.

The Golden Hour. 12mo. Boston, 1862.

Address in . . . . Manchester, England, on the Civil War in America. 12mo. Manchester, 1863.

Epistle of Jonathan to John. 8vo. London, 1864.

Testimonies Concerning Slavery. 12mo. London, 1864.

In Memoriam. William Johnson Fox. Discourse, June 12, 1864. 12mo. London, 1864.

Benjamin Banneker, the Negro Astronomer. Reprinted from The Atlantic Monthly. 12mo. London, 1864.

Passages from the Note Books of Nathaniel' Hawthorne. With Introduction by M. D. Conway. 12mo. London, 1869.

The Earthward Pilgrimage. 12mo. London, 1870.

The Voysey Case from an Heretical Standpoint. 12mo. Ramsgate [England], 1871.

The Spiritual Serfdom of the Laity. 12mo. Ramsgate, 1871.

Mazzini. A Discourse, March 17, 1872. 12mo. [London, 1872.]

Demonology. Four Lectures given in the Royal Institution. 8vo. London, 1872.

On Mythology. Read before the London Anthropological Society. 8vo. [London, 1872.]

Republican Superstitions; as illustrated in the Political History of America. 12mo. London, 1872.

The Parting of the Ways: Sterling and Maurice. 12mo. London, 1872.

The Sacred Anthology. A Book of [Oriental] Ethnical Scriptures. 8vo. London, 1873.

John Stuart Mill. 12mo. London, 1873.

David Friederich Strauss. Discourse and Commemorative Services. 12mo. London, 1874.

Consequences. 8vo. London, 1875.

Revivalism. 8vo. [London, 1875.]

Intellectual Suicide. 8vo. [London, 1875.]

Christianity. 12mo. London, 1876.

James Waterlow. A Memorial Address. 12mo. London, 1876.

Human Sacrifices in England. 12mo. London, 1876.

Our Cause and its Claims upon us. (Privately printed.) 8vo. [London, 1876.]

Our Cause and its Accusers. 12mo. London, 1876.

The First Love Again. Discourse . . . Cincinnati, Nov. 28, 1875. 12mo London, 1876.

Entering Society. 12mo. London, 1877.

Unbelief, its Nature, Causes and Cure. 12mo. London, 1877.

Alcestis in England. 12mo. London, 1877.

The Religion of Children. 12mo. London, 1877.

Idols and Ideals. 8vo. London and New York, 1877.

Unitarianism and its Grandchildren. 8vo. London, 1877.

Unscientific Punishments. 12mo. London, 1878.

The Peril of War. A Discourse. 12mo. London, 1878.

Atheism, a Spectre. A Discourse. 12mo. London, 1878.

Demonology and Devil-Lore. Illustrations. 2 volumes, 8vo. London, 1878.

Liberty and Morality. 12mo. London, 1878.

What is Religion? A Discourse. 12mo. [London, 1878.]

A Necklace of Stories. Illustrations. Square 16mo. London, 1879.

The Criminal's Ascension. A Discourse. 12mo. London, 1879.

The Rising Generation. 12mo. London, 1880.

A Last Word. A Discourse. 12mo. London, 1880.

What is the Religion of Humanity? 12mo. London. 1880.

Laureate Despair. 12mo. London, 1881.

The Wandering Jew and the Pound of Flesh. 12mo. London and New York, 1881.

Thomas Carlyle. A Memorial Discourse. 8vo. London, 1881.

Thomas Carlyle. Illustrations. 12mo. New York, 1881.

Garfield. A Discourse. 12mo. London, 1881.

The Oath and its Ethics. 12mo. London, 1881.

The Philosophy of Persecution. 8vo. London, 1881.

Emerson at Home and Abroad. 8vo. London, 1882.

Travels in South Kensington. With Notes on Decorative Art and Architecture in England. Illustrations. Square 8vo. London, 1882.

Lessons for the Day. 2 volumes, 8vo. London, 1882-83.

Emerson and his Views of Nature. An Address. 8vo. London, 1882.

Farewell Discourses. Delivered at South Place Chapel. 8vo. London, 1884.

A Charge to be kept at South Place. A Discourse. 12mo. London, 1885.

Pine and Palm. A Novel. 8vo. London and New York, 1887.

Omitted Chapters of History, disclosed in the Life and Papers of Edmund Randolph, Governor of Virginia .... Illustrations. 8vo. New York and London, 1888.

George Washington and Mount Vernon. Illustrations. Royal 8vo. New York, 1889.

George Washington's Rules of Civility traced to their Sources and Restored. 16mo. New York [1890].

Life of Nathaniel Hawthorne. 8vo. [and 16mo.] London, 1890.

Prisons of Air. A Novel. 12mo. New York, 1891.

History of Thomas Paine. With a History of his Literary, Political, and Religious Life in America, France and England. Portrait. 2 volumes, 8vo. New York and London, 1892.

Civilizing the Sabbath. 12mo. London, 1892.

Barons of the Potomac and the Rappahannock. Portrait and fac-simile. (360 copies.) 8vo. New York: The Grolier Club, 1892.

Centenary History of the South Place Society. Illustrations. 12mo. London, 1894.

The Writings of Thomas Paine. Collected and Edited by Moncure D. Conway. Portraits. 4 volumes, 8vo. New York and London, 1894–1895.
  *₀*See also THOREAU, H. D.

COOKE, JOHN ESTEN. 1830–1886.

Leather Stocking and Silk; or Hunter John Myers and his Times. A Story of the Valley of Virginia. 12mo. New York, 1854.

The Virginia Comedians: or Life in the Old Dominion. Edited from the MSS. of C. Effingham, Esq. 2 volumes, 12mo. New York, 1854.

[Anonymous.] The Youth of Jefferson; or a Chronicle of College Scrapes at Williamsburg, in Virginia, 1754. 12mo. New York, 1854.

Ellie; or, the Human Comedy. Illustrations by Strother. 12mo. Richmond, 1855.

The Last of the Foresters; or, Humors on the Border; a Story of the old Virginia Frontier. 12mo. New York, 1856.

Henry St. John, Gentleman, of "Flower of Hundreds" in the County of Prince George, Virginia. A Tale of 1774–75. 12mo. New York, 1859.
  *₀*Republished as Bonnybel Vane. 12mo. New York, 1883.

The Life of Stonewall Jackson, from Official Papers. By A Virginian. Portrait. 8vo. Richmond, 1863.
  *₀*Republished as Stonewall Jackson: a Military Biography. New York, 1871.

Surry of Eagle's Nest; or, the Memoirs of a Staff Officer serving in Virginia. Edited from the MSS. of Col. Surry. Illustrations. 12mo. New York, 1866.

Wearing of the Gray: being Personal Portraits, Scenes and Adventures of the War. 8vo. New York, 1867.

Fairfax; or the Master of Greenway Court. A Chronicle of the Valley of the Shenandoah. 12mo. New York, 1868.

Hilt to Hilt, or Days and Nights in the Shenandoah in the Autumn of 1864. 12mo. New York, 1869.

Mohun; or, the Last Days of Lee and his Paladins. Final Memoirs of a Staff-Officer serving in Virginia. From the MSS. of Col. Surry of Eagle's Nest. Portrait and plates. 12mo. New York, 1869.

Hammer and Rapier. 12mo. New York, 1870.

The Heir of Graymount. 12mo. New York, 1870.

Out of the Foam. A Novel. 12mo. New York, 1871.

A Life of General Robert E. Lee. Portraits and maps. 8vo. New York, 1871.

Pretty Mrs. Gaston, and other Stories. Illustrations. 12mo. New York, 1871.

Doctor Vandike. A Novel. 8vo. New York, 1873.

Her Majesty the Queen. A Novel. 12mo. Philadelphia, 1873.

Justin Harley. A Romance of Old Virginia. 12mo. Philadelphia, 1874.

Life of Samuel J. Tilden, of New York. Portraits. 12mo. New York, 1876.

Canolles: the Fortunes of a Partizan of '81. 12mo. Detroit, 1877.

Professor Pressensee, Materialist and Inventor: a Story. 32mo. New York, 1878.

Mr. Grantley's Idea. 32mo. New York, 1879.

Stories of the Old Dominion from the Settlement to the End of the Revolution. Illustrations. 12mo. New York, 1879.

The Virginia Bohemians. A Novel. 8vo. New York, 1880.

Virginia : a History of the People. Map. 12mo. Boston, 1883.

Fanchette. By One of her Admirers. 12mo. Boston, 1883.

My Lady Pocahontas : a True Relation of Virginia. Writ by Anas Todkill, Puritan and Pilgrim. With Notes by J. E. Cooke. 12mo. Boston, 1885.

The Maurice Mystery. 12mo. New York, 1885.

COOKE, ROSE TERRY. 1827-1892.

Poems. By Rose Terry. 12mo. Boston, 1861.

Happy Dodd ; or "she hath done what she could." 12mo. Boston, 1878.

Somebody's Neighbors. 12mo. Boston, 1881.

The Deacon's Week. 32mo. Boston [1884].

Root-Bound, and other Sketches. Illustrations. 12mo. Boston, 1885.

No : a Story for Boys. 12mo. New York, 1886.

The Sphinx's Children and other People's. 12mo. Boston, 1886.

The Old Garden. Arranged by Kate Sanborn. Illustrations. Small 4to. Boston, 1888.

Steadfast. The Story of a Saint and a Sinner. 12mo. Boston, 1889.

Huckleberries gathered from New England Hills. 12mo. Boston, 1891.

COOPER, JAMES FENIMORE. 1789-1851.

[Anonymous.] Precaution ; a Novel. 2 volumes, 12mo. New York, 1820.

The Spy ; a Tale of the Neutral Ground. 2 volumes, 12mo. New York, 1821.

The Pioneers ; or the Sources of the Susquehanna. A Descriptive Tale. 2 volumes, 12mo. New York, 1823.

The Pilot; a Tale of the Sea. 2 volumes, 12mo. New York, 1823.

Lionel Lincoln; or the Leaguer of Boston. 2 volumes, 12mo. New York, 1825.

The Last of the Mohicans. A Narrative of 1757. 2 volumes, 12mo. Philadelphia, 1826.

The Prairie; a Tale. 2 volumes, 12mo. Philadelphia, 1827.

The Red Rover; a Tale. 2 volumes, 12mo. Philadelphia, 1828.

Notions of the Americans: picked up by A Travelling Bachelor. 2 volumes, 12mo. Philadelphia, 1828.

The Wept of Wish-ton-Wish; a Tale. 2 volumes, 12mo. Philadelphia, 1829.

The Water-Witch; or the Skimmer of the Seas. A Tale. 2 volumes, 12mo. Philadelphia, 1830.

The Bravo: a Tale. 2 volumes, 12mo. Philadelphia, 1831.

Letter to Gen. Lafayette on the Expenditure of the United States of America. 8vo. Paris, 1831.

The Heidenmauer; or the Benedictines: a Legend of the Rhine. 2 volumes, 12mo. Philadelphia, 1832.

The Headsman; or, the Abbaye des Vignerons. A Tale. 2 volumes, 12mo. Philadelphia, 1833.

A Letter to his Countrymen. 8vo. New York, 1834.

The Monikins. 2 volumes, 12mo. Philadelphia, 1835.

Sketches in Switzerland in 1828. By An American. 2 volumes, 12mo. Philadelphia, 1836.

Sketches in Switzerland in 1832. 2 volumes, 12mo. Philadelphia, 1836.

Hints on manning the Navy. [Reprinted from the Naval Magazine, March, 1836.] 8vo. Philadelphia, 1837.

Gleanings in Europe. [France.] By An American. 2 volumes, 12mo. Philadelphia, 1837.

Gleanings in Europe. England. 2 volumes, 12mo. Philadelphia, 1837.

Gleanings in Europe. Italy. 2 volumes, 12mo. Philadelphia, 1838.

The American Democrat; or Hints on the Social and Civic Relations of the United States of America. 12mo. Cooperstown, 1838.

[Anonymous.] The Chronicles of Cooperstown. 12mo. Cooperstown, 1838.

Homeward Bound; or the Chase. A Tale of the Sea. 2 volumes, 12mo. Philadelphia, 1838.

Home as Found. [A sequel to Homeward Bound.] 2 volumes, 12mo. Philadelphia, 1838.

The History of the Navy of the United States of America. 2 volumes, 12mo. Philadelphia, 1839.
 *˳*The same. Second Edition, with corrections. 2 volumes, 8vo. New York, 1840.

The Pathfinder; or the Inland Sea. 2 volumes, 12mo. Philadelphia, 1840.

Mercedes of Castile; or the Voyage to Cathay. 2 volumes, 12mo. Philadelphia, 1840.

History of the Navy of the United States. Abridged. 12mo. Philadelphia, 1841.

The Deerslayer: or, the First War-Path. A Tale. 2 volumes, 12mo. Philadelphia, 1841.

The Two Admirals; a Tale. 2 volumes, 12mo. Philadelphia, 1842.

The Wing-and-Wing; or Le Feu Follett. A Tale. 2 volumes, 12mo. Philadelphia, 1842.

Le Mouchoir; an Autobiographical Romance. 4to. New York, 1843.
 *˳*Originally published in Graham's Magazine, January-March, inclusive, 1843.

A Brief Statement of the Pleadings and Argument in the Case of J. Fenimore Cooper *versus* Horace Greeley and Thomas McElrath, in an Action for Libel, tried at Saratoga, Dec. 9, 1842. 8vo. New York, 1843.

The Battle of Lake Erie; or Answers to Messrs. Burges, Duer, and Mackenzie. Diagrams. 12mo. Cooperstown, 1843.

Wyandotte; or the Hutted Knoll. A Tale. 2 volumes, 12mo. Philadelphia, 1843.

Ned Myers; or a Life before the Mast. 12mo. Philadelphia, 1843.

Afloat and Ashore; or the Adventures of Miles Wallingford. 2 volumes, 12mo. Philadelphia, 1844.

The same. Vols. 3 and 4. 12mo. New York, 1844.

Proceedings of the Naval Court-Martial in the Case of Alexander Slidell Mackenzie . . . . To which is annexed an Elaborate Review [pp. 263-344], by J. F. Cooper. 8vo. New York, 1844.

Satanstoe; or the Littlepage Manuscripts. A Tale of the Colony. 2 volumes, 12mo. New York, 1845.

The Chainbearer; or the Littlepage Manuscripts. 2 volumes, 12mo. New York, 1845.

Elinor Wyllys; or the Young Folk at Longbridge. A Tale. By Amabel Penfeather. Edited by J. F. Cooper. 2 volumes, 12mo. Philadelphia, 1845.

*₊*Contemporaries assert that Cooper was certainly the author of this tale, the copyright proceeds of which were regularly received by him; the publishers of the work also believed him to be the author. He was so very unpopular at the time that he, very reasonably, deemed it best for the prospects of the publication that he should appear in no closer relation than that of editor.

The Redskins; or Indian and Injun: being the Conclusion of the Littlepage Manuscripts. 2 volumes, 12mo. New York, 1846.

Lives of Distinguished American Naval Officers. 2 volumes, 12mo. Philadelphia (also Auburn, N. Y.), 1846.

The Crater; or Vulcan's Peak. A Tale of the Pacific. 2 volumes, 12mo. New York, 1847.

Jack Tier; or the Florida Reefs. 2 volumes, 12mo. New York, 1848.

The Oak Openings; or the Bee-Hunter. 2 volumes, 12mo. New York, 1848.

The Sea Lions; or the Lost Sealers. 2 volumes, 12mo. New York, 1849.

The Ways of the Hour. A Tale. 12mo. New York, 1850.

The History of the Navy of the United States, with a Continuation, 1815-1853, mostly from the Author's Manuscripts. 12mo. New York, 1853.

Works. Illustrations by F. O. C. Darley. 32 volumes, small 8vo. New York, 1859-61.

COOPER, SUSAN FENIMORE. . . .

Rural Hours. By A Lady. 12mo. New York, 1850.
　*.*The same. 21 colored engravings. 8vo. New York, 1851.

The Shield; a Narrative. 12mo. New York, 1852.

Country Rambles, or Journal of a Naturalist in England. 12mo. New York, 1853.

Rural Rambles. 12mo. Philadelphia, 1854.

Rhyme and Reason of Country Life; from Fields Old and New. 8vo. New York, 1854.

[Anonymous.] Mount Vernon: a Letter to the Children of America. Portrait and vignettes. 16mo. New York, 1859.

Pages and Pictures from the Writings of James Fenimore Cooper; with Notes by Susan F. Cooper. Engravings by Darley. 4to. New York, 1861.
　*.*The same. Proofs on India paper. 4to. New York, 1861.

Appleton's Illustrated Almanac for 1870. Edited by Miss S. F. Cooper [who also supplied the literary contents]. Illustrations. 4to. New York [1869].

William West Skiles. A Sketch of Missionary Life at Valle Crucis, in Western North Carolina. 1842-1862. 12mo. New York, 1890.

COZZENS, FREDERICK SWARTWOUT. 1818-1869.

Prismatics. By Richard Haywarde. Illustrations. 12mo. New York, 1853.

Cozzens' Wine Press: a Vinous, Vivacious Monthly. [June 20, 1855–March 20, 1861.] Royal 8vo. New York, 1855–61.

The Sparrowgrass Papers: or, Living in the Country. Frontispiece and vignette title. 12mo. New York, 1856.

Acadia; or, a Month with Blue Noses. Frontispiece and vignette title. 12mo. New York, 1859.

Memorial of Colonel Peter Porter. 8vo. New York, 1865.

The Sayings of Dr. Bushwhacker and other Learned Men. 12mo. New York, 1867.

Fitz Greene Halleck: a Memorial. 2 portraits. 8vo. New York, 1868.

CRANCH, CHRISTOPHER PEARSE. 1813–1892.

A Poem delivered in . . . . Quincy, May 25, 1840. 8vo. Boston, 1840.

Poems. 12mo. Philadelphia, 1844.

Address delivered before the Harvard Musical Association, Aug. 28, 1845. 8vo. Boston, 1845.

The Last of the Huggermuggers, a Giant Story. Illustrations. 12mo. Boston, 1856.

Kobboltozo: a Sequel to The Last of the Huggermuggers. Illustrations. 12mo. Boston, 1857.

The Æneids of Virgil, translated into English Blank Verse. Royal 8vo. Boston, 1872.

Satan: a Libretto. Square 18mo. Boston, 1874.

The Bird and the Bell and other Poems. 16mo. Boston, 1875.

Ariel and Caliban, with other Poems. 16mo. Boston, 1887.

Memorial of Robert Browning. [Containing personal reminiscences, and sonnet by C. P. Cranch.] Portrait and plates. Small 4to. Cambridge [1890].

CRAWFORD, FRANCIS MARION. 1854—

Mr. Isaacs: a Tale of Modern India. 12mo. London and New York, 1882.

Dr. Claudius: a True Story. 12mo. London and New York, 1883.

To Leeward. 2 volumes, 12mo. London, 1883.
  *.*The same. 12mo. Boston, 1884.

An American Politician. 12mo. Boston, 1884.

A Roman Singer. 12mo. Boston, 1884.
  *.*The same. 2 volumes, 12mo. London, 1884.

Zoroaster. A Novel. 12mo. New York, 1885.
  *.*The same. 2 volumes, 12mo. London, 1885.

A Tale of a Lonely Parish. 12mo. New York, 1886.
  *.*The same. 2 volumes, 12mo. London, 1886.

Saracinesca. 12mo. New York, 1887.
  *.*The same. 3 volumes, 12mo. London, 1887.

Marzio's Crucifix. 12mo. New York, 1887.
  *.*The same. 2 volumes, 12mo. London, 1887.

Paul Patoff. 12mo. Boston, 1887.
  *.*The same. 3 volumes, 12mo. London, 1887.

With the Immortals. 12mo. New York, 1888.
  *.*The same. 2 volumes, 12mo. London, 1888.

Greiffenstein. 12mo. New York, 1889.
  *.*The same. 3 volumes, 12mo. London, 1889.

Sant' Ilario. A Sequel to Saracinesca. 12mo. New York, 1889.
  *.*The same. 3 volumes, 12mo. London, 1889.

A Cigarette-Maker's Romance. 12mo. New York and London, 1890.

Khaled: a Tale of Arabia. 12mo. New York and London, 1891.

The Witch of Prague. Illustrations. 12mo. New York and London, 1891.

The Three Fates. 12mo. New York and London, 1892.

Don Orsino. A Novel. 12mo. New York and London, 1892.

The Children of the King: a Tale of Southern Italy. 12mo. New York, 1893.
  *.*The same. 2 volumes, 12mo. London, 1893.

Marion Darche. 12mo. New York, 1893.
*„*The same. 2 volumes, 16mo. London, 1893.

The Novel. What it is. Portrait. 18mo New York and London, 1893.

Pietro Ghisleri. 12mo. New York, 1893.
*„*The same. 3 volumes. London, 1893.

Katherine Lauderdale. Illustrations. 2 volumes, 16mo. New York and London, 1894.

Love in Idleness: a Tale of Bar Harbour. Illustrations. 12mo. New York, 1894.

The Upper Berth [and By the Waters of Paradise]. 32mo. New York, 1894.

The Ralstons: a Sequel to Katherine Lauderdale. 2 volumes, 16mo. New York, 1895.

Casa Braccio. Illustrations. 12mo. New York, 1895.

Constantinople. Illustrations. 12mo. New York, 1895.

CURTIS, GEORGE WILLIAM. 1824–1892.

[Anonymous.] Nile Notes of a Howadji. Vignette title. 12mo. New York, 1851.

Lotus Eating: a Summer Book. Illustrations. 12mo. New York, 1852.

The Howadji in Syria. 12mo. New York, 1852.

[Anonymous.] The Potiphar Papers. (Reprinted from Putnam's Monthly.) Illustrations. 12mo. New York, 1853.

(Edited, with Memoir.) Rural Essays, by the late A. J. Downing. Portrait. 8vo. New York, 1853.

Prue and I. 12mo. New York, 1856.

Works; collected and newly revised by the Author. 5 volumes, 12mo. New York, 1856.

The Duty of the American Scholar to Politics and the Times: an Oration. . . . Middletown, Conn., August 5, 1856. 8vo. New York, 1856.

A Letter to the Young Men of Maine; in Reply to an Invitation to address the Meeting at Bangor, August 28, 1856. 8vo. [New York, 1856.]

An Address vindicating the Rights of Woman to the Elective Franchise. . . . May 15, 1858. 12mo. New York, 1858.

A Summer on the Borders of the Carribean Sea. By J. Dennis Harris. With an Introduction by G. W. Curtis. 12mo. New York, 1860.

Trumps. A Novel. Illustrations. 12mo. New York, 1861.
*₀*Of this work a few copies were issued, for presentation by the author, wholly uncut, small 8vo. New York, 1861.

A Rhyme of Rhode Island and the Times, (with address by Rev. Francis Vinton) delivered before the Sons of Rhode Island, in New York, May 29, 1863. 8vo. New York, 1863.

The Rhode Island Prisoner. A Sonnet. New York, June 22, 1865, (also a sonnet by William Pitt Palmer) suggested by a View of the Jersey Prison Ship. Broadside. [New York, 1865.]

Equal Rights for Women. A Speech at the Constitutional Convention, [at Albany] July 19, 1867. 8vo. [New York, 1867.]

An Oration delivered at the Dedication of the Statue of Major-General John Sedgwick. . . . Oct. 21, 1868. [In Report of the Ceremonies.] Plate. 8vo. New York, 1869.

Fair Play for Women. An Address. . . . May 12, 1870. 16mo. Boston, 1871.

(With others.) Reform of the Civil Service: a Report made to the President, Dec. 18, 1871. 8vo. Washington, 1871.

Report of the Advisory Board of the Civil Service: made to the President, April 11, 1872. 8vo. Washington, 1872.

Charles Sumner: a Eulogy delivered before the Legislature of Massachusetts, June 9, 1874. 8vo. [Boston, 1874.]
*₀*Also published in Memorial of Charles Sumner [from the Commonwealth of Massachusetts], Boston, 1874.

The Puritan Principle,—Liberty under the Law: a Speech . . . . December 22, 1876. 8vo. New York, 1877.

Burgoyne's Surrender. An Oration . . . . at Schuylerville, N. Y., Oct. 17, 1877. 8vo. New York, 1877.

The Public Duty of Educated Men. An Oration . . . . Schenectady, N. Y., June 27, 1877. 8vo. Albany, 1878.

William Cullen Bryant: his Life, Character and Writings. A Commemorative Address . . . . New York, Dec. 30, 1878. 16mo. New York, 1879.

Robert Burns. An Address at the Unveiling of the Statue of the Poet, in Central Park, Oct. 2, 1880. (Printed for Private Circulation.) 8vo. [New York] 1880.

The Progress of Reform. An Address. . . . Aug. 1, 1883. 12mo. New York, 1883.

An Address at the Unveiling of the Statue of Washington, ... 26th November, 1883. . . . Plate. 8vo. New York, 1883.

A Memorial of Wendell Phillips from the City of Boston [containing Eulogy by Curtis]. Portrait. 8vo. Boston, 1884.
 *.*The Eulogy was also published separately, 8vo. New York, 1884.

The Year's Work in Civil Service Reform. An Address . . . . August 6, 1884. 12mo. New York, 1884.

The Puritan Spirit: an Oration. . . . June 6, 1885. 8vo. [New York, 1885.]

Civil Service Reform under the Present National Administration. An Address . . . . Aug. 5, 1885. 12mo. New York, 1885.

The Situation. An Address. . . . Aug. 4, 1886. 12mo. New York, 1886.

The Administration and Reform. An Address. . . . Aug. 3, 1887. 12mo. New York, 1887.

The Reason and Result of Civil Service Reform. An Address . . . . May 29, 1888. 12mo. New York, 1888.

Address delivered before the Society of the Army of the Potomac . . . . July 3, 1888. [In Report of the Proceedings.] 8vo. New York, 1888.

The Situation and Prospects of Reform. An Address. . . . Oct. 1, 1889. 12mo. New York, 1889.

The Higher Education of Women. An Address. . . . June 12, 1890. 8vo. New York, 1890.

Promises and Performances. An Address .... Oct. 1,
1890. 12mo. New York, 1890.

Modern Ghosts. Selected and translated [from various
writers]. With Introduction by G. W. Curtis. 16mo.
New York, 1890.

Washington Irving. A Sketch, with a Preface and Appendix,
containing Notes and Illustrations. 2 Portraits. (347
copies.) 8vo. New York: The Grolier Club, 1891.

Ten Years of Reform. An Address .... Sept. 29, 1891,
12mo. New York, 1891.

James Russell Lowell: an Address. 2 portraits. 32mo. New
York, 1892.

Party and Patronage. An Address prepared for the National
Civil Service Reform League [April 28, 1892]. 8vo. [New
York] 1892.

Prue and I. Illustrations. Small 8vo. New York, 1892.
  *₊*The same. Large paper. (250 copies.) 8vo. New York,
1892.

Essays from the Easy Chair. [First, second, and third
series.] Portraits. 3 volumes, 16mo. New York, 1892,
'93, '94.

Orations and Addresses. Edited by Charles Eliot Norton.
Portrait. 3 volumes, 8vo. New York, 1894.

Literary and Social Essays. 12mo. New York, 1895.
  *₊*See also BRIGGS, C. F.; HOLMES, O. W.; LOWELL, J. R.;
MOTLEY, J. L.; STEDMAN, E. C.; and WINTHROP, THEODORE.

DANA, RICHARD HENRY. 1787–1879.

Oration before the Washington Benevolent Society, at Cambridge, July 4, 1814. 8vo. Cambridge, 1814.

[Anonymous.] The Idle Man. 6 parts, 8vo. New York,
1821–22.
  *₊*Five poems by William Cullen Bryant first appeared in
this publication.

Poems. 16mo. Boston, 1827.

A Poem [Thoughts on the Soul] delivered before The Porter
Rhetorical Society, Andover. 8vo. Boston, 1829.

Poems and Prose Writings. 16mo. Boston, 1833.

The Buccaneer and other Poems. 16mo. London, 1844.

Poems and Prose Writings. 2 volumes, small 8vo. New York, 1850.

DANA, RICHARD HENRY, JR. 1815-1882.

[Anonymous.] Two Years before the Mast. A Personal Narrative of Life at Sea. 18mo. New York, 1840.

The Seaman's Friend, containing a Treatise on Practical Seamanship . . . . [etc]. Plates. 12mo. New York, 1841.

To Cuba and Back: a Vacation Voyage. 12mo. Boston, 1859.

Speech at Manchester, N. H., Feb. 19, 1861. 8vo. Boston, 1861.

A Tribute to Judge Sprague: Remarks at a Dinner given to the Officers of the Kearsarge. 8vo. Boston, 1864.

Enemy's Territory and Alien Enemies. 8vo. Boston, 1864.

An Address upon the Life and Services of Edward Everett. (Privately printed; 50 copies.) 8vo. Cambridge, 1865.

Speech at a Meeting . . . . Faneuil Hall, June 21, 1865, to consider the Subject of Re-Organization of the Rebel States. 8vo. [Boston, 1865.]

Two Years before the Mast . . . . New Edition with Subsequent Matter by the Author. 12mo. New York, 1869.

Oration at Lexington, April 19, 1875. Royal 8vo. Boston, 1875.

***See also ALLSTON, WASHINGTON.

DAVIS, RICHARD HARDING. 1864 —

Gallegher and other Stories. 12mo. New York, 1891.

Stories for Boys. Illustrations. 12mo. New York, 1891.

The West from a Car-Window. Illustrations. 12mo. New York, 1892.

Van Bibber and Others. Illustrations. 12mo. New York, 1892.

Our English Cousins. Illustrations. 12mo. New York, 1894.

The Rulers of the Mediterranean. Illustrations. 12mo. New York, 1894.

The Exiles and other Stories. Portrait and illustrations. 12mo. New York, 1894.

The Princess Aline. Illustrations. 12mo. New York, 1895.

About Paris. Illustrations. 12mo. New York, 1895.

DAWES, RUFUS. • 1803-1859.

The Valley of the Nashaway and other Poems. 12mo. Boston, 1830.

Athenia of Damascus. A Tragedy. 12mo. New York, 1839.

Geraldine, Athenia of Damascus, and Miscellaneous Poems. Portrait. 12mo. New York, 1839.

Nix's Mate: an Historical Romance of America. 2 volumes, 12mo. New York, 1839.

DE KAY, CHARLES. 1848 —

The Bohemian: a Tragedy of Modern Life. 16mo. New York, 1878.

Hesperus and other Poems. 12mo. New York, 1880.

The Vision of Nimrod: an Oriental Romance. 12mo. New York, 1881.

The Vision of Esther. A Sequel to The Vision of Nimrod. 12mo. New York, 1882.

The Love Poems of Louis Barnaval, edited [and written] by Charles De Kay. 12mo. New York, 1883.

Life and Works of Antoine Louis Barye, Sculptor. Portrait and illustrations. 4to. New York, 1889.

(Translated.) The Family Life of Heinrich Heine. Portraits. 12mo. New York [1892].

DELAND, MARGARET [WADE CAMPBELL]. 1857 —

The Old Garden and other Verses. 12mo. Boston, 1886.

John Ward, Preacher. A Novel. 12mo. Boston, 1888.

Florida Days. Illustrations. 8vo. Boston, 1889.

Sidney. 12mo. Boston, 1890.

The Story of a Child. 12mo. Boston, 1892.

Mr. Tommy Dove and other Stories. 12mo. Boston, 1893.

The Old Garden. Illustrations by Walter Crane. 8vo. Boston, 1893.

Philip and his Wife. A Novel. 12mo. Boston, 1894.

DERBY, GEORGE HORATIO [JOHN PHOENIX]. 1823–1861.

Phœnixiana; or, Sketches and Burlesques. Illustrations. 12mo. New York, 1855.

The Squibob Papers. Illustrations. 12mo. New York, 1865.

DODGE, MARY ABIGAIL [GAIL HAMILTON]. 1830–1896.

Country Living and Country Thinking. 12mo. Boston, 1862.

Courage! [Reprinted from The Congregationalist, January 27, 1862.] 8vo. [New York, 1862.]

Gala-Days. 12mo. Boston, 1863.

[Anonymous.] A Call to my Countrymen. Reprinted from The Atlantic Monthly, March, 1863. 12mo. New York, 1863.

A New Atmosphere. 12mo. Boston, 1864.

Stumbling-Blocks. 12mo. Boston, 1864.

Skirmishes and Sketches. 12mo. Boston, 1865.

Red-Letter Days in Applethorpe. Illustrations. Square 12mo. Boston, 1866.

Summer Rest. 12mo. Boston, 1866.

Wool-Gathering. 12mo. Boston, 1867.

Woman's Wrongs: a Counter-Irritant. 12mo. Boston, 1868.

A Battle of the Books. . . . 12mo. Boston, 1870.

Woman's Worth and Worthlessness: Complement to "A
New Atmosphere." 12mo. New York, 1872.

Little Folk Life. 12mo. New York, 1872.

Child-World. Illustrations. 2 parts, 16mo. Boston, 1872-73.

Nursery Nooning. 12mo. New York, 1874.

(With Elizabeth Stoddard.) Little Folk Life Series. Illustrations. 3 volumes, 16mo. Boston, 1874.

Twelve Miles from a Lemon. 12mo. New York, 1874.

Sermons to the Clergy. 16mo. Boston, 1876.

First Love is Best. 16mo. Boston, 1877.

What think ye of Christ? The Testimony of the English
Bible. 16mo. Boston, 1877.

Our Common School System. 12mo. Boston [1880].

Divine Guidance. Memorial of Allen W. Dodge. Portrait.
12mo. New York, 1881.

New England Bygones, by Ellen Hobbs Rollins . . . .
With Introduction by Gail Hamilton. Portrait and illustrations. 8vo. Philadelphia, 1883.

The Insuppressible Book. A Controversy between Herbert
Spencer and Frederick Harrrison . . . . with Comments
by Gail Hamilton. 12mo. Boston, 1885.

A Washington Bible-Class. 12mo. New York, 1891.

English Kings in a Nutshell: an Aid to the Memory. Illustrations. Square 12mo. New York, 1893.

Biography of James G. Blaine. Portrait and illustrations. 8vo.
Norwich, 1895.

*.*See also LARCOM, LUCY.

DODGE, MARY MAPES. 1838 —

Irvington Stories. Illustrations. 16mo. New York, 1864.

Hans Brinker; or, the Silver Skates: a Story of Life in Holland. 12mo. New York, 1864.

A Few Friends and how they amused Themselves: a Tale in
Nine Chapters. 16mo. Philadelphia, 1869.

Rhymes and Jingles. Illustrations. Small 4to. New York, 1874.

Theophilus and Others. 12mo. New York, 1876.

Along the Way. Poems. 12mo. New York, 1879.

Donald and Dorothy. Illustrations. 12mo. Boston, 1883.

(Edited.) Baby Days: Stories, Rhymes and Pictures for Little Folks. Illustrations. Square 8vo. New York, 1883.

(Edited.) Baby·World. Stories, Rhymes and Pictures. . . . . Square 8vo. New York, 1884.

The Land of Pluck. Illustrations. 12mo. New York, 1894.

When Life is Young. Illustrations. 12mo. New York, 1894.

DONNELLY, IGNATIUS. 1831 —

Atlantis: the Antedeluvian World. Illustrations. 12mo. New York, 1882.

Ragnarök: the Age of Fire and Gravel. Illustrations. 12mo. New York, 1883.

The Great Cryptogram: Francis Bacon's Cipher in the So-Called Shakspere Plays. Portraits and illustrations. Royal 8vo. Chicago, 1888.
*.*Also 2 volumes, 8vo. London, 1888.

Cæsar's Column. By Edmond Boisgilbert, M. D. 12mo. Chicago, 1890.

Doctor Huguet. 12mo. Chicago, 1891.

The Golden Bottle: or the Story of Ephraim Benezet of Kansas. 12mo. New York and St. Paul, 1892.

The American People's Money. Illustrations. 12mo. Chicago, 1895.

DRAKE, JOSEPH RODMAN. 1795-1820.

(With Fitz-Greene Halleck.) Poems by Croaker, Croaker & Co., and Croaker, Jr., as published in The Evening Post. 18mo. New York, 1819.

The Culprit Fay and other Poems. Portrait and engraved title. 8vo. New York, 1835.

The Culprit Fay. [First separate edition.] Vignettes. 12mo. New York, 1859.

(With Fitz-Greene Halleck.) The Croakers. First Complete Edition [with notes]. Portraits. (150 copies.) Royal 8vo. New York: The Bradford Club, 1860.

The American Flag. [First separate edition.] Illustrations. 4to. New York, 1861.

DUGANNE, AUGUSTINE JOSEPH HICKEY. 1823-1875.

Massachusetts. 32mo. Boston, 1843.

Home Poems. 18mo. Boston, 1844.

The Iron Harp. 18mo. Philadelphia, 1847.

The Gospel of Labor: a Poem read before the Mechanics Library Association, Feb. 22, 1849. 16mo. Boston, 1849.

Parnassus in Pillory. A Satire by Motley Manners, Esq. 12mo. New York, 1851.

The Mission of Intellect: a Poem delivered at Metropolitan Hall, New York, Dec. 20, 1852. 12mo. New York, 1853.

Art's True Mission in America. 2 plates. 16mo. New York, 1853.

The True Republic: a Poem. 8vo. New York, 1854.

Poetical Works. Illustrations. 8vo. Philadelphia, 1855.

The War in Europe; being a Retrospect of Wars and Treaties. Portraits and illustrations. 8vo. New York, 1859.

The Tenant-House; or Embers from Poverty's Hearth-Stone. 12mo. New York, 1860.

A History of Governments. 12mo. New York, 1861.

Ballads of the War, — Sumter;— March to the Capital. Illustrations. 2 parts, 4to. New York, 1862.

The Ring of Destiny; or the Astrologer's Plot: a Tale of Ancient Days. 4to. Boston, 1863.

Utterances. Royal 8vo. New York, 1864.

Prison Life in the South. 12mo. New York, 1865.

Camps and Prisons: Twenty Months in the Department of the Gulf. Illustrations. 12mo. New York, 1865.

The Fighting Quakers: a True Story of the War for our Union. Frontispiece. 12mo. New York, 1866.

A History of Livingston County, N. Y., . . . by Lockwood Lyon Doty. With Biographical Introduction by A. J. H. Duganne. Portraits and illustrations. 8vo. Geneseo, 1876.
   *.*Mr. Duganne was also author of several juvenile publications, and is credited by Allibone with MDCCCXLVIII; or the Year of the People; and The Mysteries of Three Cities.

DUNLAP, WILLIAM. 1766-1839.

Darby's Return. 8vo. New York, 1787.

The Father; or, American Shandyism. Written by A Citizen of New York. A Comedy in Five Acts. . . . 8vo. New York, 1789.

The Archers; or, Mountaineers of Switzerland: an Opera in Three Acts. 8vo. New York, 1796.

Life of William Gutherie. 12mo. Exeter, N. H., 1796.

Tell Truth and shame the Devil. A Comedy. 8vo. New York, 1797.

André; a Tragedy in Five Acts: as performed by the Old American Company, New York, March 30, 1798. 8vo. New York, 1798.

André: a Tragedy. . . . To which is added the Cow-Chace: a Satirical Poem, by Major André: with the Proceedings of the Court-Martial and Authentic Documents concerning him. 8vo. London, 1799.

The Virgin of the Sun. 8vo. New York, 1800.

Pizarro in Peru. 8vo. New York, 1800.

False Shame: a Comedy. 18mo. New York, 1800.

[Anonymous.] The Wild-Goose Chace: a Play in Four Acts. With Songs. From the German of Augustus Von Kotzebue. . . . Portrait. 18mo. New York, 1800.

Blue Beard: a Dramatic Romance. 18mo. New York, 1802.

Aballino: the Great Bandit. 18mo. New York, 1803.

Ribbemont: or, the Feudal Baron: a Tragedy. 18mo. New York, 1803.

[Anonymous.] The Glory of Columbia her Yeomanry. A Play in Five Acts. 12mo. New York, 1803.

The Voice of Nature: a Drama in Three Acts. . . . 18mo. New York, 1803.

The Wife of Two Husbands. 18mo. New York, 1804.

Lord Leicester; a Tragedy . . . . 18mo. New York, 1804.

Fontainville Abbey. A Tragedy. . . . 18mo. New York, 1807.

The Father of an Only Child. A Comedy. 18mo. New York, 1807.

The Blind Boy. 18mo. New York, 1808.

Fraternal Discord. A Drama. Altered from the German. 18mo. New York, 1809.

Rinaldo Rinaldini. 18mo. New York, 1810.

The Italian Father. 18mo. New York, 1810.

[Anonymous.] The Africans; or, War, Love, and Duty. A Play. 18mo. Philadelphia, 1811.

Yankee Chronology; or, Huzza for the Constitution! A Musical Interlude in One Act. To which are added Patriotic Songs of the Freedom of the Seas and Yankee Tars. 12mo. New York, 1812.

Memoirs of the Life of George Frederick Cooke, Esquire. . . . . Portrait. 2 volumes, 16mo. New York, 1813.

(With others.) A Record, Literary and Political, of Five Months in the Year 1813. 8vo. New York [1813]. .

A Narrative of the Events which followed Bonaparte's Campaign in Russia, to the Period of his Dethronement. 12mo. Hartford, 1814.

Life of the . . . . Duke of Wellington, by Francis L. Clarke. With Supplementary Chapters by William Dunlap. Portrait and map. 8vo. New York, 1814.

Peter the Great; or, the Russian's Mother. 18mo. New York, 1814.

The Good Neighbor: an Interlude. 18mo. New York, 1814.

Lovers' Vows: a Play. 18mo. New York, 1814.

The Life of Charles Brockden Brown; together with Selections from the Rarest of his printed Works, from his Original Letters and from his Manuscripts before unpublished. 2 volumes, 8vo. Philadelphia, 1815.

A Trip to Niagara; or Travellers in America: a Farce. 18mo. New York, 1830.

Address to the Students of the National Academy of Design, New York, 18th April, 1831. 8vo. New York, 1831.

A History of the American Theatre. 8vo. New York, 1832.

Statistical Sketches of Upper Canada for the Use of Emigrants. By A Backwoodsman. 18mo. London, 1832.

History of the Rise and Progress of the Arts of Design in the United States. 2 volumes, 8vo. New York, 1834.

[Anonymous.] Thirty Years Ago, or, the Memoirs of a Water Drinker. 2 volumes, 12mo. New York, 1836.

A History of New York for Schools. Plates. 2 volumes, 18mo. New York, 1837.

History of the New Netherlands, Province of New York, and State of New York, to the Adoption of the Federal Constitution. 2 volumes, 8vo. New York, 1839-40.

EGAN, MAURICE FRANCIS. 1852 —

[Anonymous.] That Girl of Mine. 12mo. Philadelphia, 1877.

[Anonymous.] That Lover of Mine. 12mo. Philadelphia, 1877.

Preludes. 16mo. Philadelphia, 1880.

The Theatre and Christian Parents. 12mo. New York, 1885.

The Life around us. 12mo. New York, 1885.

A Garden of Roses. 12mo. Boston, 1888.

Modern Novels and Novelists. 12mo. New York [1888].

Lectures on English Literature. 12mo. New York [1889].

A Primer of English Literature. 16mo. New York, 1890.

How they worked their Way and other Tales: Stories of Duty. 12mo. New York, 1892.

Songs and Sonnets and other Poems. 16mo. Chicago, 1892.

The Disappearance of John Longworthy. 12mo. Notre Dame, Ind., 1893.

The Vocation of Patrick Desmond. 12mo. Notre Dame, 1893.

A Gentleman. 16mo. New York, 1893.

A Marriage of Reason. 12mo. Baltimore, 1893.

The Flower of the Flock. 12mo. New York, 1894.

EGGLESTON, EDWARD. 1837 — 1902

Mr. Blake's Walking-Stick. 16mo. Chicago, 1870.

The Book of Queer Stories. 12mo. Chicago, 1870.

The Sunday-School Manual: a Practical Guide to Sunday-School Work. 18mo. Chicago, 1870.

The Hoosier Schoolmaster. Illustrations. 12mo. New York, 1871.

The End of the World. Illustrations. 12mo. New York, 1872.

The Mysteries of Metropolisville. Illustrations. 12mo. New York, 1873.

A Schoolmaster's Stories for Boys and Girls. Illustrations. 12mo. Boston, 1874.

The Circus Rider: a Tale of the Heroic Age. Illustrations. 12mo. New York, 1874.

Christ in Literature: being a Treasury of Choice Readings in Prose and Verse. . . . Illustrations. Royal 8vo. New York, 1875.

Christ in Art: the Story of the Words and Acts of Jesus Christ arranged in One Continuous Narrative. Illustrations. 4to. New York, 1875.

Roxy. Illustrations. 12mo. New York, 1878.

(With Lillie E. Seelye and George Cary Eggleston.) Famous American Indians. Illustrations. 5 volumes, 12mo. New York, 1878–80.

The Hoosier Schoolboy. Illustrations. 12mo. New York, 1883.

Queer Stories for Boys and Girls. Illustrations. 12mo. New York, 1884.

The Graysons. Illustrations. 12mo. New York, 1888.

A History of the United States and its People. For the Use of Schools. Maps and illustrations. 8vo. New York, 1888.

The Household History of the United States and its People. Maps and illustrations. 8vo. New York, 1889.

First Book in American History: with Special Reference to the Lives and Deeds of Great Americans. Illustrations. Square 12mo. New York, 1889.

(Edited.) The Story of Columbus. By Elizabeth E. Seelye. Illustrations. 12mo. New York, 1892.

Duffels. 12mo. New York, 1893.

EMERSON, RALPH WALDO. 1803–1882.

A Sermon at the Ordination of Hersey Bradford Goodwin, in Concord, Mass., Feb. 17, 1830, by James Kendall [and Right Hand of Fellowship by Rev. Ralph Waldo Emerson]. 8vo. Concord, 1830.

A Sermon delivered at the Ordination of Rev. Chandler Robbins over the South Congregational Church in Boston, Dec. 4, 1833, by Rev. Henry Ware, Jr. [With hymn by Rev. R. W. Emerson.] 8vo. Boston, 1833.

An Historical Discourse delivered before the Citizens of Concord, Sept. 12, 1835. . . . 8vo. Concord, 1835.

[Anonymous.] Nature. 12mo. Boston, 1836.

(Edited.) Sartor Resartus, by Thomas Carlyle. 12mo. Boston, 1836.

An Oration [The American Scholar] delivered before the Phi Beta Kappa Society. . . . Cambridge, August 31, 1837. 8vo. Boston, 1837.
*˳*Republished as Man Thinking. 16mo. London, 1844.

An Address delivered before the Senior Class in Divinity College, Cambridge, 15 July, 1838. 8vo. Boston, 1838.

An Oration [Literary Ethics], delivered before the Literary Societies of Dartmouth College, July 24, 1838. 8vo. Boston, 1838.

(Edited.) Critical and Miscellaneous Essays, by Thomas Carlyle. 2 volumes, 12mo. Boston, 1838.

The Dial: a Magazine for Literature, Philosophy, and Religion. Edited anonomously by R. W. Emerson, S. Margaret Fuller, and George Ripley. 4 volumes, or 16 numbers [July, 1840–April, 1844, inclusive], 8vo. Boston, 1840–44.
*˳*For list of Emerson's contributions to The Dial see appendix to his biography by James E. Cabot; for general list of contributors see G. W. Cooke's article in the Journal of Speculative Philosophy, July, 1885.

The Method of Nature. An Oration delivered before the Society of the Adelphi, in Waterville College, in Maine, August 11, 1841. 8vo. Boston, 1841.

Essays. 12mo. Boston, 1841.

Notice on the Death of E. Ripley. 8vo. Boston, 1841.

Essays, with Preface by Thomas Carlyle. 12mo. London, 1841.

(Edited.) Past and Present, by Thomas Carlyle. 12mo. Boston, 1843.

Man the Reformer. A Lecture. 12mo. London [1844].

The Young American. A Lecture read before the Mercantile Library Association, in Boston, February 7, 1844. 8vo. London, 1844.

Essays. Second Series. 12mo. Boston, 1844.

Orations, Lectures, and Addresses. 16mo. London, 1844.

An Address delivered in the Court-House, in Concord, Mass., on 1st August, 1844, on the Anniversary of the Emancipation of the Negroes in the British West Indies. 8vo. Boston, 1844.

Our Pastor's Offering. A Compilation from the Writings of the Pastors of the Second Church. For the Ladies' Fair to assist in furnishing the New Church Edifice. [Including three poems, one specially contributed, with letter, by R. W. Emerson.] 16mo. Boston, 1845.

Poems. 12mo. Boston, 1847.
***Also 16mo. London, 1847.

The Massachusetts Quarterly Review. Edited by R. W. Emerson [who also contributed the editorial address, Dec. 1847], Theodore Parker, and James Eliot Cabot. 3 volumes, 8vo. Boston, 1847-50.

Nature; Addresses and Lectures. 12mo. Boston, 1849.

Representative Men: Seven Lectures. 12mo. Boston, 1850.

Memoirs of Margaret Fuller Ossoli. [By J. F. Clarke, R. W. Emerson, who contributed the chapters on Concord and Boston, vol. i., pp. 199-351, and W. H. Channing.] 2 volumes, 12mo. Boston, 1852.

Kossuth in New England . . . . with his Speeches and the Addresses that were made to him [including address at Concord, by R. W. Emerson; pp. 222-224]. Portrait. 8vo. Boston, 1852.

English Traits. 12mo. Boston, 1856.

Miscellanies; embracing Nature, Addresses and Lectures. 12mo. Boston, 1856.

The John Brown Invasion. An Authentic History of the Harper's Ferry Invasion; . . . [including Emerson's speech at the Boston meeting in Tremont Temple, Nov. 18, 1859, pp. 103-105]. 8vo. Boston, 1860.

The Conduct of Life. 12mo. Boston, 1860.

Tributes to Theodore Parker, comprising the Exercises at the Music Hall, ... June 17, 1860 [including tribute by Emerson, pp. 14-19]. With the Proceedings of the New England Anti-Slavery Convention. ... May 31. ... 12mo. Boston, 1860.

The Gulistan, or Rose Garden, by Musle-Huddeen Sheik Saadi of Shiraz. Translated from the Original by F. Gladwyn. With an Essay on Saadi's Life and Character by James Ross, and a Preface by R. W. Emerson. 12mo. Boston, 1865.

The Lincoln Memorial. A Record of the Life, Assassination and Obsequies of the Martyred President. [Including address by Emerson, pp. 146-150.] Edited by John Gilmary Shea. Portrait. Royal 8vo. New York, 1865.

Poems [newly revised]. Portrait. 24mo. Boston, 1865.

Essays. First and Second Series. 24mo. Boston, 1865.

May Day and other Pieces. 12mo. Boston, 1867.

Remarks on the Character of George L. Stearns, at Medford, April 14, 1867. 8vo. [Boston, 1867.]

Ceremonies at the Dedication of the Soldiers' Monument in Concord, Mass. [Address by Emerson, pp. 27-52.] Frontispiece. 12mo. Concord, 1867.

Prose Works. New and Revised Edition. Portrait. 2 volumes, 12mo. Boston, 1870.

Society and Solitude. Twelve Chapters. 12mo. Boston, 1870.

Plutarch's Morals. Translated by William Watson Goodwin, with Introduction by R. W. Emerson. 5 volumes, 8vo. Boston, 1870.

Tribute to Walter Scott, on the 100th Anniversary of his Birthday, Aug. 15, 1871.) Privately printed.) 8vo. Boston, 1871.
 *₊*This tribute was originally published, with remarks by O. W. Holmes and others, in Massachusetts Historical Society Proceedings, vol. xii.

Dedication of the New Building for the Free Public Library of Concord, Mass., October 1, 1873. [Including address by Emerson, pp. 37-45.] 8vo. Boston, 1873.

(Edited.) Parnassus. [Poems by various authors.] 8vo. Boston, 1875.

Letters and Social Aims. 12mo. Boston, 1876.

Selected Poems [including many not previously collected]. 18mo. Boston, 1876.

Works. New and Revised Edition. 9 volumes, 18mo. Boston, 1876.

The Fortune of the Republic: a Lecture delivered at the Old South Church, March 30, 1878. 16mo. Boston, 1878.

The Hundred Greatest Men. With an Introduction by R. W. Emerson. Portraits. 4to. London, 1879.

The Preacher. [Reprinted from The Unitarian Review of January, 1880.] 8vo. Boston, 1880.

Sketches and Reminiscences of the Radical Club of Chestnut Street, Boston. Edited by Mrs. J. T. Sargent. Illustrations. 12mo. Boston, 1880.
  *.*Including essays by Emerson (Religion), Holmes (Jonathan Edwards), John Fiske (Language), two poems by Whittier, and numerous original letters, verses, remarks, etc., by Emerson, Whittier, Stedman and others.

The Centennial of the Social Circle in Concord, March 21, 1882. [Containing memoir of Rev. Ezra Ripley, D. D., by Emerson, pp. 168-176.] 8vo. Cambridge, 1882.

Tributes to Longfellow and Emerson by the Massachusetts Historical Society. [Tributes by Holmes, pp. 13-22, and 39-50; also Emerson's addresses on Carlyle, Burns, and Scott, pp. 51-62, now first collected.] Portraits. Square 8vo. Boston, 1882.

Boston [a poem]. Read in Faneuil Hall .... Dec. 16, 1873. 12mo. [Boston, 1883.]
  *.*Issued as No. 8 of Old South Leaflets series.

Complete Works. Revised with Prefaces by James Eliot Cabot. Portrait. 11 volumes, 12mo. Boston, 1883-84.
  *.*The same. Large paper. (500 copies.) 11 volumes, 8vo. Cambridge, 1883-84.
  *.*Also 11 volumes, 18mo. Boston, 1883-84.
  *.*i., Nature, Addresses and Lectures; ii., iii., Essays; iv., Representative Men; v., English Traits; vi., The Conduct o Life; vii., Society and Solitude; viii., Letters and Social Aims;

ix., Poems; x., Lectures and Biographical Sketches [now first collected]; xi., Miscellanies [now first collected]. The two concluding volumes contain articles not previously published, and vol. ix. contains poems not included in any previous edition.

Poems. Household Edition. 12mo. Boston, 1884.

Natural History of Intellect and other Papers. 18mo. Boston, 1893.
⁂ The same. With General Index to Emerson's collected works. 12mo. Boston, 1893.
⁂ Also, large paper. (250 copies.) 8vo. Cambridge, 1893.
⁂ See also BRYANT, W. C.; CHANNING, W. E.; HAWTHORNE, N.; HOLMES, O. W.; LOWELL, J. R.; THOREAU, H. D.; and VERY, J.

ENGLISH, THOMAS DUNN. 1819 —

Zephaniah Doolittle. 12mo. Philadelphia, 1838.

Walter Woolfe. 12mo. Philadelphia, 1842.

1844; or, the Power of the "S. F.," a Tale developing the Secret Actions of Parties during the Presidential Campaign of 1844. 12mo. New York, 1847.

Poems. 12mo. New York, 1855.

[Edited, anonymously.] The Book of Rubies: a Collection of the Most Notable Love Poems in the English Language. 8vo. New York, 1866.

Ambrose Fecit; or, the Peer and the Painter. 12mo. New York, 1869.

American Ballads. 32mo. New York, 1880.

The Boy's Book of [American] Battle Lyrics . . . . with Historical Notes. Illustrations. 8vo. New York, 1885.

Jacob Schuyler's Millions. 12mo. New York, 1886.

EVERETT, EDWARD. 1794-1865.

American Poets. 8vo. [Cambridge, 1812.]

A Defence of Christianity against the Work of George B. English, A. M., entitled The Grounds of Christianity examined, by comparing the New Testament with the Old. 12mo. Boston, 1814.

Greek Grammar, translated from the German of Philip Buttman. 8vo. Boston, 1822.

Orations and Speeches on Various Occasions. 8vo. Boston, 1836.

Orations and Speeches from 1826 to 1850. 2 volumes, 8vo. Boston, 1850.

Orations and Speeches. Complete Edition. 4 volumes, 8vo. Boston, 1859.

The Mount Vernon Papers. 12mo. New York, 1860.

Life of George Washington. Portrait. 12mo. New York 1860.
  *₊*The same. Large paper. 8vo. New York, 1860.
  *₊*For dates, etc., of Everett's numerous addresses and orations, see 1859 edition. See also HOLMES, O. W.

FAIRFIELD, SUMNER LINCOLN. 1803-1844.

The Siege of Constantinople. 8vo. Charleston, 1822.

Poems. 18mo. New York, 1823.

Lays of Melpomene. 16mo. Portland, 1824.

Mina: a Dramatic Sketch. 12mo. Baltimore, 1825.

The Cities of the Plain. A Scripture Poem. 16mo. Boston, 1827.

The Heir of the World and Lesser Poems. 12mo. Philadelphia, 1829.

Abaddon, the Spirit of Destruction; and other Poems. 8vo. New York, 1830.

The Last Night of Pompeii; a Poem: and Lays and Legends. 8vo. New York, 1832.

Poems and Prose Writings. 2 volumes, 8vo. Philadelphia, 1841.

FAWCETT, EDGAR. 1847 —

Short Poems for Short People. 12mo. New York, 1872.

Purple and Fine Linen. 12mo. New York, 1873.

Ellen Story. A Novel. 8vo. New York, 1876.

Fantasy and Passion. 16mo. Boston, 1877.

A Hopeless Case. 18mo. Boston, 1880.

A Gentleman of Leisure. A Novel. 18mo. Boston, 1881.

The False Friend. 4to. New York [1881].

An Ambitious Woman. 12mo. Boston, 1884.

Tinkling Cymbals: a Novel. 12mo. Boston, 1884.

Song and Story. Later Poems. 12mo. Boston, 1884.

The Adventures of a Widow. 12mo. Boston, 1884.

Rutherford. 12mo. New York, 1884.

[Anonymous.] The Buntling Ball: a Græco-American Play. Being a Poetical Satire on New York Society. Illustrations. Square 12mo. New York, 1884.

[Anonymous.] The New King Arthur: an Opera without Music. Illustrations. Square 12mo. New York, 1885.

Social Silhouettes; being the Impressions of Mr. Mark Manhattan. 12mo. Boston, 1885.

Romance and Revery. Poems. 12mo. Boston, 1886.

The Confessions of Claud. A Romance. Portrait. 12mo. Boston, 1886.

The House at High Bridge. A Novel. 12mo. Boston, 1887.

Miriam Balestier. A Novel. 12mo. New York [1888].

Divided Lives. A Novel. 12mo. New York, 1888.

A Man's Will. A Novel. 12mo. New York, 1888.

Olivia Delaplaine. A Novel. 12mo. Boston, 1888.

Agnosticism and other Essays. With a Prologue by Robert G. Ingersoll. 12mo. New York, 1889.

A Demoralizing Marriage. 8vo. Philadelphia, 1889.

A Daughter of Silence. 12mo. New York, 1890.

How a Husband forgave. Illustrations. 12mo. New York [1890].

Fabian Dimitry. A Novel. 12mo. Chicago, 1890.

The Evil that Men do. 12mo. New York, 1890.

Loaded Dice. A Novel. 12mo. New York [1891].

A New York Family. Illustrations. 12mo. New York [1891].

Songs of Doubt and Dream. 8vo. New York, 1891.

A Romance of Two Brothers. 12mo. New York, 1891.

Blooms and Brambles. 12mo. London, 1891.

An Heir to Millions. A Novel. 12mo. Chicago [1892].

Women must weep. A Novel. 12mo. Chicago [1892].

The Adopted Daughter. 12mo. Chicago [1892].

American Push. A Novel. 12mo. Chicago, 1893.

A Mild Barbarian. 12mo. New York, 1894.

Her Fair Fame. A Novel. 12mo. New York, 1894.

Outrageous Fortune. 12mo. New York, 1894.
*.*See also, HAWTHORNE, JULIAN.

FAY, THEODORE SEDGWICK. 1807—

Dreams and Reveries of a Quiet Man. . . . By One of the Editors of The New York Mirror. 2 volumes, 12mo. New York, 1832.

Views in the City of New-York and its Environs . . . . by Celebrated Artists . . . . with Historical, Topographical and Critical Illustrations by T. S. Fay [and others]. 4to. New York, 1832.

Crayon Sketches. By An Amateur [W. Cox]. Edited by T. S. Fay. 2 volumes, 12mo. New York, 1833.

Norman Leslie. A Tale of the Present Time. 2 volumes, 12mo. New York, 1835.

[Anonymous.] Sydney Clifton; or, Vicissitudes in both Hemispheres. 2 volumes, 12mo. New York, 1839.

The Countess Ida. 2 volumes, 12mo. New York, 1840.

Hoboken: a Romance of New York. 2 volumes, 12mo. New
York, 1843.

Robert Rueful. 8vo. New York, 1844.

Ulric; or, the Voices. 12mo. New York, 1851.

Views of Christianity. 8vo. [Berne, 1856.]

Great Outlines of Geography. 12mo. [and folio atlas of
maps]. New York, 1867.

The Three Germanys. Glimpses into their History. Portraits. 2 volumes, 8vo. New York [1889].
 „ See also PAULDING, J. K.

FIELD, EUGENE. 1850–1895.

The Tribune Primer. 24mo. Denver, 1882.

A Model Primer. Illustrations. 16mo. Brooklyn, 1882.

Culture's Garland; being Memoranda of the Gradual Rise of
Literature, Art, Music and Society in Chicago and other
Western Ganglia. With an Introduction by Julian Hawthorne. 16mo. Boston, 1887.

A Little Book of Western Verse. (Privately printed; 250
copies.) Small 8vo. Chicago, 1889.

A Little Book of Profitable Tales. (Privately printed; 250
copies.) Small 8vo. Chicago, 1889.

A Little Book of Western Verse. 12mo. New York, 1890.

A Little Book of Profitable Tales. 12mo. New York, 1890.

Echoes from the Sabine Farm, being Certain Horatian Lyrics,
now for the First Time discreetly and delectably done into
English Verse by Eugene and Roswell M. Field, with Sundry Little Picturings by E. H. Garrett. (70 copies.) 8vo.
The Orchard, New Rochelle, 1891.
 „ Also 30 copies printed on Japan paper, each containing
an autograph poem. 8vo. New Rochelle, 1891.

With Trumpet and Drum. 16mo. New York, 1892.
 „ The same. Large paper. (250 copies.) Small 8vo. New
York, 1892.

 „ A few copies were also printed on Japan paper for presentation by the author.

Second Book of Verse. (Privately printed; 300 copies.) Small 8vo. Chicago, 1893.
 *₊*Also a few copies on Japan paper for presentation by the author.
 *₊*The same. 12mo. New York, 1893.

Echoes from the Sabine Farm .... (500 copies.) Royal 8vo. Chicago, 1893.

The Holy Cross and other Tales. 16mo. Cambridge, 1893.
 *₊*The same. Large paper. (100 copies). Small 4to Cambridge, 1893.
 *₊*Also a few copies on Japan paper for presentation by the author.

First Editions of American Authors, a Manual for Book-Lovers, compiled by Herbert S. Stone, with an Introduction by Eugene Field. 16mo. Cambridge, 1893.
 *₊*The same. Large paper. (50 copies.) Small 4to. Cambridge, 1893.

Love Songs of Childhood. 16mo. New York, 1894.
 *₊*The same. Large paper. (100 copies.) Small 8vo. New York, 1894.
 *₊*Also a few copies on Japan paper for presentation by the author.

Memoir of Mrs. Ruth C. Gray. (Privately printed.) 12mo. St. Louis, 1894.

FIELDS, ANNIE ADAMS (MRS. JAMES T. FIELDS). 1834 —

Ode recited by Charlotte Cushman, at the Inauguration of the Great Organ in Boston, Nov. 2, 1863. 8vo. [Boston, 1863.]

Under the Olive. 18mo. Boston, 1881.

[Anonymous.] James T. Fields. Biographical Notes and Personal Sketches, with Unpublished Fragments, and Tributes from Men and Women of Letters [including memorial poems by Whittier and Longfellow]. 8vo. Boston, 1881.

How to help the Poor. 16mo. Boston, 1883.

[With others, anonymously.] A Week away from Time. 12mo. Boston, 1887.

Whittier: Notes of his Life and of his Friendships. Illustrations. 32mo. New York, 1893.

A Shelf of Old Books. Illustrations. 8vo. New York, 1894.

The Singing Shepherd and other Poems. 16mo. Boston, 1895.
  *₊*See also THAXTER, CELIA.

FIELDS, JAMES THOMAS. 1820-1881.

Anniversary Poem delivered before the Mercantile Library Association of Boston, Sept. 13, 1838. 8vo. Boston, 1838.

The Post of Honor . . . . read before the Boston Mercantile Library Association . . . . 8vo. Boston, 1848.

Poems. Square 12mo. Boston, 1849.

(Edited, anonymously.) The Boston Book. Being Specimens of Metropolitan Literature [including The Yankee Zincali, pp. 240–252, by Whittier, The Morning Visit, pp. 89–92, by Holmes, and contributions, original and selected, by Parsons, Lowell, Longfellow, Hawthorne and others]. 12mo. Boston, 1850.

Poems. Illustrations. (Privately printed.) Square 18mo. Cambridge [1854].

[Anonymous.] A Few Verses for a Few Friends. (Privately printed.) 16mo. [Boston, 1858.]

Religio Medici, A Letter to a Friend, Christian Morals, Urn-Burial, and other Papers. By Sir Thomas Browne. [With biographical sketch of the author, pp. vii.–xviii., by Fields.] Portrait. 16mo. Boston, 1862.
  *₊*The same. Large paper. (25 copies.) 8vo. Boston, 1862.

Early and Late Papers, hitherto uncollected, by W. M. Thackeray. [Edited, with prefatory note, by Fields.] Portrait. 12mo. Boston, 1867.

(Edited.) The Mystery of Edwin Drood and some Uncollected Pieces, by Charles Dickens. Illustrations. 8vo. Boston, 1870.

Yesterdays with Authors. 12mo. Boston, 1872.

(With E. P. Whipple, and others.) Variegated Leaves. A Book of Prose and Verse in Aid of the Children's Hospital. 16mo. Boston, 1873.

Hawthorne. Illustrations. 32mo. Boston, 1876.

Old Acquaintance. Barry Cornwall and some of his Friends. 15 portraits. 32mo. Boston, 1876.

In and out of Doors with Charles Dickens. 32mo. Boston, 1876.

Underbrush. 18mo. Boston, 1877.

A Conversational Pitcher. 16mo. Boston [1877].

(Edited, with E. P. Whipple.) The Family Library of British Poetry, . . . 1350–1878. Portraits. 8vo. Boston, 1878.

Ballads and other Verses. 16mo. Boston, 1881.
*_{*}*See also FIELDS, ANNIE A.

FISKE, JOHN. 1842 —

Tobacco and Alcohol: i., It does pay to smoke; ii., The coming Man will drink Wine. 16mo. New York, 1868.

Myths and Myth-Makers: Old Tales and Superstitions interpreted by Comparative Mythology. 12mo. Boston, 1873.

Outlines of Cosmic Philosophy. Based on the Doctrine of Evolution, with Criticisms on the Positive Philosophy. 2 volumes, 8vo. London, 1874.
*_{*}*Also 2 volumes. 8vo. Boston, 1875.

The Unseen World and other Essays. 12mo. Boston, 1876.

Darwinism and other Essays. 12mo. London and New York, 1879.

The Presidents of America, a Series of Original Steel Engravings . . . . With Biographical Sketches and an Introductory Essay by John Fiske. 4to. Boston, 1879.

Excursions of an Evolutionist. 12mo. Boston, 1884.

The Destiny of Man Viewed in the Light of his Origin. 12mo. Boston, 1884.

American Political Ideas viewed from the Standpoint of Universal History. Three Lectures given at the Royal Institution of Great Britain, in May, 1880. 12mo. New York, 1885.

Darwinism and other Essays. New Edition, revised and enlarged. 12mo. Boston, 1885.

The Idea of God as affected by Modern Knowledge. 16mo. Boston, 1885.

Washington and his Country; being Irving's Life of Washington abridged for the Use of Schools. With Introduction and Continuation to the End of the Civil War, by John Fiske. 16mo. Boston, 1887.

(Edited, with James Grant Wilson.) Appleton's Cyclopædia of American Biography. Portraits. 6 volumes, 8vo. New York, 1887-89.

The Critical Period of American History, 1783-1789. 12mo. Boston, 1888.

The War of Independence. Map. 12mo. Boston, 1889.

The Reconstruction of Europe, by H. Murdock. With Introduction by John Fiske. 12mo. Boston, 1889.

A Memorial of Crispus Attucks, Samuel Gray, and Patrick Carr, from the City of Boston. [Address by John Fiske, and poem by John Boyle O'Reilly.] 3 plates. Royal 8vo. Boston, 1889.

Civil Government in the United States, considered with some Reference to its Origins. 12mo. Boston, 1890.

The American Revolution. Portrait and maps. 2 volumes, 12mo. Boston, 1891.

The Doctrine of Evolution. 12mo. New York, 1891.

The Discovery of America. With some Account of Ancient America and the Spanish Conquest. Portrait and illustrations. 2 volumes, 8vo. Boston, 1892.
 *.*The same. Large paper. (250 copies.) 4 volumes, royal 8vo. Cambridge, 1892.

A Memorial of Christopher Columbus from the City of Boston . . . . [with oration by John Fiske]. Portrait and illustrations. Royal 8vo. Boston, 1893.

Edward Livingston Youmans. . . . A Sketch of his Life, with Selections from his Writings and Correspondence. Portraits. 8vo. New York, 1894.

A History of the United States for Schools. Illustrations. 12mo. Boston, 1894.
  *₊*See also Proctor, Edna Dean.

FLAGG, WILSON. 1805-1884.

Analysis of Female Beauty. 12mo. Boston, 1834.

The Tailor's Shop; or Crowns of Thorns and Coats of Thistles. Designed to tickle some, and nettle others; intended chiefly for Politicians. 16mo. Boston, 1844.

Studies in the Field and Forest. 12mo. Boston, 1857.

Mount Auburn: its Scenes, its Beauties, and its Lessons. Illustrations. 12mo. Boston, 1861.

The Woods and By-Ways of New England. Illustrations. 8vo. Boston, 1872.

The Birds and Seasons of New England. Illustrations. 8vo. Boston, 1875.

Halcyon Days. 12mo. Boston, 1881.

A Year among the Trees. 12mo. Boston, 1881.

A Year with the Birds. 12mo. Boston, 1881.
  *₊*These three volumes are composed of the text of the 1872 and 1875 titles.

FLINT, TIMOTHY. 1780-1840.

A Sermon preached May 11, 1808 . . . . 8vo. Newburyport, 1808.

Recollections of the Last Ten Years, passed . . . . in the Valley of the Mississippi. 8vo. Boston, 1826.

[Anonymous.] Francis Berrian, or the Mexican Patriot. . . . 2 volumes, 12mo. Boston, 1826.

(Edited.) The Western Monthly Review. [May, 1827-June, 1830.] 3 volumes, 8vo. Cincinnati, 1828-30.

A Condensed Geography and History of the Western States, or, the Mississippi Valley. 2 volumes, 8vo. Cincinnati, 1828.

[Anonymous.] Arthur Clenning. . . . 2 volumes, 12mo. Philadelphia, 1828.

George Mason, the Young Backwoodsman ; or Don't give up the Ship. A Story of the Mississippi. 12mo. Boston, 1829.

The Shoshonee Valley: a Romance. 2 volumes, 12mo. Cincinnati, 1830.

The Lost Child. 16mo. Boston, 1830.

(Translated.) The Art of being Happy. From the French of Droz. . . . 12mo. Boston, 1832.

Indian Wars of the West: combining Biographical Sketches of the Early Pioneers. 12mo. Cincinnati, 1833.

Lectures upon Natural History. . . . and Discourses on the Arts. 12mo. Boston, 1833.

Biographical Memoir of Daniel Boone, the First Settler of Kentucky. 12mo. Cincinnati, 1833.
 *₁*Reissued as The First White Man: or, the Life and Exploits of Col. Daniel Boone. Illustrations. 12mo. Cincinnati, 1849.

(Translated.) Celibacy vanquished, or the Old Bachelor Reclaimed. 12mo. Philadelphia, 1834.

FOOTE, MARY HALLOCK. 1847—

The Led-Horse Claim: a Romance of a Mining Camp. Illustrations. 12mo. Boston, 1883.

John Bodewin's Testimony. 12mo. Boston, 1886.

The Last Assembly Ball. 12mo. Boston, 1889.

The Chosen Valley. 16mo. Boston, 1892.

In Exile and other Stories. 16mo. Boston, 1894.

The Cup of Trembling and other Stories. 16mo. Boston, 1895.

FORD, PAUL LEICESTER. . . .

(Edited.) The Webster Genealogy. . . . 4to. Brooklyn, 1876.

Bibliotheca Chaunciana. A List of the Writings of Charles Chauncy. (Privately printed.) 8vo. Brooklyn, 1884.

(Edited.) Lines to Mr. Dodson. . . . by Frances Sargent Osgood. (10 copies.) 4to. Brooklyn, 1885.

Bibliotheca Hamiltoniana : a List of Books written by, or relating to Alexander Hamilton. (500 copies.) 8vo. New York, 1886.

A List of Treasury Reports and Circulars issued by Alexander Hamilton, 1789-1795. (50 copies.) 8vo. Brooklyn, 1886.

A List of Editions of The Federalist. (50 copies.) 8vo. Brooklyn, 1886.

(Edited.) Pamphlets on the Constitution of the United States, published during its Discussion by the People, 1787-1788, with Notes and a Bibliography. (500 copies.) 8vo. Brooklyn, 1888.

Some Materials for a Bibliography of the Official Publications of the Continental Congress for 1774-1789. (250 copies.) 8vo. Brooklyn, 1888.

A List of the Federal Convention of 1787. (100 copies.) 8vo. Brooklyn, 1888.

Bibliography and Reference List of the History and Literature relative to the Adoption of the Constitution of the United States. (250 copies.) 8vo. Brooklyn, 1888.

Check List of American Magazines printed in the 18th Century. (250 copies.) 8vo. Brooklyn, 1889.

Check List of Bibliographies, Catalogues, Reference Lists and Lists of Authorities of American Books and Subjects. (500 copies.) 8vo. Brooklyn, 1889.

Franklin Bibliography. A List of Books written by or relating to Benjamin Franklin. (500 copies.) 8vo. Brooklyn, 1889.

List of Some Briefs in Appeal Cases relating to America tried before the Land Commissioners of Appeal, 1738-1758. (250 copies.) 8vo. Brooklyn, 1889.

Who was the Mother of Franklin's Son ? An Historical Conundrum, hitherto given up, now partly answered. (100 copies.) 8vo. Brooklyn, 1889.

The Best Laid Plans. [A play, printed as manuscript for private use.] (50 copies.) 4to. [Brooklyn] 1889.
  *⁎*The same, Second Edition. (100 copies.) Small 4to. [Brooklyn] 1889.

The Origin, Purpose, and Result of the Harrisburg Convention of 1788. A Study in Popular Government. 8vo. Brooklyn, 1890.

(Edited.) The Sayings of Poor Richard, etc. Originally printed in Poor Richard's Almanac, 1733-1758. Portrait. 16mo. New York, 1890.

(Edited.) The Writings of Christopher Columbus. 12mo. New York, 1892.

(Edited.) A Summary View. By Thomas Jefferson. (100 copies.) 8vo. Brooklyn, 1892.

(Edited.) Essays on the Constitution of the United States published during its Discussion by the People, 1787-1788. 8vo. Brooklyn, 1892.

(With others.) Memorial Volume of the Washington Centennial. 4to. New York, 1893.

Some Notes towards an Essay on the Beginnings of American Dramatic Literature, 1606-1789. [25 copies printed as manuscript for suggestion and revision.] Small 4to. [Brooklyn] 1893.

(With others.) James Lorimer Graham, Jr. January 17th, 1894. The Century Association: New York, 1894.

Josiah Tucker and his Writings. Royal 8vo. Chicago [1894].

(Edited.) Notes on Virginia. By Thomas Jefferson. (100 copies.) 8vo. Brooklyn, 1894.

The Hon. Peter Stirling and what People thought of him. 12mo. New York, 1894.

(Edited.) Writings of John Dickinson. 3 volumes, 8vo. Philadelphia, 1895.
  *⁎*For historical writings see Reports of American Historical Association, for 1889, 1890, 1891, 1892.

FREDERICK, HAROLD. 1856—

Seth's Brother's Wife: a Study of Life in the Greater New York. 12mo. New York, 1887.

The Lawton Girl. 12mo. New York, 1890.

In the Valley. Illustrations. 12mo. New York, 1890.

The Young Emperor, William II. Portraits. 12mo. New York, 1892,

The New Exodus, a Study of Israel in Russia. Portraits. 8vo. New York, 1892.

The Return of the O'Mahony. Illustrations. 12mo. New York [1892].

The Copperhead. 12mo. New York, 1893.

Marsena, and other Stories of the Wartime. 12mo. New York, 1894.
***Mr. Frederic's works, except Marsena, appeared simultaneously in London and New York; a French translation of The Young Emperor was also published in Paris, 1894.

FRENCH, ALICE (OCTAVE THANET). 1850—

Knitters in the Sun. 12mo. Boston, 1887.

Expiation. Illustrations. 12mo. New York, 1890.

Otto the Knight and other Trans-Mississippi Stories. 12mo. Boston, 1891.

We all. 12mo. New York, 1891.

Stories of a Western Town. Illustrations. 12mo. New York, 1893.

An Adventure in Photography. Illustrations. 12mo. New York, 1893.

FRENEAU, PHILIP. 1752–1832.

[Anonymous.] A Poem on the Rising Glory of America: being an Exercise delivered at the Public Commencement at Nassau-Hall, September 25, 1771. 8vo. Philadelphia, 1772.

A Voyage to Boston: a Poem. 8vo. Philadelphia, 1775.

[Anonymous.] The British Prison-Ship: a Poem in Four Cantoes. . . . To which is added a Poem on the Death of Captain N. Biddle, who was blown up with the Yarmouth near Barbadoes. 8vo. Philadelphia, 1781.

[Anonymous.] New Travels through North America: in a Series of Letters; exhibiting the History of the Victorious Campaign of the Allied Armies under General Washington and the Count de Rochambeau, in 1781. Interspersed with Political and Philosophical Observations upon the Genius, Temper, and Customs of the Americans. Also Narrations of the Capture of General Burgoyne and Lord Cornwallis. . . . Translated from the Original of the Abbé Robin. 8vo. Boston, 1784.

Poems. Written Chiefly during the Late War. 12mo. Philadelphia, 1786.

A Journey from Philadelphia to New York, by Way of Burlington and South-Amboy. By Robert Slender, Stocking Weaver. 8vo. Philadelphia, 1787.

Miscellaneous Works, containing Essays and Additional Poems. 12mo. Philadelphia, 1788.

[Anonymous.] The Village Merchant: a Poem. To which is added, The Country Printer. 12mo. Philadelphia, 1794.

Poems written between the Years 1768 & 1794. A New Edition, revised and corrected by the Author; including a Considerable Number of Pieces never before published. 8vo. Monmouth, N. J., 1795.

The Probationary Odes of 'Jonathan Pindar, Esq., a Cousin of Peter's, and Candidate for the Post of Poet Laureate to the C [ongress of the]. U [nited]. S [tates]. 12mo. Philadelphia, 1796.
*.*Quoted by Sabin as attributed to Freneau.

(Edited.) The Time-Piece and Literary Companion. 3 volumes [148 numbers], 8vo. New York, 1797–98.
*.*No. 1 was published March 13, 1797; No. 148, August 25, 1798.

Letters on Various Interesting and Important Subjects, many of which have appeared in The Aurora. Corrected and much enlarged. By Robert Slender, O. S. U. 8vo. Philadelphia, 1799.

Poems written and published during the American Revolutionary War, and now republished from the Original Manuscripts, interspersed with Translations from the Ancients, and other Pieces not heretofore in-Print. 2 plates. 2 volumes, 12mo. Philadelphia, 1809.
  *₀*Designated on title-page, third edition.

A Laughable Poem; or, Robert Slender's Journey from Philadelphia to New York, by Way of Burlington and South Amboy. 12mo. Philadelphia, Dec. 20, 1809.

A Collection of Poems on American Affairs, and a Variety of other Subjects, chiefly Moral and Political; written between the Year 1797 and the Present Time. 2 volumes, 16mo. New York, 1815.

FULLER, HENRY BLAKE. 1857 —

The Chevalier of Pensieri-Vani, together with Frequent References to the Prorege of Arcopia. By Stanton Page. 12mo. Boston [1890].

The Chevalier of Pensieri-Vani. Second Edition, revised and enlarged. 12mo. New York, 1892.

The Chatelaine of La Trinite. Illustrations. 12mo. New York, 1892.

The Cliff-Dwellers: a Novel. Illustrations. 12mo. New York, 1893.

With the Procession: a Novel. 12mo. New York, 1895.

FULLER (OSSOLI), S. MARGARET. 1810–1850.

Conversations with Goethe in the Last Years of his Life, translated from the German of Eckermann. 12mo. Boston, 1839.

[Anonymous.] Günderode. [A translation from the German, of the correspondence between the Canoness Günderode and Bettine Brentano.] 12mo. Boston, 1842.

Summer on the Lakes in 1843. 12mo. Boston, 1844.
  *₀*Some copies were issued with engravings.

Woman in the Nineteenth Century. 12mo. New York, 1845.

Papers on Literature and Art. 2 volumes, 12mo. New York, 1846.

Woman in the Nineteenth Century and Kindred Papers relating to the Sphere, Condition, and Duties of Woman. Edited by Arthur B. Fuller, with an Introduction by Horace Greeley. Portrait. 12mo. New York, 1855.

At Home and Abroad, or Things and Thoughts in America and Europe [in 4 parts, of which only part 1, Summer on the Lakes, was previously published]. Edited by Arthur B. Fuller. [With biographical notices by Bayard Taylor and Horace Greeley, and memorial poems by W. S. Landor, G. P. R. James and others.] 12mo. Boston, 1856.

Life Without and Life Within ; or, Reviews, Narratives, Essays, and Poems [now first collected]. Edited by Arthur B. Fuller. 12mo. Boston, 1860.
  *.*See also EMERSON, R. W.

GARLAND, HAMLIN. 1861 —

Under the Wheel : a Play in Six Scenes. (Privately printed.) 8vo. Boston, 1890.

Main-Travelled Roads : Six Mississippi Valley Stories. 12mo. Boston, 1891.

A Member of the Third House. 12mo. Chicago, 1892.

Jason Edwards. An Average Man. 12mo. Boston, 1892.

A Little Norsk : Ol' Pap's Flaxen. 16mo. New York, 1892.

A Spoil of Office. Frontispiece. 12mo. Boston, 1892.

Prairie Folks. 12mo. Chicago, 1893.

Main-Travelled Roads. Revised Edition, with Introduction by W. D. Howells. Frontispiece. 16mo. Cambridge, 1893.
  *.*The same. Large paper. (110 copies.) 8vo. Cambridge, 1893.

Prairie Songs : Verses. 16mo. Cambridge, 1893.
  *.*The same. Large paper. (110 copies.) 8vo. Cambridge, 1893.

Crumbling Idols : Twelve Essays on Art. 16mo. Chicago, 1894.

GIBSON, WILLIAM HAMILTON. 1850-1896.

 The Complete American Trapper; or the Tricks of Trapping and Trap-making; containing also an extended Chapter on Life in the Woods. Illustrations. 12mo. New York, 1876.
  ⁎ Republished as Camp Life in the Woods. 12mo. New York, 1881.

 Pastoral Days; or Memories of a New England Year. Illustrations. 4to. New York, 1881.

 Highways and Byways; or, Saunterings in New England. Illustrations. 4to. New York, 1883.

 Happy Hunting-Grounds: a Tribute to the Woods and Fields. Illustrations. 4to. New York, 1887.

 (Edited.) The Master of the Gunnery: a Memorial of Frederick William Gunn, by his Pupils. Portrait and illustrations. 4to. New York, 1888.

 Strolls by Starlight and Sunshine. Illustrations. Royal 8vo. New York, 1891.

 Sharp Eyes: a Rambler's Calendar of Fifty-Two Weeks among Insects, Birds and Flowers. 8vo. New York, 1892.

 Our Edible Toadstools and Mushrooms, and how to distinguish them: a Selection of Thirty Native Food Varieties easily recognizable by their marked Individualities, with Simple Rules for the Identification of Poisonous Species. 87 illustrations, of which 30 are colored, by the author. 8vo. New York. 1895.

GILDER, RICHARD WATSON. 1844 —

 The New Day: a Poem in Songs and Sonnets. Decorations. Square 16mo. New York, 1875.

 The Poet and his Master and other Poems. Decorations. 16mo. New York, 1878.

 Lyrics and other Poems. Decorations. 16mo. New York, 1881.

 Poems. In Three Parts: i., The New Day; ii., The Celestial Passion; iii., Lyrics. Decorations. 3 volumes, 16mo. New York [1887].

Two Worlds and other Poems. Decorations. 16mo. New York, 1891.

The Great Remembrance and other Poems. Decorations. 16mo. New York, 1893.

Five Books of Song. [Including The New Day, The Celestial Passion, Lyrics, Two Worlds, The Great Remembrance.] Illustrations. 12mo. New York, 1894.

GOODRICH, SAMUEL GRISWOLD (PETER PARLEY). 1793-1860.

The Outcast and other Poems. Illustrations. 12mo. Boston, 1836.

Sow well, and reap well; or Household Education. 12mo. Boston, 1838.

Five Letters to my Neighbor Smith. 12mo. Boston, 1839.

Sketches from a Student's Window. 12mo. Boston, 1841.

Ireland and the Irish. 12mo. Boston, 1842.

Poems. [Complete edition.] Illustrations. 12mo. New York, 1851.

Recollections of a Lifetime; or Men and Things I have seen. Portrait and illustrations. 2 volumes, 12mo. New York, 1856.

*₀*Mr. Goodrich, in his "Recollections," claimed to "stand before the public as the author and editor of about one hundred and seventy volumes," of which a list is given in the work referred to. Of these here given he is sole author; in the compilation of the others he "had the aid" of many of the best names in American literature, but their contributions were in most cases published anonymously.

GOULD, HANNAH FLAGG. 1789-1865.

Poems. 18mo. Boston, 1832.

Poems. Vol. 2. 18mo. Boston, 1835.

Poems. [Revised, with additions.] 2 volumes, 16mo. Boston, 1839.

Poems. Vol. 3. 16mo. Boston, 1841.

The Golden Vase; a Gift for the Young. 16mo. Boston, 1843.

Gathered Leaves; or Miscellaneous Papers. 16mo. Boston, 1846.

New Poems. 16mo. Boston, 1850.

Esther: a Scripture Narrative. 16mo. New York, 1850.

The Diosma. A Perennial. 16mo. Boston, 1851.

The Youth's Coronal. 16mo. New York, 1851.

The Mother's Dream, and other Poems. 16mo. Boston, 1853.

Hymns and other Pieces for Children. Illustrations. 16mo. Boston, 1854.

GRANT, ROBERT. 1852 —

Verses from The Harvard Advocate [by Robert Grant, G. E. Woodberry and others]. 12mo. New York, 1876.

The Little Tin-Gods-on-Wheels; or Society in our Modern Athens. [Also, Oxygen: a Mount Desert Pastoral.] Illustrations. Square 16mo. Cambridge, 1879.

The Confessions of a Frivolous Girl. Illustrations. 12mo. Boston, 1880.

[Anonymous.] Rollo's Journey to Cambridge. [By Robert Grant and John T. Wheelwright.] Illustrations. Small 4to. Boston, 1880.

[Anonymous.] The Lambs. A Tragedy. Illustrations. Square 12mo. Boston, 1883.

Yankee Doodle. A Poem before the Phi Beta Kappa Society of Harvard University, June 28, 1883. 12mo. Boston, 1883.

The King's Men; a Tale of To-Morrow. By Robert Grant, John Boyle O'Reilly, J. S. of Dale, and J. T. Wheelwright. 12mo. New York, 1884.

An Average Man. A Novel. 12mo. Boston, 1884.

The Oldest School in America. An Oration by Phillips Brooks and a Poem by Robert Grant at the Celebration of the 250th Anniversary of the Boston Latin School, April 23, 1885. 12mo. Boston, 1885.

The Knave of Hearts. A Fairy Story. 12mo. Boston, 1886.

Face to Face. 12mo. New York, 1886.

A Romantic Young Lady. 12mo. Boston, 1886.

Jack Hall; or the School-Days of an American Boy. Illustrations. 12mo. Boston, 1888.

Jack in the Bush; or, a Summer on a Salmon River. Illustrations. 12mo. Boston, 1888.

Mrs. Harold Stagg. Illustrations. 12mo. New York [1891].

The Carletons. Illustrations. 12mo. New York [1891].

The Reflections of a Married Man. Illustrations. 12mo. New York, 1892.

The Opinions of a Philosopher. Illustrations. 12mo. New York, 1893.

The Bachelor's Christmas and other Stories. Illustrations. 12mo. New York, 1895.

The Art of Living. Illustrations. 12mo. New York, 1895.

GRISWOLD, RUFUS WILMOT. 1815-1857.

[Anonymous.] Poems. 12mo. New York, 1841.

Sermons. 12mo. New York, 1841.

(Edited.) The Biographical Annual; consisting of Memoirs of Eminent Persons recently deceased. Portraits. 2 volumes, 12mo. New York, 1841-42.

The Poets and Poetry of America, with an Historical Introduction. Frontispiece. 8vo. Philadelphia, 1842.

(Edited.) Gems from American Poets. 32mo. New York, 1842.

Gems from the American Female Poets, with Brief Biographical Notices. 32mo. Philadelphia, 1842.

Readings in American Poetry. 12mo. New York, 1843.

The Cypress Wreath: a Book of Consolation for those who mourn. 32mo. Boston, 1844.

(Edited.) The Prose Works of John Milton [first American edition]. 2 volumes, 8vo. New York, 1845.

The Poets and Poetry of England in the Nineteenth Century. 8vo. New York, 1845.

Curiosities of Literature, by Isaac D'Israeli. With Supplement, — Curiosities of American Literature, by R. W. Griswold. Portrait. 8vo. New York, 1846.

The Prose and Prose Writers of America, with a Survey of the History, Conditions, and Prospects of American Literature. Portraits. 8vo. Philadelphia, 1847.

Washington and the Generals of the American Revolution. Portraits. 2 volumes, 12mo. Philadelphia, 1847.
***Suppressed, owing to legal proceedings threatened by J. T. Headley, who had published some time previous his work bearing the same title.

(With Horace B. Wallace.) Napoleon and the Marshals of the Empire. Portraits. 2 volumes, 12mo. Philadelphia, 1848.

The Female Poets of America. Portrait. 8vo. Philadelphia, 1848.

The Republican Court; or American Society in the Days of Washington. Portraits. Royal 8vo. New York, 1855.

The Cyclopædia of American Literature, by E. A. Duycinck and G. L. Duycinck. A Review. 8vo. New York, 1856.

Statement of the Relations of Rufus W. Griswold with Charlotte Myers (called Charlotte Griswold), Elizabeth F. Ellet, Ann S. Stephens, Samuel J. Waring, Hamilton R. Searles, and Charles D. Lewis, with Particular Reference to their late Unsuccessful Attempt to have set aside the Decree granted in 1852, by the Court of Common Pleas of Philadelphia County, in the Case of Griswold vs. Griswold. 8vo. Philadelphia, 1856.
***Mr. Griswold also edited editions of the writings of John Sterling, 1843; James Montgomery, 1845; Mrs. Norton, 1846; W. M. Praed, 1852; and others, besides compiling or editing several annuals and gift-books.
***See also POE, E. A.; and SMITH, ELIZABETH O.

GUINEY, LOUISE IMOGEN. 1861 —

Songs at the Start. 16mo. Boston, 1884.

Goose-Quill Papers. 16mo. Boston, 1885.

The White Sail and other Poems. 16mo. Boston [1887].

Brownies and Bogles. Illustrations. 12mo. Boston [1888].

Monsieur Henri. A Footnote to French History. Portrait and map. 16mo. New York, 1892.
  . Also 37 copies bound in Chollet plaid, each signed by the author.

A Roadside Harp. A Book of Verse. 12mo. Boston, 1893.

A Little English Gallery. Portrait. 16mo. New York, 1894.

Robert Louis Stevenson. A Study by A[lice] B[rown], with a Prelude and Postlude by L. I. G[uiney]. (Privately printed.) 8vo. Boston, 1895.

Three Sonnets written at Oxford. (Privately printed.) Square 16mo. [Boston] 1895.

Lovers' Saint Ruth's and Three other Tales. 12mo. Boston, 1895.
  . The same. China paper. (30 copies.) 8vo. Boston, 1895.
  . See also PARSONS, T. W.; and SPOFFORD, HARRIET P.

HALLECK, FITZ-GREENE. 1795-1867.

[Anonymous.] Fanny. 8vo. New York, 1819.

Fanny: a Poem [revised, with additions]. 8vo. New York, 1821.

[Anonymous.] Alnwick Castle, with other Poems. 8vo. New York, 1827.

Alnwick Castle, with other Poems [including some now first published]. 8vo. New York, 1836.

Fanny, with other Poems. Engraved title. 12mo. New York, 1839.

Selections from the British Poets. 2 volumes, 18mo. New York, 1840.

Alnwick Castle. . . . [with further additions]. 12mo. New York, 1845.

Poetical Works, now First Collected. 7 engravings, including portrait of the author. 8vo. New York, 1847.

Young America: a Poem. 12mo. New York, 1865.

Fanny: a Poem. With Notes. Portrait. Royal 8vo. New York, 1866.
 ***Seventy-five copies privately printed for W. L. Andrews, of which five are printed throughout on India paper and two on paper of various colors.

Lines to the Recorder. Royal 8vo. New York, 1866.
 ***Uniform in style and number of issue with Fanny.

Poetical Writings. With Extracts from those of Joseph Rodman Drake. Edited by James Grant Wilson. Portrait. 12mo. New York, 1869.
 ***The same, with additional portraits and illustrations. Large paper. (150 copies.) Royal 8vo. New York, 1869.

Life and Letters. Edited by James Grant Wilson. Portrait. 12mo. New York, 1869.
 ***The same, with additional portraits and illustrations. Large paper. (100 copies.) Royal 8vo. New York, 1869.

 ***See also DRAKE, J. R., and PAULDING, J. K.

HALPINE, CHARLES GRAHAME. 1829-1868.

Lyrics, by the Letter H. 12mo. New York, 1854.

The Life and Adventures, Songs, Services, and Speeches of Private Miles O'Reilly. Illustrations. 12mo. New York, 1864.

Baked Meats of the Funeral: Essays, Poems, Speeches, Histories, and Banquets. . . . Illustrations. 12mo. New York, 1866.

Poetical Works, with a Biographical Sketch and Explanatory Notes. Edited by Robert B. Roosevelt. Portrait. 12mo. New York, 1869.

The Patriot Brothers; or, the Willows of the Golden Vale. 12mo. Dublin, 1870.

Mountcashel's Brigade; or, the Defence of Cremona. 12mo. Dublin, 1870.

HARDY, ARTHUR SHERBURNE. 1847 —

    Francesca of Rimini. By A. S. H. 12mo. Philadelphia, 1878.

    Imaginary Quantities: their Geometrical Interpretation. Translated from the French. 24mo. New York, 1881.

    Elements of Quaternions. Plates. 8vo. Boston, 1881.

    But yet a Woman. 12mo. Boston, 1883.

    The Wind of Destiny. 12mo. Boston, 1886.

    Passé Rose. 12mo. Boston, 1889.

    Elements of Analytic Geometry. 8vo. Boston, 1889.

    Elements of the Differential and Integral Calculus. 8vo. Boston, 1890.

    Life and Letters of Joseph Hardy Neesima. Portraits. 12mo. Boston, 1891.

HARRIS, JOEL CHANDLER. 1848 —

    Uncle Remus: his Songs and his Sayings; the Folk-Lore of the Old Plantation. Illustrations. 12mo. New York, 1881.

    Nights with Uncle Remus: Myths and Legends of the Plantation. Illustrations. 12mo. Boston, 1883.

    Mingo and other Sketches in Black and White. 12mo. Boston, 1884.

    Free Joe and other Georgian Sketches. 12mo. New York, 1887.

    Daddy Jake the Runaway, and other Stories told after Dark. Illustrations. Small 4to. New York [1889].

    (Edited.) Life of Henry W. Grady, including his Writings and Speeches. A Memorial Volume compiled by Mr. Grady's Co-Workers on The Constitution [Joel C. Harris, Henry Watterson, and others]. Portrait and illustrations. 8vo. New York [1890].

    Balaam and his Master, and other Sketches and Stories. 12mo. Boston, 1891.

On the Plantation. A Story of a Georgia Boy's Adventures during the War. Illustrations. 12mo. New York, 1892.

(Translated.) Evening Tales, by Frederic Ortoli. 12mo. New York, 1893.

Uncle Remus and his Friends. Old Plantation Stories, Songs, and Ballads, with Sketches of Negro Character. Illustrations. 12mo. Boston, 1893.

Little Mr. Thimblefinger and his Queer Country: what the Children saw there. Illustrations. 12mo. Boston, 1894.

Mr. Rabbit at Home: a Sequel to Mr. Thimblefinger. Illustrations. 8vo. Boston, 1895.

HARRISON, CONSTANCE CARY. 1845—

[Anonymous.] Golden-Rod: an Idyl of Mount Desert. 32mo. New York, 1880.

The Story of Helen Troy. 16mo. New York, 1881.

Woman's Handiwork in Modern Homes. Illustrations. 8vo. New York, 1881.

The Old-Fashioned Fairy-Book. Illustrations. Square 16mo. London, 1884.

Folk and Fairy Tales. Illustrations. 12mo. London, 1885.

Bric-a-Brac Stories. Illustrations. 12mo. New York, 1885.

Bar Harbor Days. A Tale of Mount Desert. Illustrations. 16mo. New York, 1887.

(Translated.) Short Comedies for Amateur Players. 16mo. New York, 1889.

Flower de Hundred. The Story of a Virginia Plantation. 12mo. New York, 1890.

[Anonymous.] The Anglomaniacs. A Story of New York. 12mo. New York [1890].

Alice in Wonderland. 8vo. New York, 1890.

A Daughter of the South and Shorter Stories. 12mo. New York [1892].

An Edelweiss of the Sierras and other Tales. 12mo. New York, 1892.

Belhaven Tales, Crow's Nest, Una and King David. Illustrations. 12mo. New York, 1892.

Sweet Bells out of Tune. Illustrations. 12mo. New York, 1893.

A Bachelor Maid. Illustrations. 12mo. New York, 1894.

(Edited.) Short Stories. 12mo. New York, 1894.

An Errant Wooing. Illustrations. 12mo. New York, 1895.

A Virginia Cousin [and Bar Harbor Tales]. 12mo. Boston, 1895.

HARRISON, GABRIEL . . . .

The Stratford Bust of William Shakespeare, and a Critical Enquiry into its Authenticity and Artistic Merits. 3 photographic views, by the author, from the bust at Stratford. (75 copies.) 4to. Brooklyn, 1864.

The Life and Writings of John Howard Payne. Portraits. (250 copies.) Royal 8vo. Brooklyn, 1875.
***The same. Large paper. (15 copies.) 4to. Brooklyn, 1875.

The Scarlet Letter: a Romantic Drama in Four Acts. Dramatized from Nathaniel Hawthorne's Masterly Romance. Portrait of the author and photographic plate (Hester Prynne). (100 copies.) 8vo. Brooklyn, 1876.

A History of the Progress of the Drama, Music, and the Fine Arts in the City of Brooklyn. Portraits and illustrations. (100 copies.) 4to. Brooklyn, 1884.

John Howard Payne: Dramatist, Poet, Actor, and Author of "Home, Sweet Home." Portrait and illustrations. 8vo. Philadelphia, 1885.
***The same. Large paper. (25 copies.) 4to. Philadelphia, 1885.

Edwin Forrest, the Actor and the Man, Critical and Reminiscent. 11 photogravure portraits by the author. (200 copies.) Royal 8vo. Brooklyn, 1889.

HARTE, FRANCIS BRET. 1839—

(Edited, anonymously.) Outcroppings: being Selections of California Verse. Square 16mo. San Francisco, 1866.

The Lost Galleon and other Tales. 12mo. San Francisco, 1867.

Condensed Novels and other Papers. With Comic Illustrations by Frank Bellew. 12mo. New York, 1867.

The Luck of Roaring Camp and other Sketches. 12mo. Boston, 1870.

Plain Language from Truthful James. [A series of nine original sketches, by Hull, with engraved text.] 8vo. Western News Co. [Chicago, 1870.]

Fac-Simile of the Original Manuscript of The Heathen Chinee as written for The Overland Monthly, together with the Corrected Letter Press as published in the Issue of September, 1870. Portrait. 8vo. San Francisco [1871].
*.*Also twelve copies printed for presentation by the author. 4to. San Francisco [1871].

The Heathen Chinee. Illustrations by Sol Eytinge, Jr. 12mo. Boston, 1871.

The Pliocene Skull. Sketches by E. M. Schaffer, M.D. Dec. 8, 1870. Square 8vo. [Washington, 1871.]
*.*The second issue of The Pliocene Skull contains extract from the proceedings of the California Academy of Natural Sciences, July 16, 1866; also additional design on wrapper, neither of which appeared in first issue. Square 8vo. [Washington, 1871.]

Condensed Novels. Illustrations by S. Eytinge, Jr. 12mo. Boston, 1871.
*.*The "other papers" of the New York edition of 1867 are omitted in this issue.

Poems. 12mo. Boston, 1871.

East and West Poems. 12mo. Boston, 1871.

That Heathen Chinee and other Poems, mostly Humorous. Illustrations, and music of The Heathen Chinee. 12mo. London [1871].

Stories of the Sierras. 12mo. Boston, 1872.

The Luck of Roaring Camp and other Sketches. Illustrations. 4to. Boston, 1872.

Poetical Works. Illustrations. Square 16mo. Boston, 1872.

Proceedings at the 3rd Annual Re-Union of the Society of the Army of the Potomac in Boston, May 12th, 1871. [Poem, The Old Major Explains, by Bret Harte, p. 22.] 8vo. New York, 1872.

Mrs. Skaggs's Husbands and other Sketches. 16mo. Boston, 1873.

M'liss: an Idyl of Red Mountain. 8vo. New York, 1873.

Complete Works in Prose and Poetry, with an Introductory Essay by J. M. Bellew. Portrait. Small 8vo. London [1873].

An Episode of Fiddletown and other Sketches. 8vo. London, 1873.

Echoes of the Foot-Hills. 16mo. Boston, 1875.

Tales of the Argonauts and other Sketches. 16mo. Boston, 1875.

Gabriel Conroy. Illustrations. 8vo. Hartford, 1876.

Two Men of Sandy Bar. A Drama. 18mo. Boston, 1876.

Thankful Blossom: a Romance of the Jerseys, 1779. Illustrations. 18mo. Boston, 1877.

The Story of a Mine. 18mo. Boston, 1878.

West Point Jic Jacs. A Collection of Military Verse, together with the Special Poem, Cadet Grey, by Bret Harte. Illustrations. Oblong 16mo. New York, 1878.

The Hoodlum Band and other Stories. 4to. London, 1878.

Drift from Two Shores. 18mo. Boston, 1878.

An Heiress of Red Dog and other Tales. 16mo. London, 1879.

The Twins of Table Mountain and other Stories. 18mo. Boston, 1879.

Jeff Briggs's Love Story and other Sketches. 16mo. London, 1880.

Complete Works. Collected and revised by the Author. 5 volumes, 12mo. Boston, 1882.

Flip, and Found at Blazing Star. 18mo. Boston, 1882.

Flip and other Stories. 12mo. London, 1882.
 *‗*This edition contains "A Gentleman of La Porte," not included in the Boston issue.

Poetical Works [newly revised by the author]. Household Edition. Portrait. 12mo. Boston, 1883.

In the Carquinez Woods. 18mo. Boston, 1884.

On the Frontier. 18mo. Boston, 1884.

Maruja. 18mo. Boston, 1885.

By Shore and Sedge. 18mo. Boston, 1885.

Snow-Bound at Eagle's. 18mo. Boston, 1885.

The Queen of the Pirate Isle. Illustrations in colors by Kate Greenaway. Square 8vo. London [1886].
 *‗*The imported copies bear Boston imprint and are dated 1887.

A Millionaire of Rough and Ready, and Devil's Ford. 18mo. Boston, 1887.

Devil's Ford. A Novel. 12mo. London, 1887.

The Crusade of the Excelsior. Illustrations. 16mo. Boston, 1887.

The Argonauts of North Liberty. 18mo. Boston, 1888.

A Phyllis of the Sierras, and Drift from Redwood Camp. 18mo. Boston, 1888.

Cressy. 16mo. Boston, 1889.

The Heritage of Dedlow Marsh, and other Tales. 16mo. Boston, 1889.

A Waif of the Plains. 18mo. Boston, 1890.

A Ward of the Golden Gate. 16mo. Boston, 1890.

A Sappho of Green Springs and other Stories. 16mo. Boston, 1891.

Colonel Starbottle's Client and other People. 16mo. Boston, 1892.

A First Family of Tasajera. 16mo. Boston, 1892.

Susy: a Story of the Plains. 16mo. Boston, 1893.

Sally Dows and other Stories. 16mo. Boston, 1893.

A Protégée of Jack Hamlin's and other Stories. 16mo. Boston, 1894.

The Bell-Ringer of Angel's and other Stories. 16mo. Boston, 1894.

(With Robert Louis Stevenson, Rudyard Kipling and others.) My First Book. Portraits and illustrations. Square 8vo. London, 1894.

Clarence. 16mo. Boston, 1895.

In a Hollow of the Hills. 16mo. Boston, 1895.
*.*See also JAMES, HENRY.

HAWTHORNE, JULIAN. 1846 —

Bressant. A Novel. 12mo. New York, 1873.

Idolatry: a Romance. 12mo. Boston, 1874.

Saxon Studies. 12mo. Boston, 1876.

Garth. A Novel. 8vo. New York, 1877.

Mrs. Gainsborough's Diamonds. 16mo. New York, 1877.

Sebastian Strome. 3 volumes, 12mo. London, 1879.
*.*Also, 8vo. New York, 1880.

The Laughing Mill and other Stories. 12mo. London, 1879.

Archibald Malmaison. 12mo. London, 1879.

Ellice Quentin and other Stories. 2 volumes, 12mo. London, 1880.

Yellow Cap and other Fairy Stories. 12mo. London, 1880.

Prince Saroni's Wife and other Stories. 2 volumes, 12mo. London, 1882.

Dust: a Novel. Portrait and illustrations. 12mo. New York, 1883.

Beatrix Randolph. A Novel. 3 volumes, 12mo. London, 1883.
*.*Also, 12mo. Boston, 1884.

Fortune's Fool. 12mo. Boston, 1883.

Prince Saroni's Wife, and The Pearl Shell Necklace. 12mo. New York, 1884.

Nathaniel Hawthorne and his Wife. A Biography. Portraits and illustrations. Large paper. (350 copies.) 2 volumes, 8vo. Cambridge, 1884.
  *.*The same. 2 volumes, 12mo. Boston, 1885.

Love — or, a Name. A Story. 12mo. Boston, 1885.

Miss Cadogna: a Romance. 12mo. London, 1885.

Noble Blood. 12mo. New York, 1885.

John Parmelee's Curse. 16mo. New York [1886].

The Trial of Gideon. 12mo. New York, 1886.

Confessions and Criticisms. Portrait. 12mo. Boston, 1887.

A Tragic Mystery. 12mo. New York, 1887.

An American Penman. 12mo. New York, 1887.

The Great Bank Robbery. 12mo. New York, 1887.

Another's Crime. 12mo. New York, 1888.

Section 588; or, the Fatal Letter. 12mo. New York, 1888.
  *.*The preceding five volumes are edited from the diary of Police Inspector Byrnes, of New York.

A Dream and a Forgetting. 12mo. New York, 1888.

The Professor's Sister. 12mo. New York, 1888.
  *.*Published in London as The Spirit of the Camera.

Sinfire [with Douglas Duane, by Edgar Fawcett]. 12mo. Philadelphia, 1888.

Constance. 12mo. New York, 1889.

Kildhurm's Oak. 12mo. New York [1890].

Pauline. 12mo. New York [1890].

(With Leonard Bacon.) American Literature. An Elementary Text-Book. Portraits. 12mo. Boston, 1891.

The Story of Oregon. 2 volumes, 8vo. New York, 1892.

Six Cent Sam's. Illustrations. 12mo. St. Paul, 1893.

Humors of the Fair. Illustrations. 12mo. Chicago, 1893.
*.*See also FIELD, EUGENE; and HAWTHORNE, N.

HAWTHORNE, NATHANIEL. 1804-1864.

[Anonymous.] Fanshawe, a Tale. 12mo. Boston, 1828.

The American Magazine of Useful Knowledge. Vol. II. Illustrations. Royal 8vo. Boston, 1836.
 *.*The six concluding numbers of this volume, March–August, inclusive, 1836, were edited, anonymously, by Hawthorne, who, with his sister, wrote or revised almost the entire contents. His contributions to this magazine have never been reprinted.

[Anonymous.] Peter Parley's Universal History, on the Basis of Geography. For the Use of Families. Maps and illustrations. 2 volumes, square 12mo. Boston, 1837.

Twice-Told Tales. 12mo. Boston, 1837.

The Gentle Boy: A Thrice-Told Tale. With an Original Illustration. 4to. Boston, 1839.

The Sister Years: being the Carrier's Address to the Patrons of The Salem Gazette, 1st January, 1839. 8vo. Salem, 1839.

Grandfather's Chair: a History for Youth. 18mo. Boston, 1841.
*.*Reissued, with revisions and additions. Frontispiece. 18mo. Boston, 1842.

Famous Old People: being the Second Epoch of Grandfather's Chair. 18mo. Boston, 1841.

Liberty Tree: with the Last Words of Grandfather's Chair. 18mo. Boston, 1841.
*.*The same. Second Edition [with revisions]. Frontispiece. 18mo. Boston, 1842.

Famous Old People. Second Edition [with revisions]. Frontispiece. 18mo. Boston, 1842.

Twice-Told Tales. [Vol. ii., now first published; second issue of vol. i.] 2 volumes, 16mo. Boston, 1842.

Biographical Stories for Children. 18mo. Boston, 1842.

Historical Tales for Youth. 2 volumes, 18mo. Boston, 1842.
  *_{*}*i., Grandfather's Chair, and Famous Old People; ii., Liberty Tree and Biographical Stories for Children.

Samuel Johnson. The Sunday School Society's Gift. 18mo. Boston, 1842.

The Celestial Railroad. 32mo. Boston, 1843.

[Anonymous.] A Visit to the Celestial City. Revised by the Committee of Publication of the American Sunday-School Union. 4 illustrations. 16mo. Philadelphia [1843].

(Edited.) Journal of an African Cruiser. 12mo. New York, 1845.
  *_{*}*The edition consisted of two thousand copies, of which five hundred were sent to England and appeared with the publishers' London imprint.

Mosses from an Old Manse. 2 parts, 12mo. New York, 1846.

The Celestial Railroad. 32mo. Lowell, 1847.

Æsthetic Papers, edited by Elizabeth P. Peabody. [Including Main Street, by Hawthorne, pp. 145-174; also War, an unpublished lecture, by Emerson, and Resistance to Civil Government, by Thoreau.] 8vo. Boston, 1849.

The Scarlet Letter; a Romance. 12mo. Bóston, 1850.
  *_{*}*In the first issue the word " re-duplicate " occurs on page 21, line 20, for which the word " repudiate " was substituted in the second issue (although, in his preface to the latter, the author asserts its publication " without the change of a word"); the word " resuscitate " appears in subsequent issues.

The Scarlet Letter. [Second issue, with additional preface, and alteration of text.] 12mo. Boston, 1850.

The House of the Seven Gables, a Romance. 12mo. Boston, 1851.

Twice-Told Tales. A New Edition [revised, with preface, pp. 5-12, now first published]. 2 volumes, 12mo. Boston, 1851.

True Stories from History and Biography. Illustrations. 12mo. Boston, 1851.
  *_{*}*The same [second issue, with revisions and additions]. Illustrations. 12mo. Boston, 1851.

The Memorial: written by Friends of the Late Mrs. [Frances S.] Osgood, [including Hawthorne, who specially contributed The Snow Image, pp. 41-58, Simms, Stoddard, Bayard Taylor, Willis, Boker and others,] and edited by Mary Hewitt. Portrait and illustrations. 8vo. New York, 1851.

The Snow-Image and other Tales. 12mo. London, 1851.

The Snow Image and other Twice-Told Tales. 12mo. Boston, 1852.

The Blithedale Romance. 12mo. Boston, 1852.
*.*Also issued in 2 volumes, 8vo. London, 1852.

A Wonder-Book for Girls and Boys. Illustrations. 12mo. Boston, 1852.

Life of Franklin Pierce. Portrait. 12mo. Boston, 1852.

Tanglewood Tales for Girls and Boys: being a Second Wonder-Book. Illustrations. 12mo. Boston, 1853.

Mosses from an Old Manse. Carefully revised by the Author [with an additional sketch, Feathertop]. 2 volumes, 12mo. Boston, 1854.

[Anonymous.] A Rill from the Town Pump. [With remarks by Telba.] 16mo. London, 1857.

The Philosophy of the Plays of Shakespere Unfolded. By Delia Bacon. With a Preface [pp. vii.-xi.] by Nathaniel Hawthorne. 8vo. London, 1857.
*.*The imported copies bear the date here given, but with Boston imprint.

The Weal-Reaf: a Record of the Essex Institute Fair. [Containing letter and original contribution by Hawthorne.] Small 4to. Salem, 1860.

The Marble Faun; or the Romance of Monte Beni. 2 volumes, 12mo. Boston, 1860.
*.*The same. Second issue, with additional "conclusion" pp. 284-288. 2 volumes, 12mo. Boston, 1860.
*.*Issued in London as Transformation . . . . 3 volumes, small 8vo. 1860.

Our Old Home: a Series of Sketches. 12mo. Boston, 1863.

The Snow Image: a Childish Miracle. Colored illustrations. [First separate edition.] Square 12mo. New York, 1864.

Pansie: a Fragment. 12mo. London [1864].

Twice-Told Tales. A New Edition [including The Snow Image]. Portrait. 2 volumes, 24mo. Boston, 1865.

Passages from the American Note-Books. 2 volumes, 12mo. Boston, 1868.

Passages from the English Note-Books. 2 volumes, 12mo. Boston, 1870.

Passages from the French and Italian Note-Books. 2 volumes, 8vo. London, 1871.
 *₀*The same. 2 volumes, 12mo. Boston, 1872.

Septimius Felton; or, the Elixir of Life. 12mo. Boston, 1872.

Memoir of Nathaniel Hawthorne [by H. A. Page] with Stories now First Published. 12mo. London, 1872.

The Dolliver Romance and other Pieces. 12mo. Boston, 1876.

Fanshawe and other Pieces [now first collected]. 12mo. Boston, 1876.
 *₀*The two preceding volumes were also issued uniform with the Little Classic edition of Hawthorne's works, 18mo. 1876.

Legends of New England. Illustrations. 32mo. Boston, 1877.

Legends of the Province House. Frontispiece. 32mo. Boston, 1877.

Tales of the White Hills. 32mo. Boston, 1877.

A Virtuoso's Collection, and other Tales. Frontispiece. 32mo. Boston, 1877.

Doctor Grimshawe's Secret, a Romance. Edited, with Preface and Notes, by Julian Hawthorne. 12mo. Boston, 1883.

Sketches and Studies. 18mo. Boston [1883].

Tales, Sketches and other Papers. With a Biographical Sketch by George Parsons Lathrop. Portrait and facsimiles. 12mo. Boston, 1883.

Complete Works. With Introductions and Bibliographical Notes by George Parsons Lathrop. Portraits and illustrations. 13 volumes, 12mo. Boston, 1883.

*⁎*The same. Large paper. (250 copies.) 13 volumes, royal 8vo. Cambridge, 1883.

Delia Bacon. By Theodore Bacon. 8vo. London, 1888.

*⁎*Contains twenty letters, mostly relative to the Bacon-Shakespeare theory, by Hawthorne, now first published.

*⁎*Twenty-seven original contributions by Hawthorne appeared, anonymously, in The Token (Boston), for 1830, 1831, 1832, 1833, 1835, 1836, 1837 and 1838; The New England Magazine, for 1834 and 1835, contained seventeen; The Democratic Review (New York), for 1838, 1839, 1840, 1843, 1844, 1845 and 1846 contained twenty-five, among others. Papers of an Old Dartmouth Prisoner, never reprinted; and The Atlantic Monthly for 1860, 1862, 1863, 1865 and 1868, several, including the posthumous fragments of Septimius Felton and The Dolliver Romance. Besides the annual and the magazines here named, he contributed to The Knickerbocker, 1837; American Monthly, 1838; The Pioneer, 1843; Dollar Magazine, 1851; International Magazine, 1852; and Harper's Monthly Magazine, 1857.

HAY, JOHN. 1838 —

Pike County Ballads, and other Pieces. 12mo. Boston, 1871.

Jim Bludsoe of the Prairie Belle, and Little Breeches. Illustrations. 12mo. Boston, 1871.

Little Breeches: a Pike County View of Special Providence. Illustrations. 8vo. New York, 1871.

Little Breeches and other Pieces: Humourous, Descriptive and Pathetic. 12mo. London, 1871.

Castilian Days. 12mo. Boston, 1871.

Amasa Stone. Born April 27, 1818. Died May 11, 1883. (Privately printed; 95 copies.) 8vo. New York, 1883.

Memorial of Dr. Charles Hay. (Privately printed.) 8vo. New York, 1885.

The Enchanted Shirt. Illustrations. Square 16mo. Chicago [1889].

Poems. 12mo. Boston, 1890.

(With John G. Nicolay.) Abraham Lincoln: a History. Portraits and illustrations. 10 volumes, 8vo. New York, 1890.

(Edited, with J. G. Nicolay.) The Complete Works of Abraham Lincoln. Comprising his Speeches, State Papers, and Miscellaneous Writings. Portraits and facsimiles. 2 volumes, 8vo. New York, 1894.

HAYNE, PAUL HAMILTON. 1831–1886.

Poems. 16mo. Boston, 1855.

Sonnets and other Poems. 12mo. Charleston, 1857.

Avolio: a Legend of the Island of Cos. With Poems Lyrical, Miscellaneous and Dramatic. 16mo. Boston, 1860.

Legends and Lyrics. 12mo. Philadelphia, 1872.

The Mountain of the Lovers; with Poems of Nature and Tradition. 12mo. New York, 1875.

W. Gilmore Simms. A Poem delivered at the Charleston Academy of Music, on 13th Dec., 1877, as Prologue to the Dramatic Entertainment in Aid of the Simms Memorial Fund. 8vo. [Charleston; 1877.]

Poems. Complete, with Biographical Sketch. Portrait and illustrations. Square 8vo. Boston, 1882.
  *.*See also TIMROD, HENRY.

HEARN, LAFCADIO. 1850 —

(Translated.) One of Cleopatra's Nights, and other Fantastic Romances, by Theophile Gautier. Portrait. 8vo. New York, 1882.

Strange Leaves from Strange Literature. Stories reconstructed from the Anvari—Soheili, Baitál—Pachísí, Mahabharata, Gulistan, Talmud . . . . 16mo. Boston, 1884.

(Translated.) Gombo Zhébes. Little Dictionary of Creole Proverbs; selected from Six Creole Dialects, with Notes . . . . Square 8vo. New York, 1885.

Some Chinese Ghosts. 12mo. Boston, 1887.

Chita: a Memory of Last Island. 12mo. New York, 1889.

Youma. 12mo. New York, 1890.

(Translated.) The Crime of Sylvestre Bonnard (Member of the Institute), by Anatole France. 8vo. New York, 1890.

Glimpses of Unfamiliar Japan. 2 volumes, 8vo. Boston, 1894.

Out of the East; Reveries and Studies in New Japan. 12mo. Boston, 1895.

HIBBARD, GEORGE A. 1858 —

Iduna and other Stories. 12mo. New York, 1891.

The Governor and other Stories. 12mo. New York, 1892.

Nowadays and other Stories. Illustrations. 16mo. New York, 1893.

HIGGINSON, THOMAS WENTWORTH. 1823 —

Man shall not live by Bread Alone; a Thanksgiving Sermon. 8vo. Newburyport, 1848.

The Tongue: Two Practical Sermons. 8vo. Newburyport, 1850.

The Birthday in Fairyland: a Story for Children. 18mo. Boston, 1850.

Address to the Voters of the Third Congressional District of Massachusetts. 8vo. Lowell, 1850.

Merchants: a Sunday Evening Lecture. 8vo. Newburyport, 1851.

Things New and Old: an Installation Sermon . . . . 8vo. Worcester, 1852.

Elegy without Fiction. Sermon, Oct. 31, 1852. Suggested by the Deaths of Webster and Rantoul. Broadside. Worcester, 1852.

Thalatta: a Book for the Seaside. [Edited, anonymously, by Higginson and Samuel Longfellow.] 12mo. Boston, 1853.

The Unitarian Autumnal Convention, a Sermon. 8vo. Boston, 1853.

Woman and her Wishes: an Essay. Inscribed to the Massachusetts Constitutional Convention. 8vo. Boston, 1853.

Massachusetts in Mourning. A Sermon. . . . Worcester, June 4, 1854. 8vo. Boston, 1854.

A Ride through Kansas. 8vo. [Boston] 1856.

Does Slavery Christianize the Negro? 12mo. New York [1857].

The New Revolution: a Speech before the Anti-Slavery Society. . . . New York, May 12, 1857. 8vo. Boston, 1857.

Out-Door Papers. 12mo. Boston, 1863.

(Translated.) The Works of Epictetus. Consisting of his Discourses, the Enchiridion, and Fragments. 8vo. Boston, 1865.
  ***Also 2 volumes, 12mo. Boston, 1890.

(Edited.) Harvard Memorial Biographies. 2 volumes, 8vo. Cambridge, 1865.
  ***The same, revised. 2 volumes, 12mo. Cambridge, 1867.

Memoir of Dr. Thaddeus William Harris. 8vo. Boston, 1869.
  ***Reprinted from Harris's Entomological Correspondence.

Malbone: an Oldport Romance. 12mo. Boston, 1869.

Ought Women to learn the Alphabet? . . . . 12mo. Boston, 1869.

Army Life in a Black Regiment. 12mo. Boston, 1870.

Atlantic Essays. 12mo. Boston, 1871.

The Sympathy of Religions. Royal 8vo. Boston, 1871.

Oldport Days. Illustrations. 12mo. Boston, 1873.

Young Folks' History of the United States. Illustrations. Square 16mo. Boston, 1875.
  ***Gradually enlarged in subsequent editions.

Brief Biographies of European Public Men. 4 volumes, square 16mo. Boston, 1875-77.

History of Education in Rhode Island [prepared for the State of Rhode Island]. 8vo. Providence, 1876.

Young Folks' Book of American Explorers. Illustrations. 12mo. Boston, 1877.

Short Studies of American Authors. 12mo. Boston, 1880.

Common Sense about Women. 16mo. Boston, 1882.

Wendell Phillips. Reprinted from The Nation. 8vo. Boston, 1884.

Margaret Fuller Ossoli. Portrait. 16mo. Boston, 1884.

A Larger History of the United States. . . . to the Close of President Jackson's Administration. Maps and illustrations. Square 8vo. New York, 1886.

The Monarch of Dreams. 24mo. Boston, 1887.

Hints on Writing and Speech-Making. 24mo. Boston, 1887.

Women and Men. 16mo. New York, 1888.

Travellers and Outlaws: Episodes in American History. 12mo. Boston, 1889.

The Afternoon Landscape. Poems and Translations. 12mo. New York, 1889.

In a Fair Country. Essays from Out-Door Papers. 54 illustrations. Oblong 8vo. Boston [1890].

Life of Francis Higginson, First Minister in Massachusetts Bay Colony . . . . 12mo. New York [1891].

(Edited, with Ella H. Bigelow.) American Sonnets. 24mo. Boston, 1891.

Concerning all of us. Portrait. 16mo. New York, 1892.

The New World and the New Book . . . . With Kindred Essays. 12mo. Boston, 1892.

(With Mary Thacher Higginson.) Such as they are. Poems. Illustrations. Square 16mo. Boston, 1893.

(With Edward Channing.) English History for American Readers. Maps and illustrations. 12mo. New York, 1893.

(Edited.) Massachusetts in the Civil War. 2 volumes, 8vo. Boston, 1895.
  . See also HOLMES, O. W.

HILLHOUSE, JAMES ABRAHAM. 1789-1841.

The Education of a Poet. An Oration delivered at Yale University. 8vo. New Haven, 1811.

[Anonymous.] Percy's Masque, a Drama, in Five Acts. From the London Edition. 16mo. New York, 1820.
  . No London edition is believed to have been published.

The Judgment: a Vision. Pronounced before the Phi Beta Kappa Society, Yale University. 8vo. New York, 1821.

Oration at New Haven, Aug. 19, 1834, in Commemoration of the Life and Services of General Lafayette. 8vo. New Haven, 1834.

Hadad. A Dramatic Poem. 8vo. New York, 1838.

Sachem's Wood. A Short Poem. 8vo. New Haven, 1838.

Dramas, Discourses, and other Pieces. 2 volumes, 16mo. Boston, 1839.

HIRST, HENRY BECK. 1813-1874.

The Coming of the Mammoth, The Funeral of Time and other Pieces. 12mo. Boston, 1845.

Endymion. A Tale of Greece. 12mo. Boston, 1848.

The Penance of Roland: a Romance of the Peine Forte et Dure and other Poems. 12mo. Boston, 1849.

HOFFMAN, CHARLES FENNO. 1806-1884.

A Winter in the West. By A New Yorker. 2 volumes, 12mo. New York, 1835.

(Edited, anonymously.) The New York Book of Poetry [containing original poems by Washington Irving and others]. 8vo. New York, 1837.

(Edited.) The American Monthly Magazine. 8vo. New York, 1838.

Wild Scenes in the Forest and Prairie. 2 volumes, 12mo. London, 1839.

Greyslaer: a Romance of the Mohawk. 2 volumes, 12mo. New York, 1840.

The Vigil of Faith and other Poems. 12mo. New York, 1842.

Wild Scenes in the Forest and Prairie, with Sketches of American Life. 2 volumes, 12mo. New York, 1843.

Proceedings of the New York Historical Society, 1843. [Containing The People of New York, by Hoffman.] 8 vo. New York, 1843.

The Echo: or, Borrowed Notes for Home Circulation. Royal 8vo. Philadelphia, 1844.

Report of the Committee of the New York Historical Society, on a National Name, March 31, 1845. [Signed, David Dudley Field, Henry R. Schoolcraft and Charles F. Hoffman.] 8vo. [New York, 1845.]

Lays of the Hudson. Illustrations. 32mo. New York, 1846.

Love's Calendar, Lays of the Hudson, and other Poems. 32mo. New York, 1847.

(Edited.) The Literary World. A Gazette for Authors, Readers, and Publishers. 2 volumes, 4to. New York, 1847.

The Pioneers of New York; a Discourse before the St. Nicholas Society. 8vo. New York, 1848.

Poems [including several now first published]. Collected and edited by E. F. Hoffman. Portrait. 12mo. Philadelphia, 1873.

HOLLAND, JOSIAH GILBERT. 1819–1881.

(Edited.) Cut-Flowers: a Collection of Poems. By Mrs. D. Ellen Goodman Shepard. Portrait. 12mo. Springfield, 1854.

History of Western Massachusetts. Map. 2 volumes, 12mo. Springfield, 1855.

Address at the Dedication of the New City Hall, Springfield, Mass., Jan. 1, 1856. 8vo. Springfield, 1856.

The Bay-Path. 12mo. New York, 1857.

Poems. 12mo. New York, 1858.

Letters to Young People, Married and Single. 12mo. New York, 1858.

Bitter Sweet. A Poem. 12mo. New York, 1859.

Gold-Foil, hammered from Popular Proverbs. 12mo. New York, 1859.

Miss Gilbert's Career. An American Story. 12mo. New York, 1860.

Lessons in Life: a Series of Familiar Essays. 12mo. New York, 1862.

Letters to the Joneses. 12mo. New York, 1863.

The Laboring Man's Sabbath. To Benjamin Franklin Jones, Mechanic, concerning his Habit of staying away from Church. 16mo. Springfield, 1863.

Eulogy on Abraham Lincoln . . . . April 19, 1865. 8vo. Springfield, 1865.

The Life of Abraham Lincoln. Portrait and illustrations. 8vo. Springfield, 1865.

Plain Talks on Familiar Subjects. A Series of Popular Lectures. 12mo. New York, 1866.

Kathrina: her Life and mine, in a Poem. 12mo. New York, 1867.

(Edited.) Christ and the Twelve Scenes in the Life of our Saviour and his Apostles. Illustrations. 8vo. Springfield, 1867.

The Marble Prophecy and other Poems. Frontispiece. 12mo. New York, 1872.

Arthur Bonnicastle: an American Novel. Illustrations. 12mo. New York, 1873.

Garnered Sheaves. 12mo. New York, 1873.

(Edited.) Illustrated Library of Favorite Song. Square 8vo. New York, 1873.

The Mistress of the Manse. 12mo. New York, 1874.

The Story of Sevenoaks. Illustrations. 12mo. New York, 1875.

Nicholas Minturn. Study in a Story. Illustrations. 12mo. New York, 1876.

Every-Day Topics. A Book of Briefs. 12mo. New York, 1876.

Complete Poetical Writings. 12mo. New York, 1879.
***The same. Portrait and illustrations. 8vo. New York, 1880.

Works. Newly revised. 9 volumes, 12mo. New York, 1881-82.

Every-Day Topics. Second Series. 12mo. New York, 1882.

HOLMES, OLIVER WENDELL. 1809-1894.

Harvard Register. [Containing Holmes' first published poems.] 12 numbers, 8vo. Cambridge, 1827-28.

The Collegian. In Six Parts. [February–July, inclusive, 1830.] 8vo. Cambridge, 1830.
***Published by the undergraduates of 1830 and 1831, and edited by a club consisting of two members of the class of 1830 (one of whom was John Osborne Sargent), and three members of the class of 1831. The six numbers contain twenty-four poems by Holmes, only a few of which were retained in the 1836 and subsequent editions of Poems; and contain also the first printed composition of John Lothrop Motley.

The Amateur. A Journal of Literature and the Fine Arts. [June 15, 1830–June 4, 1831, inclusive.] 22 parts, 4to. Boston, 1830-31.
***This publication contained seventeen poems, at least, by Holmes, of which only eight were included in the collective editions of his poems. The paintings of the Athenæum Gallery formed the subjects of several of Holmes' early poems, which may explain why the publication entitled "Poetical Illustrations of the Athenæum Gallery of Paintings" (8vo., Boston, 1827), has been frequently ascribed to him. The real author of the volume was William G. Crosby.

[Anonymous.] The Harbinger: a May-Gift. 8vo. Boston, 1833.
***In three parts: part i., by Park Benjamin; ii., pp. 31-60, by Holmes, and iii., by John Osborne Sargent.

Poems. 12mo. Boston, 1836.

Boylston Prize Dissertations for 1836, by Oliver W. Holmes, M.D. [pp. 189-288], Robert W. Haxall, M.D., and Luther V. Bell, M.D. 8vo. Boston, 1836.
*_**Issued as Library of Practical Medicine, vol. vii.

Boylston Prize Dissertations for the Years 1836 and 1837. 8vo. Boston, 1838.

Principles of the Theory and Practice of Medicine. By Marshall Hall, M.D. . . . First American Edition. Revised and much enlarged by Jacob Bigelow, M.D., ... and Oliver W. Holmes, M.D . . . . 8vo. Boston, 1839.

The Allston Exhibition. [North American Review, April, 1840, pp. 358-381.] 8vo. Boston, 1840.

Homœopathy and its Kindred Delusions ; Two Lectures before the Boston Society of Useful Knowledge. 12mo. Boston, 1842.

Report of the Dinner to Charles Dickens, in Boston, February 1, 1842. [Including song sung on the occasion by Holmes, and speeches by Dickens, Bancroft and others.] 16mo. Boston, 1842.

[Review of] Elliotson's Principles and Practice of Medicine. [Boston Medical and Surgical Journal, Dec. 13, 1843, pp. 369-376.] 8vo. Boston, 1843.

The Position and Prospects of the Medical Student : an Address delivered before the Boylston Medical Society of Harvard University, January 12, 1844. 8vo. Boston, 1844.

The Contagiousness of Puerperal Fever. Read before the Boston Society for Medical Improvement, and published at the Request of the Society, from The New England Quarterly Journal of Medicine and Surgery. 8vo. [Boston, 1844.]

The Berkshire Jubilee, celebrated at Pittsfield, Mass., August 22 and 23, 1844. [Poem and speech by Holmes, pp. 161-163.] Illustrations. 8vo. Albany, 1845.

History of the Old Township of Dunstable : including Nashua . . . . [etc.]. By Charles J. Fox. [Containing poem, pp. 51-54, recited by Holmes at the Pilgrims' Dinner at Plymouth, N. H., Dec. 22, 1845.] Illustrations. 12mo. Nashua, 1846.

Urania: a Rhymed Lesson. Pronounced before the Mercantile Library Association, October 14, 1846. 8vo. Boston, 1846.

Poems [including eight now first collected]. 16mo. London, 1846.

Some Account of the Letheon, or who was the Discoverer? [Containing Holmes' letter suggesting Anæsthesia as a name for the new discovery.] 8vo. Boston, 1847.

An Introductory Lecture delivered at the Massachusetts Medical College, November 3, 1847. 8vo. Boston, 1847.

(With others.) Report of the Committee on Medical Literature, of the American Medical Society. 8vo. [Philadelphia, 1849.]
*.*Reprinted from Transactions of the Society, vol. i., pp. 249-288, 8vo. Philadelphia, 1848.

Poems. New and Enlarged Edition. [Containing prefatory note " from a letter to the publishers," and nine poems, including Urania, now first collected.] Vignettes. 12mo. Boston, 1849.

Poems. New and Enlarged Edition. [Containing prefatory note " to the publishers," and five additional poems, pp. 182-195.] Vignettes. 12mo. Boston, 1849.
*.*The prefatory note of first issue of Poems, 1849, is not dated, and is entirely distinct from that of the second, which is dated January 13th, 1849. In the contents of the latter, the poems, Cambridge Churchyard, and Old Ironsides, forming a portion of Poetry: a Metrical Essay, are for the first time indexed separately. The first issue consists of pp. vi+272; the second, of pp. vi+286.

Astræa: the Balance of Illusions. A Poem delivered before the Phi Beta Kappa Society of Yale College, August 14, 1850. 12mo. Boston, 1850.

Poem (with address by Rev. Henry Neill) delivered at the Dedication of Pittsfield (Rural) Cemetery, September 9th, 1850. Map and plate. 8vo. Pittsfield, 1850.
*.*The poem was also issued separately, 8vo. [Boston, 1850.]

The Benefactors of the Medical School of Harvard University; an Introductory Lecture at the Massachusetts Medical College, Nov. 7, 1850. With a Biographical Sketch of the Late Dr. George Parkman. 8vo. Boston, 1850.

Proceedings of the American Academy of Arts and Sciences. Vol. II. [Containing Holmes' article, On the Use of Direct Light in Microscopic Researches, pp. 326–332.] 8vo. Boston, 1852.

Poetical Works. Illustrations. First English Edition. 24mo. London, 1852.
*₊*In this edition the poem, To an English Friend, is published for the first time; and two poems, The Ploughman, and Pittsfield Cemetery, are now first collected; with these exceptions, and the prefatory memoir, the text of second issue of Poems, 1849, is copied.

Microscopic Preparation. [Boston Medical and Surgical Journal, May 25, 1853, pp. 337–340.] 8vo. Boston, 1853.

Songs of the Class of 1829. (Printed for the Use of the Class only.) 12mo. Boston, 1854.
*₊*Five songs, of which three are by O. W. H[olmes], and two by S. F. S[mith].

God Bless our Yankee Girls. Written by O. W. Holmes, composed .... by T. Comer. 4to. Boston [1854].

The Late Dr. Elisha Bartlett. [Boston Medical and Surgical Journal, Aug. 16, 1855, pp. 49–52.] 8vo. Boston, 1855.

Dr. Jackson's Letters to a Young Physician. A Review. [Boston Medical and Surgical Journal, Oct. 4, 1855, pp. 197–206.] 8vo. Boston, 1855.

Puerperal Fever as a Private Pestilence. [Reprinted, with additions, from The New England Quarterly Journal of Medicine and Surgery, 1843.] 8vo. Boston, 1855.

Oration delivered before the New England Society, in the City of New York, at their Semi-Centennial Anniversary, December 22, 1855. 8vo. [New York, 1855.]
*₊*Also published in the Society's report of the Celebration, New York, 1856; and, with address by John Pierpont, 8vo. New York, 1856.

The 74th Anniversary of the Birth-Day of Daniel Webster, celebrated at the Revere House, Boston, January 18, 1856. [Poem, by Holmes, pp. 49–51.] 8vo. Boston, 1856.

Mechanism of Vital Actions. [North American Review, July, 1857, pp. 39–77.] 8vo. Boston, 1857.

New Stand for the Compound Microscope. [Boston Medical and Surgical Journal, Dec. 10, 1857, pp. 373-680.] 8vo. Boston, 1857.

Valedictory Address delivered to the Medical Graduates of Harvard University, at the Annual Commencement, March 10, 1858. (Reprinted from Boston Medical and Surgical Journal.) 8vo. Boston, 1858.

[Anonymous.] The Autocrat of the Breakfast-Table. Every Man his own Boswell. Engraved false title, and illustrations. 12mo. Boston, 1858.
***The engraved false title was omitted from a large portion of the edition, and from all later issues.
***The same. Large paper. 8vo. Boston, 1859.

The Professor at the Breakfast-Table ; with the Story of Iris. 12mo. Boston, 1860.

Memorial of the Commemoration by the Church of the Disciples, on the Fiftieth Birth-Day of their Pastor, James Freeman Clarke, April 4, 1860. [Poem by Holmes, pp. 19-20, also poem by Julia Ward Howe, pp. 14-15.] Portrait. 12mo. Boston, 1860.

Currents and Counter-Currents in Medical Science. An Address before the Massachusetts Medical Society, at the Annual Meeting, May 30, 1860. 8vo. Boston, 1860.

Addresses at the Inauguration of Cornelius C. Felton, LL.D., as President of Harvard College, July 19, 1860. [Address, pp. 121-124, and remarks, p. 132, by Holmes.] 8vo. Cambridge, 1860.

Currents and Counter-Currents in Medical Science. With other Addresses and Essays. 12mo. Boston, 1861.

Elsie Venner : a Romance of Destiny. 2 volumes, 12mo. Boston, 1861.

The Address of Mr. Everett, and the Poem of Dr. O. W. Holmes, at the Dinner given to H. I. H. Monseigneur the Prince Napoleon, September 25th, 1861. (Privately printed.) 8vo. Cambridge, 1861.

Border Lines of Knowledge in some Branches of Medical Science. An Introductory Lecture, delivered before the Medical Class of Harvard University, Nov. 6th, 1861. 12mo. Boston, 1862.

Songs in many Keys. 12mo. Boston, 1862.

Poems [newly revised]. Portrait. 24mo. Boston, 1862.

Medical Directions written for Governor Winthrop, by Edmund Stafford, of London, in 1643. With Notes by O. W. Holmes. Reprinted from the Proceedings of the Massachusetts Historical Society. 8vo. Boston, 1862.

Oration delivered before the City Authorities of Boston, July 4, 1863. (12 copies printed for the author.) 4to. Boston 1863.
 . The same. 8vo. Boston, 1863.
 . Also reprinted for gratuitous distribution. 8vo. Philadelphia, 1863.

Soundings from the Atlantic. Vignettes. 12mo. Boston, 1864.

Humorous Poems. Illustrations. Square 16mo. Boston, 1865.

Tribute of the Massachusetts Historical Society, to the Memory of Edward Everett, January 30, 1865. [Poem by Holmes, pp. 65–67; and letter from Whittier, pp. 87–90.] Portrait. Royal 8vo. Boston, 1865.
 . Reprinted in A Memorial of Edward Everett from the City of Boston. 2 portraits. Royal 8vo. Boston, 1865.
 . The same. Large paper. (100 copies.) 4to. Boston, 1865.

A Memorial of Abraham Lincoln. . . . [Poem by Holmes, pp. 84–85.] Royal 8vo. Boston, 1865.
 . The same. Large paper. 4to. Boston, 1865.

Proceedings of the Massachusetts Historical Society, for May, 1865. [Containing remarks on Dante, pp. 277–278, by Holmes.] 8vo. [Boston, 1865.]

The Flower of Liberty. [Poems specially contributed by Holmes, Whittier, Curtis, Bryant, Aldrich, Bayard Taylor, Longfellow, Parsons, Emerson, and others.] Edited and illustrated [with 50 engravings of patriotic emblems] by Julia A. M. Furbish. Square 8vo. Boston, 1866.

Tribute of the Massachusetts Historical Society to the Memory of George Livermore [containing tribute by Holmes, pp. 17–19]. 8vo. Boston, 1866.

The Guardian Angel. 12mo. Boston, 1867.

Teaching from the Chair and at the Bedside. An Introductory Lecture delivered before the Medical Class of Harvard University, November 6, 1867. 8vo. Boston, 1867.

(Edited, with D. G. Mitchell.) The Atlantic Almanac [for] 1868. Illustrations. 4to. Boston [1867].

Poems and Songs of the Class of 1829 [including 20 poems by Holmes]. Third Edition. Printed for the Use of the Class only. 8vo. Boston, 1868.
***Earnest efforts, during the past five years, have resulted in failure to discover any information relative to the "second edition" which would seem indicated by the preceding title. No such edition was known to surviving members of the class or their relatives (Dr. Holmes' copy was one of the 1868 issue); and considering that the volume was intended for members of the class, only, some purpose, humorous or otherwise, may have suggested the "third edition" inscription.

Lectures delivered in a Course before the Lowell Institute in Boston, by Members of the Massachusetts Historical Society, on Subjects relating to the Early History of Massachusetts. [Including The Medical Profession in Massachusetts, pp. 257-301, read by Holmes, Jan. 29, 1869.] Royal 8vo. Boston, 1869.

Review of The Dental Cosmos. [Boston Medical and Surgical Journal, March 11, 1869, pp. 99-102.] Royal 8vo. Boston, 1869.

Official Monthly Bulletin of the . . . . Celebration of Peace, and Musical Festival . . . . Boston, June 15-19, 1869. [Poem by Holmes, p. 4.] Illustrations. Royal 8vo. Boston, 1869.

Address delivered on the Centennial Anniversary of the Birth of Alexander von Humboldt . . . . by Louis Agassiz. With an Account of the Evening Reception. [Including poem written for the occasion, by Holmes, address by Emerson, poem by Julia Ward Howe, and letter by Whittier.] 8vo. Boston, 1869.

Celebration of the 111th Anniversary of Robert Burns' Natal Day, at Delmonico's Hotel, New York, January 25th, 1870. [Tributes by Holmes, pp. 10-11; Bryant, pp. 12-14; and Sage, pp. 18-20.] 8vo. New York, 1870.

Rip Van Winkle, M. D. An After-Dinner Prescription taken by the Massachusetts Medical Society . . . . May 25th, 1870. [Boston Medical and Surgical Journal, June 9, 1870, pp. 444-446.] Royal 8vo. Boston, 1870.

Harvard College. [Programme of] Services on the Laying of the Corner Stone of Memorial Hall, October 6, 1870 [with Hymn by Holmes, pp. 3-4]. Square 12mo. [Cambridge, 1870.]

Mechanism in Thought and Morals. An Address delivered before the Phi Beta Kappa Society of Harvard University, June 29, 1870. With Notes and Afterthoughts. 12mo. Boston, 1871.

Valedictory Address to the Graduating Class of the Bellevue Hospital, March 2, 1871. [New York Medical Journal, April, 1871, pp. 420-440.] 8vo. New York, 1871.

Proceedings of the Massachusetts Historical Society, May-August, 1871. [Containing tributes to Sir Walter Scott, by Holmes, Emerson, and Bryant.] 8vo. [Boston, 1871.]

Tribute to Walter Scott on the 100th Anniversary of his Birthday, August 15, 1871. (Privately printed.) 8vo. Boston, 1872.

The Poet at the Breakfast-Table. His Talks with his Fellow-Boarders. Frontispiece. 12mo. Boston, 1872.

The Claims of Dentistry. An Address delivered at the Commencement Exercises of the Dental Department in Harvard University, February 14, 1872. [Reprinted from Boston Medical and Surgical Journal, Feb. 29, 1872.] 8vo. Boston, 1872.

Centennial of the Boston Pier, or the Long Wharf Corporation. 1873. [Remarks and poem, by Holmes, pp. 18-20.] 8vo. Cambridge, 1873.

Proceedings of a Special Meeting of the Massachusetts Historical Society, Dec. 16, 1873; being the 100th Anniversary of the Destruction of the Tea in Boston Harbor. [Ballad of the Boston Tea Party, by Holmes, pp. 56-58.] 8vo. Boston, 1874.

Proceedings of the Massachusetts Historical Society from January to June, 1874. [Containing remarks on Scaligerana, by Holmes, pp. 315-317.] 8vo. [Boston, 1874.]

Prof. Jeffries Wyman. A Memorial Outline. [Reprinted from The Atlantic Monthly for November, 1874.] 8vo. [Boston, 1874.]
*˳*Reprinted also in Proceedings of the Massachusetts Historical Society for April, 1875.

Songs of many Seasons. 1862-1874. 12mo. Boston, 1875.

The Physiology of Versification. Harmonies of Organic and Animal Life. [Boston Medical and Surgical Journal, Jan. 7, 1875, pp. 6-9.] 8vo. Boston, 1875.

Memorial. Bunker Hill. [Containing Grandmother's Story of Bunker-Hill Battle: as she saw it from the Belfry, pp. 1-4, specially written for the Memorial, by Holmes.] Illustrations. Royal 8vo. Boston, 1875.

Fair Play. [A collection of charades in aid of a fair at Waltham, October, 1875.] 16mo. Waltham [1875].

Grandmother's Story of Bunker Hill Battle: as she saw it from the Belfry. (6 copies privately printed for the author.) 4to. [Cambridge, 1876.]

His Royal Highness Prince Oscar at the National Celebration of the Centennial Anniversary of American Independence .... July 4, 1876 [with ode by Holmes]. Portraits. (Privately printed.) 8vo. Boston, 1876.

Poetical Works. Household Edition. [Including additional poems to 1877, together with additional poems, to 1877, of the class of 1829.] 12mo. Boston, 1877.
*˳*The same, with portrait and illustrations. 8vo. Boston, 1878.

An Address delivered at the Annual Meeting of the Boston Microscopical Society. [Reprinted from Boston Medical and Surgical Journal, May 24, 1877.] 8vo. Cambridge, 1877.

A Family Record. Woodstock, Conn., July 4, 1877. 4to. [Cambridge, 1877.]
*˳*Only a few copies printed for the author.

The Story of Iris. [First separate edition.] 32mo. Boston, 1877.

Favorite Poems. Illustrations. 32mo. Boston, 1877.

Visions: a Study of False Sight. By Edward Clarke, M.D. With an Introduction and Memorial Sketch by O. W. Holmes. Portrait. 12mo. Boston, 1878.

Proceedings of the Harvard Club of New York City, at their 12th Annual Dinner . . . . Feby. 21st, 1878. [Containing two sonnets and letter, by Holmes, pp. 16-17, and address by D. G. Mitchell, pp. 17-21.] 8vo. New York, 1878.
*.*Printed copies of the sonnets were presented to the guests on this occasion.

Proceedings of the Massachusetts Historical Society for November and December, 1878. [Containing Memoir, by Holmes, of the Hon. John Lothrop Motley, LL.D., pp. 404-473.] 8vo. [Boston, 1878.]
*.*The memoir, as here given, is an abridgment (so as to bring it within suitable limits for publication in the Proceedings) of the memoir about to be published at the time by Houghton, Osgood & Co.

John Lothrop Motley. A Memoir. Reprinted from the Proceedings of the Massachusetts Historical Society, 1878. 8vo. Boston, 1879.

John Lothrop Motley. A Memoir. [Unabridged, and containing memorial poems by Bryant and Story.] Portrait. 12mo. Boston, 1879.
*.*The same. Memorial Edition. Small 4to. Boston, 1879.
*.*Also 12mo. London, 1878.

The School-Boy. Illustrations. 8vo. Boston, 1879.

Proceedings of the Massachusetts Historical Society, January to April, 1879. [Containing Holmes' tributes to George S. Hillard and Jacob Bigelow, pp. 38-44.] 8vo. Boston, 1879.

Nautilus. [A privately printed issue of The Chambered Nautilus, with a translation into Latin, signed E. S. D.] 12mo. [Cambridge, 1879.]

The Iron Gate and other Poems. Portrait. 12mo. Boston, 1880.

Seventieth Birthday of James Freeman Clarke. Memorial of the Celebration by the Church of the Disciples, Monday, April 5th, 1880. [Poem by Holmes, pp. 11-12.] Portrait. 8vo. Boston, 1880.

Exercises in celebrating the 250th Anniversary of the Settlement of Cambridge, September 28, 1880. [Remarks and poem by Holmes, pp. 32-35 ; remarks by Longfellow, pp. 29-30 ; oration by T. W. Higginson, pp. 44-65 ; and letter from J. R. Lowell, p. 127.] Portraits and illustrations. Royal 8vo. Cambridge, 1881.

Benjamin Peirce. A Memorial Collection by Moses King. [Containing memorial poem by Holmes, pp. 63-64, and verses by T. W. Parsons, pp. 3, 6, and 37.] Portrait. Square 12mo. Cambridge, 1881.

The Poets' Tribute to Garfield . . . . Poems written for The Boston Daily Globe [by Holmes, Joaquin Miller, John Boyle O'Reilly and others] and many Selections. With Biography and Portrait. 8vo. Cambridge, 1881.

Dedication of the New Building and Hall of the Boston Medical Library Association . . . . December 3, 1878. . . . Address of the President, Dr. O. W. Holmes [pp. 1-21, reprinted from Boston Medical and Surgical Journal, Dec. 12, 1878]. . . . Small 4to. Cambridge, 1881.

Songs and Poems of the Class of 1829. Part 2. 1868-1881. [Consisting of twenty-six poems, of which seventeen are by Holmes.] 8vo. [Boston, 1881.]
*.*The pagination is continued from the issue of 1868.

Poem written by Dr. . . . Holmes for the Centennial Anniversary Dinner of the Massachusetts Medical Society, June 8, 1881, and read by him on that Occasion. [Boston Medical and Surgical Journal, June 23, 1881, pp. .577-580.] 4to. Boston, 1881.

Proceedings of the Massachusetts Historical Society from January to June, 1882. [Containing tributes, by Holmes, at January meeting, to R. H. Dana, pp. 197-199 ; at April meeting, to H. W. Longfellow, pp. 269-275 ; and at May meeting, to R. W. Emerson, pp. 303-310.] 8vo. [Boston, 1882.]

Medical Highways and By-Ways. A Lecture delivered before the Medical Department of Harvard University, May 10, 1882. [Reprinted from Boston Medical and Surgical Journal, June 1, 1882.] 12mo. Cambridge, 1882.

Farewell Address at Harvard Medical School, Nov. 28, 1882. 8vo. Boston, 1882.

Pages from an Old Volume of Life. 1857–1881. 12mo. Boston, 1883.

Medical Essays. 1842–1882. 12mo. Boston, 1883.

The New Century and the New Building of the Harvard Medical School. 1783–1883. Addresses and Exercises at the 100th Anniversary of the Foundation of the Medical School of Harvard University, Oct. 17, 1883. [Address by Holmes, pp. 3–35; also Appendix, Endowment of the Harvard Medical School, pp. 51–55.] Illustrations. 8vo. Cambridge, 1884.

Ralph Waldo Emerson. Portrait. 12mo. Boston, 1885.

A Mortal Antipathy. First Opening of the New Portfolio. 12mo. Boston, 1885.

Illustrated Poems. Portrait and 70 illustrations. 4to. Boston, 1885.

Services at the Celebration of the 250th Anniversary of the Origin of the First Church in Cambridge, February 7–14, 1886. [Poem and remarks by Holmes, pp. 22 and 120.] 8vo. Cambridge, 1886.

Speeches at the First Dinner of the Phillips Academy Alumni Association, Parker House, Boston, March 24, 1886. [Including speech and poem by Holmes, pp. 21–26.] 8vo. Boston, 1886.

The Last Leaf. [Printed in facsimile of manuscript, with history of the poem and notes by the author.] Illustrations. 4to. Cambridge, 1886.

1686–1886. [Programme of] Commemorative Services, King's Chapel, Boston, upon the Completion of 200 Years, Wednesday, December 15, 1886 [including hymn by Holmes]. Facsimile and vignettes. Small 4to. [Boston, 1886.]

The Commemoration by King's Chapel, Boston, of the Completion of 200 Years since its Foundation. [Poem by Holmes, pp. 131–134.] Illustrations. 8vo. Boston, 1887.

Our Hundred Days in Europe. 12mo. Boston, 1887.
  *₊*The same. Large paper. (100 copies.) Small 4to. London, 1888.

Before the Curfew and other Poems, chiefly Occasional.
16mo. Boston, 1888.
  *₀*Of this work 250 copies were issued wholly uncut, with paper labels.

Proceedings of the Massachusetts Historical Society for June, 1888. [Containing Holmes' tribute to James Freeman Clarke, pp. 144–147.] 8vo. [Boston, 1888.]

The Latest Poems of the Class of 1829. Part 3. 1882–1889. [Consisting of thirteen poems, of which eight are by Holmes.] 8vo. [Boston, 1889.]
  *₀*The pagination, pp. 199–232, is continued from part 2, 1861.

Proceedings on the Occasion of laying the Corner-Stone of the New Library Building of the City of Boston. November 28, 1888. [Poem by Holmes, pp. 19–20.] Illustrations. Royal 8vo. Boston, 1889.

Proceedings of the Massachusetts Historical Society, for June, 1889. [Containing Memoir of William Amory, pp. 414–417, by Holmes.] 8vo. [Boston, 1889.]

Typical Elms of Massachusetts. Introductory Chapter by O. W. Holmes. Descriptive Text by Lorin L. Dame. Plates [58] by Henry Brooks. 4to. Boston, 1890.

Over the Tea-Cups. Vignette. 12mo. Boston, 1891.

Complete Collected Writings [newly revised]. Portraits and illustrations. 13 volumes, 12mo. Boston, 1891.
  *₀*The same. Large paper. (275 copies.) 13 volumes, 8vo. Cambridge, 1891.

The One-Hoss Shay and Companion Poems. With Preface [now first published] by the Author. Illustrations. 12mo. Boston, 1892.

Dorothy Q., together with A Ballad of the Boston Tea-Party and Grandmother's Story of Bunker Hill Battle. [With original preface by the author.] Illustrations. 12mo. Boston, 1893.
  *₀*The same. Large paper. (250 copies.) 8vo. Boston, 1893.

Horatian Echoes. Translations of the Odes of Horace, by John Osborne Sargent, with Introduction by O. W. Holmes. 12mo. Boston, 1893.

Complete Poetical Works [including many poems now first collected]. Cambridge Edition. Portrait and vignette. 8vo. Boston [1895].

※※Many of Dr. Holmes' contributions to medical literature have never been reprinted, which will explain why so much more space is given to separate titles of his magazine articles than to those of other authors included in this publication. Besides the articles contributed to the Boston Medical and Surgical Journal which are named in this list, the numbers of that journal for May 17, 1855, August 2, and September 5, 1867, June 17, 1875, September 28, 1876, June 16, and 23, 1881, February 23, 1882, and February 7, 1889, contain letters, sonnets, and papers of lesser importance. A list of his numerous contributions to The Atlantic Monthly is rendered unnecessary by the index volume. The New England Magazine, 1831-1835, published several of his early writings, including the first portion of The Autocrat of the Breakfast-Table. With few exceptions the magazines named contain all his contributions to periodical literature.

※※See also BRYANT, W. C.; EMERSON, R. W.; HOWE, JULIA WARD; LONGFELLOW, H. W.; LOWELL, J. R.; WARNER, C. D.; WHITTIER, J. G.; and WINSOR, JUSTIN.

HOSMER, WILLIAM HENRY CUYLER. 1814-1877.

The Fall of Tecumseh: a Drama. 12mo. Avon, 1830.

Themes of Song: a Poem. 12mo. Rochester, 1834.

The Pioneers of Western New York, a Poem at Geneva, N. Y., ... August 1, 1838. 12mo. Geneva [1838].

Yonnondio; or, Warriors of the Genessee: a Tale of the Seventeenth Century. 12mo. New York, 1844.

An Address by Henry R. Schoolcraft and a Poem by W. H. C. Hosmer before the New Confederation of the Iroquois. 8vo. New York, 1846.

The Months. 12mo. Boston, 1847.

Poetical Works. 2 volumes, 12mo. New York, 1854.

Later Lays and Lyrics. 12mo. Rochester, N. Y., 1873.

HOWARD, BLANCHE WILLIS. 1847 —

[Anonymous.] One Summer. Illustrations. 18mo. Boston, 1875.

One Year Abroad. 18mo. Boston, 1877.

Aunt Serena. 16mo. Boston, 1881.

Guenn. A Wave on the Breton Coast. Illustrations. 12mo. Boston, 1883.

Aulnay Tower. 12mo. Boston, 1885.

Tony the Maid. Illustrations. 16mo. New York, 1887.

The Open Door. 12mo. Boston, 1889.

A Battle and a Boy. 12mo. New York [1892].

(With William Sharp.) A Fellowe and his Wife. 12mo. Boston, 1892.

No Heroes. A Story for Boys. Illustrations. 12mo. Boston, 1893.

HOWE, JULIA WARD. 1819 —

[Anonymous.] Passion Flowers. 12mo. Boston, 1854.

Words for the Hour. 12mo. Boston, 1857.

The World's Own. 12mo. Boston, 1857.

Leonore; or, the World's Own; a Tragedy. 8vo. New York, 1857.

Hippolytus. A Tragedy. 12mo. New York, 1858.

A Trip to Cuba. 12mo. Boston, 1860.

(Edited.) The Boatswain's Whistle. [Containing original contributions by Holmes, Whittier, Emerson and others.] Published at the National Sailors' Fair, November 10–19, 1864. 10 numbers, 4to. Boston, 1864.

Later Lyrics. 12mo. Boston, 1866.

From the Oak to the Olive: a Plain Record of a Pleasant Journey. 12mo. Boston, 1868.

(Edited.) Sex in Education. A Reply to E. H. Clarke's "Sex in Education." 12mo. Boston, 1874.

Memoir of Samuel Gridley Howe. With other Memorial Tributes [by Holmes, Bryant and others]. Portrait. 8vo. Boston, 1876.

The Golden Eagle ; or, the Privateer of 1776. A National Drama. 12mo. New York, 1876.

Modern Society. 12mo. Boston, 1881.

Margaret Fuller (Marchesa Ossoli). 12mo. Boston, 1883.

Is Polite Society Polite? and other Essays. Portrait. 12mo. Boston, 1895.
***See also HOLMES, O. W., and WARNER, C. D.

HOWELLS, WILLIAM DEAN. 1837 —

(With John James Piatt.) Poems of Two Friends. 12mo. Columbus, 1860.

Lives and Speeches of Abraham Lincoln and Hannibal Hamlin. Portraits. 12mo. Columbus, 1860.
***Life of Lincoln, by Howells, pp. 10-94; Memorabilia of the Chicago Convention, pp. 97-111; Speeches of Lincoln, pp. 115-304; Life and Speeches of Hamlin, by J. L. Hayes, pp. 305-406.

The Poets and Poetry of the West. With Biographical and Critical Notices by William T. Coggeshall [and others]. 8vo. Columbus, 1860.
***This volume contains six poems by Howells, together with four biographical notices, those of Mary R. Whittesley, Gordon A. Stewart, Helen L. Bostwick, and John H. A. Bone.

Venetian Life. 12mo. New York, 1866.

Italian Journeys. 12mo. New York, 1867.

No Love Lost : a Romance of Travel. Illustrations. Square 16mo. New York, 1869.

Suburban Sketches. 12mo. New York, 1871.
***The same, revised and enlarged. Illustrations. 12mo. Boston, 1872.

Their Wedding Journey. Illustrations. 12mo. Boston, 1872.
***The same, with additional chapter, Niagara Revisited. 12mo. Boston, 1887.

A Chance Acquaintance. 18mo. Boston, 1873.

Poems. 18mo. Boston, 1873.
***The poem, Naming the Bird, pp. 163-169, is omitted from the Poems of 1886.

A Foregone Conclusion. 12mo. Boston, 1875.

The Cambridge of 1776: .... with .... the Diary of
Dorothy Dudley [containing an introductory sonnet by
Howells]. Edited for the Ladies' Centennial Committee
by A[rthur] G[ilman]. Illustrations. 8vo. Cambridge,
1876.

Sketch of the Life and Character of Rutherford B. Hayes
[pp. vi.+195]. Also [by another author] A Biographical
Sketch of William A. Wheeler. 2 portraits. 16mo. New
York, 1876.

A Day's Pleasure. Illustrations. 32mo. Boston, 1876.

The Parlor Car. Farce. 32mo. Boston, 1876.

Out of the Question. A Comedy. 18mo. Boston, 1877.

A Counterfeit Presentment. Comedy. 18mo. Boston, 1877.

(Edited, with introductory essays.) Choice Autobiographies.
8 volumes, 18mo. Boston, 1877.
*_{*}*i., ii., Margravine of Baireuth; iii., Lord Herbert of Cherbury and Thomas Elwood; iv., Vittoria Alfieri; v., Carlo Goldoni; vi., Edward Gibbon; vii., viii., Francois Marmontel.

The Lady of the Aroostook. 12mo. Boston, 1879.

The Undiscovered Country. 12mo. Boston, 1880.

A Fearful Responsibility and other Stories. 12mo. Boston,
1881.

Dr. Breen's Practice. A Novel. 12mo. Boston, 1881.

Buying a Horse. 32mo. Boston, 1881.

A Modern Instance. A Novel. 12mo. Boston, 1882.

The Sleeping Car. A Farce. 32mo. Boston, 1883.

A Woman's Reason. 12mo. Boston, 1883.

A Little Girl [Mildred Howells] among the Old Masters.
With Introduction and Comment by W. D. Howells. 54
illustrations. Oblong 16mo. Boston, 1884.

Niagara Revisited, 12 Years after their Wedding Journey, by
the Hoosac Tunnel Route. Colored illustrations. Small
4to. Chicago [1884].
*_{*}*Reprinted, with alteration of text, from The Atlantic
Monthly, 1883; but, owing to threatened litigation, not circulated, the entire issue being, with the exception of a few copies,
destroyed.

The Register. Farce. 18mo. Boston. 1884.

Three Villages. 18mo. Boston, 1884.

The Rise of Silas Lapham. 12mo. Boston, 1885.

The Elevator. Farce. 18mo. Boston, 1885.

Indian Summer. 12mo. Boston, 1885.

Tuscan Cities. Illustrations. 8vo. Boston, 1886.

The Garroters. Farce. 12mo. Boston, 1886.

Poems [including four now first collected]. 12mo. Boston, 1886.

George Fuller: his Life and Works. A Memorial Volume. [Containing biographical sketch by Howells, and contributions by Stillman, Whittier and others.] Portrait and plates, India paper proofs. (300 copies.) 4to. Boston, 1886.

Modern Italian Poets: Essays and Versions. Portraits. 12mo. New York, 1887.

The Minister's Charge; or, the Apprenticeship of Lemuel Barker. 12mo. Boston, 1887.

(Edited, with Thomas S. Perry.) Library of Universal Adventure by Sea and Land. Including Original Narratives and Authentic Stories of Personal Prowess and Peril . . . . from the year 79, A. D., to 1888. Illustrations. 8vo. New York, 1888.

April Hopes. 12mo. New York, 1888.

A Sea-Change; or, Love's Stowaway. A Lyricated Farce. . . . . 18mo. Boston, 1888.

Annie Kilburn. 12mo. New York, 1889.

The Mouse-Trap and other Farces. Illustrations. 12mo. New York, 1889.

The Sleeping-Car and other Farces. 12mo. Boston, 1890.

A Hazard of New Fortunes. Illustrations. 8vo. New York, 1890.
   *₀*Also issued (without illustrations), 2 volumes, 12mo. New York, 1890.

The Shadow of a Dream. 12mo. New York, 1890.

The House by the Medlar-Tree. Translated by Mary A. Craig. Introduction by W. D. Howells. 16mo. New York, 1890.

A Boy's Town. Described for "Harper's Young People." Illustrations. 12mo. New York, 1890.

Pastels in Prose. From the French. Translated by Stuart Merrill, with Introduction by W. D. Howells. Illustrations. 16mo. New York, 1890.

Criticism and Fiction. Portrait. 16mo. New York, 1891.

(Edited, with introduction.) Poems, by George Pellew. 8vo. Boston [1892].

Venetian Life. [A new edition.] Illustrations. 2 volumes, 12mo. Boston, 1892.
   *₊*The same. Large paper. (250 copies.) 2 volumes, 8vo. Cambridge, 1892.

An Imperative Duty. 12mo. New York, 1892.

The Albany Depot. Illustrations. 32mo. New York, 1892.

A Letter of Introduction. Farce. Illustrations. 32mo. New York, 1892.

A Little Swiss Sojourn. Illustrations. 32mo. New York, 1892.

The Quality of Mercy. 12mo. New York, 1892.

The World of Chance. 12mo. New York, 1893.

The Coast of Bohemia. 12mo. New York, 1893.

(With S. L. Clemens and others.) The Niagara Book. Illustrations. 12mo. Buffalo, 1893.

Christmas Every Day and other Stories told for Children. Illustrations. 16mo. New York, 1893.

Evening Dress. Farce. 32mo. New York, 1893.

My Year in a Log Cabin. Illustrations. 32mo. New York, 1893.

The Unexpected Guests. Farce. 32mo. New York, 1893.

A Likely Story. Farce. 32mo. New York, 1894.

Five o'Clock Tea. Farce. Illustrations. 32mo. New York, 1894.

A Traveller from Altruria. Romance. 12mo. New York, 1894.

Their Wedding Journey. Holiday Edition. Illustrations. Small 8vo. Boston, 1895.
　*.*The same. Large paper. (250 copies.) 8vo. Boston, 1895.

Recollections of Life in Ohio, 1813-1840. By William Cooper Howells. With Introduction by W. D. Howells. Portrait. 8vo. Cincinnati, 1895.

My Literary Passions. 12mo. New York, 1895.

Stops of Various Quills. Illustrations. Square 8vo. New York, 1895.
　*.*The same. Edition de Luxe, printed in sepia. (50 copies.) Square.8vo. New York, 1895.
　*.*See also ALDRICH, T. B.; GARLAND, HAMLIN; JAMES, HENRY; LONGFELLOW, H. W.; LOWELL, J. R.; STODDARD, C. W.; THOREAU, H. D.

HUTTON, LAWRENCE. 1843 —

Plays and Players. 8vo. New York, 1875.
　*.*The same. Large paper. (25 copies.) 4to. New York, 1875.

Literary Landmarks of London. 12mo. Boston and London, 1877.

(With Clara Erskine Clement.) Artists of the Nineteenth Century and their Works. 2 volumes, 12mo. Boston, 1879.

(Edited.) American Actor Series. Portraits and illustrations. 6 volumes, 12mo. Boston, 1881-82.
　*.*The same. Large paper. (100 copies.) 6 volumes, 4to. Boston, 1881-82.

Memories of Fifty Years, by Lester Wallack. With an Introduction by Lawrence Hutton. Portrait and illustrations. 12mo. New York, 1887.
　*.*The same. Large paper. (500 copies.) 8vo. New York, 1887.

(Collected and annotated.) Opening Addresses written for
and delivered at the First Performances in many American
Theatres, from Boston to San Francisco, 1752-1880.
Illustrations. (175 copies.) 8vo. New York: The
Dunlap Society, 1887.

Occasional Addresses, 1773-1890. (185 copies.) 8vo.
New York: The Dunlap Society, 1890.

Curiosities of the American Stage. Portraits and illustrations.
8vo. New York and London, 1891.

(Edited.) Letters of Charles Dickens to Wilkie Collins.
Portraits and facsimiles. 16mo. New York, 1892.

Literary Landmarks of Edinburgh. Illustrations. 12mo.
New York and London, 1892.

From the Books of Lawrence Hutton. Portrait. 16mo.
New York, 1892.

Edwin Booth. Portrait and illustrations. 32mo. New
York, 1893.

Portraits in Plaster. From the Collection of Lawrence Hutton. Illustrations. 8vo. New York and London, 1894.

Literary Landmarks of Jerusalem. Illustrations. 12mo.
New York and London, 1895.

Other Times and other Seasons. Portrait. 16mo. New
York, 1895.
  *.*See also MATTHEWS, BRANDER.

IRELAND, JOSEPH NORTON. 1817—

Fifty Years of a Play-Goer's Journal; or Annals of the New
York Stage. 1798-1848. By H. N. D. 2 parts, 12mo.
New York [1860].

Records of the New York Stage from 1750 to 1860. Portraits. (200 copies.) 2 volumes, royal 8vo. New York,
1866.
  *.*The same. Large paper. (60 copies, 2 of same on
Whatman paper.) 4to. New York, 1866.

Some Account of the Ireland Family, originally of Long
Island, N. Y., 1644-1880. 8vo. Bridgeport, 1880.

Mrs. Duff. Portraits and illustrations. 12mo. Boston, 1882.
*⁎*The same. Large paper. (100 copies.) 4to. Boston, 1882.

Thomas Abthorpe Cooper. A Memoir of his Professional Life. Portrait. (195 copies.) 8vo. New York: The Dunlap Society, 1888.

Charlotte Cushman, a Lecture by Lawrence Barrett [with letter from J. N. Ireland]. Portrait. 8vo. New York: The Dunlap Society, 1889.

IRVING, WASHINGTON. 1783–1859.

A Voyage to the Eastern Part of Terra Firma, or the Spanish Main in South-America, during the Years 1801, 1802, 1803 and 1804. By F. Depons. . . . Translated by An American Gentleman. 3 volumes, 8vo. New York, 1806.

(With J. K. Paulding and William Irving.) Salmagundi; or the Whim-Whams and Opinions of Launcelot Langstaffe, Esq., and Others. 2 volumes, or 20 numbers [January, 1807–January, 1808], 12mo. New York, 1807–1808.

A History of New York from the Beginning of the World to the End of the Dutch Dynasty. . . . By Diedrich Knickerbocker. Folded view of New Amsterdam. 2 volumes, 12mo. New York, 1809.

The Poetical Works of Thomas Campbell. Including Several Poems from the Original Manuscript, never before published in this Country. To which is prefixed a Biographical Sketch of the Author, by A Gentleman of New-York. 2 volumes, 12mo. Philadelphia, Baltimore, Albany [etc.], 1810.
⁎"Published by Edward Earle, Philadelphia. Also by D. Mallory & Co., Boston; P. H. Nicklin & Co., Baltimore; Lyman, Hall & Co., Portland; and Swift and Chipman, Middlebury, Vt. Fry and Kammerer, Printers, 1810." So reads the imprint on the original board covers of the copy from which this title is transcribed; the corresponding inscription on title page reads, "Printed for D. W. Farrand & Green, Albany. Also for E. Earle, Philadelphia," etc.; on the title page of the Boston Public Library copy this is changed to "Printed for P. H. Nicklin & Co., Baltimore, also for D. W. Farrand and Green, Albany," etc., and it seems safe to assume that on the title pages of copies assigned to any of the booksellers named their business place would take precedence—the original covers retaining the Philadelphia imprint as here indicated.

(Edited, anonymously.) The Analectic Magazine, containing Selections from Foreign Reviews and Magazines of such Articles as are Most Valuable, Curious, or Entertaining. Portraits and Illustrations. 6 volumes, 8vo. Philadelphia, 1813-15.

*.*The first number, January, 1813, was issued with the title "Select Reviews, and Spirit of Foreign Magazines. New Series;" the note, "To Readers," on last page of wrapper, conveying the editor's apologies for his inability to attend to the editorial work of that number, his remonstrance against unwelcome compliments, extravagant panegyrics, etc., and the announcement that the title of next number "will probably vary from that hitherto adopted." The publication contained, in addition to the selections, several original poems, sketches, reviews, and biographies, by Irving, Paulding and others. Commencing with vol. vii., the title was changed to The Analectic Magazine and Naval Chronicle.

Biography of James Lawrence, late Captain in the Navy of the United States; together with a Collection of Papers relative to the Action between the Chesapeake and Shannon, and the Death of Captain Lawrence. Portrait. 18mo. New Brunswick, 1813.

*.*The biographical sketch by Irving, pp. 9-60, is reprinted from The Analectic Magazine for August, 1813.

The Poetical Works of Thomas Campbell. Comprising Several Pieces not contained in any Former Edition. To which is prefixed a Revised and Improved Biographical Sketch of the Author [pp. 1-24], by A Gentleman of New-York. 24mo. [Philadelphia, 1815.]

*.*The engraved false title bears the imprint of the publisher, Edward Earle, which is omitted on title page. The false title makes no reference to revision of the biographical sketch, which is considerably altered from that of the 1810 edition; nor to the "several pieces" referred to on title page, and which may have been absorbed by Caroline, pp. 204-209, the only poem here added to those of the previous collection. The biographical sketch, in its revised form, was first published in The Analectic Magazine for March, 1815.

The Sketch-Book of Geoffrey Crayon, Gent. 7 parts, 8vo. New York, 1819-20.

*.*Arranged for two volumes; the pagination of parts i., ii., iii., iv., forming vol. 1., occurs in regular volume sequence; whilst the separate pagination of each part is retained in parts v., vi., vii., or second volume.

Bracebridge Hall; or, the Humourists. A Medley, by Geoffrey Crayon, Gent. 2 volumes, 12mo. New York, 1822.

*.*After 1820, Irving's works were published simultaneously in New York and London.

Letters of Jonathan Oldstyle, Gent. By The Author of The Sketch-Book, with a Biographical Notice. 8vo. New York, 1824.

Tales of a Traveller. 4 parts, 8vo. New York, 1824.

History of the Life and Times of Christopher Columbus. Map. 3 volumes, 8vo. New York, 1828.
*₀*The same. Abridged by the author. 12mo. New York, 1829.

A Chronicle of the Conquest of Granada. By Fray Antonio Agapida. 2 volumes, 12mo. Philadelphia, 1829.

(Edited.) Miscellaneous Works of Oliver Goldsmith, with an Account of his Life and Writings. Portrait. 8vo. Philadelphia, 1830.
*₀*Published in Paris some time previous to publication in Philadelphia.

Voyages and Discoveries of the Companions of Columbus. 8vo. Philadelphia, 1831.

The Alhambra: a Series of Tales and Sketches of the Moors and Spaniards. 2 volumes, 12mo. Philadelphia, 1832.

Poems, by William Cullen Bryant, an American. Edited [with introductory dedication, 4 pp., to Samuel Rogers,] by Washington Irving. 12mo. London, 1832.

Works [now first collected]. Portrait. Royal 8vo. Paris, 1834.

The Crayon Miscellany. 3 volumes, 16mo. Philadelphia, 1835.
*₀*i., A Tour on the Prairies; ii., Abbotsford and Newstead Abbey; iii., Legends of the Conquest of Spain.

Astoria; or, Incidents of an Enterprise beyond the Rocky Mountains. 2 volumes, 8vo. Philadelphia, 1836.

The Rocky Mountains: or, Scenes, Incidents, and Adventures in the Far West. Digested from the Journal of Captain B. L. E. Bonneville . . . . 2 volumes, 12mo. Philadelphia, 1837.

The Life of Oliver Goldsmith, with Selections from his Writings. Portrait. 2 volumes, 18mo. New York, 1840.
*₀*The biography occupies pp. 9-186 of first volume.

Works. Portrait. 2 volumes, royal 8vo. Philadelphia, 1840.

Biography and Poetical Remains of the Late Margaret Miller Davidson. 12mo. Philadelphia, 1841.

The Poetry and History of Wyoming: containing Campbell's Gertrude, with a Biographical Sketch of the Author by W. Irving; and the History of Wyoming .... by William L. Stone. Illustrations. 12mo. New York, 1841.

A Book of the Hudson. Collected from the Various Works of Diedrich Knickerbocker. Edited by Geoffrey Crayon. Vignette title. 18mo. New York, 1849.

Oliver Goldsmith: a Biography. Illustrations. Square 8vo. New York, 1849.

Mahomet and his Successors. 2 volumes, 12mo. New York, 1849-50.

Wolfert's Roost, and other Papers now First Collected. Frontispiece and vignette title. 12mo. New York, 1855.

The Life of Washington. Portraits and illustrations. 5 volumes, 8vo. New York, 1855-59.
 *.*i., 1855; ii., iii., 1856; iv., 1857; v., 1859.
 *.*The same. Large paper. (110 copies.) 5 volumes, 4to. New York, 1855-59.

Irvingiana. [A memorial volume, including tributes by Longfellow and Bancroft, together with an unpublished letter by Irving.] Square 8vo. New York, 1860.

Life and Letters. Edited by Pierre M. Irving. Portraits. 4 volumes, 12mo. New York, 1862-64.
 *.*i., ii., 1862; iii., 1863; iv., 1864.
 *.*The same. Large paper. (50 copies.) 4 volumes, 4to. New York, 1862-64.

Spanish Papers and other Miscellanies hitherto Unpublished or Uncollected. Edited by Pierre M. Irving. Portrait and frontispiece. 2 volumes, 12mo. New York, 1866.
 *.*The same. Large paper. (110 copies.) 2 volumes, 4to. New York, 1866.
 *.*The following titles have also been attributed to Irving, but without any satisfactory proof that he was, directly or remotely, connected with their publication:
 The Literary Picture Gallery, etc., to the Visitors of Ballston Spa. 1808.
 Fragment of a Journal of a Sentimental Philosopher. 8vo. New York, 1809.

A Word in Season touching the Present Misunderstanding in the Episcopal Church. By A Layman. 8vo. New York, 1811.
Brief Remarks on "The Wife." 8vo. New York, 1819.
***See also BRYANT, W. C.; HOFFMAN, C. F.; and LOWELL, J. R.

JACKSON, HELEN MARIA HUNT. (H. H.) 1831-1885.

Bathmendi: a Persian Tale. Translated for the Children from the French .... 12mo. Boston, 1867.

Nathan the Wise, a Dramatic Poem by G. E. Lessing. Translated by Ellen Frothingham. Preceded by a Brief Account of the Poet and his Works [by H. H., pp. v.-xxiii.], and followed by an Essay on the Poem by Kuno Fischer. 16mo. New York, 1868.

Verses. 16mo. Boston, 1870.

Bits of Travel. 18mo. Boston, 1872.

Bits of Talk about Home Matters. 18mo. Boston, 1873.

The Story of Boon. Square 16mo. Boston, 1874.

[Anonymous.] Mercy Philbrick's Choice. 16mo. Boston, 1876.

Bits of Talk in Verse and Prose for Young Folks. 18mo. Boston, 1876.

[Anonymous.] Hetty's Strange History. 16mo. Boston, 1877.

Bits of Travel at Home. 18mo. Boston, 1878.

Nelly's Silver Mine. 16mo. Boston, 1878.

Letters from a Cat. Illustrations. Square 12mo. Boston, 1879.

Mammy Tittleback and her Family. A True Story of Seventeen Cats. Illustrations. Square 12mo. Boston, 1881.

A Century of Dishonor: a Sketch of the United States Government's Dealings with some of the Indian Tribes. 12mo. New York, 1881.

The Training of Children. 16mo. New York, 1882.

(With Abbott Kinney.) Report on the Condition and Needs of the Mission Indians of California. 8vo. Washington, 1883.

Ramona. A Story. 12mo. Boston, 1884.

The Hunter Cats of Connorloa. Illustrations. Square 12mo. Boston, 1884.

Zeph. A Posthumous Story. 12mo. Boston, 1885.

Glimpses of Three Coasts. 12mo. Boston, 1886.

Sonnets and Lyrics. 24mo. Boston, 1886.

Between Whiles. 12mo. Boston, 1887.

The Procession of Flowers in Colorado. Illustrations in colors. (100 copies.) 4to. Boston, 1887.

Poems. Complete. Portrait and illustrations. 12mo. Boston, 1892.
*.*The same. Edition de Luxe. (250 copies.) 8vo. Boston, 1892.

JAMES, HENRY. 1843 —

Balloon Post. [Consisting of original contributions by Henry James, W. D. Howells, Bret Harte and others.] Published at the French Fair [in aid of the destitute people of France], April 11-17, 1871. 6 numbers, 4to. Boston, 1871.

Transatlantic Sketches. 12mo. Boston, 1875.

A Passionate Pilgrim and other Tales. 12mo. Boston, 1875.

Roderick Hudson. 12mo. Boston, 1876.

The American. 12mo. Boston, 1877.

Watch and Ward. 18mo. New York, 1878.

French Poets and Novelists. 12mo. New York, 1878.

Daisy Miller. A Study. 32mo. New York, 1878.

The Europeans. A Sketch. 2 volumes, 12mo. London, 1878.
*.*Also, one volume, 12mo. Boston, 1879.

An International Episode. 32mo. New York, 1879.

The Madonna of the Future and other Tales. 2 volumes, 12mo. London, 1879.

Hawthorne. 12mo. London, 1879.
*₊*Also, 12mo. New York, 1880.

A Bundle of Letters. (Reprinted from the Parisian.) Square 12mo. Boston [1880].

Confidence. 12mo. Boston, 1880.

The Diary of a Man of Fifty [and A Bundle of Letters]. 32mo. New York, 1880.

Washington Square. Illustrations. 12mo. New York, 1880.

The Portrait of a Lady. 12mo. Boston, 1882.

Daisy Miller. A Comedy in Three Acts. 16mo. Boston, 1883.

The Siege of London; The Pension Beaurepas; and The Point of View. 12mo. Boston, 1883.

Portraits of Places. 12mo. London, 1883.
*₊*Also, 12mo. Boston, 1884.

Tales of Three Cities. 12mo. Boston, 1884.

A Little Tour in France. 12mo. Boston, 1885.

The Art of Fiction [with companion essay, bearing the same title, by Walter Besant]. 12mo. Boston, 1885.

Stories Revived. First and Second Series. 2 volumes, 12mo. London, 1885.

The Author of Beltraffio [and other stories]. 12mo. Boston, 1885.

The Bostonians: a Novel. 12mo. New York, 1886.

The Princess Cassamassima: a Novel. 12mo. New York, 1886.

Partial Portraits. 12mo. New York, 1888.

The Aspern Papers and other Stories. 12mo. New York, 1888.

The Reverberator: a Novel. 12mo. New York, 1888.

A London Life [and other stories]. 12mo. New York, 1889.

The Tragic Muse. 2 volumes, 16mo. Boston, 1890.

The Odd Number. Thirteen Tales by Guy de Maupassant. Translated by Jonathan Sturges. Introduction by H. James. 16mo. New York, 1890.

(Translated.) Port Tarascon. The Last Adventures of the Illustrious Tartarin. Illustrations. 8vo. New York, 1891.

The Lesson of the Master [and other stories]. 12mo. New York, 1892.

Daisy Miller, and An International Episode. Illustrations. Small 8vo. New York, 1892.
  *_{*}*The same. Edition de Luxe. (250 copies.) 8vo. New York, 1892.

The Real Thing and other Tales. 12mo. New York, 1893.

Picture and Text. Portrait and illustrations. 16mo. New York, 1893.

The Private Life [and other stories]. 16mo. New York, 1893.

Essays in London and Elsewhere. 12mo. New York, 1893.

Theatricals. 2 volumes, 16mo. New York, 1894.

The Wheel of Time. 16mo. New York, 1894.

Terminations. 12mo. New York, 1895.

[Anonymous.] "The Quest of the Holy Grail." The First Portion of a Series of Paintings to be done for the Decoration of the Public Library of Boston, U. S. A. By Edwin A. Abbey. 8vo. [London] 1895.
  *_{*}*After the death of Henry James, Sr., in 1882, Mr. James omitted the "Jr.," which previously had been appended to his name on the title pages of his published works.

JANVIER, THOMAS ALLIBONE. 1849 —

Color Studies. 12mo. New York, 1885.

The Mexican Guide. 16mo. New York, 1886 [*et seq.*].

The Aztec Treasure House. A Romance of Contemporaneous Antiquity. Illustrations. 12mo. New York, 1890.

Stories of Old New Spain. Illustrations. 12mo. New York, 1891.

The Uncle of an Angel and other Stories. Illustrations. 12mo. New York, 1891.

Color Studies and a Mexican Campaign. 12mo. New York, 1891.

An Embassy to Provence. Frontispiece. 12mo. New York, 1893.

The Women's Conquest. 16mo. New York, 1893.

In Old New York. Maps and illustrations. 12mo. New York, 1894.

JEWETT, SARAH ORNE. 1849 —

Deephaven. 18mo. Boston, 1877.

Play Days. 18mo. Boston, 1878.

Old Friends and New. 18mo. Boston, 1879.

Country By-Ways. 18mo. Boston, 1881.

The Mate of the Daylight and Friends Ashore. 18mo. Boston, 1883.

A Country Doctor. 16mo. Boston, 1884.

A Marsh Island. A Novel. 16mo. Boston, 1885.

A White Heron and other Stories. 18mo. Boston, 1886.

The Story of the Normans told chiefly in Relation to their Conquest of England. Illustrations. 12mo. New York, 1887.

The King of Folly Island and other People. 16mo. Boston, 1888.

Betty Leicester. 18mo. Boston, 1890.

Tales of New England. 16mo. Boston, 1890.

Strangers and Wayfarers. 16mo. Boston, 1890.

A Native of Winby and other Tales. 16mo. Boston, 1893.

Deephaven. Holiday Edition. Illustrations. Small 8vo. Boston, 1894.
*₀*The same. Large paper. (250 copies.) 8vo. Cambridge, 1894.

Betty Leicester's English Christmas. (Privately printed.) 12mo. Baltimore, 1894.

The Life of Nancy. 12mo. Boston, 1895.

JOHNSON, ROSSITER. 1840 —

(Edited.) Little Classics. 18 volumes, 18mo. Boston, 1874–80.

(Edited.) Works of the British Poets, from Chaucer to Morris, with Biographical Sketches. Illustrations. 3 volumes, 8vo. New York, 1876.

(Edited.) Famous Single and Fugitive Poems. 12mo. New York, 1877.

(Edited.) Play-Day Poems. 16mo. New York, 1878.

Phaeton Rogers: a Novel of Boy Life. Illustrations. 12mo. New York, 1881.

A History of the War of 1812–15 between the United States and Great Britain. 12mo. New York, 1882.

A History of the French War, ending in the Conquest of Canada. 12mo. New York, 1882.

(Edited, with Charles A. Dana.) Fifty Perfect Poems. Illustrations. 8vo. New York, 1882.

Idler and Poet. (Poems.) 12mo. Boston, 1883.

A History of the War of Secession, 1861–1865. Illustrations. 8vo. Boston, 1892.

The End of a Rainbow: an American Story. Illustrations. 12mo. New York, 1892.

(Edited, with John D Champlin and George Cary Eggleston.) Liber Scriptorum: the First Book of the Authors Club. 4to. New York, 1893.

Three Decades. (Privately printed.) 12mo. New York, 1895.

JOHNSTON, RICHARD MALCOLM. 1822—

Georgia Sketches. By An Old Man. 16mo. Augusta, Ga., 1864.

Dukesborough Tales. By Philemon Perch. Square 12mo. Baltimore, 1871.

(With William Hand Browne.) A Historical Sketch of English Literature. 12mo. New York, 1872.

(With W. H. Browne.) Life of Alexander H. Stephens. 8vo. Philadelphia, 1878.

Old Mark Langston. A Tale of Duke's Creek. 16mo. New York, 1884.

Two Gray Tourists. 12mo. Baltimore, 1885.

Mr. Absalom Billingslea and other Georgia Folk. Illustrations. 16mo. New York, 1888.

Ogeechee Cross-Firings. Illustrations. 8vo. New York, 1889.

The Widow Guthrie. Illustrations. 12mo. New York, 1890.

The Primes and their Neighbors. Ten Tales of Middle Georgia. Illustrations. 12mo. New York, 1891.

Studies, Literary and Social. 2 volumes, 12mo. Indianapolis, 1891–92.

Dukesborough Tales. Chronicles of Mr. Bill Williams. 12mo. New York, 1892.

Mr. Billy Downs and his Likes. Frontispiece. 12mo. New York, 1892.

Mr. Fortner's Marital Claims and other Stories. 16mo. New York, 1892.

Little Ike Templin and other Stories. 16mo. Boston, 1894.

JONES, JAMES ATHEARN. 1790–1853.

[Anonymous.] Tales of an Indian Camp. Illustrations by W. H. Brooke. 3 volumes, small 8vo. London, 1820.

A Letter to an English Gentleman, on the Libels and Calumnies on America by English Writers and Reviewers. 8vo. Philadelphia, 1826.

Traditions of the North American Indians: being a Second and Revised Edition of Tales of an Indian Camp. 3 volumes, small 8vo. London, 1830.

Haverhill; or, Memoirs of an Officer in the Army of Wolfe. 2 volumes, 12mo. New York, 1831.
*.*Also, 3 volumes, small 8vo. London, 1831.

A Biographical Account of the Late Ichabod Norton, Esq., of Edgartown, Mass. (Printed for private distribution.) 8vo. Boston, 1848.

JONES, JOHN B. 1810–1866.

Thoughts on the Literary Prospects of America. 8vo. Baltimore, 1839.

Wild Western Scenes; a Narrative of Adventures in the Western Wilderness, Forty Years ago; wherein the Conduct of Daniel Boone, the Great American Pioneer, is particularly described. By A Squatter. 12mo. Philadelphia, 1845.

The Spanglers and Tinglers; or, the Rival Belles. A Tale unveiling some of the Mysteries of Society and Politics as they exist at the Present Time in the United States. 12mo. Philadelphia, 1852.

Adventures of Col. Gracchus Vanderbomb, of Sloughcreek, in Pursuit of the Presidency: also the Exploits of Mr. Numerius Plutarch Kipps, his Private Secretary. 12mo. Philadelphia, 1852.

The Monarchist. An Historical Novel, embracing Real Characters and Romantic Adventures. 12mo. Philadelphia, 1853.

Life and Adventures of a Country Merchant: a Narrative of his Exploits at Home, during his Travels, and in the Cities. Designed to amuse and instruct. 12mo. Philadelphia, 1854.

The Winkles; or, the Merry Monomaniacs. An American Picture with Portraits of the Natives. 12mo. New York, 1855.

The War-Path. A Narrative of Adventures in the Wilderness. .... 12mo. Philadelphia, 1856.

Wild Southern Scenes. A Tale of Disunion! and Border War! 12mo. Philadelphia [1859].

Wild Western Scenes; or, the White Spirit of the Wilderness. Being a Narrative of Adventures embracing the same Characters portrayed in the Original Wild Western Scenes. 12mo. Richmond, 1863.

The Rival Belles; or, Life in Washington. 12mo. Philadelphia, 1864.

A Rebel War Clerk's Diary at the Confederate States' Capital, 1861–1865. 2 volumes, 12mo. Philadelphia, 1866.

JUDAH, SAMUEL B. H. . . . .

The Mountain Torrent. A Melo-Drama. 18mo. New York, 1820.

Odofriede, the Outcast; a Dramatic Poem. 8vo. New York, 1822.

The Rose of Arragon. 16mo. New York, 1822.

[Anonymous.] Gotham and the Gothamites, a Medley. 18mo. New York, 1823.
  **A satire on New York society, which resulted in the imprisonment of the author, who was also the publisher, and the suppression of the work.

[Anonymous.] A Tale of Lexington: a National Comedy, founded on the Opening of the Revolution. 18mo. New York, 1823.

The Buccaneers; a Romance of our own Country in its Ancient Days; illustrated with Divers Marvellous Histories, and Antique and Facetious Episodes; gathered from the Most Authentic Chronicles of the Settlement of the Niew Nederlandts . . . . [by] Terentius Phlogobombos. . . . 2 volumes, 12mo. Boston and New York, 1827.
  **Suppressed, owing to the libelous passage in the introduction. Sabin discovered some copies of the work from which the offensive passage was omitted.

JUDD, SYLVESTER. 1813-1853.

    Margaret. A Tale of the Real and Ideal, Blight and Bloom; including Sketches of a Place not before described, called Mons Christi. 12mo. Boston, 1845.

    [Anonymous.] Richard Edney and the Governor's Family. A Rus-Urban Tale. 12mo. Boston, 1850.

    Philo: an Evangeliad. 12mo. Boston, 1850.

    The Church; in a Series of Discourses. 12mo. Boston, 1854.
       *₀*For separate titles and dates of the author's published sermons and discourses, consult the last-named work.

KENNEDY, JOHN PENDLETON. 1795-1870.

    (With Peter Hoffman.) The Red Book. 2 volumes, 8vo. Baltimore, 1818-19.

    [Anonymous.] Swallow Barn, or, a Sojourn in the Old Dominion. 2 volumes, 12mo. Philadelphia, 1832.

    Horse-Shoe Robinson: a Tale of the Tory Ascendancy. 2 volumes, 12mo. Philadelphia, 1835.

    [Anonymous.] Rob of the Bowl: a Legend of St. Inigoes. 2 volumes, 12mo. Philadelphia, 1838.

    Quodlibet: containing some Annals thereof, with an Authentic Account of the Origin and Growth of the Borough, and the Sayings and Doings of Sundry of the Townspeople. . . . . Edited by Solomon Second Thoughts, Schoolmaster. 12mo. Philadelphia, 1840.
       *₀*A satire on the methods which resulted in the election of William Henry Harrison to the presidency.

    Memoirs of the Life of William Wirt, Attorney-General of the United States. Portrait and facsimile. 2 volumes, 8vo. Philadelphia, 1849.

    Swallow Barn. Revised Edition, with 20 illustrations by Strother. 12mo. New York, 1852.

    The Blackwater Chronicle: a Narrative of an Expedition into the Land of Canaan, in Randolph County, Virginia, in 1851. By The Clerke of Oxenforde. Illustrations by Strother. 12mo. New York, 1853.

> Narrative of an Expedition of Five Americans into a Land of Wild Animals. Illustrations by Watts Phillips. 16mo. London, 1854.
>
> Works [first collected edition]. 3 volumes, 12mo. New York, 1854.
>
> (Edited, with Alexander Bliss.) Autograph Leaves of our Country's Authors. [Selections in facsimile of the authors' manuscript.] Illustrations. 4to. Baltimore, 1864.
>
> Mr. Ambrose's Letters on the Rebellion. 16mo. New York, 1865.
>
> Works [including biography by H. T. Tuckerman]. 10 volumes, 12mo. New York, 1870-72.
>
> At Home and Abroad; a Series of Essays: with a Journal in Europe in 1867-8. 12mo. New York, 1872.
> ***Also numerous lectures, essays and addresses, for separate titles of which see Works.

KEY, FRANCIS SCOTT. 1779-1843.

> Oration in the Capitol of the United States, on the Fourth of July, 1831. 8vo. Washington, 1831.
>
> The Power of Literature and its Connexion with Religion. An Oration, delivered at Bristol College, July 23, 1834, before the Philologian Society. 8vo. Bristol, 1834.
>
> Poems. With an Introductory Letter by Chief Justice Taney. 16mo. New York, 1857.
>
> The Star Spangled Banner. Illustrations by Darley. 4to. New York [1861].

KIRKLAND, JOSEPH. 1830-1894.

> Zury: the Meanest Man in Spring County. A Novel of Western Life. Frontispiece. 12mo. Boston, 1887.
>
> The McVeys. (An Episode.) 16mo. Boston, 1888.
>
> The Captain of Company K. 12mo. Chicago, 1891.
>
> (With Caroline Kirkland.) The Story of Chicago. Illustrations. 2 volumes, 8vo. Chicago, 1892-94.
>
> The Chicago Massacre of 1812. Illustrations. 12mo. Chicago, 1893.

LAIGHTON, ALBERT. 1829-1887.

    Poems. 16mo. Boston and Portsmouth, 1859.

    (Edited, with Aurin M. Payson.) The Poets of Portsmouth. Small 8vo. Boston and Portsmouth, 1865.

    Poems. 16mo. Boston, 1878.
        *₊*Only a few of the poems published in 1859 are retained in this edition.

LANIER, SIDNEY. 1842-1881.

    Tiger-Lilies. A Novel. 16mo. New York, 1867.

    The Centennial Celebration of Columbia. A Cantata for the Inaugural Ceremonies at Philadelphia, May 10, 1876. Music by Dudley Buck. Royal 8vo. New York [1876].

    Florida : its Scenery, Climate, and History. With an Account of Charleston, Savannah, Augusta, and Aiken. . . . Illustrations. 12mo. Philadelphia, 1876.

    Poems. 16mo. Philadelphia, 1877.

    Sketch of the Life of J. F. D. Lanier. Printed for the Use of his Family only. [With genealogical appendix, pp. 75-87, by Sidney Lanier.] Portrait. 8vo. [New York, 1877.]

    (With others.) Some Highways and Byways of American Travel. Illustrations. 8vo. Philadelphia, 1878.
        *₊*The articles on St. Augustine in April, and Ocklaroaha in May, were contributed by Lanier.

    (Edited.) The Boys' Froissart. Illustrations. 8vo. New York, 1878.

    (Edited.) The Boys' King Arthur. Illustrations. 8vo. New York, 1880.

    The Science of English Verse. 12mo. New York, 1880.

    (Edited.) The Boys' Mabinogion. Illustrations. 8vo. New York, 1881.

    (Edited.) The Boys' Percy. Illustrations. 8vo. New York, 1882.

    The English Novel and the Principle of its Development. 12mo. New York, 1883.

Poems. Edited by his Wife. With a Biographical Sketch by William Hayes Ward. Portrait. 12mo. New York, 1884.

LANIGAN, GEORGE THOMAS. 1845-1886.

(Edited.) National Ballads of Canada. 8vo. Montreal, 1865.

Fables by G. Washington Æsop. Taken "Anywhere, Anywhere, out of The World." Illustrations. Small 4to. New York, 1878.

The World's Almanac for 1879. Illustrations. Small 4to. New York [1878].

LARCOM, LUCY. 1826-1893.

Ships in the Mist and other Stories. 18mo. Boston, 1859.

The Sunbeam and other Stories. 16mo. Boston, 1860.

Similitudes. 16mo. Boston, 1860.

Leila among the Mountains. 16mo. Boston, 1861.

Our Young Folks. A Magazine for Boys and Girls. Illustrations. 6 volumes, 8vo. Boston, 1865-70.
   *₊*Vols. i., ii., iii., were edited by Lucy Larcom, J. T. Trowbridge, and Gail Hamilton; vols. iv., v., vi., by Lucy Larcom and J. T. Trowbridge.

(Edited.) Breathings of the Better Life. Square 16mo. Boston, 1866.

Poems. 12mo. Boston, 1869.

Childhood Songs. Illustrations. 12mo. Boston, 1875.

An Idyl of Work. 16mo. Boston, 1875.

(Edited.) Roadside Poems for Summer Travellers. Square 16mo. Boston, 1876.

(Edited.) Hill-Side and Sea-Side in Poetry. Square 16mo. Boston, 1877.

Landscape in American Poetry. Illustrations. Royal 8vo. New York [1879].

Wild Roses of Cape Ann and other Poems. 16mo. Boston, 1881.

Poetical Works. Portrait. 12mo. Boston, 1885.

(Edited.) Beckonings for every Day: a Calendar of Thought. 16mo. Boston, 1886.

A New England Girlhood; Outlines from Memory. 16mo. Boston, 1889.

Easter Gleams. 16mo. Boston, 1890.

As it is in Heaven. 16mo. Boston, 1891.

At the Beautiful Gate and other Songs of Faith. 16mo. Boston, 1892.

The Unseen Friend. 16mo. Boston, 1892.

Life, Letters, and Diary of Lucy Larcom, by Daniel D. Addison. Portrait. 16mo. Boston, 1894.

*₀*Miss Larcom's earliest printed compositions appeared in the pages of The Lowell Offering, to which she and her sister were regular contributors. The numbers of this publication for October and December, 1840, and January and February, 1841, Nos. 1–4, were issued in quarto form, with the title "The Lowell Offering: a Repository of Original Articles on Various Subjects, written by Operatives;" the number for April, 1841, issued as Vol. 1, No. 1, appeared as "The Lowell Offering; a Repository of Original Articles, written exclusively by Females employed in the Mills"—and in octavo form, as did all subsequent issues, the sub-title undergoing occasional slight alterations. Vol. 1 consisted of the numbers for April to December, inclusive, 1841; vol. 2, January to September, inclusive, 1842; vol. 3, October, 1842, to September, 1843, inclusive; vol. 4, November, 1843, to October, 1844, inclusive; and vol. 5, January to December, inclusive, 1845. At this date the publication was discontinued, but was resumed, April, 1848, as "The New England Offering: written by Females who are or have been Factory Operatives. Harriet Farley, Editor." The numbers for April to December, inclusive, 1848, appeared as "new series, Nos. 1–9;" the number for January, 1849, as "Vol. 1, No. 1," whilst some of the subsequent numbers, including the last issued, March, 1850, appeared with the imprint, vols. vi., vii., viii., indicating the publication as a continuation of The Lowell Offering. Two short-lived Lowell rivals of The Offering, and now of almost equal scarcity, were The Operatives' Magazine, published in 1842, and The Ladies' Pearl, 1841–43. Whittier contributed original poems to the latter publication.

LATHROP, GEORGE PARSONS. 1851—

Rose and Roof-Tree. Frontispiece. 16mo. Boston, 1875.

A Study of Hawthorne [in which is included Hawthorne's Diary, reprinted from The Portland Transcript]. Vignette. 18mo. Boston, 1876.

[Anonymous.] Afterglow. 16mo. Boston, 1877.

Somebody Else. 16mo. Boston, 1878.

[Edited, anonymously.] A Masque of Poets. [Original poems, by fifty living authors, specially written for this collection.] 16mo. Boston, 1878.

Presidential Pills: being a Vade-Mecum of Matters concerning Generals Hanfield and Garcock. Illustrations. 18mo. Boston, 1880.

An Echo of Passion. 12mo. Boston, 1882.

In the Distance. A Novel. 16mo. Boston, 1882.

Spanish Vistas. Illustrations. Square 8vo. New York, 1883.

History of the Union League of Philadelphia from its Origin and Foundation to 1882. 8vo. Philadelphia, 1883.

Newport. 16mo. New York, 1884.

True, and other Stories. 12mo. New York, 1884.

Representative Poems of Living Poets, American and English. Selected by the Poets themselves, with an Introduction [pp. vii.-xxvi.] by G. P. Lathrop. Illustrations. 8vo. New York [1886].

Behind Time. Illustrations. 12mo. New York [1886].

Gettysburg, a Battle Ode. 8vo. New York, 1888.

Two Sides of a Story. 12mo. New York [1889].

Would you kill him? A Novel. 12mo. New York, 1889.

(With W. H. Rideing.) The Letter of Credit. Square 16mo. New York, 1890.

Dreams and Days. Poems. 12mo. New York, 1892.

(With Rose Hawthorne Lathrop.) A Story of Courage: Annals of the Georgetown Convent of the Visitation. Illustrations. 12mo. Boston, 1894.
   *₀*The same. Large paper. (250 copies.) 8vo. Boston, 1894.
   *₀*See also HAWTHORNE, N.

LAZARUS, EMMA. 1849-1887.

Poems and Translations, written between the Ages of Fourteen and Seventeen. 12mo. New York, 1867.

Admetus and other Poems. 8vo. New York, 1871.

Alide: an Episode of Goethe's Life. 16mo. Philadelphia, 1874.

The Spagnoletto: a Play. (Privately printed.) 8vo. [New York] 1876.

(Translated.) Poems and Ballads of Heinrich Heine. To which is prefixed a Biographical Sketch of Heine [by the translator]. 12mo. New York, 1881.

Songs of a Semite; The Dance to Death, and other Poems. 8vo. New York, 1882.

Poems. With Biographical Sketch [by Josephine Lazarus]. Portrait. 2 volumes, 16mo. Boston, 1889.

LEGGETT, WILLIAM. 1802-1840.

Poems. 12mo. Edwardsville, 1822.
   *₀*Privately printed, and bound, by the author.

Leisure Hours at Sea; being a Few Miscellaneous Poems. By A Midshipman of the United States Navy. 12mo. New York, 1825.

(Edited.) The Critic; a Weekly Journal of Literature, Fine Arts, and the Drama. Royal 8vo. New York, 1828-29.

Tales and Sketches. By A Country Schoolmaster. Portrait. 16mo. New York, 1829.

(Edited.) The Plain Dealer. 4to. New York, 1829.

Naval Stories. 16mo. New York, 1834.

Political Writings. Selected and arranged by Theodore Sedgwick, Jr. 2 volumes, 12mo. New York, 1840.
***William Cullen Bryant, by whom the work was copyrighted, was assistant editor.
***See also BRYANT, W. C., and PAULDING, J. K.

LELAND, CHARLES GODFREY. 1824—

Meister Karl's Sketch-Book. 12mo. Philadelphia, 1855.

The Poetry and Mystery of Dreams. 12mo. Philadelphia, 1856.

(Translated.) Heine's Pictures of Travel. 12mo. Philadelphia, 1856.
***Commenced, in numbers, London and Philadelphia, 1855.

Sunshine and Thought. 12mo. New York, 1863.

Centralization, or, "State Rights." 8vo. New York, 1863.

[Anonymous.] Ye Book of Copperheads. Illustrations. Oblong 8vo. Philadelphia, 1863.

Life of Abraham Lincoln. 12mo. London, 1863.

Legends of the Birds. Illustrations. Small 4to. Philadelphia, 1864.

(Translated.) Letters to a Lady, by Wilhelm von Humboldt. 16mo. Philadelphia, 1864.

(Translated.) Heine's Book of Songs. 16mo. Philadelphia, 1864.

(Translated.) Memoirs of a Good-for-Nothing. Vignettes. 12mo. Philadelphia, 1866.

The Union Pacific Railway, Eastern Division, or 3,000 Miles in a Railway Car. 8vo. Philadelphia, 1867.

Hans Breitman's Party and other Ballads. 8vo. Philadelphia [1868].

Hans Breitman about Town and other Ballads. 8vo. Philadelphia [1869].

Hans Breitman and his Philosopede Illustrations. 12mo. New York, 1869.

Hans Breitman in Politics. A Humorous Poem. Frontispiece. 8vo. Philadelphia, 1869.

Hans Breitman's Christmas, with other Ballads. 12mo. London, 1869.

Hans Breitman in Church. With other Ballads. 18mo. London, 1870.
   *.*Also 8vo. Philadelphia [1870].

Hans Breitman as an Uhlan. Vignette. 18mo. London, 1871.

Hans Breitman as a Uhlan and other New Ballads. 8vo. Philadelphia [1871].

Hans Breitman in Europe. 8vo. Philadelphia [1871].

Hans Breitman's Ballads. [First collected edition.] 2 volumes, 8vo. Philadelphia [1871].

The Music-Lesson of Confucius, and other Poems. 18mo. Boston, 1872.

(Translated.) Gaudeamus! Humorous Poems. 16mo. Boston, 1872.

The Egyptian Sketch-Book. 12mo. New York, 1873.

The English Gypsies and their Language. 12mo. New York, 1873.

Fusang; or the Discovery of America by Chinese Buddhist Priests in the Fifth Century. 16mo. London, 1875.

(With E. H. Palmer and Janet Tuckey.) English Gypsy Songs. In Romany. With Metrical English Translations. 16mo. London, 1875.

Johnnykin and the Goblins. Illustrations. 12mo. New York, 1876.

Pidgin-English Sing-Song; or, Songs and Stories in the China-English Dialect. With a Vocabulary. 12mo. London and Philadelphia, 1876.

Abraham Lincoln and the Abolition of Slavery in the United States. 12mo. New York, 1879.

The Gypsies. 12mo. Boston, 1882.

The Algonquin Legends of New England; or, Myths and Folk-Lore of the Micmac, Passamaquoddy and Penobscot Tribes. 8vo. Boston, 1884.

The Breitman Ballads. A New Edition. Small 8vo. London, 1889.
　*.*The same. Large paper. (100 copies.) Square 8vo. London, 1889.

(With Albert Barrére.) A Dictionary of Slang Jargon and Cant. Embracing English, American, and Anglo-Indian Slang, Tinkers' Jargon and other Irregular Phraseology. 2 volumes, small 4to. London, 1889-90.

Gypsy Sorcery and Fortune Telling, illustrated by Numerous Incantations, Specimens of Medical Magic, Anecdotes and Tales. Illustrations by the author. Square 8vo. London, 1891.

Etruscan Roman Remains in Popular Tradition. Illustrations by the author. Square 8vo. London, 1892.
　*.*The same. Edition de Luxe. (100 copies, each numbered and signed, and containing an additional original drawing, by the author.) 4to. London, 1892.

The Hundred Riddles of the Fairy Bellaria. Illustrations. Square 16mo. London, 1892.
　*.*The same. Large paper. (100 copies.) Small 4to. London, 1892.

(Edited.) The Life and Adventures of James P. Beckwith. . . . . Illustrations. 12mo. London, 1892.

(Translated.) The Family Life of Heinrich Heine, illustrated by 122 Unpublished Letters, edited by Baron von Embden. Portraits. 12mo. London, 1893.

Voodoo Tales, by Mary Alicia Owen. With Introduction by C. G. Leland. 8vo. New York, 1893.

Memoirs. Portraits. 2 volumes, 8vo. London, 1893.

Songs of the Sea and Lays of the Land. Square 12mo. London, 1895.

Legends of Florence, collected from the People and re-told. 12mo. London, 1895.

Hans Breitman in Germany: Tyrol. 16mo. London, 1895.
　*.*A complete edition of the works of Heinrich Heine, translated and edited, with copious notes and introductions, by Mr. Leland, was announced in 1891, but for some cause only a few volumes seem to have been published. Mr. Leland has also edited several art handbooks and educational publications.

LEWIS, ALONZO. 1794-1861.

 Poems. 12mo. Portsmouth, 1823.

 The History of Lynn, Mass., 1629-1829. 4 plates. 8vo. Boston, 1829.

 Poems. Portrait. 12mo. Boston, 1831.

 Forest Flowers and Sea Shells. 12mo. Boston, 1831.

 The Picture of Nahant. 12mo. Lynn, 1845.

 Love, Forest Flowers, and Sea Shells. 32mo. Boston, 1845.

 A Guide through Nahant, with an Account of the First Inhabitants. 8vo. Lynn, 1851.

LEWIS, ESTELLE ANNA BLANCHE. 1824-1880.

 Records of the Heart: Lyrical and Narrative Poems. 12mo. New York, 1844.

 The Child of the Sea and other Poems. 12mo. New York, 1848.

 Myths of the Minstrel. 12mo. New York, 1852.

 Records of the Heart. [Complete poetical works.] Illustrations. 8vo. New York, 1857.

 Helémah; or, the Fall of Montezuma: a Tragedy. 12mo. New York, 1864.

 Sappho, a Tragedy. By Stella. Frontispiece. 8vo. London, 1868.

 The King's Stratagem; or, the Pearl of Poland: a Tragedy. 12mo. London, 1869.

LOCKE, DAVID ROSS (PETROLEUM V. NASBY). 1833-1888.

 The Nasby Papers: Letters and Sermons containing Views on the Topics of the Day. 8vo. Indianapolis, 1864.

 Divers Views, Opinions, and Prophecies. Illustrations. 8vo. Cincinnati, 1866.

 Swingin' round the Cirkle. Ideas of Men, Politics, and Things. Illustrations. 12mo. Boston, 1867.

Ekkoes from Kentucky. Illustrations. 12mo. Boston, 1868.

Struggles, Social, Political, and Financial. 12mo. Boston, 1873.

The Moral History of America's Life-Struggle. 8vo. Boston, 1874.

The Morals of Abou Ben Adhem; Eastern Fruit on Western Dishes. 12mo. Boston, 1875.

Inflation at the Cross Roads. Illustrations. 12mo. New York, 1875.

A Paper City. 12mo. Boston, 1879.

Hannah Jane. Illustrations. Square 8vo. Boston, 1881.

Nasby in Exile; or Six Months of Travel. Illustrations. 8vo. Boston, 1882.

The Demagogue. A Political Novel. 12mo. Boston, 1891.

LONGFELLOW, HENRY WADSWORTH. 1807-1882.

The United States Literary Gazette. 3 volumes. Boston, 1825-26.
***Many of Longfellow's early poems first appeared in this publication; of these fourteen were retained in Miscellaneous Poems selected from The United States Literary Gazette (for which see BRYANT, W. C.), but all except five were omitted from subsequent collections of his poems. The first volume of The Gazette was issued in quarto form, the second and third in octavo. In October, 1826, W. C. Bryant assumed editorial charge of the publication, the title of which was altered to The United States Review and Literary Gazette; two volumes were issued bearing this title.

(Edited, with preface.) Novelas Españolas. El Serrano de Las Alpujarras; y el Cudaro Misterioso. [By George W. Montgomery.] 12mo. Brunswick, 1830.

Elements of French Grammar, by M. L' Homond. Translated, with Preface and Notes, by An Instructor. 12mo. Brunswick, 1830.

(Edited, with preface.) Manuel de Proverbes Dramatiques. 12mo. Portland, 1830.

French Exercises, selected chiefly from Wanostrocht, by An Instructer. 12mo. Brunswick, 1830.
*.*On the title page, the word "Instructor" is spelled as here given.

[Anonymous.] Le Ministre de Wakefield. Traduction Nouvelle, précédée d'un Essai sur la Vie et les Ecrits d'Olivier Goldsmith, par M. Hennequin, Editeur de L'Esprit de L' Encyclopédie, et l'un des Collaborateurs de la Biographie Universelle. D'Apres l'Edition de Paris. 12mo. Boston, 1831.

Manuel de Proverbes Dramatiques. Second Edition [containing 8 additional pieces]. 12mo. Boston, 1832.
*.*The two preceding titles were issued as Cours de Langue Francaise.

Syllabus de la Grammaire Itallienne. 12mo. Boston, 1832.

Saggi de Novellieri Italiani. D'ogni Secolo: Tratti dá piu Celebri Scrittori, con Brevi Notizie interno alla Vita di Ciascheduno. 12mo. Boston, 1832.

Coplas de Don Jorge Manrique. Translated from the Spanish, with an Introductory Essay on the Moral and Devotional Poetry of Spain [and nine sonnets, of which only seven were retained in subsequent issues]. 16mo. Boston, 1833.

[Anonymous.] Outre Mer, a Pilgrimage beyond the Sea. Nos. 1 and 2 [all published in serial form]. 2 numbers, 8vo. Boston, 1833-34.

Outre-Mer. 2 volumes, 12mo. New York, 1835.

Outre-Mer: or, a Pilgrimage to the Old World. By An American. 2 volumes, 8vo. London, 1835.

Hyperion. 2 volumes, 12mo. New York, 1839.

Voices of the Night. 16mo. Cambridge, 1839.
*.*The same; third edition. Large paper. 8vo. Cambridge, 1840.
*.*Also issued in pamphlet form, 8vo. Boston, 1845.

The Bowdoin Poets [including four poems by Longfellow]. Edited by E. P. Weston. Frontispiece. 12mo. Brunswick, 1840.

Ballads and other Poems. 16mo. Cambridge, 1842.
*.*The same; third edition. Large paper. 8vo. Cambridge, 1842.

Poems on Slavery. 16mo. Cambridge, 1842.
*⁎*The same; third edition. Large paper. 8vo. Cambridge, 1843.

The Spanish Student. A Play in Three Acts. 16mo. Cambridge, 1843.
*⁎*The same; third edition. Large paper. 8vo. Cambridge, 1843.

Hyperion. Second Edition [revised]. 12mo. Cambridge, 1845.

(Edited, with proem.) The Waif: a Collection of Poems. 16mo. Cambridge, 1845.

The Poets and Poetry of Europe. Edited, with Introductions and Biographical Notices. Portrait [of Schiller]. 8vo. Philadelphia, 1845.
*⁎*Of this work the earlier copies were printed, under the editor's supervision, by Metcalf and Company, Cambridge; the later, and more numerous, copies were printed by T. K. and P. G. Collins, Philadelphia.

Poems [including nineteen now first published]. Illustrations. 8vo. Philadelphia, 1845.

Poems. Complete in One Volume [containing poems not included in Philadelphia edition]. 8vo. New York, 1846.
*⁎*Reissued with additions, including Evangeline. 8vo. New York, 1849.

The Belfry of Bruges and other Poems. 16mo. Cambridge, 1846.
*⁎*The illuminated wrapper is dated 1845; the title page, 1846.
*⁎*The same; fourth edition. Large paper. 8vo. Cambridge, 1846.

Outre-Mer. Second Edition [revised]. 12mo. Boston, 1846.

(Edited, with proem.) The Estray; a Collection of Poems. 16mo. Boston, 1847.

Evangeline, a Tale of Acadie. 16mo. Boston, 1847.
*⁎*The same. Large paper. 8vo. Boston, 1848.

Kavanagh, a Tale. 12mo. Boston, 1849.

The Seaside and the Fireside. 12mo. Boston, 1850.
*⁎*The same. Large paper. 8vo. Boston, 1850.

Poems. A New Edition [including The Seaside and the Fireside]. 2 volumes, 12mo. Boston, 1850.

The Golden Legend. 12mo. Boston, 1851.

The Song of Hiawatha. 12mo. Boston, 1855.
    *₊*The same. Large paper. 8vo. Boston, 1856.

Prose Works [including Driftwood, a series of essays now first collected]. Portrait. 2 volumes, 24mo. Boston, 1857.

Poems. Complete Edition. Portrait. 2 volumes, 24mo. Boston, 1857.

The Courtship of Miles Standish, and other Poems. 12mo. Boston, 1858.

Report of the Proceedings of a Special Meeting of the Massachusetts Historical Society, December, 1859, on the Occasion of the Death of Washington Irving. [Containing tributes by Longfellow, Holmes, and others.] 8vo. Boston, 1860.

Tales of a Wayside Inn. Vignette title. 12mo. Boston, 1863.

Household Poems. Illustrations. Square 16mo. Boston, 1865.

Poetical and Prose Works. Revised Edition. Portrait. 7 volumes, 12mo. Boston, 1866.
    *₊*The same. Large paper. (100 copies.) 7 volumes, small 8vo. Boston, 1866.
    *₊*In the 1866 edition two essays, Dante, and The Divina Commedia (vol. i., pp. 419-449. 1857 edition), are omitted; the essay on Ancient French Romances is now first published in book form, vol. iii., pp. 191-240.

Poetical Works [newly revised]. 18mo. Boston, 1867.

Flower-de-Luce. Illustrations. Square 16mo. Boston, 1867.

Noël. [The original French text by Longfellow, with translation into English by John E. Norcross. Privately printed; 50 copies.] Square 12mo. Philadelphia, 1867.
    *₊*Longfellow's English version of the poem appears in Flower-de-Luce.

(Translated.) The Divine Comedy of Dante Alighieri. 3 volumes, royal 8vo. Boston, 1867.

*₊*A special issue of three copies was printed on India paper, at a cost of $1,000, for three gentlemen of Chicago.

The New England Tragedies. 12mo. Boston, 1868.

The Building of the Ship. [First separate edition.] Illustrations. Square 16mo. Boston, 1870.

The Divine Tragedy. 12mo. Boston, 1871.

*₊*Also, large type edition, 8vo. Boston, 1871.

Fair for our Dumb Animals, Boston, December, 1871. "Justice Table" (Mrs. William Appleton's). The Alarm-Bell of Atri. Printed by permission from The Atlantic Monthly, July, 1870. 8vo. [Boston, 1871.]

The Poets and Poetry of Europe. New Edition, revised and enlarged. 8vo. Philadelphia, 1871.

Three Books of Song. 12mo. Boston, 1872.

Excelsior. Illustrations. 12mo. Excelsior Life Insurance Company: New York, 1872.

Christus: a Mystery. [Comprising The Divine Tragedy, The Golden Legend, and The New England Tragedies, with connecting interludes.] 3 volumes, 16mo. Boston, 1872.

*₊*Also issued, with illustrations, square 16mo. Boston, 1873; and library edition, large type, 8vo. Boston, 1873.

Aftermath. Frontispiece. 12mo. Boston, 1873.

The Hanging of the Crane. Illustrations. 12mo. Boston, 1875.

*₊*The same, with additional illustrations. 8vo. Boston, 1875.

The Masque of Pandora and other Poems. 12mo. Boston, 1875.

(Edited.) Poems of Places. 31 volumes, 18mo. Boston, 1876–79.

*₊*i.–iv., England and Wales; v., Ireland; vi.–viii., Scotland, Denmark, Iceland, Norway, and Sweden; ix., x., France and Savoy; xi.–xiii., Italy; xiv., xv., Spain, Portugal, Belgium and Holland; xvi., Switzerland and Austria; xvii., xviii., Germany; xix., Greece and Turkey; xx., Russia; xxi.–xxiii., Asia; xxiv., Africa; xxv.–xxx., America (North, South and British); xxxi., Oceanica.

Laurel Leaves. Original Poems, Stories, and Essays by H. W. Longfellow, J. G. Whittier, O. W. Holmes, W. C. Bryant, J. R. Lowell .... [and others]. Illustrations. Square 8vo. Boston, 1876.

Poems of the Old South [church]. By H. W. Longfellow, O. W. Holmes, J. G. Whittier, Julia Ward Howe .... [and others]. Illustrations. Square 12mo. Boston, 1877.

The Skeleton in Armor. [First separate edition.] Illustrations. 8vo. Boston, 1877.

Favorite Poems. Illustrations. 32mo. Boston, 1877.

The Courtship of Miles Standish. [First separate edition.] Illustrations. 32mo. Boston, 1877.

Excelsior. [First separate published edition.] Illustrations. Square 12mo. Boston, 1878.

Kéramos and other Poems. 12mo. Boston, 1878.

Early Poems [including four not reprinted elsewhere]. Edited by R. H. Shepherd. 16mo. London, 1878.

From my Arm-Chair. To the Children of Cambridge who presented to me .... this Chair made from the Wood of the Village Blacksmith's Chestnut Tree. [A privately printed four-page leaflet, dated Feb. 27, 1879.] 12mo. [Cambridge, 1879.]

Ultima Thule. Portrait. 16mo. Boston, 1880.

Complete Poetical and Prose Works, with Later Poems. With a Biographical Sketch by Octavius B. Frothingham. Portraits and illustrations. 3 volumes, or 45 parts, 4to. Boston [1880–83].

"The City and the Sea," with other Cambridge Contributions [by Child, Howells, Higginson and others] in Aid of the Hospital Fund. Square 12mo. Cambridge, 1881.

In the Harbor; Ultima Thule. Part 2. Portrait. 16mo. Boston, 1882.

Selections from the Poems of H. W. Longfellow. Published by the Massachusetts Society for the Prevention of Cruelty to Animals. 16mo. Boston, 1882.

"There was a Little Girl." [First separate edition.] Illustrations. Oblong 16mo. New York, 1883.

Michael Angelo. A Dramatic Poem. Illustrations. 4to. Boston, 1884.
*.*An edition was also issued in London, dated 1883.

Fourth Annual Report of the Dante Society. May 19, 1885. With an Appendix, containing Additional Notes to The Divine Comedy [pp. 15–31] by H. W. Longfellow. 8vo. Cambridge, 1885.

Writings, with Biographical Notes. Portraits. 11 volumes, 12mo. Boston, 1886.
*.*The same. Large paper. (500 copies.) 11 volumes, royal 8vo. Cambridge, 1886.

Life, with Extracts from his Journals and Correspondence. Edited by Samuel Longfellow. Portraits and illustrations. 2 volumes, 8vo. Boston, 1886.
*.*The same. Large paper. (300 copies.) 2 volumes, royal 8vo. Cambridge, 1886.

Final Memorials [containing journals and correspondence, 1866–1882, with many letters of an earlier date, and bibliography, pp. 431–435]. Edited by Samuel Longfellow. Portraits and illustrations. 8vo. Boston, 1887.
*.*For a list of Longfellow's contributions to The North American Review and The Atlantic Monthly, see indices to these journals; he was also a frequent contributor to Graham's Magazine, Putnam's Magazine, The Liberty Bell, and other annual and monthly publications.
*.*See also BRYANT, W. C.; FIELDS, ANNIE; HOLMES, O. W.; IRVING, W.; LOWELL, J. R.

LOWELL, JAMES RUSSELL. 1819–1891.

Harvardiana. Vol. IV. 8vo. Cambridge, 1838.
*.*Of the one hundred and sixteen articles comprising the contents of this volume, sixty-seven were contributed by its editors, J. R. Lowell, Nathan Hale, Jr., Charles W. Scates, Rufus King, and G. W. Lippitt. Lowell's prose contributions have never been republished.

[Anonymous.] Class Poem. 8vo. [Cambridge] 1838.

A Year's Life. 12mo. Boston, 1841.

The Boston Miscellany of Literature and Fashion. Edited by Nathan Hale, Jr. Portraits and illustrations. 2 volumes, or 12 parts [January–December, 1842], royal 8vo. Boston, 1842.

*₊*Besides the literary notices Lowell contributed to The Miscellany eight poems; also The Old English Dramatists, which appeared in the numbers for April, May and August, and the anonymously published sketch, The First Client, with Incidental Good Precepts for Incipient Attorneys. The latter sketch has never been reprinted, nor have the literary notices contributed to this publication. In December, 1842, Henry T. Tuckerman assumed editorial charge of The Miscellany, but the issues for January and February, 1843, terminated his connection with the publication,—and its existence.

The Pioneer. A Literary and Critical Magazine. J. R. Lowell and R. Carter, Editors and Proprietors. Illustrations. 3 numbers [January, February, March, 1843], royal 8vo. Boston, 1843.
*₊*Lowell contributed to The Pioneer the introduction and book notices, three poems, an essay on song writing, and a paper on the plays of Thomas Middleton; of these only the poems were subsequently reprinted. Among the other contributors were Parsons, Poe, Hawthorne, Story and Whittier.

Poems. 12mo. Cambridge, 1844.
*₊*The same. Large paper. 8vo. Cambridge, 1844.

Conversations on some of the Old Poets. 12mo. Cambridge, 1845.

Liberty Chimes [by J. R. Lowell, Mrs. S. H. Whitman and others]. 16mo. Providence, 1845.

On the Capture of Certain Fugitive Slaves. 16mo. [Boston] 1845.

The Young American's Magazine of Self-Improvement. Edited by Geo. W. Light. Vol. I. Portrait. 12mo. Boston, 1847.
*₊*On completion of this volume, to which Lowell contributed three poems, the publication was discontinued.

Poems. Second Series. 12mo. Cambridge, 1848.

Melibœus-Hipponax. The Biglow Papers, edited with an Introduction, Notes, Glossary, and Copious Index, by Homer Wilbur, M.A. 12mo. Cambridge, 1848.

The Vision of Sir Launfal. 12mo. Cambridge, 1848.
*₊*Also published, with illustrations, square 16mo. Boston, 1867.

[Anonymous.] A Fable for Critics. 12mo. New York, 1848.
*₊*The same. [Second edition, revised; with additional preliminary (rhymed) note, 6 pp.] 12mo. New York, 1848.

Celebration of the Introduction of the Water of Cochituate Lake into the City of Boston. October 25, 1848. [Ode, by Lowell, pp. 21-22.] 8vo. Boston [1848].

Poems. 2 volumes, 12mo. Boston, 1849.

Selections from the Writings and Speeches of William Lloyd Garrison. [With prefatory poems by Lowell and Whittier.] 12mo. Boston, 1852.

Poetical Works of John Keats. With a Life [by Lowell]. Portrait. 16mo. Boston, 1854.

The Poetical Works of William Wordsworth. [With a biographical introduction, vol. i., pp. ix.-xl., by Lowell.] 7 volumes, 16mo. Boston, 1854.

(Edited.) The Poems of Maria Lowell. Portrait. (Privately printed; 50 copies.) Square 12mo. Cambridge, 1855.

The Poetical Works of Percy Bysshe Shelley, edited by Mrs. Shelley. With a memoir by J. R. Lowell [Vol. i., pp. 13-31]. Portrait. 2 volumes, 24mo. Boston, 1857.

Poetical Works. Portrait. 2 volumes, 24mo. Boston, 1858.

Poetry of the Bells, collected by S. Batchelder, Jr. [Godminster Chimes, pp. 57-60, specially contributed by Lowell.] Vignette title. 12mo. Riverside Press: printed in Aid of the Cambridge Chime. [Cambridge] 1858.

The Biglow Papers. With Additional Notes and Enlarged Glossary. Frontispiece by G. Cruikshank. 12mo. London, 1859.

The Victoria Regia: a Volume of Original Contributions in Poetry and Prose [including The Fatal Curiosity, pp. 83-84, by Lowell]. Edited by Adelaide Anne Proctor. 8vo. London, 1861.

[Anonymous.] Mason and Slidell: a Yankee Idyl. [Reprinted from The Atlantic Monthly, February, 1862.] 8vo. [Boston, 1862.]

[Anonymous.] Il Pesceballo. Opera Seria in Un Atto. [The words by F. J. Child, the English text by Lowell.] 16mo. [Cambridge, 1862.]

Fireside Travels. 12mo. Boston, 1864.

The President's Policy. [Reprinted from The North American Review.] 8vo. [Boston, 1864.]
*₊*The same. 8vo. Philadelphia, 1864.

Spirit of the Fair [in aid of the United States Sanitary Commission]. 17 numbers, 4to. New York, April, 1864.
*₊*Containing sketches by Cooper and Irving, now first published, and original contributions by Lowell, Bancroft, Bryant, Curtis, Taylor, Stedman, Stoddard, Parsons, and others.

Memorial: R[obert] G[ould] S[haw]. [Including original poems by Lowell, Emerson, and others.] Portrait. (Privately printed.) Square 12mo. Cambridge, 1864.

Ode recited at the Commemoration of the Living and Dead Soldiers of Harvard University, July 21, 1865. (Privately printed; 50 copies.) Royal 8vo. Cambridge, 1865.

The Biglow Papers. Second Series. 12mo. Boston, 1867.

Under the Willows and other Poems. 12mo. Boston, 1869.

Poetical Works. Complete Edition. 16mo. Boston, 1869.

The Atlantic Almanac [for] 1870. [Containing A Good Word for Winter, pp. 39-45, by Lowell, and Bo-Peep: a Pastoral, by Howells.] Illustrations. 4to. Boston [1869].

Among my Books. 12mo. Boston, 1870.

The Cathedral. Vignettes. 16mo. Boston, 1870.

Proceedings of the Massachusetts Historical Society, from June to September, 1870. [Including tribute by Lowell to John P. Kennedy, pp. 365-367.] 8vo. [Boston, 1870.]

My Study Windows. 12mo. Boston, 1871.

Poetical Works [newly revised]. Household Edition. Portrait. 12mo. Boston, 1873.

The Courtin'. [First separate edition.] Illustrations. Small 4to. Boston, 1874.

Cambridge in the Centennial. Proceedings, July 3, 1875, in Celebration of the Centennial Anniversary of Washington's taking Command of the Continental Army, on Cambridge Common. [Poem, pp. 27-38, by Lowell, also response, p. 87; and response and poem by Holmes, pp. 88-91.] Illustrations. 8vo. Cambridge, 1875.

Proceedings at the Centennial Celebration of Concord Fight, April 19, 1875. [Ode by Lowell, pp. 82-88; address by Emerson, pp. 79-81; and oration by Curtis, pp. 89-119.] Illustrations. Royal 8vo. Concord, 1876.

Among my Books. Second Series. 12mo. Boston, 1876.

Three Memorial Poems. Square 16mo. Boston, 1877.

My Garden Acquaintance, and A Good Word for Winter. [First separate edition.] 32mo. Boston, 1877.

A Moosehead Journal. [First separate edition.] Illustrations. 32mo. Boston, 1877.

Favorite Poems. Illustrations. 32mo. Boston, 1877.

Tribute of the Massachusetts Historical Society to the Memory of Edmund Quincy [including tribute by Lowell, pp. 9-11] and John Lothrop Motley [including tribute by Holmes, pp. 16-23]. 8vo. Boston, 1877.
 *⁎*Also printed in Proceedings, March to December, 1877, with Holmes' tribute to George T. Davis. 8vo. [Boston, 1877.]

The Rose. [First separate edition.] Illustrations. Square 12mo. Boston, 1878.

(Edited, with others.) Diary of Samuel Sewall. 1674-1729. Portrait. 3 volumes, 8vo. Boston, 1878-82.
 *⁎*Collections of the Massachusetts Historical Society. Fifth Series. Vols. v., vi., vii.

True Manliness. From the Writings of Thomas Hughes. With Introduction by J. R. Lowell. 12mo. Boston [1880].

Death of President Garfield. Meeting of Americans in London, at Exeter Hall, 24 September, 1881. [Address by Lowell, pp. 11-21.] Portrait. Square 8vo. London, 1881.

On Democracy: an Address delivered in the Town Hall, Birmingham, on the 6th of October, 1884. 8vo. Birmingham [1884].
  *₊*Also a few copies, printed in large type, for the author's use, square 8vo. [London, 1884.]

Celebration of the 250th Anniversary of the Incorporation of the Town of Concord, September 12, 1885. [Addresses by Lowell, pp. 65–69, and George W. Curtis, pp. 90–94.] 8vo. Concord, 1885.

Under the Old Elm and other Poems. 12mo. Boston, 1885.

Proceedings at the Dedication of the New Library Building, Chelsea, Mass., Dec. 22, 1885. [Address by Lowell, pp. 16–30.] Plate. 8vo. Cambridge, 1886.

Fifth Annual Report of the Dante Society . . . . Appendix I. Dante: [by] James Russell Lowell. [Reprinted from Appleton's Cyclopædia, 1859.] 8vo. Cambridge, 1886.

A Record of the Commemoration, November 5th to 8th, 1886, on 250th Anniversary of the Founding of Harvard College. [Edited by Justin Winsor.] Royal 8vo. Cambridge, 1887.
  *₊*Oration, pp. 194-236, and speech, 300-301, by Lowell; poem, pp. 237-249, and speech, 302-303, by Holmes; and speech, pp. 309-312, by Curtis.

Democracy and other Addresses. 12mo. Boston, 1887.

Proceedings of the Massachusetts Historical Society, from October, 1886, to January, 1887. [Including Lowell's tribute to Charles F. Adams, pp. 149–152.] 8vo. [Boston, 1887].

Political Essays. 12mo. Boston, 1888.

The English Poets: Lessing, Rousseau: Essays, with an Apology for a Preface. 16mo. London, 1888.

Gately's World's Progress. . . . Edited by Charles E. Beale. With Introduction by J. R. Lowell. Illustrations. 4to. Boston [1888].
  *₊*This work was originally published in 1886, but Lowell's introduction was not obtained until 1888, and bears copyright of that date, whilst the verso of titlepage bears copyright date, 1886.

Heartsease and Rue. Portrait. 12mo. Boston, 1888.
 *⁎*Of this work 250 copies were issued wholly uncut, with paper labels.

The Independent in Politics. An Address delivered before the Reform Club of New York, April 13, 1888. 8vo. New York, 1888.

The Complete Angler and The Contemplative Man's Recreation, of Isaak Walton and Charles Cotton. With Introduction by J. R. Lowell. Illustrations. 2 volumes, 12mo. Boston, 1889.
 *⁎*The same. Large paper. (500 copies.) 2 volumes, 8vo. Boston, 1889.

Areopagitica. A Speech of Mr. John Milton for the Liberty of Unlicensed Printing, to the Parliament of England, with an Introduction by J. R. Lowell. Portrait. (328 copies.) 16mo. New York: The Grolier Club, 1890.

Writings. [Newly revised, and including essays and other articles now first collected.] Portraits. 10 volumes, 12mo. Boston, 1890.
 *⁎*The same. Large paper. (300 copies.) 10 volumes, royal 8vo. Cambridge, 1890.

The Old English Dramatists. Portrait. 12mo. Boston, 1892.
 *⁎*The same. Large paper. (300 copies.) Royal 8vo. Cambridge, 1892.

Latest Literary Essays. [Edited by Charles Eliot Norton.] Portrait. 12mo. Boston, 1892.
 *⁎*The same. Large paper. (300 copies.) Royal 8vo. Cambridge, 1892.

American Ideas for English Readers. With Introduction by Henry Stone. Portrait. 16mo. Boston [1892].

Letters. Edited by Charles Eliot Norton. Portraits. 2 volumes, 8vo. New York, 1894.

Poems of John Donne, from the Text of the Edition of 1633. Revised by J. R. Lowell. With the Various Readings . . . . and Notes by Charles Eliot Norton. (380 copies.) 2 volumes, 12mo. New York: The Grolier Club, 1895.

Last Poems [edited by Charles Eliot Norton]. Portrait. 12mo. Boston, 1895.

*₊*For a list of Lowell's numerous contributions to The North American Review, and The Atlantic Monthly, including the years during which he was editorially connected with these journals, see the Index to each. To the anti-slavery annual, The Liberty Bell, for 1842, 1843, 1844, 1845, 1846, 1847, 1848, 1849, and 1850, he contributed eleven poems; and also was a frequent contributor to Graham's Magazine, Putnam's Magazine, Sartain's Magazine, The Southern Literary Messenger, The Democratic Review, and other periodicals, as well as to The National Anti-Slavery Standard, of which he was, in 1848, associate editor.

*₊*See also Bryant, W. C.; Holmes, O. W.; Longfellow, H. W.; Mitchell, D. G.; Poe, E. A.; Quincy, Edmund; and Whittier, J. G.

LOWELL, PERCIVAL. 1855 —

Chosön; the Land of the Morning Calm. A Sketch of Korea. Illustrations and maps. 8vo. Boston, 1886.

The Soul of the Far East. 12mo. Boston, 1888.

Noto: an Unexplored Corner of Japan. 12mo. Boston, 1891.

The Eve of the French Revolution. 12mo. Boston, 1892.

Occult Japan; or, the Way of the Gods. Plates. 12mo. Boston, 1895.

Mars. Illustrations. 8vo. Boston, 1895.

LOWELL, ROBERT [TRAILL SPENCE]. 1816 —

[Anonymous.] The New Priest in Conception Bay. 2 volumes, 12mo. Boston, 1858.

*₊*The same. Revised edition, with new preface. 12mo. Boston, 1889.

Fresh Hearts that failed Three Thousand Years ago, and other Things. 12mo. Boston, 1860.

Poems. A New Edition, with New Poems. 12mo. Boston, 1864.

Antony Brade. 12mo. Boston, 1874.

A Story or Two from an Old Dutch Town. 12mo. Boston, 1878.

Burgoyne's Last March. Poem for the Celebration of the Hundredth Year of Bemis's Heights (Saratoga), Sept. 19, 1877. 16mo. [Newark, N. J.] 1878.

LUDLOW, FITZ-HUGH. 1836–1870.

[Anonymous.] The Hasheesh Eater: being Passages from the Life of a Pythagorean. 12mo. New York, 1857.

Biographical Sketch of John Nelson Pattison. 8vo. [New York, 1863.]

Little Brother and other Genre Pictures. 12mo. Boston, 1867.

The Opium Habit. 12mo. New York, 1868.

The Heart of the Continent. A Record of Travel across the Plains and in Oregon, with an Examination of the Mormon Principle. Illustrations. 8vo. New York, 1870.

LUNT, GEORGE. 1803–1885.

Leisure Hours. A Series of Occasional Poems. 8vo. Boston, 1826.

The Grave of Byron, with other Poems. 16mo. Boston, 1826.

Oration delivered in Newburyport, July 4, 1833. 8vo. Newburyport, 1833.

Poems. 12mo. New York, 1839.

Culture: a Poem before the Mercantile Library Association of Boston, October 3, 1843. 12mo. Boston, 1843.

The Age of Gold and other Poems. 12mo. Boston, 1843.

An Address delivered before the Massachusetts Charitable Mechanic Association, Sept. 26, 1844. 8vo. Boston, 1844.

An Address before the Massachusetts Horticultural Society, May 15, 1845. 8vo. Boston, 1845.

[Anonymous.] The Dove and the Eagle. 12mo. Boston, 1851.

Lyric Poems, Sonnets and Miscellanies. 12mo. Boston, 1854.

Eastford; or, Household Sketches. By Wesley Brooke.
12mo. Boston, 1855.

Julia. A Poem. By Wesley Brooke. 12mo. Boston, 1855.

Three Eras of New England Life and other Addresses, with
Papers Critical and Biographical. 12mo. Boston, 1857.

Patriotism a Moral Duty. Lecture before the Democratic
Union Association, March 21, 1858. 8vo. Boston, 1858.

[Anonymous.] Radicalism in Religion, Philosophy, and
Social Life; Four Papers from The Boston Courier for
1858. 16mo. Boston, 1858.

[Anonymous.] Report of the Proceedings of Professed
Spiritual Agents and Mediums in the Presence of Professors Peirce, Agassiz . . . . [and others]. 8vo. Boston,
1859.

[Anonymous.] The Union. 16mo. Boston, 1860.

Washington and our own Times. A Lecture in Aid of the
Public Library, Newburyport, Feb. 22, 1861. 12mo.
Boston, 1861.

[Anonymous.] Requiem. Dedicated to the Memory of the
Slain in Battle. Illuminated text. (Privately printed.)
Square 12mo. [Boston, 1862.]

The Origin of the Late War: traced from the Beginning of
the Constitution to the Revolt of the Southern States.
12mo. New York, 1866.

Old New England Traits. 12mo. New York, 1873.

A Familiar Epistle to the Hon. Thomas F. Bayard. 16mo.
Boston, 1875.

Miscellaneous Poems. 12mo. Boston, 1884.

MacLELLAN, ISAAC. 1806—

The Fall of the Indian, with other Poems. 24mo. Boston,
1830.

The Year, with other Poems. 8vo. Boston, 1832.

Journal of a Residence in Scotland and a Tour through England, France [etc.]. Compiled from the MSS. of H. B.
MacLellan. 12mo. Boston, 1834.

Mount Auburn and other Poems. 12mo. Boston, 1843.

Fishing in American Waters. By Genio C. Scott. [Containing numerous verses and poetical chapter headings by Mac-Lellan.] Illustrations. 12mo. New York, 1869.
 ***The same. New edition [with additional chapters]. 8vo. New York, 1875.

Poems of the Rod and Gun; or, Sports by Flood and Field. Edited, with a Memoir of the Author, by Will Wildwood [Frederick E. Pond]. Plate. 12mo. New York, 1886.
 ***See also MELLEN, GRENVILLE.

MATHEWS, CORNELIUS. 1817–1889.

The Motley Book: by the Late Ben Smith. Illustrations. 8vo. New York, 1838.

[Anonymous.] Behemoth: a Legend of the Mound-Builders. 12mo. New York, 1839.

(Edited, with E. A. Duycinck.) Arcturus: a Journal of Books and Opinion. [Dec., 1840–May, 1842.] 3 volumes, 8vo. New York, 1841–42.

The Career of Puffer Hopkins. Illustrations. 8vo. New York, 1842.

A Speech on International Copyright delivered at the Dinner to Charles Dickens, at New York, February 19, 1842. 8vo. New York, 1842.

Appeal on Behalf of International Copyright. 8vo. New York, 1842.

Poems on Man in his Various Aspects under the American Republic. 12mo. London, 1842.
 ***Also, 12mo. New York, 1843.

Various Writings . . . . 8vo. New York, 1843.
 ***The title page date is misprinted "MDCCCLXIII."

Big Abel and the Little Manhattan. 12mo. New York, 1845.

Poems on Man. [Newly revised, with additions.] 32mo. New York, 1846.

Moneypenny, or the Heart of the World. 8vo. New York, 1850.

[Anonymous.] Chanticleer: a Thanksgiving Story of the Peabody Family. 12mo. New York, 1850.
  *.*Reprinted, with Illustrations by Darley. 12mo. New York [1856].

Witchcraft. 16mo. London, 1852.

A Pen-and-Ink Panorama of New York City. 18mo. New York, 1853.

[Anonymous.] The Indian Fairy-Book. From the Original Legends. Illustrations. 12mo. New York, 1856.

The Indian Fairy-Book. Compiled from the Manuscripts of Henry Rowe Schoolcraft. 12mo. New York, 1869.

The Enchanted Moccassins and other Legends of the American Indians. Illustrations. Square 8vo. New York, 1877.

MATTHEWS, [JAMES] BRANDER. 1852—

Songs of '71. [Columbia College] Class-Day Songs. 8vo. New York, 1871.
  *.*Of the fifteen songs, five are by J. B. Matthews.

(Edited.) Comedies for Amateur Acting. 16mo. New York, 1879.

The Theatres of Paris. Illustrations. 16mo. New York, 1880.

French Dramatists of the Nineteenth Century. 12mo. New York, 1881.
  *.*The same, enlarged edition. 12mo. New York, 1891.

(Edited.) Poems of American Patriotism. 12mo. New York, 1882.

The Rhymester; or, the Rules of Rhyme. By Tom Hood. Edited, with Additions, by Arthur Penn. 16mo. New York, 1882.

The Home Library. By Arthur Penn. Illustrations. 8vo. New York, 1883.

(With H. C. Bunner.) In Partnership. Studies in Story-Telling. 32mo. New York, 1884.

Sheridan's Comedies. The Rivals, and The School for Scandal. Edited, with an Introduction and Notes to each Play, and a Biographical Sketch of Sheridan, by Brander Matthews. Illustrations. Small 4to. London, 1884.
  *.*Also, Boston, 1885.

The Last Meeting. 12mo. New York, 1885.

A Secret of the Sea [and other stories]. 12mo. New York, 1886.

(Edited, with Laurence Hutton.) Actors and Actresses of Great Britain and the United States, from the Days of Garrick to the Present Time. 5 volumes, 12mo. New York [1886].

(Edited.) Ballads of Books. 12mo. New York, 1887.
  *˛*The same. Large paper. (100 copies.) 8vo. New York, 1887.

(Edited, with introduction.) André. A Tragedy in Five Acts, by William Dunlap. (175 copies.) 8vo. New York: The Dunlap Society, 1887.

Biennial Reports of the Treasurer [T. J. McKee] and the Secretary [Brander Matthews] of the Dunlap Society. (500 copies.) 8vo. New York: The Dunlap Society, 1888.

Pen and Ink. Papers of More or Less Importance. 12mo. New York, 1888.
  *˛*The same, with etched portrait. Large paper. (110 copies.) 8vo. New York, 1888.

Cheap Books and Good Books. 12mo. New York, 1888.

A Family Tree and other Stories. 12mo. New York, 1889.

American Authors and British Pirates. 12mo. New York, 1889.

With my Friends. Tales told in Partnership. With an Introductory Essay. 12mo. New York, 1891.

(Edited, with introduction.) Bunker Hill. A Tragedy, by John Burk. Portrait. (500 copies.) 8vo. New York: The Dunlap Society, 1891.

Ten Tales by Francois Coppée. Translated by Walter Learned. With . . . . an Introduction by Brander Matthews. 16mo. New York, 1891.

(Edited.) Dramatic Essays of Charles Lamb. Portrait. 16mo. New York [1891].

In the Vestibule Limited. A Story. 32mo. New York, 1892.

Tom Paulding. 12mo. New York, 1892.

Americanisms and Briticisms, with other Essays on other Isms. Portrait. 16mo. New York, 1892.

(With G. H. Jessop.) A Tale of Twenty-Five Hours. 16mo. New York, 1892.

The Story of a Story, and other Stories. Illustrations. 16mo. New York, 1893.

The Decision of the Court. Portrait and illustrations. 32mo. New York, 1893.

This Picture and that. A Comedy. Illustrations. 32mo. New York, 1894.

Studies of the Stage. Portrait. 16mo. New York, 1894.

Parisian Points of View. By Ludovic Halévy. Translated by E. V. B. Matthews. Introduction by Brander Matthews. 16mo. New York, 1894.

The Royal Marine. An Idyl of Narragansett Pier. Illustrations. 18mo. New York, 1894.

Vignettes of Manhattan. 12mo. New York, 1894.

Bookbindings: Old and New: Notes of a Book-Lover. With an Account of the Grolier Club. Illustrations. 12mo. New York, 1895.
    *.*The same. Large paper. (100 copies.) 8vo. New York, 1895.

(Edited.) Tales of a Traveller, by Washington Irving. 8vo. New York, 1895.

His Father's Son. 12mo. New York, 1895.
    *.*See also NORTON, C. E.

MAYO, WILLIAM STARBUCK. 1812—

Flood and Field; or, Tales of Battle on Sea and Land. 12mo. Philadelphia, 1844.

Kaloolah; or, Journeyings to the Djebel Kumri. An Autobiography of Jonathan Romer. Frontispiece and vignette title. 12mo. New York, 1849.

The Berber; or, the Mountaineer of the Atlas. 12mo. New York, 1850.

Illustrations of Natural Philosophy, in Six Large Plates. Edited [with descriptive text] by W. S. Mayo. 12mo. New York, 1850.

Romance-Dust from the Historic Placer. 12mo. New York, 1851.

Never Again. Illustrations. 12mo. New York, 1873.

MELLEN, GRENVILLE. 1799–1841.

Ode for the Celebration of the Battle of Bunker-Hill, at the Laying of the Monumental Stone, June 17, 1825. 8vo. Boston, 1825.

Address before the Citizens of North Yarmouth, July 4, 1825. 8vo. Portland, 1825.

The Rest of the Nations. [A poem.] Pronounced before the Peace Society of Maine . . . . May 10, 1826. 8vo. Portland, 1826.

[Anonymous.] Our Chronicle of '26. A Satirical Poem. 8vo. Boston, 1827.

The Light of Letters: an Anniversary Poem, before the Athenian Society of Bowdoin College. 8vo. Portland, 1828.

Sad Tales and Glad Tales. By Reginald Reverie. 12mo. Boston, 1828.

The Age of Print: a Poem delivered before the Phi Beta Kappa Society, Cambridge, 26 August, 1830. 8vo. Boston, 1830.

The Martyr's Triumph, Buried Valley; and other Poems. 12mo. Boston, 1833.

Lafayette Music. Consisting of a Dirge, Requiem and Ode, as performed at Faneuil Hall, Boston, Sept. 6, 1834. Poetry by Grenville Mellen and Isaac MacLellan, Jr. Music by Lowell Mason and Isaac MacLellan, Jr. 4to. [Boston, 1834.]

The Passions: a Poem pronounced Dec. 28, 1835, the Anniversary of the Birth of Spurzheim. 8vo. Boston, 1836.

A Book of the United States: exhibiting its Geography, Divisions, Constitution, and Government. Illustrations. 8vo. Hartford, 1837.

Poem at Amherst College . . . . Aug. 27, 1839. 8vo. Amherst, 1839.
  *_{*}*See also BRYANT, W. C.

MELVILLE, HERMAN. 1819–1891.

Typee: a Peep at Polynesian Life, during a Four Months' Residence in a Valley of the Marquesas. Map. 2 volumes, 12mo. New York, 1846.

Typee . . . . Revised Edition, with a Sequel [The Story of Toby, pp. 291–307]. Map. 12mo. New York, 1847.

Omoo; a Narrative of Adventures in the South Seas. 12mo. New York, 1847.

Mardi: and a Voyage thither. 2 volumes, 12mo. New York, 1849.

Redburn; his First Voyage; being the Sailor-Boy Confessions and Reminiscences of the Son-of-a-Gentleman in the Merchant Service. 12mo. New York, 1849.

White-Jacket; or the World in a Man-of-War. 12mo. New York, 1850.

Moby-Dick; or, the Whale. 12mo. New York, 1851.

Pierre; or, the Ambiguities. 12mo. New York, 1852.

Israel Potter: his Fifty Years of Exile. 12mo. New York, 1855.

The Piazza Tales. 12mo. New York, 1856.

The Confidence Man: his Masquerade. 12mo. New York, 1857.

Battle-Pieces and Aspects of the War. 12mo. New York, 1866.

Clarel: a Poem, and Pilgrimage in the Holy Land. 2 volumes, 12mo. New York, 1876.

John Marr and other Sailors. (Privately printed; 25 copies.) New York, 1888.

Timoleon. (Privately printed; 25 copies.) New York, 1891.

⁎ See also BRYANT, W. C.

MILES, GEORGE HENRY. 1824–1871.

A Discourse in Commemoration of the Landing of the Pilgrims of Maryland, pronounced .... May 10, 1847. 8vo. Emmittsburg, 1847.

Oration at Mt. St. Mary's College. ... 8vo. Baltimore, 1850.

Mohammed, the Arabian Prophet. A Tragedy, in Five Acts. 12mo. Boston, 1850.

⁎ This drama obtained the prize of $1,000 offered by Edwin Forrest, for the best play by an American author.

Mary's Birthday; or, the Cynic. A Comedy. 12mo. Boston [1857].

Senor Valiente. A Comedy in Five Acts. 8vo. Baltimore, 1859.

Christine: a Troubadour's Song, and other Poems. 12mo. New York, 1866.

Abou Hassan, the Wag; or the Sleeper Awakened. 12mo. Baltimore, 1868.

A Review of Hamlet. [Reprinted from The Southern Review.] 8vo. Baltimore [1870].

The Truce of God: a Tale of the Eleventh Century. 18mo. Baltimore, 1871.

⁎ Mr. Miles was also author of the dramas, De Soto. Cromwell, The Seven Sisters, and others, and was one of the contributors to Brownson's Review.

MILLER, CINCINNATUS HEINE (JOAQUIN MILLER). 1841—

Joaquin et al. 18mo. Portland, Oregon, 1869.

⁎ All subsequent works of the author bear his assumed name — Joaquin Miller.

Songs of the Sierras. 12mo. Boston, 1871.

Songs of the Sunlands. 12mo. Boston, 1873.

Unwritten History; or, Life among the Modocs. Illustrations. 8vo. Hartford, 1873.

The Ship in the Desert. 12mo. Boston, 1875.

First Families of the Sierras. 12mo. Chicago, 1876.

The One Fair Woman. 3 volumes, 12mo. London, 1876.
 *₀*The same. Three Volumes in One, 12mo. New York, 1876.

Mae Madden. By Mary Murdock Mason. With an Introductory Poem [pp. 3-10], by Joaquin Miller. 18mo. Chicago, 1876.

The Baroness of New York. 12mo. New York, 1877.

The Danites in the Sierras, and other Choice Selections. Edited by A. V. D. Honeyman. 12mo. New York, 1877.

Songs of Italy. 12mo. Boston, 1878.

Shadows of Shasta. 12mo. Chicago, 1881.

Paquita, the Indian Heroine. A True Story, Wild and Sad. Illustrations. 8vo. Hartford, 1881.

Poetical Works [revised]. Household Edition. 12mo. Boston, 1882.

Memorie and Rime. 12mo. New York, 1884.

The Destruction of Gotham. 12mo. New York, 1886.

Songs of the Mexican Seas. 12mo. Boston, 1887.

(With others.) Tennyson's Fairies and other Stories. Illustrations. 12mo. Boston [1889].

My own Story. Portrait and illustrations. 12mo. New York, 1890.

Songs of the Sierras [and Sunlands]. Revised Edition. Portrait. 12mo. Chicago, 1892.

Songs of Summer Lands. Portrait. 12mo. Chicago, 1892.

The Building of the City Beautiful. A Poetic Romance. 16mo. Cambridge, 1893.
 *₀*The same. Large paper. (50 copies.) 8vo. Cambridge, 1893.
 *₀*See also HOLMES, O.W.

MITCHELL, DONALD GRANT (IK MARVEL). 1822—

Valedictory Oration [The Dignity of Learning] before the Senior Class of 1841. 8vo. New Haven, 1841.

Fresh Gleanings; or, a New Sheaf from the Old Fields of Continental Europe. 12mo. New York, 1847.

The Battle Summer: being Transcripts from Personal Observation in Paris, during the Year 1848. Frontispiece and vignette title. 12mo. New York, 1850.

The Lorgnette; or, Studies of the Town. By An Opera Goer. 24 semi-monthly parts, 12mo. New York, 1850.
*₊*The same. Second Edition [the first in book form]. Illustrations by Darley. 2 volumes, 12mo. New York [1850].

Reveries of a Bachelor: or, a Book of the Heart. Frontispiece and vignette title. 12mo. New York, 1850.

A Bachelor's Reveries: in Three Parts. (12 copies.) 8vo. Wormsloe, 1850.

Dream Life: a Fable of the Seasons. Frontispiece and vignette title. 12mo. New York, 1851.

Fresh Gleanings [with a new preface]. 12mo. New York, 1851.

The Lorgnette .... Fourth Edition [with preface, now first published]. Illustrations. 2 volumes, 12mo. New York, 1851.

Reveries of a Bachelor. Numerous illustrations by Darley. [First illustrated edition.] Square 8vo. New York, 1852.

Fudge Doings: being Tony Fudge's Record of the Same. In Forty Chapters. Frontispieces. 2 volumes, 12mo. New York, 1855.

Report of the Proceedings of the 25th Anniversary of the Brotherhood of Alpha Delta Phi in New York, 24th and 25th June, 1857. [Oration by Mitchell, pp. 14–37.] Issued by the Fraternity. 8vo. New York, 1858.

Address before the Connecticut Agricultural Society, at Bridgeport, Oct. 15, 1857. 8vo. Hartford, 1858.

My Farm of Edgewood: a Country Book. 12mo. New York, 1863.

Seven Stories, with Basement and Attic. 12mo. New York, 1864.

Wet Days at Edgewood; with Old Farmers, Old Gardeners, and Old Pastorals. 12mo. New York, 1865.

Doctor Johns: being a Narrative of Certain Events in the Life of an Orthodox Minister of Connecticut. 2 volumes, 12mo. New York, 1866.

Rural Studies, with Hints for Country Places. 12mo. New York, 1867.
  ***Republished as Out of Town Places. 12mo. New York, 1884.

(Edited.) The Atlantic Almanac [for] 1869. [Containing My Garden Acquaintance, pp. 32–37, by Lowell; Talk Concerning the Human Body and its Management, pp. 47–58, by Holmes, and contributions by the editor, Harriet Beecher Stowe, and others.] Illustrations. 4to. Boston [1868].

Pictures of Edgewood, being Photographic Views with Text and Illustrative Diagrams [by D. G. Mitchell]. (300 copies.) 4to. New York, 1869.

An Address delivered before the American Dairymen's Association, at Utica, N. Y., Jan. 11, 1871. On some of the Relations of Science to Farm Practice. 8vo. Utica, 1871.

A Freehold Villa for Nothing; or, how I became my own Landlord without Capital. [With appendix by D. Smith.] Illustrations. 16mo. London [1873].

Address: Fences and Division of Farm Lands, before Connecticut Board of Agriculture, at Winsted, Dec. 17, 1875. 8vo. Hartford, 1876.

Address before Massachusetts Board of Agriculture, at Worcester, Nov. 15, 1876. 8vo. Boston, 1877.

About Old Story Tellers: of how and when they lived, and what Stories they told. Illustrations. Square 12mo. New York, 1878.

A Report to the Commissioners on Lay-Out of East-Rock Park. 8vo. New Haven, 1882.

Address before the Alpha Delta Phi Society, at the Academy of Music, N. Y. 8vo. New York, 1883.

(Edited.) Daniel Tyler. A Memorial Volume, containing his Autobiography and War Record, some Account of his Later Years, with Various Reminiscences and the Tributes of Friends. (Privately printed; 200 copies.) 4to. New Haven, 1883.

The Woodbridge Record, being an Account of the Descendants of the Rev. John Woodbridge, of Newbury, Mass. Compiled from the Papers left by the Late Louis Mitchell, Esq. [By D. G. Mitchell.] (Privately printed; 200 copies.) 4to. New Haven, 1883.

Washington Irving. Commemoration of 100th Anniversary of his Birth by the Washington Irving Association at Tarry-on-Hudson. . . . April 3, 1883. [Address by Mitchell, pp. 37-48; and by Charles Dudley Warner, pp. 48-52.] Portraits. Square 8vo. New York, 1884.

Bound Together: a Sheaf of Papers. 12mo. New York, 1884.

Reveries of a Bachelor. [Newly revised, with additional preface.] Illustrations. 12mo. New York, 1884.
  *₊*The same. Large paper. (250 copies.) 8vo. New York, 1884.
  *₊*Uniform editions of Dream Life were issued simultaneously; and limited editions of each (200 copies) were reissued in 1889.

Readings from Macaulay. Italy. With an Introduction by D. G. Mitchell. 16mo. Boston, 1887.

Works. [Revised edition.] 8 volumes, 12mo. New York, 1888.

English Lands, Letters, and Kings. From Celt to Tudor. 12mo. New York, 1889.

English Lands, Letters, and Kings. From Elizabeth to Anne. 12mo. New York, 1890.

(With others.) Homes in City and Country. Illustrations. 8vo. New York, 1893.

English Lands, Letters, and Kings. Queen Anne and the Georges. 12mo. New York, 1895.
  *₊*See also HOLMES, O. W.

MITCHELL, SILAS WEIR. 1829 —

[Anonymous.] The Wonderful Story of Fuz-Buz, the Fly, and Mother Grabem, the Spider. Illustrations. Square 16mo. Philadelphia, 1867.

Hephzibah Guiness; Thee and you; and A Draft on the Bank of Spain. 12mo. Philadelphia, 1880.

The Hill of Stones and other Poems. 12mo. Boston, 1883.

In War Time. A Novel. 12mo. Boston, 1885.

Roland Blake. A Novel. 12mo. Boston, 1886.

A Masque and other Poems. 8vo. Boston, 1887.

Prince Little Boy and other Tales of Fairy-Land. Illustrations. 12mo. Philadelphia, 1888.

Far in the Forest: a Story. 12mo. Philadelphia, 1889.

The Cup of Youth and other Poems. 8vo. Boston, 1889.

A Psalm of Death and other Poems. 8vo. Boston, 1890.

Francis Drake. A Tragedy of the Sea. 8vo. Boston, 1892.

The Mother and other Poems. 8vo. Boston, 1892.

Characteristics. 12mo. New York, 1892.

When all the Woods are Green. Portrait. 12mo. New York, 1894.

Mr. Kris Kringle. A Christmas Tale. 12mo. Philadelphia, 1894.

A Madeira Party. Frontispiece. 24mo. New York, 1895.

Philip Vernon. A Tale in Prose and Verse. 12mo. New York, 1895.
***Dr. Mitchell is also author and editor of several medical addresses and publications.

MORFORD, HENRY. 1823-1881.

Music of the Spheres. 12mo. Granville, Middleton, N. J., 1840.

[Anonymous.] The Rest of Don Juan. Inscribed to the Shade of Byron. 8vo. New York, 1846.

Rhymes of Twenty Years. Portrait. 12mo. New York, 1859.

Sprees and Splashes, or Droll Recollections of Town and Country. Portrait. 12mo. New York, 1863.

The Great Rebellion: Grand National Allegory and Tableaux. 16mo. Chicago, 1863.

Shoulder Straps. A Novel of New York and the Army, in 1862. Illustrations. 12mo. Philadelphia, 1863.

The Days of Shoddy. A Novel of the Great Rebellion of 1861. 12mo. Philadelphia [1863].

The Coward. A Novel of Society and the Field in 1861. 12mo. Philadelphia [1864].

Utterly Wrecked. 8vo. New York, 1866.

Paris in '67; or the Great Exposition. 12mo. New York, 1867.

Over Sea; or England, France, and Scotland, as seen by a Live American. 12mo. New York, 1867.

Turned from the Door. 8vo. New York, 1869.

Only a Commoner. 3 volumes, 12mo. London, 1871.

John Jasper's Secret. Illustrations. 12mo. Philadelphia [1871].

Rhymes of an Editor. Including Almost. Portrait and illustrations. 12mo. London, 1873.

Short-Trip Guide to Europe. Map. 12mo. New York [1875].

The Spur of Monmouth, or Washington in Arms. By An Ex-Pension Agent. Portrait. 12mo. Philadelphia, 1876.

MORRIS, GEORGE POPE. 1802-1864.

(Edited, with S. Woodworth.) The New York Mirror and Ladies' Literary Gazette [Aug. 2, 1823-Dec. 31, 1842]. Plates. 20 volumes, 4to. New York, 1823-42.

The Deserted Bride and other Poems. 8vo. New York, 1838.

The Little Frenchman and his Water Lots, with other
Sketches of the Times. Illustrations. 12mo. Philadelphia, 1839.

(Edited.) American Melodies containing a Single Selection
from the Productions of 200 Writers. 16mo. New York,
1841.
*₊*Reprinted as The Gift-Book of American Melodies.
Philadelphia, 1854.

The Maid of Saxony [an opera]. Square 12mo. New York,
1842.

The Whip-Poor-Will. Illustrations. Square 12mo. New
York [1843].

The Deserted Bride and other Poems [including The Maid
of Saxony, and The Whip-Poor-Will]. Illustrations. Square
12mo. New York, 1843.

(Edited, with N. P. Willis.) The New Mirror. A Weekly
devoted to Literature, Art, Drama, etc. [April 8, 1843–
Sept. 28, 1844.] 3 volumes, royal 8vo. New York, 1843–
44.

Songs and Ballads. Royal 8vo. New York, 1844.

(Edited, with N. P. Willis.) The Prose and Poetry of
Europe and America. 8vo. New York, 1845.

The Deserted Bride and other Productions. Portrait and
illustrations. 8vo. New York, 1853.

Poems. With a Memoir of the Author. Portrait. 24mo.
New York, 1860.
*₊*See also, BRYANT, W. C.; NACK, JAMES; and PAULDING,
J. K.

MOTLEY, JOHN LOTHROP. 1814–1877.

Morton's Hope; or, the Memoirs of a Provincial. By An
American. 2 volumes, 12mo. New York, 1839.

[Anonymous.] Morton of Morton's Hope. An Autobiography. 3 volumes, 12mo. London, 1839.
*₊*A reissue of the New York edition, with extensive revisions and alterations.

[Anonymous.] Merry Mount; a Romance of the Massachusetts Colony. 2 volumes, 12mo. Boston, 1849.

The Rise of the Dutch Republic. A History. Portrait. 3 volumes, 8vo. New York, 1856.

Letters of J. L. Motley and Joseph Holt [on the Government's position relative to the rebellious States]. 12mo. New York, 1861.

The Causes of the American Civil War. A Letter to The London Times. 8vo. New York, 1861.
  *₊*Also published in London, 8vo. 1861; and in The Pulpit and the Rostrum, New York, 1861.

History of the United Netherlands: from the Death of William the Silent to the Twelve Years' Truce — 1609. With a Full View of the English-Dutch Struggle against Spain, and the Origin and Destruction of the Spanish Armada. Portraits. 4 volumes, 8vo. New York, 1861–68.

Four Questions for the People, at the Presidential Election. Address. . . . Oct. 20, 1868. 8vo. Boston, 1868.

Historic Progress and American Democracy: an Address . . . . Dec. 16, 1868. 8vo. New York, 1869.

The Life and Death of John of Barneveld, with a View of the Primary Causes and Movements of the Thirty Years' War. Illustrations. 2 volumes, 8vo. New York, 1874.

Democracy, the Climax of Political Progress. An Historical Essay. 8vo. Glasgow [1875].

Peter the Great. 32mo. New York, 1877.

Correspondence. . . . Edited by George William Curtis. 2 volumes, 8vo. New York, 1889.
  *₊*See also HOLMES, O. W.

MOULTON, ELLEN LOUISE CHANDLER. 1835 —

The Waverley Garland, a Present for all Seasons. Edited by "Ellen Louise." Portrait and illustration. 4to. Boston, 1853.

This, that, and the other. By Ellen Louise Chandler. Vignette title. 12mo. Boston, 1854.

Juno Clifford. A Tale. By A Lady. Frontispiece and vignette title. 12mo. New York, 1856.

My Third Book. A Collection of Tales. 12mo. New York, 1859.

Bedtime Stories. Illustrations. Square 16mo. Boston, 1873.

More Bedtime Stories. Illustrations. Square 16mo. Boston, 1874.

(With Elizabeth S. Phelps and others.) Some Women's Hearts. 16mo. Boston, 1874.

Poems. By L. C. M. 18mo. Boston, 1878.

New Bedtime Stories. Illustrations. Square 16mo. Boston, 1880.

Random Rambles. 18mo. Boston, 1881.

Firelight Stories. Illustrations. Square 16mo. Boston, 1883.

Ourselves and our Neighbors. 16mo. Boston, 1887.

(Edited.) Garden Secrets. Poems by Philip Bourke Marston. Portrait. 16mo. London, 1887.

Miss Eyre from Boston, and others. 16mo. Boston, 1889.

In the Garden of Dreams: Lyrics and Sonnets. Illustrations. 16mo. Boston, 1890.

Stories told at Twilight. Illustrations. 16mo. Boston, 1890.

(Edited.) A Last Harvest. By Philip Bourke Marston. 16mo. London, 1891.
 *˳*The same. Large paper. (50 copies.) 8vo. London, 1891.

Swallow Flights. New Edition of Poems published in 1877 [1878], with Ten Additional Poems. 12mo. Boston, 1892.

(Edited.) Collected Poems of Philip Bourke Marston. Portrait. 12mo. Boston, 1892.

In the Garden of Dreams. Illustrations. 16mo. Boston, 1894.

Arthur O'Shaughnessy: his Life and his Work. With Selections from his Poems. Portrait. 16mo. Cambridge, 1894.
 *˳*The same. Large paper. (60 copies.) 8vo. Cambridge, 1894.

MULLANY, PATRICK FRANCIS (Brother Azarias). 1847–1893.

    An Essay contributing to a Philosophy of Literature. By B. A. M. 12mo. Philadelphia, 1877.

    Psychological Aspects of Education. 8vo. New York, 1877.

    The Development of English Thought: the Old English Period. 12mo. New York, 1879.

    On Thinking. Address delivered before the Students of Rock Hill College, 1881. 8vo. New York, 1881.

    Culture of the Spiritual Sense. 8vo. New York, 1884.

    Aristotle and the Christian Church. An Essay. 12mo. London, 1888.

    Books and Reading. 12mo. New York, 1890.

    Mary, Queen of May. 12mo. Notre Dame, Ind., 1891.

    Phases of Thought and Criticism. 12mo. Boston, 1892.
        *₊*Brother Azarias also contributed essays and papers to The International Review, The American Catholic Quarterly Review, The American Ecclesiastical Review and other periodicals.

MURFREE, MARY NOAILLES (Charles Egbert Craddock). 1850—

    In the Tennessee Mountains. 12mo. Boston, 1884.

    Where the Battle was fought. 12mo. Boston, 1884.

    Down the Ravine. Illustrations. 12mo. Boston, 1885.

    The Prophet of the Great Smoky Mountains. 12mo. Boston, 1885.

    In the Clouds. 12mo. Boston, 1887.

    The Story of Keedon Bluffs. 12mo. Boston, 1888.

    The Despot of Broomsedge Cove. 12mo. Boston, 1889.

    In the Stranger People's Country. Illustrations. 12mo. New York, 1891.

    His Vanished Star. 12mo. Boston, 1894.

The Phantoms of the Foot-Bridge and other Stories. Illustrations. 12mo. New York, 1895.

The Mystery of Witch-Face Mountain, and other Stories. 12mo. Boston, 1895.

MYERS, PETER HAMILTON. 1813-1878.

Ensenore. A Poem. 8vo. New York, 1840.

[Anonymous.] The First of the Knickerbockers. A Story of 1673. 12mo. New York, 1848.

The Young Patroon, or Christmas in 1690. A Tale of New York. 12mo. New York, 1849.

The King of the Hurons. 12mo. New York, 1850.

The Miser's Heir, or the Young Millionaire. 8vo. Philadelphia, 1854.

The Prisoner of the Border; a Tale of 1838. 12mo. New York, 1857.

NACK, JAMES. 1809-1879.

The Legend of the Rocks and other Poems. 12mo. New York, 1827.

Ode on the Proclamation of President Jackson. With a Memoir of the Author. 8vo. New York, 1833.

Earl Rupert, and other Tales and Poems. With a Memoir by P. M. Wetmore. 12mo. New York, 1839.

The Immortal; a Dramatic Romance, and other Poems. With a Memoir by George P. Morris. 12mo. New York, 1850.

Romance of the Ring and other Poems. 12mo. New York, 1850.

Poems. With Introduction by George P. Morris. 12mo. New York, 1852.

NEAL, JOHN. 1793-1876.

Battle of Niagara, a Poem without Notes; and Goldau, or, the Maniac Harper. By Jehu O'Cataract. 18mo. Baltimore, 1818.
  *⁎*The same. Second Edition [with additions]. 18mo. Baltimore, 1819.

[Anonymous.] Logan, a Family History. 2 volumes, 12mo. Philadelphia, 1822.

[Anonymous.] Seventy-Six. 2 volumes, 12mo. Baltimore, 1823.

Randolph: a Novel. 2 volumes, 12mo. [New York] 1823.

Errata; or, the Works of Will Adams. A Tale. 2 volumes, 12mo. New York, 1823.

[Anonymous.] Brother Jonathan; or, the New Englanders. 3 volumes, 12mo. Edinburgh, 1825.

Rachel Dyer: a North American Story. 12mo. Portland, 1828.

(Edited.) The Yankee. A Literary Paper. Portland and Boston, 1828-29.
   ***Of this publication numbers 1-52, inclusive, forming vol. i., and vol. ii., numbers 1-26, inclusive, January 2, 1828, to June 25, 1829, were issued in quarto form; the subsequent numbers, July-December, inclusive, 1829, in octavo. The number for October 15, 1828, appeared with Boston imprint, as did all subsequent numbers. One of the principal contributors to this journal was John G. Whittier, many of whose early compositions first appeared in its pages.

Address delivered before the Portland Association for the Promoting of Temperance, Feb. 11th, 1829. 8vo. Portland, 1829.

Authorship, a Tale. By A New Englander Over-Sea. 12mo. Boston, 1830.

Our Country. An Address before the Alumni of Waterville College, July 29, 1830. 8vo. Portland, 1830.

Principles of Legislature: from the MS. of Jeremy Bentham. By M. Dupont. Translated from the Second Corrected and Enlarged Edition; with Notes and a Biographical Notice of Jeremy Bentham and M. Dupont by John Neal. Portrait. 8vo. Boston, 1830.

The Down Easters. 2 volumes, 12mo. New York, 1831.

Banks and Banking. A Letter to the Bank Directors of Portland. 18mo. Portland, 1837.

Oration delivered at Portland July 4, 1838. 8vo. Portland, 1838.

Man. A Discourse, before the United Brothers' Society of Brown University, Sept. 4, 1838. 8vo. Providence, 1838.

From the American Press to the American People. In Behalf of John Bratish Eliovitch. 8vo. Portland, 1840.

One Word More; intended for the Reasoning and Thoughtful among Unbelievers. 12mo. Portland and Boston, 1854.

True Womanhood. 12mo. Boston, 1859.

The White-Faced Pacer; or, before and after the Battle. 16mo. New York, 1864.

The Moose-Hunter; or, Life in the Maine Woods. 16mo. New York [1864].

Account of the Great Conflagration in Portland, July 4th and 5th, 1866, and a New Business Guide. 8vo. Portland, 1866.

Wandering Recollections of a Somewhat Busy Life. An Autobiography. 12mo. Boston, 1869.

Great Mysteries and Little Plagues. Frontispiece. 12mo. Boston, 1870.

Little Moccasin; or, Along the Madawaska. A Story of Life in the Lumber Region. Frontispiece. 16mo. London [1870].

Portland Illustrated. Portrait and illustrations. 8vo. Portland, 1874.

NEAL, JOSEPH CLAY. 1807-1847.

Charcoal Sketches; or, Scenes in a Metropolis. Illustrations by D. C. Johnston. 12mo. Philadelphia, 1838.

Peter Ploddy and other Oddities. 12mo. Philadelphia, 1844.

Charcoal Sketches. Second Series. Illustrations by Darley. 8vo. New York, 1848.

The Misfortunes of Peter Faber and other Sketches. Illustrations by Darley. 12mo. Philadelphia, 1854.

NEWELL, ROBERT HENRY (ORPHEUS C. KERR). 1836—

The Orpheus C. Kerr Papers. 3 volumes, 12mo. New York, 1862-65.

The Palace Beautiful and other Poems. 12mo. New York, 1865.

The Martyr-President: a Poem. 12mo. New York, 1865.

Avery Glibun; or between Two Fires: a Romance. 8vo. New York, 1867.

Smoked Glass. Illustrations. 12mo. New York, 1868.

The Cloven Foot; an [American] Adaptation of " The Mystery of Edwin Drood " . . . . 12mo. New York, 1870.

Versatilities. 16mo. Boston, 1871.

The Walking Doll; or the Asters and Disasters of Society. 12mo. New York, 1872.

Studies in Stanzas. 16mo. New York, 1882.

There was once a Man. 12mo. New York, 1884.

NOAH, MORDECAI MANUEL. 1785–1851.

The Fortress of Sorrento: a Petit Historical Drama. 16mo. New York, 1808.

Shakspeare Illustrated: or, the Novels and Histories on which the Plays of Shakspeare are founded. Collected and translated from the Originals, by Mrs. Lenox. With Critical Remarks and Biographical Sketches of the Writers, by M. M. Noah. 2 volumes, 8vo. Philadelphia, 1809.

Correspondence and Documents relative to the Attempt to negociate for the Release of the American Captives at Algiers. 8vo. Washington, 1816.

Discourse at the Consecration of the Synagogue in New-York, ... 17th of April, 1818. 8vo. New York, 1818.

She would be a Soldier, or the Plains of Chippewa. An Historical Drama in Three Acts. 24mo. New York, 1819.

Travels in England, France, Spain, and the Barbary States, in the Years 1813–15. Portrait. 8vo. New York, 1819.

[Anonymous.] The Wandering Boys: or, the Castle of Olival. A Melo Drama. In Two Acts. 24mo. Boston, 1821.

The Grecian Captive, or, the Fall of Athens. 16mo. New York, 1822.

Marion : or, the Hero of Lake George : a Drama .... founded on Events of the Revolutionary War. 16mo. New York, 1822.

An Address delivered .... on the Opening of the Mechanic Institution .... 8vo. New York, 1822.

A Statement of Facts relative to the Conduct of Henry Eckford, Esq., as connected with The National Advocate. 8vo. New York, 1824.

Discourse on the Evidences of the American Indians being the Descendants of the Lost Tribes of Israel. 8vo. New York, 1837.

.... The Book of Jasher; referred to in Joshua and Second Samuel. Faithfully translated from the Original Hebrew into English. [Edited, with preface, pp. iii.-vii., by M. M. Noah.] 8vo. New York, 1840.

Discourse on the Restoration of the Jews. With a Map of the Land of Israel. 8vo. New York, 1845.

Gleanings of a gathered Harvest. 12mo. New York, 1845.

A Letter addressed to the Southern Delegates of the Baltimore Democratic Convention, on the Claims of the "Barn-Burners" to be admitted to Seats in that Convention. 8vo. New York, 1848.

The Jews, Judea, and Christianity. A Discourse on the Restoration of the Jews. 12mo. London, 1849.

NORTON, CHARLES ELIOT. 1827—

[Anonymous.] Considerations on some Recent Social Theories. 16mo. Boston, 1853.

The New Life, of Dante : an Essay, with Translations. (100 copies.) Square 12mo. Cambridge, 1859.

Notes of Travel and Study in Italy. 12mo. Boston, 1860.

A Review of a Translation into Italian [by Giovanni Tamburini] of the Commentary by Benvenuto da Imola on the Divina Commedia. (50 copies.) Small 4to. Cambridge, 1861.

The Soldier of the Good Cause. 24mo. Boston, 1861.

The Poems of Arthur Hugh Clough. With a Memoir [pp. xi.-xxxvi.] by C. E. Norton. 24mo. Boston, 1862.

(Translated.) The New Life of Dante Alighieri. Royal 8vo. Boston, 1867.

William Blake's Illustrations of the Book of Job reproduced in Heliotype, with Descriptive Letter-Press and Sketch of Blake's Life and Works. 4to. Boston, 1875.

A Catalogue of the Plates of Turner's Liber Studiorum. 4to. Boston, 1875.

Philosophical Discussions, by Chauncey Wright. With Biographical Sketch of the Author by C. E. Norton. 8vo. New York, 1877.

List of the Principal Books relating to the Life and Work of Michael Angelo. With Notes. 8vo. Cambridge, 1879.

Historical Study of Church-Building in the Middle Ages: Venice, Siena, Florence. 8vo. New York, 1880.
 *₀*The same. Large paper. Royal 8vo. New York, 1880.

[Edward C. Cabot's] Letter to the President of the Archæological Institute [C. E. Norton]. And his Reply, concerning the Work at Assos and the Contribution of the Boston Society of Architects towards the Cost of printing the Report of the Assos Expedition. 8vo. Boston, 1884.

(Edited.) Early Letters of Thomas Carlyle. 2 portraits. 2 volumes, 12mo. London, 1886.

(Edited.) Reminiscences of Thomas Carlyle. 2 maps. 2 volumes, 8vo. London, 1887.

(Edited.) Correspondence between Goethe and Carlyle. 12mo. London, 1887.

(Edited.) Letters of Thomas Carlyle. 1826-1836. Frontispiece and facsimile. 2 volumes, 12mo. London, 1888.

(Translated.) The Divine Comedy, and The New Life of Dante Alighieri. 4 volumes, 16mo. Boston, 1891-92.
 *₀*The same. Large paper. (250 copies.) 12mo. Boston, 1891-92.

(Edited.) Scott's Complete Poetical Works. Illustrations. 2 volumes, 12mo. New York, 1894.

(With Brander Matthews, and others.) Four American Universities. [Harvard, by Norton, pp. 1-43.] Illustrations. Square 8vo. New York, 1895.

(Edited.) The Heart of Oak Books. 6 volumes, 12mo. Boston, 1895.
*₊*See also Curtis, G. W.; Emerson, R. W.; Lowell, J. R.; and Parsons, T. W.

O'CONNOR, WILLIAM DOUGLAS. 1833-1889.

[Anonymous.] Harrington: a Story of True Love. 12mo. Boston, 1860.

The Good Gray Poet: a Vindication [of Walt Whitman]. 8vo. New York, 1866.

The Ghost. Illustrations. Square 16mo. New York, 1867.

The United States Life-Saving Service. Reprint from Appleton's Annual Cyclopædia of the Year 1878. Illustrations. 8vo. New York, 1884.
*₊*The original pagination is retained in the reprint.

Hamlet's Note Book. 12mo. Boston, 1886.

Three Tales. The Ghost, The Brazen Android, The Carpenter. [With a preface, pp. iii.-vii., by Walt Whitman.] 12mo. Boston, 1892.

O'REILLY, JOHN BOYLE. 1844-1890.

Songs from the Southern Seas, and other Poems. 12mo. Boston, 1873.

Songs, Legends and Ballads. 12mo. Boston, 1878.

Moondyne. A Story from the Under World. 12mo. Boston, 1879.

The Statues in the Block and other Poems. 12mo. Boston, 1881.

America. [A poem.] Read at the Reunion of the Army of the Potomac, at Detroit, June 14, 1882. 4to. [Boston, 1882.]

In Bohemia. 12mo. Boston, 1886.

The Irish Question : its Commercial and Industrial Aspects. Address before the Beacon Society of Boston, Feb. 28, 1886. 8vo. [Boston, 1886.]

The Ethics of Boxing and Manly Sport. Illustrations. 12mo. Boston, 1888.

The Proceedings at the Celebration by the Pilgrim Society at Plymouth, August 1st, 1889, of the Completion of the National Monument to the Pilgrims. [Containing poem for the occasion, by O'Reilly.] Illustrations. 8vo. Plymouth, 1889.

Life of John Boyle O'Reilly, by James Jeffrey Roche. Together with his Complete Poems and Speeches, edited by Mrs. J. B. O'Reilly. Portrait and illustrations. 8vo. New York [1891].
*₀*See also FISKE, JOHN; GRANT, ROBERT; and HOLMES, O. W.

OSBORN, LAUGHTON. 1809-1878.

[Anonymous.] Sixty Years of the Life of Jeremy Levis. 2 volumes, 12mo. New York, 1831.

[Anonymous.] The Confessions of a Poet. 2 volumes, 12mo. Philadelphia, 1835.

The Vision of Rubeta, an Epic Story of the Island of Manhattan. Illustrations. 8vo. Boston, 1838.

The Critique of The Vision of Rubeta. A Dramatic Sketch in One Act. By Autodicus. 8vo. Philadelphia, 1838.
*₀*A brochure evidently intended to stimulate the sale of the work criticised.

Arthur Carryl. A Novel. . . . Odes . . . . Epigrams. Parodies and Minor Pieces. 8vo. New York, 1841.

The Silver Head and the Double Heart. 12mo. New York, 1867.

Calvary — Virginia. Tragedies. 12mo. New York, 1867.

Alice ; or, the Painter's Story. 12mo. New York, 1867.

Dramatic Works. 2 volumes, 12mo. New York, 1868.

Bianca Capello. A Tragedy. 12mo. New York, 1868.

The School of Critics : a Comedy. 12mo. New York, 1868.

Montanini : a Tragedy. 12mo. New York, 1868.

Travels by Sea and Land. By Alethitheras. 12mo. New York, 1868.

The Magnetizer. The Prodigal. Comedies in Prose. 8vo. New York, 1869.

Ugo da Este ; Uberto ; The Cid of Seville. Tragedies. 12mo. New York, 1869.

The Last Mandeville . . . . [and other] Tragedies. 12mo. New York, 1870.

Meleagros ; The New Calvary. Tragedies. 12mo. New York, 1871.

Mariamne. 12mo. New York, 1873.

OSGOOD, FRANCES SARGENT. 1812-1850.

A Wreath of Wild Flowers from New England. 12mo. London, 1838.

The Casket of Fate. 48mo. Boston, 1840.

The Poetry of Flowers, and Flowers of Poetry. Illustrations. 12mo. New York, 1841.

Interpretation of Flora. 12mo. Philadelphia, 1841.

The Rose. 18mo. Providence, 1842.

The Snow-Drop. 18mo. Providence, 1842.

Poems. Frontispiece and engraved title page. 12mo. New York, 1846.

The Floral Offering. Illustrations. 4to. Philadelphia, 1849.

A Letter about the Lions : addressed to Mabel in the Country. 8vo. New York, 1849.

Poems. Complete Edition. Illustrations. 8vo. Philadelphia, 1850.
⁂ See also FORD, P. L.

PAGE, THOMAS NELSON. 1853—

In Ole Virginia ; or, Marse Chan and other Stories. 12mo. New York, 1887.

Two Little Confederates. Illustrations. Square 8vo. New York, 1888.

(With A. C. Gordon.) Befo' de War: Echoes in Negro Dialect. 12mo. New York, 1888.

On Newfound River. 12mo. New York, 1891.

Among the Camps: Young People's Stories of the War. Illustrations. Square 8vo. New York, 1891.

Elsket and other Stories. 12mo. New York, 1891.

The Old South: Essays Social and Political. Portrait. 12mo. New York, 1892.

Marse Chan. A Tale of Old Virginia. Illustrations. Square 8vo. New York, 1892.

Meh Lady. A Story of the War. Illustrations. Square 8vo. New York, 1893.

Works. Library Edition. Portrait. 4 volumes, 12mo. New York, 1893.

Pastime Stories. Illustrations. 12mo. New York, 1894.

Polly. A Christmas Recollection. Illustrations. Square 8vo. New York, 1894.

The Burial of the Guns. 12mo. New York, 1894.

Unc' Edinburg: a Plantation Echo. Illustrations. Square 8vo. New York, 1895.

PALMER, JOHN WILLIAMSON. 1825—

The Golden Dragon; or, up and down the Irrawaddy: being Passages of Adventure in the Burman Empire. By An American. 12mo. New York, 1856.

The Queen's Heart; a Comedy. 12mo. Boston, 1858.

The New and the Old; or California and India in Romantic Aspects. 12mo. New York, 1859.

(Translated.) Love. From the French of Michelet. 12mo. New York, 1860.

(Translated.) Woman. From the French of Michelet. 12mo. New York, 1860.

(Edited.) Folk-Songs : a Book of Poems made for the Popular Heart. Illustrations. Royal 8vo. New York, 1860.

(Translated.) The Moral History of Woman. From the French of Legouvé. 12mo. New York, 1860.

(Edited.) The Poetry of Compliment and Courtship. 16mo. Boston, 1868.
  ***Also issued with engravings. Square 12mo. Boston, 1868.

Beauties and Curiosities of Engraving. Illustrations. Folio. Boston [1879].

(Edited.) Home Life in the Bible. By Henrietta Lee Palmer. Illustrations. 8vo. Boston, 1881.

After his Kind. By John Coventry. 12mo. New York, 1886.

PARKMAN, FRANCIS. 1823-1893.

The California and Oregon Trail ; being Sketches of Prairie and Rocky Mountain Life. 12mo. New York, 1849.

History of the Conspiracy of Pontiac and the War of the North American Tribes against the English Colonies, after the Conquest of Canada. Maps. 8vo. Boston, 1851.
  ***The same. Large paper. (75 copies.) Royal 8vo. Boston, 1866.

Vassall Morton. A Novel. 12mo. Boston, 1856.

France and England in North America : a Series of Historical Narratives :—

I. The Pioneers of France in the New World. Portrait and maps. 8vo. Boston, 1865.

II. The Jesuits in North America in the Seventeenth Century. Map. 8vo. Boston, 1867.

III. The Discovery of the Great West. Map. 8vo. Boston, 1869.
  ***Reprinted as La Salle, or the Discovery of the Great West. 8vo. Boston, 1879.

IV. The Old Regime in Canada. Map. 8vo. Boston, 1874.

V. Count Frontenac and New France under Louis XIV. Map. 8vo. Boston, 1877.

VI. A Half-Century of Conflict. Maps. 2 volumes, 8vo. Boston, 1892.

VII. Montcalm and Wolfe. Portraits and maps. 2 volumes, 8vo. Boston, 1884.
*₊*A large paper edition, 75 copies, of each part was published on the dates indicated.

The Book of Roses. Square 12mo. Boston, 1866.

Historical Account of Boquet's Expedition against the Indians in 1764. With Preface by Francis Parkman. 8vo. Cincinnati, 1868.
*₊*The same. Large paper. Royal 8vo. Cincinnati, 1868.

Some of the Reasons against Woman Suffrage. Printed at the Request of an Association of Women. 8vo. [Boston, 1884.]

Historical Hand-Book of the Northern Tour. Lakes George and Champlain; Niagara; Montreal; Quebec. Illustrations and maps. 8vo. Boston, 1885.

Braddock's Defeat. 12mo. New York, 1890.

Champlain and his Associates. 12mo. New York, 1890.

Our Common Schools. 8vo. [Boston, 1890.]

The Oregon Trail . . . . With New Introduction by the Author. Illustrations. 8vo. Boston, 1893.

Proceedings of the Massachusetts Historical Society, October and November, 1893. [Containing autobiography of Francis Parkman, pp. 350–360, and memorial poem, by Holmes, pp. 360–361.] 8vo. [Boston, 1893.]
*₊*See also CATHERWOOD, MARY HARTWELL.

PARSONS, THOMAS WILLIAM. 1819–1892.

[Anonymous.] The First Ten Cantos of the Inferno of Dante Alighieri, newly translated into English Verse. Portrait. (Privately printed.) 8vo. Boston, 1843.

Twenty-Fourth of October, 1852. [Poem on the death of Daniel Webster.] 4to. [Boston, 1852.]

Poems. 12mo. Boston, 1854.

Seventeen Cantos of the Inferno of Dante Alighieri. (Privately printed.) Small 4to. Boston, 1865.

The Rosary. (Privately printed; 80 copies.) Small 4to. Cambridge, 1865.

The Magnolia. (Privately printed.) 4to. Boston, 1866.

The First Canticle : Inferno, of the Divine Comedy of Dante Alighieri. Small 4to. Boston, 1867.
*„*Also issued with portrait and 75 illustrations. Small 4to. Boston, 1867.

The Old House at Sudbury. (Privately printed.) 12mo. Cambridge, 1870.

The Shadow of the Obelisk and other Poems. Square 12mo. London, 1872.

The Willey House and Sonnets. Illustrations. (Privately printed.) 12mo. Cambridge, 1875.

The Birthday of •Michael Angelo. (Privately printed.) Square 18mo. London, 1875.

The Ante-Purgatorio of Dante Alighieri. (Privately printed.) 8vo. Cambridge, 1875.

A Memorial of the American Patriots who fell at the Battle of Bunker Hill, June 17, 1775. With an Account of the Dedication of the Memorial Tablets on Winthrop Square, Charlestown, June 17, 1889 and an Appendix containing Illustrative Papers. [Ode by Parsons, pp. 20–23.] Illustrations. Royal 8vo. Boston, 1889.

Circum Præcordia : the Collects of the Holy Catholic Church as they are set forth by the Church of England in her Book of Common Prayer, for every Sunday in the Year. Together with a Few Poems. 16mo. Boston [1892].

Poems. [Edited by Charles Eliot Norton.] 12mo. Boston, 1893.

The Divine Comedy of Dante Alighieri. With a Preface by Charles Eliot Norton, and a Memorial Sketch by Louise Imogen Guiney. 12mo. Boston, 1893.
*„*See also HOLMES, O. W.; LOWELL, J. R.; and WHITTIER, J. G.

PARTON, JAMES. 1822-1891.

 The Life of Horace Greeley, Editor of The New York Tribune. Portraits and illustrations. 12mo. New York, 1855.

 The Humorous Poetry of the English Language from Chaucer to Saxe, with Notes Explanatory and Biographical. 8vo. New York, 1856.

 The Life and Times of Aaron Burr. . . . 2 portraits. 8vo. New York, 1858.

 Life of Andrew Jackson. Portraits. 3 volumes, 12mo. New York, 1860.
  *.*The same. Large paper. 3 volumes, royal 8vo. New York, 1860.

 General Butler in New Orleans: History of the Administration of the Department of the Gulf in 1862. . . . Portraits and plan. 12mo. New York, 1863.

 The Life and Times of Benjamin Franklin. 4 portraits. 2 volumes, 12mo. New York, 1864.
  *.*The same. Large paper. (100 copies.) 2 volumes, royal 8vo. New York, 1864.

 Life of John Jacob Astor. To which is appended a Copy of his Last Will. 12mo. New York, 1865.

 How New York City is governed. 12mo. Boston, 1866.

 Life of Aaron Burr. New and Enlarged Edition. Portrait. 2 volumes, 8vo. New York, 1866.

 (Edited.) Manual for the Instruction of Rings Railroad and Political: with a History of the Grand Chicago and North-Western Ring. 24mo. New York, 1866.

 Famous Americans of Recent Times. Portrait. 8vo. Boston, 1867.

 Smoking and Drinking. (Reprinted from The Atlantic Monthly.) 16mo. Boston, 1868.

 The People's Book of Biography; or Short Lives of Most Interesting Persons of all Ages and Countries. 12 portraits. 8vo. Hartford, 1868.

 (Edited.) Eminent Women of the Age: being Narratives of the Lives and Deeds of the Most Prominent Women of the Present Generation. 14 plates. 8vo. Hartford, 1869.

The Danish Islands: are we bound in Honor to pay for them?
8vo. Boston, 1869.

George W. Childs. A Biographical Sketch. 12mo. Philadelphia, 1870.

(Edited.) Sketches of Men of Progress [by the editor, Bayard Taylor and others]. Portraits. [50 parts, or 1 volume.] 4to. New York, 1870–71.

Topics of the Times. 12mo. Boston, 1871.

Triumphs of Enterprise, Ingenuity and Public Spirit. 8vo. Hartford, 1871.
***Reprinted, with illustrations, 8vo. New York, 1874.

(Edited.) The Words of Washington. 16mo. Boston, 1872.

Fanny Fern: a Memorial Volume. Her Select Writings and Memoir. 12mo. New York, 1873.

Taxation of Church Property. 12mo. Boston [1873].

Life of Thomas Jefferson. . . . Portrait. 8vo. Boston, 1874.

Caricature and other Comic Art in all Times and many Lands. 203 illustrations. 8vo. New York, 1877.

(Edited.) Le Parnasse Francaise. A Book of French Poetry from 1550 to the Present Time. 12mo. Boston, 1877.
***Also issued (with portrait), 8vo. Boston, 1877.

Lives of Illustrious Men: the People's Book of Biography. . . . . 8vo. New York, 1881.

François Marie Arouet (Voltaire). Portraits and illustrations. 2 volumes, 8vo. Boston, 1881.

Noted Women of Europe and America. Portraits. 8vo. Hartford, 1883.

Captains of Industry; or Men of Business who did Something besides making Money. 4 portraits. 12mo. Boston, 1884.

(Edited.) Some Noted Princes, Authors and Statesmen of our Times. By James Parton, J. T. Fields, E. P. Whipple, Louise Chandler Moulton and others. Portraits and illustrations. 8vo. Norwich, 1885.

Daughters of Genius. Illustrations. 12mo. Philadelphia, 1886.

Captains of Industry. Second Series. 12mo. Boston, 1891.

PAULDING, JAMES KIRKE. 1779-1860.

The Diverting History of John Bull and Brother Jonathan. By Hector Bull-Us. 18mo. New York, 1812.

[Anonymous.] The Lay of the Scottish Fiddle: a Tale of Havre de Grace. Supposed to be written by W — S — Esq. 18mo. New York, 1813.
*₊*Also, 18mo. London, 1814.

Jokeby, a Burlesque on Rokeby, a Poem in Six Cantos. By An Amateur of Fashion. To which are added Notes by our Most Popular Characters. 18mo. New York, 1813.

[Anonymous.] The United States and England: being a Reply to the Criticism [by Robert Southey] on Inchiquin's Letters, contained in The Quarterly Review for January, 1814. 8vo. New York, 1815.

[Anonymous.] Letters from Virginia. Translated from the French. 12mo. Baltimore, 1816.

[Anonymous.] Letters from the South, written during an Excursion in the Summer of 1816. 2 volumes, 16mo. New York, 1817.

The Backwoodsman. A Poem. 16mo. Philadelphia, 1818.

Salmagundi. Second Series. [May 30, 1819-August 19, 1820.] 12mo. New York, 1819-20.

A Sketch of Old England, by A New-England Man. 2 volumes, 12mo. New York, 1822.

[Anonymous.] Koningsmarke, the Long Finne; a Story of the New World. 2 volumes, 12mo. New York, 1823.

John Bull in America; or, the New Munchausen. 12mo. New York, 1825.

The Merry Tales of the Three Wise Men of Gotham. 12mo. New York, 1826.

New Mirror for Travellers and Guide to the Springs. By An Amateur. 12mo. New York, 1828.

Tales of the Good Woman by A Doubting Gentleman. 12mo. New York, 1829.

Chronicles of the City of Gotham, from the Papers of a Retired Councilman. 8vo. New York, 1830.

The Dutchman's Fireside. A Tale. 2 volumes, 12mo. New York, 1831.

The Lion of the West: a Comedy. 12mo. New York, 1831.

Westward Ho! A Tale. 2 volumes, 12mo. New York, 1832.

The Atlantic Club-Book: being Sketches in Prose and Verse [compiled by G. P. Morris, from The New York Mirror,] by Various Authors. [Paulding, Halleck, Bryant, Leggett, Fay, Morris, Simms, Willis, Woodworth and others.] 2 volumes, 12mo. New York, 1834.

A Life of Washington. 4 plates. 2 volumes, 18mo. New York, 1835.

Letters from the South. By A Northern Man. 2 volumes, 12mo. New York, 1835.
 *.*A new revision of the 1817 edition, with many alterations and additions.

[Anonymous.] The Book of Saint Nicholas. Translated from the Original Dutch of Dominie Nicholas Aegidius Oudenarde. 12mo. New York, 1836.

Slavery in the United States. 18mo. New York, 1836.

[Anonymous.] A Christmas Gift from Fairy Land. Illustrations. 12mo. New York [1838].

The Old Continental; or, the Price of Liberty. 2 volumes, 12mo. New York, 1846.

(With William I. Paulding.) American Comedies. 12mo. Philadelphia, 1847.
 *.*Of the four comedies, three are by J. K. Paulding.

The Puritan and his Daughter. 2 volumes, 12mo. New York, 1849.

Literary Life [including unpublished letters and hitherto uncollected sketches]. Compiled by W. I. Paulding. Portrait. 12mo. New York, 1867.

***See also BRYANT, W. C.; and IRVING, W.

PAYNE, JOHN HOWARD. 1791-1852.

(Edited.) The Thespian Mirror. [December 28, 1805-March 22, 1806.] 22 numbers, 8vo. New York, 1805-1806.

Lovers' Vows. 18mo. Baltimore, 1809.

Juvenile Poems, principally written between the Age of Thirteen and Seventeen. 18mo. Baltimore, 1813.

Lispings of the Muse: a Selection from Juvenile Poems, chiefly written at, and before, the Age of Sixteen. (Privately printed.) 8vo. London, 1815.

Accusation; or, the Family of D'Anglade: a Melo Drama in Three Acts, from the French with Alterations. 18mo. Boston, 1818.

Brutus; or, the Fall of Tarquin. An Historical Tragedy in Five Acts. 18mo. London [1818].

***Also, 8vo. London, 1819; and 16mo. New York, 1819.

Therese, the Orphan of Geneva, a Drama in Three Acts .... 18mo. New York, 1821.

Adeline, the Victim of Seduction, a Melo Drama in Three Acts. ... 18mo. New York, 1822.

Clari; or, the Maid of Milan. An Opera in Three Acts [containing the lyric "Home, Sweet Home"]. 18mo. New York, 1823.

Ali Pacha; or, the Signet-Ring. A Melo-Drama in Two Acts. 18mo. New York, 1823.

The Two Galley Slaves: a Melo Drama in Two Acts. Frontispiece. 18mo. London [1823].

Richelieu: a Domestic Tragedy, founded on Fact. (As adapted for performance at the Theatre Royal, Covent Garden, London; before it was altered by order of the Lord Chamberlain, and produced under a new name.) Now First printed from the Author's Manuscript. 18mo. New York, 1826.

'Twas I, or the Truth a Lie. A Farce in Two Acts. 18mo. New York, 1828.

Charles the Second; or, the Merry Monarch. A Comedy. 18mo. Philadelphia, 1829.

Prospectus of a New Periodical [Jam Jehan Nima, a Weekly Periodical. . . .]. 8vo. [New York, 1833.]

PERCIVAL, JAMES GATES. 1795-1856.

(Translated.) Physiological and Chemical Researches on the Use of Prussic Acid. . . . by F. Magendie. 12mo. New Haven, 1820.

Poems [including Prometheus, part I]. 18mo. New Haven, 1821.

Oration delivered before the Phi Beta Kappa Society of Connecticut, Sept. 10, 1822, on some of the Moral and Poetical Truths derivable from the Study of History. 8vo. New Haven, 1822.

Prometheus, Part II, and other Poems. 18mo. New Haven, 1822.

Clio. Part I. 12mo. Charleston, S. C., 1822.

Clio. Part II. 18mo. New Haven, 1822.

Poems. 8vo. New York, 1823.

Poem [The Mind] delivered before the Connecticut Phi Beta Kappa Society, September 13th, 1825. 8vo. New Haven, 1825.
*.*Reprinted, 8vo. Boston, 1826.

Geographical View of the World, by Rev. J. Goldsmith. Revised by J. G. Percival. Illustrations. 12mo. New York, 1826.

(Edited.) Elegant Extracts in Prose and Verse. Portraits. 6 volumes, 8vo. Boston, 1826.

Clio. Part III. 18mo. New York, 1827.

(Edited.) Malte Brun's System of Universal Geography. Plates and maps. 3 volumes, 4to. Boston, 1834.

Report on the Geology of the State of Connecticut. Map. 8vo. New Haven, 1842.

The Dream of a Day and other Poems. 12mo. New Haven, 1843.

Poems. 18mo. New Haven, 1851.

Report on the Kensington Lead Mines, Berlin, Conn. 8vo. New Haven, 1853.

(With W. H. Stevens.) Geological Reports on the Middletown Silver Lead Mines. 8vo. New York, 1853.

Report on the Iron of Dodge and Washington Counties, Wisconsin. Plate. 8vo. Milwaukee, 1855.

Poems. With Biographical Sketch [by L. W. Fitch]. Portrait. 2 volumes, 24mo. Boston, 1859.

Life and Letters. Edited by Julius H. Ward. Portrait. 12mo. Boston, 1866.

PHELPS [WARD], ELIZABETH STUART. 1844 —

The Gates Ajar. 12mo. Boston, 1868.

Men, Women and Ghosts. 12mo. Boston, 1869.

Hedged in. A Novel. 12mo. Boston, 1870.

The Silent Partner. 12mo. Boston, 1871.

What to wear? 12mo. Boston, 1873.

Poetic Studies. Square 16mo. Boston, 1875.

The Story of Avis. 12mo. Boston, 1877.

My Cousin and I. 12mo. Boston, 1879.

An Old Maid's Paradise. 16mo. Boston, 1879.

Sealed Orders and other Stories. 16mo. Boston, 1879.

Friends: a Duet. 16mo. Boston, 1881.

Doctor Zay. A Novel. 16mo. Boston, 1882.

Beyond the Gates. 16mo. Boston, 1883.

Songs of the Silent World and other Poems. Portrait. 16mo. Boston, 1885.

The Gates Between. 16mo. Boston, 1887.

The Madonna of the Tubs. Illustrations. 12mo. Boston, 1887.

Jack the Fisherman. Illustrations. Square 12mo. Boston, 1887.

Burglars in Paradise. 16mo. Boston, 1887.

The Struggle for Immortality. 16mo. Boston, 1889.

A Lost Winter. Illustrations. Oblong 8vo. Boston, 1889.

(With H. D. Ward.) The Master of the Magicians. A Novel. 16mo. Boston, 1890.

(With H. D. Ward.) Come Forth. A Novel. 16mo. Boston, 1891.

Austin Phelps. A Memoir. Portrait and illustrations. 8vo. New York, 1891.

Fourteen to One. 16mo. Boston, 1891.

Donald Marcy. 16mo. Boston, 1893.

A Singular Life. 16mo. Boston, 1895.
***Also the Trotty Series, and other juvenile and Sunday-school works. See also MOULTON, LOUISE CHANDLER.

PIATT, JOHN JAMES. 1835—

(With Mrs. S. M. B. Piatt.) The Nests at Washington and other Poems. 12mo. New York, 1864.

Poems in Sunshine and Twilight. 16mo. Cincinnati, 1866.

Western Windows and other Poems. 12mo. New York, 1869.

Landmarks and other Poems. 12mo. Boston, 1871.

(Edited.) Poems of George Denison Prentice. Portrait. 12mo. Cincinnati, 1876.

The Lost Farm and other Poems. 12mo. Boston, 1877.

May Festival, 1878. Ode for the Opening of the Cincinnati Music Hall. 12mo. Cincinnati, 1878.

Poems of House and Home. 12mo. Boston, 1879.

Pencilled Fly-Leaves. Square 16mo. Chicago, 1880.

Idyls and Lyrics of the Ohio Valley. 16mo. Cincinnati, 1881.

(Edited.) The Union of American Poetry and Art. A Collection of Poems by American Poets. Illustrations. 4to. Cincinnati, 1882.

(With Mrs. S. M. B. Piatt.) The Children out of Doors. 12mo. Edinburgh, 1884.

At the Holy Well: a Handful of New Verses. 12mo. Cincinnati, 1887.

A Dream of Church Windows. Poems of House and Home. 12mo. Boston, 1888.

A Return to Paradise and other Fly-Leaf Essays in Town and Country. 12mo. London, 1891.

Little New-World Idyls and other Poems. Portrait. 12mo. London, 1893.
   ***See also HOWELLS, W. D.

PIATT, SARAH MORGAN BRYAN. 1835—

[Anonymous.] A Woman's Poems. 12mo. Boston, 1871.

A Voyage to the Fortunate Islands and other Poems. 12mo. Boston, 1874.

That New World, and other Poems. 12mo. Boston, 1877.

Poems in Company with Children. Small 4to. Boston, 1877.

Dramatic Persons and Moods, with other New Poems. 12mo. Boston, 1880.

An Irish Garland. 12mo. Edinburgh, 1884.
   ***Also Boston, 1885.

In Primrose Time: a New Irish Garland. 12mo. London and Boston, 1886.

Child's World Ballads. 12mo. London, 1887.

The Little Emigrants. 16mo. Chicago, 1887.

The Witch in the Glass and other Poems. Illustrations. 12mo. Boston, 1889.

Irish Wild Flowers. 16mo. New York, 1891.

An Enchanted Castle and other Poems. 12mo. New York, 1893.

Poems. Portraits. 2 volumes, 12mo. New York, 1894.
  *.*See also PIATT, J. J.

PICKERING, HENRY. 1781-1831.

[Anonymous.] The Ruins of Pœstum: and other Compositions in Verse. Small 4to. Salem, 1822.

Athens and other Poems. 8vo. Salem, 1824.

Poems. By An American. (Privately printed; 25 copies.) 8vo. Boston, 1830.

[Anonymous.] The Buckwheat Cake. A Poem. Frontispiece. (Privately printed.) 8vo. Boston, 1831.

PIERPONT, JOHN. 1785-1866.

The Portrait: a Poem delivered before the Washington Benevolent Society of Newburyport, October 27, 1812. 8vo. Boston, 1812.

Airs of Palestine. 8vo. Baltimore, 1816.

(Edited.) Sabbath Recreations; or Select Poetry of a Religious Kind, Chiefly taken from the Works of Modern Poets with Original Pieces never before published. By Miss Emily Taylor. First American Edition [containing many poems by the editor, W. C. Bryant, N. P. Willis, J. G. Whittier, and others]. 16mo. Boston, 1839.

Airs of Palestine and other Poems. 16mo. Boston, 1840.

Cold Water Melodies and Washingtonian Songster. 18mo. Boston, 1842.

Anti-Slavery Poems. 18mo. Boston, 1843.

Lays for the Sabbath. A Collection of Religious Poetry. 12mo. Boston, 1850.

The Pilgrims of Plymouth: a Poem delivered before the New England Society, in New York, Dec. 22, 1855. 8vo. Boston, 1856.
  *.*Besides the titles here given Mr. Pierpont published numerous sermons, temperance addresses and educational works.
  *.*See also HOLMES, O. W.

PIKE, ALBERT. 1809-1891.

> Prose Sketches and Poems written in the Western Country. 12mo. Boston, 1834.
>
> (Edited.) Reports of Cases argued and determined in the Supreme Court of Arkansas. 5 volumes, 8vo. Little Rock, 1840-45.
>
> The Arkansas Form-Book. 8vo. Little Rock, 1845.
>
> Nugæ. (Privately printed; 150 copies.) 12mo. Philadelphia, 1854.
>
> Kansas State Rights. Appeal to the Democracy of the South. 8vo. Washington, 1857.
>
> (With others.) The Life-Wake of the Fine Arkansas Gentleman who died before his Time. 8vo. Washington, 1859.
> *⁎*Only a few copies printed, as souvenirs of a reception given to Albert Pike, following a premature announcement of his death, which appeared in the daily press. Several stanzas written on the event, together with a speech, by Mr. Pike, are here given.
>
> State or Province? Bond or Free? Addressed particularly to the people of Arkansas. 8vo. [Washington] 1869.

PINKNEY, EDWARD COATE. 1802-1828.

> [Anonymous.] Rodolph. 8vo. Baltimore, 1823.
>
> Poems. 18mo. Baltimore, 1825.
>
> Poems. [Second edition, from a copy revised and corrected by the author.] 18mo. Baltimore, 1838.
> *⁎*Reprinted, with introduction by N. P. Willis, and biographical sketch by William Leggett, royal 8vo. New York, 1844.

POE, EDGAR ALLAN. 1809-1849.

> Tamerlane and other Poems. By A Bostonian. 16mo. Boston, 1827.
> *⁎*Of this work only three copies are known, one of which is in the library of the British Museum, London, and one was sold by Messrs. Libbie and Co., Boston, in April, 1892, for $1,850. A reprint of the British Museum copy, then considered unique, was published in London, 1884, 100 copies, 16mo.
>
> Al Aaraaf, Tamerlane and Minor Poems. 8vo. Baltimore, 1829.

Poems. Second Edition [including many poems now first published].' [16mo. New York, 1831.

Southern Literary Messenger [August, 1835-January, 1837, inclusive]. 3 volumes, 8vo. Richmond, 1835-37.
*₊*Poe was associate editor of the eighteen numbers indicated of the Messenger, and contributed the literary notices, together with several poems and sketches.

The Narrative of Arthur Gordon Pym, of Nantucket. . . . 12mo. New York, 1838.

The Conchologist's First Book : a System of Testaceous Malacology, arranged expressly for the Use of Schools. . . . 12 colored plates, illustrating 215 shells. 12mo. Philadelphia, 1839.
*₊*The same. Second Edition [with new preface and several corrections and additions]. 12 colored plates. 12mo. Philadelphia, 1840.
*₊*Also reprinted, anonymously, 12mo. Philadelphia, 1845.

(Edited, with William E. Burton.) The Gentleman's Magazine [July, 1839-June, 1840, inclusive]. Illustrations. 2 volumes, royal 8vo. Philadelphia, 1839-40.

Tales of the Grotesque and Arabesque. (750 copies.) 2 volumes, 12mo. Philadelphia, 1840.
*₊*In a few of the first copies issued, page 213 of vol. ii. is misprinted " 231."

(Edited.) Graham's Magazine [April, 1841-March, 1842, inclusive]. Portraits and illustrations. 2 volumes, 8vo. Philadelphia, 1841-42.

The Prose Romances of Edgar A. Poe. No. 1. [All published.] The Murders in the Rue Morgue, and The Man that was used up. 8vo. Philadelphia, 1843.
*₊*Only two copies known, one of which, with a collection of newspaper and magazine clippings, was in 1894 catalogued at $250.

The Raven and other Poems. 12mo. New York, 1845.
*₊*Also, 12mo. London, 1846.

Tales. 12mo. New York, 1845.

(Edited, with Charles F. Briggs and Henry C. Watson.) The Broadway Journal. 2 volumes, 4to. New York, 1845.

Mesmerism : In Articulo Mortis. 8vo. London, 1846.

Eureka: a Prose Poem. (500 copies.) 12mo. New York, 1848.

Works; with Notices of his Life and Genius. By N. P. Willis, J. R. Lowell, and R. W. Griswold. Portrait. 2 volumes, 12mo. New York, 1850.

The Literati: some Honest Opinions about Autorial Merits and Demerits, with Occasional Words of Personality. Together with Marginalia, Suggestions and Essays. With a Sketch of the Author by R. W. Griswold. 12mo. New York, 1850.

Tales of Mystery, Imagination and Humour; and Poems. 26 illustrations [by the editor, Henry Vizetelly]. 16mo. London, 1852.

Works. Vol. IV. Arthur Gordon Pym &c. [Tales of humor and miscellanies.] 12mo. New York, 1856.

Works. Newly collected and edited, with a Memoir, Critical Introductions, and Notes, by Edmund Clarence Stedman and George Edward Woodberry. Portraits and illustrations. 10 volumes, 12mo. Chicago, 1894-95.
*.*The same, with additional illustrations by Aubrey Beardsley. Large paper. (250 copies.) 10 volumes, 8vo. Chicago, 1894-95.
*.*In this edition the works are, for the first time, revised after the author's final manuscript corrections, with exhaustive bibliographical notices, by Mr. Woodberry, of the several tales, reviews, sketches, and poems, and variorum readings of the latter. These make it unnecessary to give here a detailed list, with dates of publication, of Poe's contributions to the Southern Literary Messenger, The Gentleman's Magazine, Graham's Magazine, Broadway Journal, Godey's Lady's Book, and the numerous periodicals and annuals with which his connection was less permanent. Vol. x. contains, pp. 267-281, a bibliography, also by Mr. Woodberry, of the various collective editions of Poe's writings.

PRESCOTT, WILLIAM HICKLING. 1796-1859.

[Anonymous.] The Club-Room. [Edited, with three original contributions, by W. H. Prescott.] 4 numbers [February, March, April, July, 1820], 8vo. Boston, 1820.

History of the Reign of Ferdinand and Isabella the Catholic. 5 portraits. 3 volumes, 8vo. Boston, 1838.

History of the Conquest of Mexico, with a Preliminary View of the Ancient Mexican Civilization, and the Life of the Conqueror, Hernando Cortes. 3 portraits, 2 maps and facsimile. 3 volumes, 8vo. New York, 1843.

Life in Mexico, by Madame C[alderon] de la B[arca]. With Preface by W. H. Prescott. 2 volumes, 12mo. Boston, 1843.
***Also, 8vo. London, 1843.

Biographical and Critical Miscellanies. Portrait. 8vo. New York, 1845.

History of the Conquest of Peru; with a Preliminary View of the Civilization of the Incas. 2 portraits and facsimile. 3 volumes, 8vo. New York, 1847.

A Memoir of Hon. John Pickering, LL.D. 8vo. Boston, 1848.

History of the Reign of Philip the Second, King of Spain. 6 portraits. 3 volumes, 8vo. Boston, 1855-58.
*** i., ii., 1855; iii., 1858.

Memoir of the Honorable Abbott Lawrence, prepared for the National Portrait Gallery. Portrait and folded pedigree. (Privately printed.) 8vo. Philadelphia, 1856.
***Also, 4to. [Boston] 1856.

(Robertson's) History of the Reign of Charles the Fifth, with Supplement embracing the Life of Charles after his Abdication, by W. H. Prescott. Portrait. 3 volumes, 8vo. Boston, 1857.
***See also BRYANT, W. C.

PRIME, WILLIAM COWPER. 1825 —

The Owl Creek Letters and other Correspondence. By W. 12mo. New York, 1848.

[Anonymous.] The Old House by the River. 12mo. New York, 1853.

Later Years. 12mo. New York, 1854.

Boat-Life in Egypt and Nubia. 12mo. New York, 1857.

Tent-Life in the Holy Land. 12mo. New York, 1857.

Coins, Medals, and Seals, Ancient and Modern. Illustrations. Square 8vo. New York, 1861.

Gautier's Romance of the Mummy. With Introduction by W. C. Prime. 12mo. New York, 1863.

O Mother Dear, Jerusalem: the Old Hymn, its Origin and Genealogy. 12mo. New York, 1865.

Passio Christi: the Little Passion of Albert Durer. 37 illustrations. (500 copies.) Small 4to. New York, 1868.

I go a-Fishing. Small 8vo. New York, 1873.
*.*Also, 12mo. London, 1873.

Holy Cross; a History of the Invention, Preservation, and disappearance of the Wood known as the True Cross. Illustrations. 12mo. New York, 1877.

Pottery and Porcelain of all Times and Nations, with Tables of Factory and Artists' Marks for Collectors. 8vo. New York, 1878.

The China Hunters' Club. By The Youngest Member. With Introduction by W. C. Prime. Illustrations. Square 12mo. New York, 1878.

McLellan's Own Story. [Edited, with biographical sketch, pp. 1–24, by Prime.] Portraits. 8vo. New York, 1887.

Along New England Roads. 12mo. New York, 1892.

Among the Northern Hills. 12mo. New York, 1895.

PROCTOR, EDNA DEAN. 1838—

Life Thoughts gathered from the Extemporaneous Discourses of Henry Ward Beecher. Edited by One of his Congregation. 12mo. Boston, 1858.

Poems. 18mo. New York, 1866.

A Russian Journey. 12mo. Boston, 1872.

The Song of the Ancient People. With Preface and Notes by John Fiske. Illustrations. 8vo. Boston, 1893.

PUTNAM, MARY LOWELL. 1810—

(Translated.) The Bondmaid. By Frederika Bremer. 16mo. Boston, 1844.

[Anonymous.] Record of an Obscure Man. 16mo. Boston, 1861.
⁂ The same. Large paper. (50 copies.) 4to. Boston, 1861.

[Anonymous.] Tragedy of Errors. [A dramatic poem illustrating the slavery system in America.] 16mo. Boston, 1862.
⁂ The same. Large paper. (50 copies.) 4to. Boston, 1862.

[Anonymous.] Tragedy of Success. 16mo. Boston, 1862.
⁂ The same. Large paper. (50 copies.) 4to. Boston, 1862.

[Anonymous.] [Memorial of William] Lowell Putnam. Portrait. (Privately printed.) 4to. Cambridge, 1863.

[Anonymous.] Fifteen Days. An Extract from Edward Colvil's Journal. 16mo. Boston, 1866.

Guépin of Nantes: a French Republican. By M. L. P. 24mo. Dayton, O., 1874.

QUINCY, EDMUND. 1808–1877.

Introductory Lecture before the Adelphic Union, November 19, 1838. 8vo. Boston, 1839.

An Examination of the Charges of Mr. John Scoble & Mr. Lewis Tappan against the American Anti-Slavery Society. 8vo. Dublin, 1852.

[Anonymous.] Wensley: a Story without a Moral. 16mo. Boston, 1854.

[Anonymous.] Where will it end? A View of Slavery in the United States . . . . [Reprinted from The Atlantic Monthly.] 8vo. Providence, 1863.

Life of Josiah Quincy of Massachusetts. Portraits. 12mo. Boston, 1867.

Notice of Horace Binney, from the Report of the Council of the American Academy of Arts and Sciences, May, 1876. 8vo. Boston, 1876.

Wensley and other Stories. Edited by his Son, Edmund Quincy [with memorial poem, Bankside, pp. v.–vii., by J. R. Lowell]. 12mo. Boston, 1885.

The Haunted Adjutant and other Stories. . . . 12mo. Boston, 1885.

*₊*Many of the shorter stories included in the two latter titles were originally published in The Liberty Bell, an anti-slavery annual to which Mr. Quincy was one of the principal contributors.

QUINCY, JOSIAH PHILLIPS. 1829—

[Anonymous.] Lyteria: a Dramatic Poem. 12mo. Boston, 1854.

(Edited, anonymously.) Manuscript Corrections from a Copy of the Fourth Folio of Shakespeare's Plays. 8vo. Boston, 1854.

Tax-Exemption no Excuse for Spoliation: Considerations in Opposition to the Petition . . . . to permit the Sale of the Old South Church. 8vo. Boston, 1874.

The Protection of Majorities; or, Considerations relating to Electoral Reform. With other Papers. 16mo. Boston, 1875.

Alexandre Vattemare; his Service in Connection with the Boston City Library. 8vo. Cambridge [1883].

Double Taxation in Massachusetts. 12mo. Boston, 1889.

READ, THOMAS BUCHANAN. 1822–1872.

Paul Redding: a Tale of the Brandywine. 12mo. Boston, 1845.

Poems. 12mo. Boston, 1847.

(Edited.) The Female Poets of America, with Portraits, Biographical Notices and Specimens of their Writings. 8vo. Philadelphia, 1848.

Lays and Ballads. 12mo. Philadelphia, 1849.

Poems. Illustrations by Kenny Meadows. 8vo. London, 1852.

The Onward Age; an Anniversary Poem. 12mo. Cincinnati, 1852.

Poems. A New and Enlarged Edition. 12mo. Philadelphia, 1853.

*₊*Reprinted, with Illustrations, 8vo. Philadelphia, 1854.

The New Pastoral. Portrait. 12mo. Philadelphia, 1855.

The House by the Sea. A Poem. 12mo. Philadelphia, 1855.

Sylvia, or the Last Shepherd. An Eclogue. And other Poems. 12mo. Philadelphia, 1857.

Rural Poems. 12mo. London, 1857.

Poems. New and Enlarged Edition. 2 volumes, 12mo. Boston, 1860.

The Wagoner of the Alleghanies. A Poem of the Days of Seventy-Six. 12mo. Philadelphia, 1862.

A Summer Story. Sheridan's Ride and other Poems. 12mo. Philadelphia, 1865.

Poetical Works. [Newly revised, with additions.] 3 volumes, 12mo. Philadelphia, 1866.

Good Samaritans. A Poem. Square 12mo. Cincinnati, 1867.

Sheridan's Ride. (Privately printed.) 4to. New York, 1867.

Poetical Works. Complete Edition. Portrait and illustrations. 8vo. Philadelphia, 1882.
  *₊*See also TAYLOR, BAYARD.

REPPLIER, AGNES. 1855—

Books and Men. 16mo. Boston, 1888.

Points of View. 16mo. Boston, 1892.

(Edited.) A Book of Famous Verse. 16mo. Boston, 1892.

Essays in Miniature. 16mo. New York, 1892.

Essays in Idleness. 16mo. Boston, 1893.

In the Dozy Hours and other Papers. 16mo. Boston, 1894.

RICE, GEORGE EDWARD. 1822–1861.

[Anonymous.] Ephemera [a collection of poems by George E. Rice and John H. Wainwright]. 12mo. Boston, 1852.

An Old Play in a New Garb: Hamlet, Prince of Denmark. In Three Acts. 5 plates. 12mo. Boston, 1852.

Myrtilla: a Fairy Extravaganza in One Act. 12mo. Boston, 1854.

Blondel: a Historic Fancy. In Two Acts. 12mo. Boston, 1854.

Nugamenta; a Book of Verses. 16mo. Boston, 1860.

RIDEING, WILLIAM HENRY. 1853—

[Anonymous.] Scenery of the Pacific Railways, and Colorado. Map and illustrations. 8vo. New York [1878].

A-Saddle in the Wild West. 16mo. New York, 1879.

A Floating City of the Atlantic. 18mo. New York, 1879.

(Edited.) The Alpenstock: a Book about the Alps and Alpine Adventure. 16mo. New York, 1880.

Stray Moments with Thackeray: his Humor, Satire, etc. 16mo. New York, 1880.

Boys in the Mountains and on the Plains. Illustrations. Square 8vo. New York, 1882.

Boys Coastwise. Illustrations. Square 8vo. New York, 1883.

Young Folks' History of London. Illustrations. 16mo. Boston, 1884.

A Little Upstart. A Novel. 16mo. Boston, 1885.

Thackeray's London: his Haunts and the Scenes of his Novels. Illustrations. 16mo. Boston, 1885.
***The same. Large paper. (100 copies.) Small 4to. Boston, 1885.

The Boyhood of Living Authors. Illustrations. 12mo. New York [1887].

In the Land of Lorna Doone, and other Pleasurable Excursions in England. 16mo. New York [1895].
***See also LATHROP, G. P.

RILEY, JAMES WHITCOMB. 1852—

> The Old Swimmin'-Hole and 'Leven more Poems, by Benj. F. Johnson, of Boone. 16mo. Indianapolis, 1883.
>
> The Boss Girl, a Christmas Story, and other Sketches. 12mo. Indianapolis, 1886.
>
> Character Sketches and Poems. 12mo. Indianapolis, 1887.
>
> Afterwhiles. 12mo. Indianapolis, 1888.
>
> Old-Fashioned Roses: Verses and Sonnets. 16mo. London, 1888.
> *₊*The imported copies bear the Importers' imprint, with altered date, Indianapolis, 1889.
>
> (With Edgar W. Nye.) Nye and Riley's Railway Guide. Illustrations. 12mo. Chicago, 1889.
> *₊*Reissued as Fun, Wit and Humor. 12mo. Chicago, 1889.
>
> Pipes o' Pan: at Zekesbury. 12mo. Indianapolis, 1889.
>
> Rhymes of Childhood. 12mo. Indianapolis, 1890.
>
> The Flying Islands of the Night. 12mo. Indianapolis, 1891.
>
> Neighborly Poems. 12mo. Indianapolis, 1891.
>
> Sketches in Prose and Occasional Verses. 12mo. Indianapolis, 1891.
>
> An Old Sweetheart of Mine. Illustrations. 4to. Indianapolis, 1891.
>
> (With Edgar W. Nye.) Poems and Yarns. 12mo. Chicago [1892].
>
> Green Fields and Running Brooks. 12mo. Indianapolis, 1893.
>
> Poems here at Home. Illustrations. 12mo. New York, 1893.
>
> Armazindy. Frontispiece. 12mo. Indianapolis, 1894.

RITCHIE, ANNA CORA MOWATT. 1819-1870.

> Pelayo, or the Cavern of Covadonga: a Romance in Five Cantos, by Isabel. 12mo. New York, 1836.

Reviewers Reviewed; a Satire. 12mo. New York, 1837.

Gulzara, the Persian Slave. 12mo. New York, 1840.

The Fortune-Hunter: a Novel. By Helen Berkeley. 12mo. Philadelphia, 1842.

Memoirs of Madame d'Arblay. Compiled from her Diaries and Letters by Mrs. Helen Berkeley. 2 volumes, 16mo. [New York] 1844.

Fashion; or Life in New York: a Comedy in Five Acts. 12mo. New York, 1845.

Evelyn; or a Heart unmasked. A Tale of Domestic Life. 2 volumes, 12mo. Philadelphia, 1845.

Armand; or the Peer and the Peasant. A Play in Five Acts. 12mo. New York, 1848.

Autobiography of an Actress; or Eight Years on the Stage. Portrait. 12mo. Boston, 1854.

Mimic Life; or before and behind the Curtain. Frontispiece. 12mo. Boston, 1855.

Plays. 12mo. Boston, 1855.

Twin Roses: a Narrative. 12mo. Boston, 1857.

Fairy Fingers: a Novel. 12mo. New York, 1865.

The Mute Singer. A Novel. 12mo. New York, 1867.

The Clergyman's Wife and other Sketches. 12mo. New York, 1867.

Italian Life and Legends. Illustrations. 12mo. New York, 1870.

RIVES, AMELIE. 1863—

A Brother to Dragons and other Old-Time Tales. 12mo. New York, 1888.

Virginia of Virginia. A Story. Illustrations. 12mo. New York, 1888.

The Quick or the Dead. 8vo. Philadelphia, 1889.

Herod and Mariamne. 8vo. Philadelphia, 1889.

The Witness of the Sun. Portrait. 12mo. Philadelphia, 1889.

According to St. John. Portrait and illustrations. 12mo. New York [1891].

Barbara Dering. 12mo. Philadelphia, 1892.

Athelwold. Illustrations. 16mo. New York, 1893.

Tanis, the Sang-Digger. 12mo. New York, 1893.

ROBINSON, ROWLAND E. 1833—

[Anonymous.] Forest and Stream Fables. 12mo. New York, 1886.

Uncle Lisha's Shop. Life in a Corner of Yankeeland. 12mo. New York, 1887.

Sam Lovel's Camp: Uncle Lisha's Friends under Bark and Canvas. 12mo. New York, 1889.

Vermont: a Study of Independence. 12mo. Boston, 1892.

Danvis Folks. 12mo. Boston, 1894.

ROCHE, JAMES JEFFREY. 1847—

The Mahogany Tree, by W. M. Thackeray. With Introduction by J. J. Roche. Portrait and illustrations. 4to. Boston, 1887.

Songs and Satires. 12mo. Boston, 1887.

The Story of the Filibusters; and [edited] the Life of Col. David Crockett. Illustrations. 12mo. New York, 1891.

Ballads of Blue Water and other Poems. 12mo. Boston, 1895.
***See also CARPENTER, H. B.; and O'REILLY, J. B.

ROE, EDWARD PAYSON. 1838–1888.

Barriers Burned away. 12mo. New York, 1872.

Play and Profit in my Garden. 12mo. New York, 1873.

What can she do? 12mo. New York, 1873.

Gentle Woman Roused. A Story of the Temperance Movement in the West. 16mo. New York, 1874.

The Opening of a Chestnut Burr. 12mo. New York, 1874.

From Jest to Earnest. 12mo. New York, 1875.

A Manual on the Culture of Small Fruits. 8vo. Newburgh, N. Y., 1876.

Near to Nature's Heart. 12mo. New York, 1876.

A Knight of the Nineteenth Century. 12mo. New York, 1877.

A Face Illumined. 12mo. New York, 1878.

A Day of Fate. 12mo. New York, 1880.

Success with Small Fruits. Illustrations. Square 8vo. New York, 1880.

Without a Home. 12mo. New York, 1881.

His Sombre Rivals. 12mo. New York, 1883.

An Unexpected Result and other Stories. 12mo. New York, 1883.

A Young Girl's Wooing. 12mo. New York, 1884.

Nature's Serial Story. Illustrations. Square 8vo. New York, 1885.

Driven back to Eden. 12mo. New York, 1885.

An Original Belle. 12mo. New York, 1885.

He Fell in Love with his Wife. 12mo. New York, 1886.

The Earth Trembled. 12mo. New York, 1887.

A Hornet's Nest. 12mo. New York, 1887.

Found, yet Lost. 12mo. New York, 1887.

Miss Lou. 12mo. New York, 1888.

The Home Acre. 12mo. New York, 1889.

ROOSEVELT, ROBERT BARNEWELL. 1829 —

Game Fish of the Northern States of America and the British Provinces. By Barnewell. Illustrations. 12mo. New York, 1862.

Superior Fishing; or, the Striped Bass, Trout, and Black Bass of the Northern States. Illustrations. 12mo. New York, 1865.

The Game-Birds of the Coasts and Lakes of the Northern States of America. 12mo. New York, 1866.

Florida and the Game Water-Birds of the Atlantic Coast and the Lakes of the United States. Illustrations. 12mo. New York, 1868.

Five Acres too Much: a Truthful Elucidation of the Attractions of the Country. Illustrations. 12mo. New York, 1869.

Progressive Petticoats; or, Dressed to Death. 12mo. New York, 1871.

(With Seth Greene.) Fish Hatching and Fish Catching. 12mo. Rochester, 1879.

Love and Luck: the Story of a Summer's Loitering in the Great South Bay. 16mo. New York, 1886.
***See also HALPINE, C. G.

ROOSEVELT, THEODORE. 1858 —

The Naval War of 1812; or the History of the United States Navy during the Last War with Great Britain. Diagrams. 8vo. New York, 1882.

Hunting Trips of a Ranchman: Sketches of Sport on the Northern Cattle Plains. Illustrations. (500 copies.) 4to. New York, 1885.
***Also issued 8vo. New York, 1885.

Thomas Hart Benton. 12mo. Boston, 1887.

The Wilderness Hunter. An Account of the Big Game of the United States and its Chase with Horse, Hound and Rifle. Illustrations. (200 copies.) 4to. New York, 1887.
***Reissued 8vo. New York, 1893.

Gouverneur Morris. 12mo. Boston, 1888.

Essays on Practical Politics. 12mo. New York, 1888.

The Winning of the West. Maps. 8vo. New York, 1889—
 ***Vols. i., ii., From the Alleghanies to the Mississippi, 1769-1783. 1889; vol. iii., The Founding of the Trans-Alleghany Commonwealths, 1784-1790. 1894; other volumes to follow.

American Big-Game Hunting. The Book of the Boone and Crockett Club. Plates. 8vo. New York, 1893.

Report to the United States Civil Service Commission upon a Visit to Certain Indian Reservations, and Indian Schools in South Dakota, Nebraska and Kansas. 8vo. Philadelphia, 1893.

Claws and Antlers of the Rocky Mountains. Photographic Reproductions of the Wild Game, from Life, with an Introduction. 35 plates. 4to. Denver, 1894.

RYAN, ABRAM JOSEPH. 1839-1886.

Poems. Portrait. 8vo. Mobile, 1879.

The Conquered Banner and other Poems. 18mo. Mobile, 1880.

Poems. Portrait and illustrations. Square 12mo. Baltimore, 1880.

A Crown for our Queen. 12mo. Baltimore, 1882.

SALTUS, EDGAR EVERTSON. 1858—

Balzac. Portrait. 12mo. Boston, 1884.

The Philosophy of Disenchantment. 12mo. Boston, 1885.

The Anatomy of Negation. 12mo. New York, 1886.

After-Dinner Stories, by H. de Balzac, done into English by Myndart Verelst. With an Introduction by Edgar Saltus. 16mo. New York, 1886.

Mr. Incoul's Misadventure. 12mo. New York, 1887.

Tales before Supper. From Théophile Gautier and Prosper Mérimée. Told in English by Myndart Verelst, and Delayed with a Proem by Edgar Saltus. 16mo. New York, 1887.

The Truth about Tristrem Varick. A Novel. 12mo. New
York [1888].

Eden: an Episode. 12mo. New York [1888].

A Transaction in Hearts. 12mo. New York [1888].

The Pace that Kills. A Chronicle. 8vo. New York [1889].

The Transient Guest. 8vo. New York [1889].

Love and Lore. Portrait. 16mo. New York [1890].

Mary Magdalen: a Chronicle. 12mo. New York [1891].

The Story without a Name. Translated and introduced by
Edgar Saltus. 12mo. New York, 1891.

Imperial Purple. 12mo. Chicago, 1892.

The Facts in the Case of H. Hyrtl, Esq. 12mo. New
York, 1892.

Madam Sapphira. A Fifth Avenue Story. 12mo. New York
[1893].

Enthralled. A Story of International Life setting forth the
Curious Circumstances in the Case of Lord Cloden and
Oswald Quain. 12mo. New York, 1894.

When Dreams come True: a Story of Emotional Life. 12mo.
New York, 1895.

SALTUS, FRANCIS SALTUS. 1849-1889.

Honey and Gall. 12mo. Philadelphia, 1873.

Shadows and Ideals. Poems. Portrait. Small 4to. Buffalo,
1890.

The Witch of En-Dor, and other Poems. Portrait. Small
4to. Buffalo, 1891.

Dreams after Sunset. Poems. Portrait. Small 4to. Buffalo, 1892.

Flasks and Flagons. Pastels and Profiles. Vistas and Land-
scapes. Portrait. Small 4to. Buffalo, 1892.

The Bayadere and other Sonnets. Portrait. 8vo. New
York, 1894.

Fact and Fancy: Humorous Poems, by Cupid Jones. Portrait. 8vo. New York, 1895.

SANDS, ROBERT CHARLES. 1799–1832.

Address before the Columbian Society, of Columbia College, on the Death of J. S. Watkins. 12mo. New York, 1817.

[Anonymous.] The Bridal of Vaumond. 18mo. New York, 1817.

Yamoyden, a Tale of the Wars of King Philip: in Six Cantos. By the Late James W. Eastburn and his Friend [R. C. Sands]. Frontispiece and vignette title. 12mo. New York, 1820.

Life and Correspondence of John Paul Jones. 8vo. New York, 1830.

Writings, in Prose and Verse. With a Memoir of the Author [by G. C. Verplanck]. Portrait. 2 volumes, 8vo. New York, 1834.
***See also BRYANT, W. C.

SARGENT, EPES. 1812–1880.

The Bride of Genoa: a Play in Five Acts. 12mo. Boston, 1836.

Velasco; a Tragedy in Five Acts. 12mo. Boston, 1837.
***Only a few copies, for the theatre, were printed; republished, 12mo. New York, 1839.

Wealth and Worth; or which makes the Man? A Tale. 18mo. New York, 1840.

What's to be done? or the Will and the Way. 18mo. New York, 1841.

[Anonymous.] American Adventure, by Land and Sea; being Remarkable Instances of Enterprise and Fortitude among Americans. 2 volumes, 18mo. New York, 1841.

The Life and Public Services of Henry Clay. 8vo. New York, 1842.

(Edited.) Sargent's New Monthly Magazine of Literature, Fashion and the Fine Arts. 8vo. New York, 1843.

The Light of the Light-House. 4to. New York, 1844.

Fleetwood; or, the Stain of Birth. A Novel. 12mo. New York, 1845.

Songs of the Sea, with other Poems. 12mo. Boston, 1847.

The Mariner's Library. 12mo. Boston, 1847.

(Edited.) Selections in Poetry for Exercises at School and Home. 12mo. Philadelphia, 1852.

The Priestess: a Tragedy in Five Acts. (Privately printed; 20 copies.) 8vo. Boston, 1854.

The Critic Criticized: a Reply to a Review of Webster's System, in The Democratic Review for March, 1856. 8vo. Springfield, 1856.

(Edited.) Arctic Adventures by Sea and Land, from the Earliest Date to the Last Expedition in Search of Sir John Franklin. Maps and illustrations. 8vo. Boston, 1857.

Poems. 12mo. Boston, 1858.

Original Dialogues. 12mo. Boston, 1861.

Peculiar. A Tale of the Great Transition. 12mo. New York, 1864.

(Edited.) The Emerald. A Collection of Tales, Poems and Essays, gleaned chiefly from the Fugitive Literature of the Nineteenth Century. 12mo. Boston, 1866.

(Edited.) The Sapphire. A Collection of Tales, Poems and Essays .... 12mo. Boston, 1867.

[Anonymous.] Planchette; or, the Despair of Science. Being a Full Account of Modern Spiritualism. 12mo. Boston, 1869.

The Woman who dared. 12mo. Boston, 1870.

The Arctic Regions by Sea and Land. 12mo. Philadelphia, 1873.

The Proof Palpable of Immortality: being an Account of the Materialization Phenomena of Modern Spiritualism. 8vo. Boston, 1876.

Materialism's Last Assault. Does Matter do it all? A Reply to Prof. Tyndall's Latest Attack on Spiritualism. 12mo. Boston, 1876.

(Edited.) Cyclopædia of British and American Poetry. Royal 8vo. New York, 1881.
　*.*Mr. Sargent also edited several educational publications and editions of the British poets.

SARGENT, LUCIUS MANLIUS. 1786–1867.

Symposius Cœlius Ænigmata : hanc Novam Editionem juxta Lectiones Optimas diligenter congestem. 12mo. Boston, 1807.

The Culex of Virgil ; with a Translation into English Verse. 8vo. Boston, 1807.

The New Milk Cheese ; or the Comi-Heroic Thunderbolt, a Semi-Globular Publication without Beginning and without End. By Van Tromp. 2 numbers, 8vo. Boston [April 16 ; May 2], 1807.

Herbert and Ellen. Billowy Water. The Plunderer's Grave. The Tear-Drop. The Billow. 8vo. Boston, 1812.
　*.*The same. Large paper. (11 copies.) Royal 8vo. Boston, 1812.

[Anonymous.] My Mother's Gold Ring. 12mo. Boston, 1833.

Temperance Tales. 6 volumes, 16mo. Boston, 1838–39.

Review of Dr. Sprague's Sermon on the Danger of being Over-Wise. 16mo. Boston, 1842.

Letter to Rev. Dr. Marsh. 8vo. Boston, 1847.

Dealings with the Dead. By A Sexton of the Old School. 2 volumes, 12mo. Boston, 1856.

Notices of The History of Boston, by Sigma. 8vo. Boston, 1857.

The Blackstone Family, being Sketches Biographical and Genealogical of William Blackstone and his Descendants. 8vo. Norwich, Conn., 1857.

Reminiscences of Samuel Dexter ; originally written for The Boston Evening Transcript, by Sigma. 16mo. Boston, 1857.

The Ballad of the Abolition Blunder-buss. [Signed, Sigma.] Illustrations. Square 16mo. Boston, 1861.

⁎ Mr. Sargent published also several temperance addresses and tracts.

SAXE, JOHN GODFREY. 1816–1887.

Progress: a Satirical Poem. 8vo. New York, 1846.

Poems. 12mo. Boston, 1850.

The Money-King and other Poems. Portrait. 12mo. Boston, 1860.

Poems. [Newly revised, with additions.] Portrait. 24mo. Boston, 1861.

The Fly-ing Dutchman; or, the Wrath of Herr Vonstoppelnose. 16 illustrations. 12mo. New York, 1862.

Clever Stories of Many Nations rendered in Rhyme. Illustrations. Square 12mo. Boston, 1865.

The Masquerade and other Poems. 12mo. Boston, 1866.

Poems. Complete Edition. Portrait. 12mo. Boston, 1868.

Fables and Legends of Many Countries. Rendered in Rhyme. 12mo. Boston, 1872.

The Proud Miss Macbride. A Legend of Gotham. Illustrations. Square 12mo. Boston, 1874.

Leisure-Day Rhymes. 12mo. Boston, 1875.

SCOLLARD, CLINTON. 1860—

Pictures in Song. 16mo. New York, 1884.

With Reed and Lyre. 16mo. Boston, 1886.

Old and New World Lyrics. 16mo. New York, 1888.

Giovio and Giulia, a Metrical Romance. (Privately printed; 250 copies.) Square 18mo. [New York] 1892.

Songs of Sunrise Lands. 16mo. Boston, 1892.

Under Summer Skies. Illustrations. 12mo. New York, 1892.

On Sunny Shores. Illustrations. 12mo. New York, 1893.

Hills of Song. 16mo. Boston, 1895.
   *₊*The same. Large paper. (50 copies.) 8vo. Boston, 1895.

SCOVILLE, JOSEPH A. 1815-1864.

Adventures of Clarence Bolton; or Life in New York. 8vo. New York, 1853.

Plan for Central Park. By Manhattan. 8vo. [New York, 1858.]

What shall be done with the Confiscated Negroes? .... A Letter to Hon. Abraham Lincoln .... and other Patriots. By Manhattan. 8vo. [New York, 1860.]

The Old Merchants of New York City. By Walter Barrett, Clerk. 5 volumes, 12mo. New York, 1862-66.

Vigor. A Novel. By Walter Barrett, Clerk. 12mo. New York, 1864.
   *₊*Suppressed, to escape legal consequences of the personalities of which the work largely consists, and which were considered too glaring for publication in Old Merchants of New York City.

Marion: a Novel, by Manhattan. 3 volumes, 12mo. London, 1864.

SCUDDER, HORACE ELISHA. 1838—

[Anonymous.] Seven Little People and their Friends. 12mo. New York, 1862.

Dream Children. Illustrations. 16mo. Cambridge, 1864.

Life and Letters of David Coitt Scudder. Portrait. 12mo. New York, 1864.

The Game of Croquet; its Appointments and Laws; with Descriptive Illustrations. By R. Fellow. 12mo. New York, 1865.

Stories from my Attic. Illustrations. 12mo. New York, 1869.

The Bodley Books. Illustrations. 8 volumes, square 8vo. New York and Boston, 1875-85.

The Dwellers in Five-Sisters' Court. 12mo. New York, 1876.

(Edited.) Recollections of Samuel Breck, with Passages from his Note-Books. Philadelphia, 1877.

(Edited.) American Poems. Illustrations. 12mo. Boston, 1879.

(Edited.) American Prose. 12mo. Boston, 1880.

Stories and Romances. 12mo. Boston, 1880.

Boston Town. The Story of Boston told to Children. Illustrations. Square 8vo. Boston, 1881.

(Edited.) The Children's Book. Illustrations. Square 8vo. Boston, 1881.

Noah Webster. Portrait. 12mo. Boston, 1882.

(Edited.) American Commonwealths. Maps and illustrations. 13 volumes, 12mo. Boston, 1883-92.
*.*Other volumes to follow.

A History of the United States .... 12mo. Philadelphia [1884].

(Edited.) The Book of Fables, chiefly from Æsop. Illustrations. 12mo. Boston, 1885.

Men and Letters. Essays in Characterization and Criticism. 12mo. Boston, 1887.

The Book of Folk-Stories re-written. Frontispiece. 12mo. Boston, 1887.

George Washington: an Historical Biography. Illustrations. 12mo. Boston, 1889.

Literature in School. 12mo. Boston, 1889.

Address at the Dedication of Mark Hopkins Memorial Hall. 12mo. [Boston, 1890.]

Childhood in Literature and Art, with some Observations on Literature for Children. A Study. 12mo. Boston, 1894.
*.*Mr. Scudder edited the Cambridge Edition of Browning, Longfellow, Whittier and Holmes; see also STODDARD, R. H. and TAYLOR, BAYARD.

SEWALL, JONATHAN MITCHEL. 1749-1808.

> [Anonymous.] Verses occasioned by reading the Answer of the President of the United States to the House of Representatives requesting Certain Papers relative to the Treaty with Great Britain. 24mo. Boston, 1797.
>
> A Versification of President Washington's Excellent Farewell Address to the Citizens of the United States. By A Gentleman of Portsmouth. Small 4to. Portsmouth, 1798.
>
> Eulogy on the Late General Washington; pronounced in Portsmouth, N. H., 31 December, 1799. Small 4to. Portsmouth [1800].
>
> Miscellaneous Poems, with Several Specimens from the Author's Version of the Poems of Ossian. 24mo. Portsmouth, 1801.

SHAW, HENRY WHEELER (JOSH BILLINGS). 1818–1885.

> Josh Billings: his Sayings. With Comic Illustrations. 12mo. New York, 1866.
>
> Josh Billings on Ice; and other Things. Illustrations. 12mo. New York, 1868.
>
> Josh Billings' Farmers' Allminax [published annually]. Illustrations. 12mo. New York, 1870–80.
>
> Everybody's Friend, or Josh Billings' Encyclopedia and Proverbial Philosophy of Wit and Humor. Portrait and illustrations. 8vo. Hartford, 1874.
>
> Josh Billings' Trump Kards: Blue Glass Philosophy. Illustrations. 12mo. New York, 1877.
>
> Old Probabilities. [Reprinted from the Farmers' Allminax, 1870–80.] Illustrations. 8vo. New York, 1880.
>
> Josh Billings' Spice-Box crammed with Droll Yarns. Illustrations. 4to. New York, 1881.

SHELTON, FREDERICK WILLIAM. 1814–1881.

> The Trollopiad; or Travelling Gentlemen in America. A Satire, by Nil Admirari, Esq. 12mo. New York, 1837.
>
> Salander and the Dragon; a Romance. 18mo. New York, 1851.

The Rector of St. Bardolph's ; or, Superannuated. Frontispiece. 12mo. New York, 1853.

Up the River. Illustrations. 12mo. New York, 1853.

Chrystalline ; or, the Heiress of Fall-Down Castle. 12mo. New York, 1854.

Peeps from a Belfry : or, the Parish Sketch Book. 12mo. New York, 1855.

SHERMAN, FRANK DEMPSTER. 1860—

Madrigals and Catches. 16mo. New York, 1887.

Lyrics for a Lute. 16mo. Boston, 1890.

Little-Folk Lyrics. 16mo. Boston, 1892.

***See also BANGS, J. K.

SHILLABER, BENJAMIN PENHALLOW (MRS. PARTINGTON). 1814-1890.

Rhymes with Reason and without. Portrait. 12mo. Boston, 1853.

Life and Sayings of Mrs. Partington and others of the Family. Illustrations. 12mo. Boston, 1854.

A very Brief and Comprehensive Life of Ben. Franklin, Printer, done into Quaint Verse, by One of the Types. Sept. 17, 1856. Broadside. [Boston, 1856.]

Knitting Work : a Web of many Textures wrought by Ruth Partington. Illustrations. 12mo. Boston, 1859.

Partingtonian Patchwork. Illustrations. 12mo. Boston, 1873.

Lines in Pleasant Places : Rhythmics of Many Moods and Quantities, Wise and Otherwise. 12mo. Boston, 1874.

Ike and his Friends. 12mo. Boston, 1879.

Cruises with Captain Bob on Sea and Land. 12mo. Boston, 1880.

The Doublerunner Club. 12mo. Boston, 1881.

Wide-Swath, embracing Lines in Pleasant Places and other Rhymes, Wise and Otherwise. Portrait. 12mo. Cambridge, 1882.

(Edited.) Memorial of Incidents and Ceremonials attending the Session of the Sovereign Grand Lodge I. O. O. F., at Boston, Mass., September, 1886. 16mo. Boston, 1887.

Mrs. Shillaber's Cook-Book. With Introduction by Mrs. Partington. 12mo. New York, 1887.

SIGOURNEY, LYDIA HUNTLEY. 1791–1865.

Moral Pieces in Prose and Verse. By Lydia Huntley. 12mo. Hartford, 1815.

Biography and Writings of Anne Maria Hyde. 12mo. Hartford, 1816.

[Anonymous.] Traits of the Aborigines of America. A Poem. 12mo. Cambridge, 1822.

[Anonymous.] Sketch of Connecticut Forty Years since. 12mo. Hartford, 1824.

Poems. 12mo. Boston, 1827.

Letters to Young Ladies. By A Lady. 18mo. Hartford, 1833.

The Farmer and Soldier. A Tale . . . . [signed L. H. S.]. 18mo. Hartford, 1833.

Memoir of Phebe Hammond. 16mo. Hartford, 1833.

Sketches and Tales. Frontispiece. 12mo. Philadelphia, 1834.

Select Poems. Illustrations. 12mo. Philadelphia, 1834.

Poems [newly revised]. 12mo. Philadelphia, 1834.

Tales and Essays for Children. Square 18mo. Hartford, 1835.

Poems for Children. 32mo. Hartford, 1836.

Zinzendorf and other Poems. 12mo. New York, 1836.

History of Marcus Aurelius Antoninus. 16mo. Hartford, 1836.

Olive Buds. Square 16mo. Hartford, 1836.

History of the Condition of Women. 12mo. Boston, 1837.

Letters to Mothers. 12mo. Hartford, 1838.

Pocahontas and other Poems. Frontispiece. 12mo. New York, 1841.

Poems, Religious and Elegiac. 16mo. London, 1841.

Poems [newly revised]. Frontispiece. 32mo. Philadelphia, 1842.

Pleasant Memories of Pleasant Lands. Illustrations. 12mo. Boston, 1842.

Scenes in my Native Land. 12mo. Boston, 1845.

Poetry for Seamen. 16mo. Boston, 1845.

The Voice of Flowers. 16mo. Hartford, 1846.

The Lovely Sisters. 16mo. Hartford, 1846.

Myrtis with other Etchings and Sketchings. Frontispiece. 12mo. New York, 1846.

The Weeping Willow. 32mo. Hartford, 1847.

Water Drops. 16mo. New York, 1848.

Songs of the Heart and other Poems. 32mo. London, 1848.

Poems. Portrait and illustrations. 8vo. Philadelphia, 1849.

Whisper to a Bride. 18mo. Hartford [1850].

Poetical Works. Edited by F. W. N. Bayley. 16mo. London, 1850.

Poems for the Sea. 12mo. Hartford, 1850.

Letters to my Pupils: with Narratives and Biographical Sketches. Frontispiece. 12mo. New York, 1850.

Examples of Life and Death. 12mo. New York, 1851.

Olive Leaves. Illustrations. 16mo. New York, 1852.

Voices of Home. 12mo. Hartford, 1852.

The Faded Hope. 16mo. New York, 1852.
 *˛*A biography of the author's son, with selections from his writings.

Memoir of Mrs. Harriet Newell Cook. 12mo. New York, 1853.

Past Meridian. 12mo. New York, 1854.

The Western Home and other Poems. Portrait. 12mo. Philadelphia, 1854.

Sayings of the Little Ones. 12mo. Hartford, 1854.

Examples from the Eighteenth and Nineteenth Centuries. 16mo. New York, 1857.

Lucy Howard's Journal. 12mo. New York, 1858.

The Daily Counsellor. 8vo. Hartford, 1858.

Gleanings. 12mo. Hartford, 1860.

The Man of Uz, and other Poems. 12mo. Hartford, 1862.

Selections from Various Sources. 12mo. Worcester, 1863.

[Anonymous.] The Transplanted Daisy. Memoir of Frances Racillia Hackley. (Privately printed.) 4to. New York, 1865.

Letters of Life. Portrait. 12mo. New York, 1866.
  *₊*In addition to the works included in this list, Mrs. Sigourney edited numerous juvenile and religious publications, and was author of others, and of some rhymed leaflets printed for special occasions.

SILL, EDWARD ROWLAND. 1841–1887.

Poem [by Edward R. Sill] and Valedictory Oration [by Sextus Shearer, Jr.], pronounced before the Senior Class in Yale College, Presentation Day, June 19, 1861. 8vo. New Haven, 1861.

The Hermitage and other Poems. 16mo. New York, 1868.

Mozart: a Biographical Romance, from the German of Herbert Rau. 12mo. New York, 1868.

The Clocks of Gnoster-Town; or, Truth by Majority. A Poem before the Phi Beta Kappa Society of Yale College, July 21, 1869. 8vo. New Haven, 1869.

Shall we have Free High Schools? 8vo. San Francisco, 1881.

Venus of Milo and other Poems. (Privately printed.) Berkeley, California, 1883.

Poems [including many now first collected]. 16mo. Boston, 1888.

The Hermitage and Later Poems. [With memorial poem by T. B. Aldrich.] 16mo. Boston, 1889.

SIMMS, WILLIAM GILMORE. 1806-1870.

A Monody on General Charles Cotesworth Pinckney. 16mo. Charleston, 1825.

Lyrical and other Poems. 12mo. Charleston, 1827.

Early Lays. 12mo. Charleston, 1827.

The Vision of Cortes, Cain, and other Poems. 18mo. Charleston, 1829.

The Tri-Color; or, the Three Days of Blood in Paris. With some other Pieces. 8vo. Charleston, 1830.

[Anonymous.] Atalantis. A Story of the Sea: in Three Parts. 8vo. New York, 1832.

[Anonymous.] Martin Faber: the Story of a Criminal. 16mo. New York, 1833.

The Book of my Lady. A Melange. By A Bachelor Knight. 12mo. Philadelphia, 1833.

The Remains of Maynard Davis Richardson, with a Memoir of his Life. By His Friend. 12mo. Charleston, 1833.

Guy Rivers: a Tale of Georgia. 2 volumes, 12mo. New York, 1834.

The Yemassee: a Romance of South Carolina. 2 volumes, 12mo. New York, 1835.

The Partizan: a Tale of the Revolution. 2 volumes, 12mo. New York, 1835.

Mellichampe. A Legend of the Santee. 2 volumes, 12mo. New York, 1836.

Martin Faber, the Story of a Criminal; and other Tales [now first collected]. 2 volumes, 12mo. New York, 1837.

Richard Hurdis; or, the Avenger of Blood. A Tale of Alabama. 2 volumes, 12mo. Philadelphia, 1838.

Pelayo: a Story of the Goth. 2 volumes, 12mo. New York, 1838.

Slavery in America. Being a Brief of Miss Martineau on that Subject. By A South Carolinian. 8vo. Richmond, 1838.

The Morals of Slavery; being a Brief Review of the Writings of Miss Martineau and other Persons, on the Subject of Negro Slavery as it now exists in the United States. 12mo. Charleston, 1838.
  *.*Originally published in Southern Literary Messenger, 1837; reprinted in The Pro-Slavery Argument as maintained by the Most Distinguished Authors of the South, pp. 175-285. 12mo. Charleston, 1852.

Carl Werner, an Imaginative Story, with other Tales of Imagination. 2 volumes, 12mo. New York, 1838.

Southern Passages and Pictures. 12mo. New York, 1839.

The Damsel of Darien. 2 volumes, 12mo. Philadelphia, 1839.

The History of South Carolina, from its First European Discovery to its Erection into a Republic; with a Supplementary Chronicle of Events to the Present Time. 12mo. Charleston, 1840.
  *.*The same. Large paper. 8vo. Charleston, 1840.
  *.*Reprinted, with additions, 1842, and 1860.

[Anonymous.] Border Beagles: a Tale of Mississippi. 2 volumes, 12mo. Philadelphia, 1840.

The Kinsmen: or, the Black Riders of the Congaree. A Tale. 2 volumes, 12mo. Philadelphia, 1841.
  *.*Reprinted as The Scout, 12mo. New York, 1854.

Confession; or, the Blind Heart. A Domestic Story. 2 volumes, 12mo. Philadelphia, 1841.

Beauchampe, or the Kentucky Tragedy. A Tale of Passion. 2 volumes, 12mo. Philadelphia, 1842.

The Social Principle: the True Source of National Permanence. An Oration before the Erosophic Society of the University of Alabama, at its Twelfth Anniversary, Dec. 13, 1842. 8vo. Tuscaloosa, 1843.

Donna Florida: a Tale. (Privately printed.) 16mo. Charleston, 1843.

The Geography of South Carolina; being a Companion to the History of that State .... Map. 12mo. Charleston, 1843.

The Prima Donna: a Passage from City Life. 8vo. Philadelphia, 1844.

The Life of Francis Marion. Frontispiece and vignette title. 12mo. New York, 1844.

The Sources of American Independence. Oration at Aikin, 'S. C., July 4, 1844. 8vo. Aikin, 1844.

Castle Dismal; or, the Bachelor's Christmas. A Domestic Legend. 12mo. New York, 1844.

(Edited.) The Southern and Western Monthly Magazine and Review. [January–December, inclusive, 1845.] 2 volumes, 8vo. Charleston, 1845.

(Edited, anonymously.) The Charleston Book: a Miscellany in Prose and Verse. 12mo. Charleston, 1845.

Grouped Thoughts and Scattered Fancies. A Collection of Sonnets. Square 16mo. Richmond, 1845.

Helen Halsey: or the Swamp State of Conelachita. A Tale of the Borders. 12mo. New York, 1845.

Count Julian; or, the Last Days of the Goth. A Historical Romance [forming sequel to Pelayo]. 8vo. Baltimore, 1845.

The Wigwam and the Cabin. 2 volumes, 12mo. New York, 1845.

Views and Reviews in American Literature, History and Fiction. 2 volumes, 12mo. New York, 1845.

Areytos; or, Songs of the South. 12mo. Charleston, 1846.

The Life of Captain John Smith, the Founder of Virginia. 13 plates. 12mo. New York [1846].

Self Development. An Oration delivered before the Literary Societies of Oglethorpe University, Ga., Nov. 10, 1847. 8vo. Milledgeville, 1847.

The Life of Chevalier Bayard; the Good Knight sans Peur et sans Reproche. Illustrations. 12mo. New York, 1847.

Atalantis; a Story of the Sea. [Also The Eye and the Wing; Poems (37) chiefly Imaginative, pp. 73-144.] 12mo. Philadelphia, 1848.

Charleston and her Satirists: a Scribblement. By A City Bachelor. 12mo. Charleston, 1848.

The Eye and the Wing: Poems chiefly Imaginative, The Cassique of Accabee, etc. 8vo. New York, 1848.

Lays of the Palmetto: a Tribute to the South Carolina Regiment in the War with Mexico. 16mo. Charleston, 1848.

A Supplement to the Plays of William Shakespeare: comprising the Seven Dramas which have been ascribed to his Pen but which are not included with his Writings in Modern Editions. Edited, with Notes, and an Introduction to each Play, by W. G. Simms. 8vo. New York, 1848.

Sabbath Lyrics; or Songs from Scripture. A Christmas Gift of Love. 8vo. Charleston, 1849.

Father Abbot; or, the Home Tourist: a Medley. 18mo. Charleston, 1849.

The Cassique of Accabee. A Tale of Ashley River. With other Pieces. Square 16mo. New York, 1849.

The Life of Nathanael Greene, Major-General in the Army of the Revolution. Portrait and 12 plates. 12mo. New York, 1849.

The City of the Silent; a Poem. Delivered at the Consecration of Magnolia Cemetery, Nov. 19, 1850. 8vo. Charleston, 1850.

The Lily and the Totem; or, the Huguenots in Florida. A series of Sketches, Picturesque and Historical of the Colonies of Coligni in North America. 12mo. New York, 1850.

Flirtation at the Moultrie House, etc. 8vo. Charleston, 1850.

[Anonymous.] Katherine Walton; or, the Rebel of Dorchester. An Historic Romance of the Revolution in Carolina. 8vo. Philadelphia, 1851.

Norman Maurice; or, the Man of the People. An American
Drama. In Five Acts. Royal 8vo. Richmond, 1851.

The Golden Christmas; a Chronicle of St. John's Berkeley.
Compiled from the Notes of a Briefless Barrister. 12mo.
Charleston, 1852.

As Good as a Comedy, or the Tennesseean's Story. By An
Editor. 12mo. Philadelphia, 1852.

Michael Bonham: or, the Fall of Bexar. A Tale of Texas.
In Five Parts. By A Southron. 8vo. Richmond, 1852.

The Sword and the Distaff, or Fair, Fat, and Forty. 12mo.
Charleston, 1852.
  *.*Republished as Woodcraft, New York, 1854.

Marie de Bernière: a Tale of the Crescent City . . . .
12mo. Philadelphia, 1853.

Vasconselos: a Romance of the New World. By Frank
Cooper. 12mo. New York, 1853.

Egeria; or, Voices of Thought and Counsel for the Woods
and Wayside. Frontispiece and vignette title. 12mo.
Philadelphia, 1853.

Poems, Descriptive, Dramatic, Legendary and Contemplative. Portrait. 2 volumes, 12mo. New York and
Charleston, 1853.

South Carolina in the Revolutionary War: being a Reply to
Certain Misrepresentations and Mistakes of Recent
Writers in Relation to the Course and Conduct of this
State. By A Southron. 12mo. Charleston, 1853.

Southward Ho! A Spell of Sunshine. 12mo. New York,
1854.

The Forayers; or, the Raid of the Dog-Days. 12mo. New
York, 1855.

Inauguration of the Spartanburg Female College, August
22nd, 1855; with the Address on that Occasion by W. G.
Simms. 12mo. Spartanburg, 1855.

The Power of Cotton. 8vo. New York, 1856.
  *.*Ascribed to Simms, but without absolute certainty.

Charlemont; or, the Pride of the Village. A Tale of Kentucky. Illustrations. 12mo. New York, 1856.

Eutaw; a Sequel to The Forayers. A Tale of the Revolution. 12mo. New York, 1856.

The Cassique of Kiawah. A Colonial Romance. Frontispiece. 12mo. New York, 1859.

Areytos, or Songs and Ballads of the South. With other Poems [including Lays of the Palmetto, etc.]. 12mo. New York and Charleston, 1860.

[Anonymous.] Sack and Destruction of the City of Columbia, S. C. To which is added a List of the Property destroyed. 8vo. Columbia, 1865.
  *˳*Printed on Confederate bond paper, at the press of The Daily Phenix.

Army Correspondence of Col. John Laurens, in 1777-78, now First printed from Original Letters addressed to his Father, Henry Laurens. With a Memoir by W. G. Simms. 8vo. New York: The Bradford Club, 1867.

A Succinct Memoir of the Life and Public Services of Colonel John Laurens, Aid-de-Camp to General Washington, and Special Envoy to the French Court during the War of the American Revolution. Together with a Series of Letters written by him relating to that Eventful Epoch and addressed to his Father, Henry Laurens, President of Congress. 8vo. Williamstadt, 1867.

(Edited.) War Poetry of the South. 12mo. New York, 1867.

The Quaker Partizans. A Story of the Revolution. Illustrations. 12mo. New York, 1869.

The Swamp Robbers. 18mo. New York, 1870.

The Sense of the Beautiful: an Address . . . . at Charleston, S. C., May 3, 1870. 8vo. Charleston, 1870.
  *˳*A uniform edition of Simms' writings, revised by the author, with new prefaces, dedications, etc., and illustrations by Darley, was published as Revolutionary and Border Romances of the South, and Poems, in 20 volumes, 12mo. New York, 1853-59.
  *˳*See also BRYANT, W. C.; and PAULDING, J. K.

SMITH, ELIZABETH OAKES. 1806—1893.

    Riches without Wings. 12mo. Boston, 1838.

    The Sinless Child. 12mo. New York, 1841.

    The Western Captive, or Times of Tecumseh. Royal 8vo. New York, 1842.

    Swaying Reed, an Indian Legend. 12mo. New York, 1842.

    The Sinless Child and other Poems. Edited by John Keese. 12mo. New York, 1843.

    Poetical Writings [with preface by R. W. Griswold]. 32mo. New York, 1845.

    The Moss Cup. Frontispiece. 32mo. Boston, 1845.

    The True Child. 32mo. Boston, 1845.

    The Dandelion. Frontispiece. 32mo. Boston, 1846.

    Stories for Children. 12mo. Boston, 1847.

    The Salamander. A Legend for Christmas. Illustrations by Darley. 8vo. New York, 1848.

    The Lover's Gift. 32mo. Hartford, 1848.

    Woman and her Needs. 12mo. New York, 1851.

    Hints on Dress and Beauty. 12mo. New York, 1852.

    Shadow Land. 12mo. New York, 1852.

    Old New York: or, Democracy in 1689. A Tragedy. 12mo. New York, 1853.

    Bertha and Lily; or, the Parsonage of Beach Glen. 12mo. New York, 1854.

    The Newsboy. 12mo. New York, 1855.

    Hugo. 12mo. New York, 1856.

    Mary and Hugo. 12mo. New York, 1856.

    The Sagamore of Saco. Frontispiece. 12mo. New York [1858].

    Bald Eagle; or, the Last of the Ramapaughs. 12mo. London, 1867.

Footprints of Time ; or, Daily Oracles. 12mo. New York, 1870.

Sister Electa, or Life Sleeping and Waking. 12mo. New York, 1871.

My Autobiography. 12mo. New York, 1871.

SMITH, FRANCIS HOPKINSON. 1838—

(With Edward Strahan.) A Book of the Tile Club. 114 illustrations. Folio. Boston, 1886.

Old Lines in New Black and White. Twelve Illustrations of Lines from the Poems of Holmes, Lowell and Whittier. Folio. Boston, 1886.
***The same. Large paper. Japan proofs. (100 copies.) Imperial folio. Boston, 1886.

Well-Worn Roads of Spain, Holland and Italy ; travelled by a Painter in Search of the Picturesque. Illustrations by the author. Folio. Boston, 1887.

A White Umbrella in Mexico. Illustrations by the author. 12mo. Boston, 1889.

Col. Carter of Cartersville. Illustrations. 12mo. Boston, 1891.

A Day at Laguerre's and other Days. 12mo. Boston, 1892.
***The same. Large paper. (250 copies.) 8vo. Boston, 1892.

American Illustrators. Illustrations. (1,000 copies.) Folio. New York, 1892.

(With W. H. Gibson and others.) Some Artists at the Fair. Illustrations. 8vo. New York, 1893.

Venice of To-day. Illustrations by the author. Folio. New York, 1895.
***The same. Edition De Luxe. Japan proofs. Imperial folio. New York, 1895.
***Other editions, two at least, were published simultaneously with those indicated.

A Gentleman Vagabond and some Others. 16mo. Boston, 1895.
***The same. Large paper. (250 copies.) 8vo. Boston, 1895.

SMITH, RICHARD PENN. 1799-1854.

The Eighth of January. A Drama. 16mo. Philadelphia, 1829.

The Deformed; or, Woman's Trial, a Play. 16mo. Philadelphia, 1830.

The Disowned; or the Prodigals. A Play. 16mo. Philadelphia, 1830.

[Anonymous.] The Forsaken. A Novel. 2 volumes, 12mo. Philadelphia, 1831.

The Actress of Padua and other Tales. 2 volumes, 12mo. Philadelphia, 1836.

Life of David Crockett. 12mo. Philadelphia, 1836.

Miscellaneous Works, collected by his Son, Horace W. Smith. 8vo. Philadelphia, 1856.

SMITH, SEBA. 1792-1868.

The Life and Writings of Major Jack Downing, of Downingville, Way Down East in the State of Maine. Written by Himself. Illustrations. 12mo. Boston, 1833.

Letters of J. Downing, Major, to his Old Friend, Mr. Dwight, of The New York Daily Advertiser. Illustrations. 12mo. New York, 1834.

Powhatan; a Metrical Historical Romance. 12mo. New York, 1841.

(Edited.) Dew-Drops of the Nineteenth Century. Plates. 12mo. New York, 1846.

New Elements of Geometry. 8vo. New York, 1850.

My Thirty Years out of the Senate. By Major Jack Downing. Illustrations. 12mo. New York, 1859.

SNELLING, WILLIAM JOSEPH. 1804-1848.

Tales of Travel West of the Mississippi. By Solomon Bell. Illustrations. 24mo. Boston, 1830.

[Anonymous.] Tales of the North West; or Sketches of Indian Life and Character. 16mo. Boston, 1830.

A Brief and Impartial History of the Life and Actions of Andrew Jackson. By A Free Man. 16mo. Boston, 1831.

The Polar Regions of the Western Continent Explored. With Adventures . . . . of Parry, Franklin, Lyon. 8vo. Boston, 1831.

[Anonymous.] Truth; a New Year's Gift for Scribblers. 16mo. Boston, 1831.

Truth, a Gift for Scribblers. Second Edition with Additions and Emendations [consisting of prologue, additional preface, and names of those pilloried, which were indicated by initials only in first edition]. 16mo. Boston, 1832.

Exposé of the Vice of Gambling as it lately existed in Massachusetts. 12mo. Boston, 1833.

Six Months in a House of Correction. 18mo. Boston, 1835.

Indian Nullification of the Unconstitutional Laws of Massachusetts, relative to the Marshpee Tribe; or the Pretended Riot explained. By William Apes. 12mo. Boston, 1835.
*₊*Ascribed to Snelling by Drake. See No. 347. Drake catalogue.

SPOFFORD, HARRIET ELIZABETH PRESCOTT. 1835—

[Anonymous.] Sir Rohan's Ghost. A Romance. 12mo. Boston, 1860.

The Amber Gods, and other Stories. 12mo. Boston, 1863.

Azarian: an Episode. 12mo. Boston, 1864.

New England Legends. Illustrations. 8vo. Boston, 1871.

The Thief in the Night. 12mo. Boston, 1872.

Art Decoration applied to Furniture. Illustrations. Small 4to. New York, 1878.

The Servant-Girl Question. 18mo. Boston, 1881.

Hester Stanley at St. Mark's. Illustrations. 16mo. Boston, 1882.

Poems. 16mo. Boston, 1882.

The Marquis of Carrabas. 16mo. Boston, 1882.

Ballads About Authors. Illustrations. 8vo. Boston [1887].
  ⁎ The same. Edition de Luxe. 4to. Boston [1887].

A Lost Jewel. Illustrations. 16mo. Boston, 1891.

House and Hearth. 16mo. New York, 1891.

Rumor. By Elizabeth Sheppard. With Memoir of the Author by Harriet P. Spofford. 12mo. Chicago, 1892.

A Scarlet Poppy and other Stories. 16mo. New York, 1894.

(With Louise I. Guiney and Alice Brown.) Three Heroines of New England History. Their True Stories herein set forth. Illustrations. 12mo. Boston, 1894.
  ⁎ The same. Large paper. (100 copies.) 8vo. Boston, 1894.

SPRAGUE, CHARLES. 1791-1875.

The Prize Ode . . . . recited at the Representation of the Shakespeare Jubilee, Boston, February 13, 1824. 8vo. [Boston, 1824.]

Prize Poems. 12mo. Boston, 1824.

An Oration delivered Fourth of July, 1825. 8vo. Boston, 1825.

Curiosity: a Poem, delivered at Cambridge, before the Phi Beta Kappa Society, August 27, 1829. 8vo. Boston, 1829.

An Ode: pronounced before the Inhabitants of Boston, Sept. 17th, 1830, at the Centennial Celebration of the Settlement of the City. 8vo. Boston, 1830.

Writings, now first collected. 8vo. New York, 1841.

Poetical and Prose Writings. Portrait. 12mo. Boston, 1850.

Poetical and Prose Writings. With Biographical Sketch [by Charles J. Sprague]. Portrait. 12mo. Boston, 1876.

STEDMAN, EDMUND CLARENCE. 1833—

Poems, Lyrical and Idyllic. 12mo. New York, 1860.

The Prince's Ball. A Brochure. From Vanity Fair. Illustrations. 12mo. New York, 1860.

The Battle of Bull Run. 12mo. New York, 1861.

Alice of Monmouth, an Idyl of the Great War, with other Poems. 12mo. New York, 1864.

[Anonymous.] A Reconstruction Letter. (Privately printed; 100 copies.) 8vo. New York, 1866.

The Blameless Prince, and other Poems. Vignette. 12mo. Boston, 1869.

Rip Van Winkle and his Wonderful Nap. Illustrations by S. Eytinge. 4to. Boston, 1870.

Proceedings at the Fourth Annual Re-Union of the Society of the Army of the Potomac .... May 7, 1872. [Poem, Gettysburg, by Stedman, pp. 23–26.] 8vo. New York, 1873.

Poetical Works. Portrait. 12mo. Boston, 1873.

Cameos. Selected from the Works of Walter Savage Landor. By E. C. Stedman and T. B. Aldrich. With an Introduction. Square 16mo. Boston, 1874.

Victorian Poets. 12mo. Boston, 1876.

Octavius Brooks Frothingham and the New Faith. Portrait. 12mo. New York, 1876.

Elizabeth Barrett Browning. Portrait. 32mo. Boston, 1877.

Favorite Poems. Illustrations. 32mo. Boston, 1877.

Hawthorne and other Poems. 16mo. Boston, 1877.

Bryant Memorial Meeting of the Century Club, Nov. 12th, 1878. [Poem, The Death of Bryant, by Stedman, pp. 69–74; also poems by R. H. Stoddard, Bayard Taylor and others.] Portrait. 8vo. New York [1878].

Proceedings at a Reception in Honor of the Rev. O. B. Frothingham .... April 22, 1879 .... [Addresses by Stedman, G. W. Curtis and others.] Small 4to. New York, 1879.

Lyrics and Idyls, with other Poems. 12mo. London, 1879.

The Lovers of Provence, Aucassin and Nicolette .... Translated into English Prose and Verse by A. R. Macdonough [with introduction by Stedman]. Small 4to. New York [1880].

Vignettes in Rhyme, and other Verses, by Austin Dobson. [With introduction by Stedman.] 12mo. New York, 1880.

Edgar Allan Poe. Vignette portrait. 16mo. Boston, 1881.

Complete Pocket-Guide to Europe. 24mo. Boston, 1882, New York, 1887.
  *.*Re-edited annually.

The Raven, by Edgar Allan Poe. With Comment by Edmund Clarence Stedman. Illustrations by Doré. Folio. New York, 1884.

Poetical Works. Household Edition. Portrait. 12mo. Boston, 1884.

Songs and Ballads. Illustrations. (100 copies.) Square 12mo. New York : The Book Fellows' Club, 1884.

Poets of America. Small 8vo. Boston, 1885.
  *.*The same. Large paper, portraits on India paper. (150 copies.) 2 volumes, 8vo. Boston, 1885.

Victorian Poets. Revised and Extended by a Supplementary Chapter, to the Fiftieth Year of the Period under Review. Small 8vo. Boston, 1887.
  *.*The same. Large paper, portraits on Japan paper. (250 copies.) 2 volumes, 8vo. Boston, 1887.

The Star Bearer. [A Christmas poem.] Illustrations. 4to. Boston, 1888.

(Edited, with Ellen Mackay Hutchinson.) A Library of American Literature, from the Earliest Settlement to the Present Time. Portraits. 11 volumes, royal 8vo. New York, 1888–90.

The Lord's Prayer Illustrated. The Poem translated from the Old German by Edmund Clarence Stedman. 8vo. New York [1890].

The Nature and Elements of Poetry. Frontispiece. 12mo. Boston, 1892.
  *.*Also, 75 copies, wholly uncut, paper labels, small 8vo. Boston, 1892.

A Victorian Anthology. Selections illustrating the Editor's Critical Review of British Poetry in the Reign of Victoria. Portrait and vignette. Small 8vo. Boston, 1895.
 *₊*The same. Large paper. 2 portraits and vignette. (250 copies.) 2 volumes, 8vo. Boston, 1895.
 *₊*See also BURROUGHS, JOHN; LOWELL, J. R., and POE, EDGAR ALLAN.

STILLMAN, WILLIAM JAMES. 1828—

(Edited, with John Durand.) The Crayon. [Containing original contributions by Lowell, Aldrich and others.] 8 volumes, 4to. New York, 1855–61.

The Acropolis of Athens illustrated picturesquely and architecturally in Photography. (Privately printed; 100 copies.) Folio. London, 1870.

The Cretan Insurrection of 1866, '67, '68. 12mo. London, 1874.

The Amateur's Photographic Guide Book. Illustrations. 8vo. London, 1874.

Poetic Localities of Cambridge. Illustrated with Heliotypes from Nature. 4to. Boston, 1876.

Herzegovina and the Late Uprising: the Causes of the Latter and the Remedy. 12mo. London, 1877.

On the Track of Ulysses: together with an Expedition in Quest of the So-Called Venus of Milo. Two Studies of Archæology made during a Cruise among the Greek Islands. Illustrations. 4to. Boston, 1888.

Old Italian Masters. Illustrations. 4to. New York, 1892.
 *₊*The same. Edition de Luxe. (18 copies.) Japan paper proofs, signed by artist and printer. Imperial folio. New York, 1892.
 *₊*See also HOWELLS, W. D.

STIMSON, FREDERICK JESUP (J. S., OF DALE). 1855 —

[Anonymous.] Rollo's Journey to Cambridge. [By F. J. Stimson and John T. Wheelwright.] Illustrations. Small 4to. Boston, 1880.
 *₊*Whilst the earlier pages were being printed, this title was mistakenly credited to Robert Grant, and so inserted, although at the time it was, as now, included in the list prepared of Mr. Stimson's writings.

Glossary of Technical Terms, Phrases and Maxims of the Common Law. 12mo. Boston, 1881.

Guerndale: an Old Story. 12mo. New York, 1882.

The Crime of Henry Vane: a Story with a Moral. 16mo. New York, 1884.

The Sentimental Calendar. Illustrations. 12mo. New York, 1886.

American Statute Law: an Analytical and Compared Digest of the Constitutions and Civil Public Statutes of all the States and Territories, relating to Persons and Property, in Force January 1, 1886. 4to. Boston, 1886.
***The same. Vol. II. 8vo. Boston, 1892.

The Residuary Legatee; or the Posthumous Jest of the Late John Austin. 12mo. New York, 1888.

First Harvests: an Episode in the Life of Mrs. Levison Gower. A Satire without a Moral. 12mo. New York, 1888.

In Three Zones. 12mo. New York, 1893.

Labor in its Relations to Law. 16mo. New York, 1895.
***See also GRANT, ROBERT.

STOCKTON, FRANCIS RICHARD. 1834—

Ting-a-Ling. Illustrations. Square 12mo. New York, 1870.

(With M. E. Stockton.) Roundabout Rambles in Lands of Fact and Fancy. Illustrations. 4to. New York, 1872.

(With M. E. Stockton.) The Home: where it should be and what to put in it. 12mo. New York, 1872.

What might have been expected. Illustrations. 12mo. New York, 1874.

Tales out of School. Illustrations. 4to. New York, 1875.

Rudder Grange. Illustrations. 12mo. New York, 1879.

A Jolly Fellowship. Illustrations. 12mo. New York, 1880.

The Floating Prince and other Fairy Tales. 8vo. New York, 1881.

The Lady, or the Tiger? and other Stories. 12mo. New York, 1884.

The Story of Viteau. 12mo. New York, 1884.

The Casting away of Mrs. Lecks and Mrs. Aleshine. 12mo. New York [1886].

The Christmas Wreck and other Stories. 12mo. New York, 1886.

The Late Mrs. Null. 12mo. New York, 1886.

The Bee-Man of Orm and other Fanciful Tales. 12mo. New York, 1887.

The Hundredth Man. 12mo. New York, 1887.

Amos Kilbright: his Adscititious Experiences; with other Stories. 12mo. New York, 1888.

The Dusantes. [Sequel to The Casting away of Mrs. Lecks and Mrs. Aleshine.] 12mo. New York [1888].

Personally Conducted. Illustrations. Square 8vo. New York, 1889.

The Great War Syndicate. 12mo. New York [1889].

* The Stories of the Three Burglars. 12mo. New York [1889].

Ardis Claverden. 12mo. New York [1890].

The Merry Chanter. Illustrations. 12mo. New York, 1890.

The Rudder Grangers Abroad and other Stories. 12mo. New York, 1891.

The Squirrel Inn. Illustrations. 12mo. New York, 1891.

The House of Martha. 12mo. Boston, 1891.

The Clocks of Rondaine, and other Stories. Illustrations. Square 8vo. New York, 1892.

The Watchmaker's Wife and other Stories. 12mo. New York, 1893.

Pomona's Travels. A Series of Letters to the Mistress of Rudder Grange from her Former Handmaiden. Illustrations. 12mo. New York, 1894.

The Adventures of Captain Horn. 12mo. New York, 1895.

A Chosen Few. Portrait. 16mo. New York, 1895.

STODDARD, CHARLES WARREN. 1843—

Poems. Illustrations. 8vo. San Francisco, 1867.

South Sea Idyls. 18mo. Boston, 1873.

Summer Cruising in the South Sea. Illustrations. 16mo. London, 1874.

Mashallah! A Flight into Egypt. 16mo. New York, 1880.

A Trip to Hawaii. Illustrations. 12mo. [San Francisco, 1885.]

The Lepers of Molokai. 16mo. Notre Dame, Ind., 1885.

[Anonymous.] A Troubled Heart and how it was comforted at Last. 16mo. Notre Dame, 1885.

South Sea Idyls. With Introductory Letter by W. D. Howells. 12mo. Boston, 1892.
*.*Two Idyls are here given for the first time, and one of those included in 1873 edition is omitted.

Hawaiian Life; or, Lazy Letters from Low Latitudes. 12mo. Chicago, 1894.

STODDARD, ELIZABETH DREW. 1823—

The Morgesons. A Novel. 12mo. New York, 1862.

Two Men. 12mo. New York, 1865.

Temple House. 12mo. New York, 1868.

Lally Dinks' Doings. Square 16mo. Boston, 1874.

(Edited, with Mary Abigail Dodge.) Little Folk Life Series. Illustrations. 3 volumes, square 16mo. Boston, 1874.

Poems. 12mo. Boston, 1895.
*.*See also DODGE, MARY A.; and STODDARD, R. H.

STODDARD, RICHARD HENRY. 1825—

    Footprints. (Privately printed.) 12mo. New York, 1849.

    Poems. 12mo. Boston, 1852.

    Adventures in Fairy-Land. Illustrations. 16mo. Boston, 1853.

    Town and Country and the Voices in the Shell. Illustrations. Square 12mo. New York, 1857.

    Songs of Summer. 12mo. Boston, 1857.

    [Anonymous.] Life, Travels and Books of A. Von Humboldt. With an Introduction by Bayard Taylor. Portrait. 12mo. New York, 1859.

    (Edited.) The Loves and Heroines of the Poets. 12 portraits. 4to. New York, 1861.

    (Edited.) Essays by George Brimley. 12mo. New York, 1861.

    (Edited.) General Lyon's Political Essays and Life. 12mo. New York, 1861.

    (Edited.) J. G. Vassar's Twenty-One Years round the World. 8vo. New York, 1862.

    The King's Bell. 12mo. New York, 1863.

    The Story of Little Red-Riding-Hood; told in Verse. Illustrations. 4to. New York, 1864.

    The Children in the Wood; told in Verse. Illustrations. 4to. New York, 1865.

    Abraham Lincoln: an Horatian Ode. 4to. New York [1865].

    (Edited.) Golden Leaves from the Late English Poets. 12mo. New York, 1865.

    (Edited.) Under Green Leaves: a Book of Rural Poems. Illustrations. 16mo. New York, 1865.

    (Edited.) Melodies and Madrigals; mostly from the Old English Poets. Illuminated title. Square 16mo. New York, 1866.

Putnam the Brave. Illustrations. 4to. Boston, 1869.

(Edited, with Elizabeth Stoddard.) Remember: a Keepsake. Illustrations. Small 8vo. New York [1869].

The Book of the East and other Poems. 12mo. Boston, 1871.

(Edited.) The Bric-a-Brac Series. [Personal reminiscences of famous poets, novelists, humorists, actors, musicians, etc.] 10 volumes, 12mo. New York, 1874-76.

(Edited.) The Sans Souci Series. A Library of Anecdote Biographies. Portraits and illustrations. 5 volumes, 12mo. New York, 1876.
*_**The volume entitled Men and Manners a Hundred Years Ago, was edited by H. E. Scudder.

A Century After: Picturesque Glimpses of Philadelphia and Pennsylvania. Illustrations. 15 parts [of which parts 4-15, inclusive, were edited by Stoddard], 4to. Philadelphia, 1876.

(Edited.) Letters addressed by Elizabeth Barrett Browning to R. H. Horne. Portrait. Square 16mo. New York, 1877.

Ninth Annual Re-Union of the Society of the Army of the Potomac, at Springfield, Mass. [Poem, by Stoddard, pp. 12-18.] 8vo. New York, 1878.

Prose and Verse, Humorous and Satirical, of Thomas Moore, with Suppressed Passages, from the Memoirs of Lord Byron, chiefly. [With preface by Stoddard.] Frontispiece. 8vo. New York, 1878.

William Cullen Bryant. 32mo. New York, 1879.

Nathaniel Hawthorne. A Memoir. Square 16mo. New York, 1879.

Poems. Complete Edition. Portrait. 8vo. New York, 1880.

(Edited, with memoir, pp. i-clxxviii.) Select Works of Edgar Poe; Prose and Verse. Portrait. 12mo. New York, 1880.

Queens of England of the House of Hanover, by Dr. Doran. With Preface by R. H. Stoddard. 2 volumes, small 8vo. New York, 1880.

(Edited.) Life and Works of Washington Irving. Portrait. Royal 8vo. New York, 1880.

Henry Wadsworth Longfellow. A Medley in Prose and Verse. Portrait. Square 8vo. New York, 1882.

(Edited, with W. J. Linton.) English Verse. 5 volumes, 12mo. New York, 1883.

Life of Washington Irving. 16mo. New York, 1886.

The Lion's Cub with other Verse. Portrait. 12mo. New York, 1890.
*⁎*The same. (100 copies.) 16mo. London, 1891.

Under the Evening Lamp. 12mo. New York, 1892.

Life, Letters and Friendships of Richard Monckton Milnes, First Lord Houghton, by T. Wemyss Reid. With Introduction by R. H. Stoddard. Portraits. 2 volumes, 8vo. New York [1893].
*⁎*See also BRYANT, W. C.; BURROUGHS, JOHN; LOWELL, J. R.; STEDMAN, E. C.; and WHITTIER, J. G.

STORY, WILLIAM WETMORE. 1819-1895.

Report of Cases argued and determined in the Circuit Court of the United States for the First Circuit. 3 volumes, 8vo. Boston, 1842-47.

Address delivered before the Harvard Musical Association. 8vo. Boston, 1842.

Nature and Art: a Poem delivered before the Phi Beta Kappa Society of Harvard University; August 29, 1844. 8vo. Boston, 1844.

Treatise on the Law of Contracts not under Seal. Royal 8vo. Boston, 1844.

Treatise on the Law of Sales of Personal Property .... Royal 8vo. Boston, 1847.

Poems. 12mo. Boston, 1847.

(Edited.) Life and Letters of Joseph Story. Portrait. 2 volumes, 8vo. Boston, 1851.

Poems [revised, with many now first published]. 12mo. Boston, 1856.

Poem delivered at the Dedication of Crawford's Statue of Beethoven at the Boston Music Hall, March 1, 1856. 8vo. Boston, 1856.

The American Question. 8vo. London, 1862.

Roba di Roma; or Walks and Talks about Rome. 2 volumes, 12mo. London, 1862.

Proportions of the Human Figure, according to a New Canon for Practical Uses. Illustrations. Royal 8vo. London, 1866.

Graffiti d' Italia. 12mo. Edinburgh and New York, 1868.

A Roman Lawyer in Jerusalem. First Century. 16mo. Boston [1870].

Rome. By Francis Wey. With an Introduction by W. W. Story. Illustrations. 4to. London, 1872.

Nero: an Historical Play. 16mo. Edinburgh, 1875.

Stephania, a Tragedy in Five Acts,—with a Prologue. (Privately printed.) 16mo. Edinburgh [1875].

Castle St. Angelo and The Evil Eye. Being Additional Chapters to Roba di Roma. Illustrations. 12mo. London, 1877.

Ode on the Anniversary of Fifth Half-Century of the Landing of John Endicott at Salem, Mass. Portrait. Small 4to. Salem, 1878.

Vallambrosa. 12mo. Edinburgh, 1881.

He and She: a Poet's Portfolio. 18mo. Boston, 1883.

Poems. 2 volumes, 16mo. Edinburgh, 1885.
 *.*Also, 2 volumes, 16mo. Boston, 1896.

Fiammetta: a Summer Idyl. 16mo. Boston, 1886.

Conversations in a Studio. 2 volumes, 16mo. Boston, 1890.

Excursions in Art and Letters. 16mo. Boston, 1891.

A Poet's Portfolio. Later Readings. 18mo. Boston, 1894.
 *.*See also HOLMES, O. W.; and NORTON, C. E.

STOWE, HARRIET BEECHER. 1812-1896.

    The Mayflower, or, Sketches of Scenes and Characters among the Descendants of the Pilgrims. 18mo. New York, 1843.

    Works of Charlotte Elizabeth (Tonna). With an Introduction by Harriet B. Stowe. Portrait. 2 volumes, 8vo. New York, 1847.

    Uncle Tom's Cabin, or, Life among the Lowly. Illustrations. 2 volumes, 12mo. Boston, 1852.

    The Two Altars; or, Two Pictures in one. 12mo. [New York, 1852.]

    Uncle Sam's Emancipation; Earthly Care a Heavenly Discipline, and other Sketches. With a Sketch of Mrs. Stowe's Family. 12mo. Philadelphia, 1853.

    A Key to Uncle Tom's Cabin, presenting the Original Facts and Documents upon which the Story is founded. Together with Corroborative Statements verifying the Truth of the Work. 8vo. Boston, 1853.

    Sunny Memories of Foreign Lands. Illustrations. 2 volumes, 12mo. Boston, 1854.

    The Mayflower and Miscellaneous Writings. 12mo. Boston, 1855.

    The Colored Patriots of the American Revolution, with Sketches of other Distinguished Colored Persons . . . . by William C. Nell. With an Introduction by H. B. Stowe. 12mo. Boston, 1855.

    First Geography for Children. Illustrations and maps. Square 12mo. Boston, 1855.

    Dred; a Tale of the Great Dismal Swamp. 2 volumes, 12mo. Boston, 1856.
        *₊*Reissued as Nina Gordon, Boston, 1866.

    Earthly Care, a Heavenly Discipline. [First separate edition.] 48mo. Boston and Cleveland, 1856.

    Father Henson's Story of his own Life. With an Introduction by Mrs. Stowe. Portrait. 12mo. Boston, 1858.

Our Charley and what to do with him. 12mo. Boston, 1858.

The Minister's Wooing. 12mo. New York, 1859.

Helen Ruthven Waterston. [A privately printed collection of memorial tributes by Mrs. Stowe, W. C. Bryant and others.] 8vo. Boston, 1860.

The Pearl of Orr's Island; a Story of the Coast of Maine. 12mo. Boston, 1862.

Agnes of Sorrento. 12mo. Boston, 1862.

Reply to the Address of Thousands of Women of Great Britain and Ireland to their Sisters of the United States. 16mo. London, 1863.

The Ravages of a Carpet. 16mo. Boston, 1864.

House and Home Papers. By Christopher Crowfield. 12mo. Boston, 1864.

Stories about our Boys. 12mo. Edinburgh and London, 1865.

Little Foxes. By Christopher Crowfield. 12mo. Boston, 1866.

Religious Poems. Illustrations. 12mo. Boston, 1867.

Queer Little People. Illustrations. Square 16mo. Boston, 1867.

Daisy's First Winter and other Stories. 12mo. Boston, 1867.

The Chimney Corner. By Christopher Crowfield. 12mo. Boston, 1868.

Men of our Times, or leading Patriots of the Day. Portraits. 8vo. Hartford, 1868.

Oldtown Folks. 12mo. Boston, 1869.

(With Catherine E. Beecher.) The American Woman's Home, or, Principles of Domestic Science. Illustrations. 8vo. New York, 1869.

Lady Byron vindicated. A History of the Byron Controversy from its Beginning in 1816 to the Present Time. 12mo. Boston, 1870.

Little Pussy Willow. Illustrations. Square 12mo. Boston, 1870.

Pink and White Tyranny. A Society Novel. Illustrations. 12mo. Boston, 1871.

Sam Lawson's Fireside Stories. Illustrations. 12mo. Boston, 1871.

My Wife and I; or, Harry Henderson's History. 12mo. New York, 1871.

(With others.) Six of One, by Half a Dozen of the Other. 12mo. Boston, 1872.

Lives and Deeds of our Self-Made Men. 19 portraits. 8vo. Hartford, 1872.

Palmetto Leaves. Illustrations. 12mo. Boston, 1873.

Woman in Sacred History: a Series of Sketches drawn from Scriptural, Historical, and Legendary Sources. Portraits. 4to. New York, 1873.
  *.*Reissued as Bible Heroines, New York, 1876.

Betty's Bright Idea and other Tales. 12mo. New York, 1875.

We and our Neighbors; or, the Records of an Unfashionable Street. 8vo. New York, 1875.

Deacon Pitkin's Farm, and Christ's Christmas Presents. 16mo. London, 1875.

Footsteps of the Master. 12mo. New York, 1876.

Captain Kidd's Money and other Stories. 12mo. London, 1876.

The Ghost in the Mill and other Stories. 12mo. London, 1876.

Poganuc People: their Loves and Lives. 12mo. New York, 1878.

A Dog's Mission, or a Story of the Old Avery House, and other Stories. Square 12mo. New York, 1881.

Life of Harriet Beecher Stowe, compiled from her Journals
and Letters By Charles E. Stowe. Portraits and illustrations. 8vo. Boston, 1889.

*_**All enquiries relative to An Elementary Geography, said
to have been published by Mrs. Stowe, in 1833, have proved
fruitless, so that more definite data cannot be given.

STREET, ALFRED BILLINGS. 1811–1881.

Nature: a Poem pronounced at the Annual Commencement
of Geneva College. 8vo. Geneva [N. Y.], 1840.

The Burning of Schenectady and other Poems. 12mo.
Albany, 1842.

Drawings and Tintings. Royal 8vo. New York, 1844.

Poems. Complete Edition. Frontispiece and vignette title.
8vo. New York, 1845.

Fugitive Poems. 8vo. New York, 1846.

Frontenac; or, the Atotarho of the Iroquois. A Metrical
Romance. Portrait. 12mo. New York, 1849.

Our State: a Poem delivered before the Literary Societies of
the N. Y. University, on the 26th of June, 1849. 8vo. New
York, 1849.

A Poem delivered at the Anniversary of the Pittsfield Young
Ladies' Institute, Sept. 30, 1852. 8vo. Albany, 1852.

Science: a Poem. 8vo. Albany, 1856.

The Pilgrim Spirit. A Poem before the Phi Beta Kappa
Society at Yale College, July 30, 1857. 8vo. New Haven,
1857.

The Council of Revision of the State of New York, its History
. . . . [etc.] 8vo. Albany, 1859.

Woods and Waters; or, the Saranac and Racket. Illustrations. 12mo. New York, 1860.

Frontenac. A Poem of the Iroquois. 4to. Albany, 1860.
*_**The same. (300 copies.) 4to. Albany, 1866.

A Digest of Taxation in the United States. 8vo. Albany,
1864.

Forest Pictures in the Adirondacks, by John A. Hows; with [16] Original Poems by A. B. Street. Small 4to. New York, 1864.

Poems. 2 volumes, 12mo. New York, 1867.

The Indian Pass. 12mo. New York, 1869.

Lake and Mountain; or, Autumn in the Adirondacks. Illustrations. 12mo. New York, 1870.

Eagle Pine; or Sketches of a New York Frontier Village. 12mo. New York, 1871.

SULLIVAN, THOMAS RUSSELL. 1849—

Roses of Shadow. 12mo. New York, 1885.

Day and Night Stories. 12mo. New York, 1891.

Day and Night Stories. Second Series. 12mo. New York, 1893.

Tom Sylvester. A Novel. 12mo. New York, 1893.

TABB, JOHN BANISTER. 1845—

Poems. (Privately printed.) Square 18mo. [Baltimore, 1883.]

An Octave to Mary. [Poems.] Frontispiece. Oblong 16mo. Baltimore, 1893.

Poems. (500 copies.) Square 18mo. Boston, 1894.
*.*Also 50 copies on hand-made paper, and 5 on China paper.

TAPPAN, WILLIAM BRIGHAM. 1794-1849.

New England and other Poems. 18mo. Philadelphia, 1819.

Songs of Judah and other Melodies. 18mo. Philadelphia, 1820.

Lyrics. 12mo. Philadelphia, 1822.

Poems. 12mo. Philadelphia, 1822.

Lyric Poems. 16mo. Philadelphia, 1826.

Poem [Missions] read before the Porter Rhetorical Society, Andover. 8vo. Boston, 1836.

The Poet's Tribute. Portrait. 16mo. Boston, 1840.

Poems and Lyrics. 16mo. Boston, 1842.

The Daughter of the Isles and other Poems. Vignette. 24mo. Boston, 1844.

Poetry of the Heart. 12mo. Worcester, 1845.

Sacred and Miscellaneous Poems. 16mo. Boston, 1846.

Poetry of Life. Portrait. 16mo. Boston, 1848.

The Sunday School and other Poems. 16mo. Boston, 1848.

Late and Early Poems. 24mo. Worcester, 1849.

The Memento. 24mo. Boston, 1849.

TAYLOR, [JAMES] BAYARD. 1825-1878.

Ximena; or the Battle of the Sierra Morena, and other Poems. 12mo. Philadelphia, 1844.

Views a-Foot; or, Europe seen with Knapsack and Staff. With a Preface by N. P. Willis. 2 volumes, 12mo. New York, 1846.
*₊*The same. Second edition, with an additional chapter, and an introduction by Thomas B. Read. 12mo. New York, 1848.

Rhymes of Travel, Ballads and other Poems. Portrait. 12mo. New York, 1849.

El Dorado; or, Adventures in the Path of Empire. Plates. 2 volumes, 12mo. New York, 1850.
*₊*Also issued, without plates, 1 volume, 12mo. New York, 1850.

The American Legend. A Poem before the Phi Beta Kappa Society of Harvard University, July 18, 1850. Published by Request. 8vo. Boston, 1850.

(Edited, with George Ripley.) A Hand-Book of Literature and the Fine Arts. 12mo. New York, 1851.

A Book of Romances, Lyrics and Songs. 12mo. Boston, 1852.

Poems and Ballads. Portrait. 12mo. New York, 1854.

A Journey to Central Africa. Life and Landscape from Egypt to the Negro Kingdoms of the White Hills. Illustrations. 12mo. New York, 1854.

A Visit to India, China and Japan, in the Year 1853. Plates. 12mo. New York, 1855.

The Lands of the Saracen; or, Pictures of Palestine, Asia Minor, Sicily and Spain. Illustrations. 12mo. New York, 1855.

Poems of the Orient. 12mo. Boston, 1855.

Poems of Home and Travel. 12mo. Boston, 1855.

A Visit to El Medina and Mecca. By Richard F. Burton. With Introduction by Bayard Taylor. Illustrations. 12mo. New York, 1856.

Northern Travel: Summer and Winter Pictures: Sweden, Norway, Lapland. 12mo. New York, 1858.

Travels in Greece and Russia: with an Excursion to Crete. 12mo. New York, 1859.

At Home and Abroad: a Sketch-Book of Life, Scenery and Men. 12mo. New York, 1859.

At Home and Abroad. Second Series. 12mo. New York, 1862.

The Poet's Journal. 12mo. Boston, 1863.

Hannah Thurston. A Story of American Life. 12mo. New York, 1863.

John Godfrey's Fortunes; related by Himself. 12mo. New York, 1864.

Poems. Portrait. 24mo. Boston, 1865.

The Story of Kennett. 12mo. New York, 1866.

The Picture of St. John. 12mo. Boston, 1866.

Colorado: a Summer Idyl. 12mo. New York, 1867.

(Edited.) Frithiof's Saga. Translated from the Swedish of Esaias Tegner, by W. L. Blackley. 16mo. New York, 1867.

By-Ways of Europe. 12mo. New York, 1869.

Joseph and his Friend. A Story of Pennsylvania. 12mo. New York, 1870.

The Ballad of Abraham Lincoln. Illustrations by Eytinge. 4to. Boston, 1870.

(Translated.) Faust: a Tragedy, by Johann Wolfgang von Goethe. 2 volumes, royal 8vo. Boston, 1870–71.

The Masque of the Gods. 12mo. Boston, 1872.

Beauty and the Beast. 12mo. New York, 1872.

(Edited.) Illustrated Library of Travel, Exploration and Adventure. Illustrations. 8 volumes, 12mo. New York, 1872–74.
*.*Japan in our Day; Wild Men and Wild Beasts; Travels in Arabia; Travels in South Africa; Wonders of the Yellowstone; The Lake Regions of Central Africa; Central Asia; Siam, the Land of the White Elephant, as it was and is.

Lars: a Pastoral of Norway. 12mo. Boston, 1873.

A School History of Germany to 1871. Illustrations. 12mo. New York, 1874.

Egypt and Iceland in the Year 1874. 16mo. New York, 1874.

The Prophet. A Tragedy. 12mo. Boston, 1874.

Home Pastorals, Ballads and Lyrics. 12mo. Boston, 1875.

The Echo Club and other Literary Diversions. 18mo. Boston, 1876.

Boys of other Countries. Stories for American Boys. Illustrations. Square 12mo. New York, 1876.

The National Ode. July 4, 1876. [Facsimile of manuscript.] 4to. [Boston, 1876.]

The National Ode. Illustrations. 8vo. Boston, 1877.

Fitz-Greene Halleck Memorial .... Edited by E. A. Duycinck. [With addresses by Bayard Taylor and William Allen Butler.] Portrait. 8vo. New York, 1877.

Prince Deukalion. Square 8vo. Boston, 1878.

(Edited.) Picturesque Europe. A Delineation by Pen and Pencil of the Natural Features and the Picturesque and Historical Places of Great Britain and the Continent. Illustrations. 3 volumes, or 60 parts, 4to. New York [1878-80].

Studies in German Literature. With an Introduction by George H. Boker. 12mo. New York, 1879.

Poetical Works. Household Edition. 12mo. Boston, 1880.

Critical Essays and Literary Notes. 12mo. New York, 1880.

Dramatic Works. Edited, with Notes, by Marie Hansen-Taylor. 12mo. Boston, 1880.

Home Ballads. Illustrations. 8vo. Boston, 1882.

Life and Letters. Edited by Marie Hansen-Taylor and H. E. Scudder. Portrait and illustrations. 2 volumes, 12mo. Boston, 1884.

Melodies of Verse. 18mo. Boston, 1884.

Who was she? 18mo. Boston, 1884.
 *⁎*See also BRYANT, W. C.; HOLMES, O. W.; LOWELL, J. R.; STEDMAN, E. C.; STODDARD, R. H.; and WHITMAN, W.

THAXTER, CELIA. 1835-1894.

Poems. 18mo. New York, 1872.

Among the Isles of Shoals. 18mo. Boston, 1873.

Poems. New and Enlarged Edition. 18mo. Boston, 1874.

Drift-Weed. 18mo. Boston, 1879.

Poems for Children. Illustrations. 4to. Boston, 1884.

The Cruise of the Mystery and other Poems. 16mo. Boston, 1886.

Idyls and Pastorals. Illustrations. Square 8vo. Boston, [1886].
 *⁎*The same. Large paper. 4to. Boston [1886].

The Yule Log. Illustrations. 8vo. Boston, 1889.

An Island Garden. Illustrations. 8vo. Boston, 1894.

Letters. Edited by her Friends A[nnie] F[ields] and R. L. Portraits. 12mo. Boston, 1895.

Stories and Poems for Children. Frontispiece. 12mo. Boston, 1895.

THOMAS, EDITH MATILDA. 1854—

A New Year's Masque and other Poems. 16mo. Boston, 1885.

The Round Year. 16mo. Boston, 1886.

Lyrics and Sonnets. 16mo. Boston, 1887.

Children of the Seasons Series. Illustrations. 4 volumes, 12mo. New York, 1888.

Babes of the Year. Illustrations. 4to. New York, 1888.

Babes of the Nations. Illustrations. 4to. New York, 1889.

Héaven and Earth. Illustrations. Oblong 16mo. New York, 1889.

The Inverted Torch. 16mo. Boston, 1890.

Fair Shadow Land. 16mo. Boston, 1893.

In Sunshine Land. Illustrations. 16mo. Boston, 1895.

In the Young World. 16mo. Boston, 1895.

THOMAS, FREDERICK WILLIAM. 1808-1866.

The Emigrant; or Reflections when descending the Ohio: a Poem. 8vo. Cincinnati, 1833.

Clinton Bradshaw; or the Adventures of a Lawyer. 2 volumes, 12mo. Philadelphia, 1835.

[Anonymous.] East and West. A Novel. 2 volumes, 12mo. Philadelphia, 1836.

Howard Pinckney. A Novel. 2 volumes, 12mo. Philadelphia, 1840.

The Beechen Tree. A Tale told in Rhyme. 12mo. New York, 1844.

Clinton Bradshaw. A New Edition, corrected and revised by the Author. 8vo. Cincinnati, 1847.

Sketches of Character and Tales founded on Fact. 12mo. Louisville, 1849.

John Randolph of Roanoke, and other Sketches of Character including William Wirt, with Tales of Real Life. 8vo. Philadelphia, 1853.

THOMPSON, DANIEL PIERCE. 1795-1868.

(Edited.) The Laws of Vermont, 1824-34 inclusive, being a Continuation of Slade's Compilation. 8vo. Montpelier, 1835.

Adventures of Timothy Peacock, Esquire, or Freemasonry practically Illustrated. Comprising a Practical History of Masonry, exhibited in a Series of Amusing Adventures of a Masonic Quixot. By A Member of the Vermont Bar. Illustrations. 12mo. Middlebury, Vt., 1835.

May Martin, or, the Money-Diggers, a Green Mountain Tale. 12mo. Burlington, Vt., 1835.

The Green Mountain Boys. A Historical Tale of the Early Settlement of Vermont. 2 volumes, 12mo. Montpelier, Vt., 1840.
***The same. Revised edition. 12mo. Boston, 1848.

Locke Amsden, or, the School-Master: a Tale. 12mo. Boston, 1845.

Lucy Hosmer; or the Guardian and the Ghost. 12mo. Boston, 1848.

An Address pronounced before the Vermont Historical Society. 8vo. Burlington, 1850.

The Rangers; or, the Tory's Daughter. A Tale Illustrative of the Revolutionary History of Vermont, and the Northern Campaign of 1777. 2 volumes, 16mo. Boston, 1851.

May Martin, and other Tales of the Green Mountains. 16mo. Boston, 1852.

Gaut Gurley; or, the Trappers of the Umbagog. A Tale of
Border Life. 12mo. Boston. 1857.

The Doomed Chief; or, Two Hundred Years ago. 16mo.
Philadelphia, 1860.

History of the Town of Montpelier, from the time it was First
chartered, in 1781, to the Year 1860. Together with Biographical Sketches of its Most Noted Deceased Citizens.
8vo. Montpelier, Vt., 1860.

Centeola; and other Tales. 16mo. New York, 1864.

THOMPSON, MAURICE. 1844 —

Hoosier Mosaics. 18mo. New York, 1875.

The Witchery of Archery. A Complete Manual. Illustrations. 16mo. New York, 1878.

(With W. H. Thompson.) How to train in Archery. Being
a Complete Study of the York Round.... Illustrations.
16mo. New York [1879].

[Anonymous.] A Tallahassee Girl. 16mo. Boston, 1882.

[Anonymous.] His Second Campaign. 16mo. Boston,
1883.

Songs of Fair Weather. 8vo. Boston, 1883.

At Love's Extremes. 12mo. New York [1885].

A Red-Headed Family [woodpeckers]. 16mo. New York
[1885].

By-Ways and Bird Notes. 12mo. New York, 1885.

The Boys' Book of Sports and Outdoor Life. Illustrations.
8vo. New York, 1886.

Fifteenth Report of the Geology and Natural History of
Indiana. Illustrations. 8vo. Indianapolis, 1886.

A Banker of Bankersville. 12mo. New York, 1886.

Sylvan Secrets in Bird-Songs and Books. 12mo. New York,
1887.

A Fortnight of Folly. A Novel. 16mo. New York, 1888.

The Story of Louisiana. Illustrations. 8vo. Boston [1888].

Poems. 12mo. Boston, 1892.

The King of Honey Island. Illustrations. 12mo. New York [1892].

The Ethics of Literary Art. 12mo. Hartford, 1893.

Lincoln's Grave. A Poem. (450 copies.) 16mo. Cambridge and Chicago, 1894.
  *₊*The same. Large paper. (50 copies.) 8vo. Cambridge, 1894.

The Ocala Boy: a Story of Florida, Town and Forest. Illustrations. 12mo. Boston, 1895.

THOMPSON, MORTIMER M. (Q. K. PHILANDER DOESTICKS). 1831-1865.

Doesticks: what he says. Illustrations 12mo. New York, 1855.

Plu-ri-bus-tah: a Song that's by no Author. Illustrations. 12mo. New York, 1856.

History and Records of the Elephant Club. Illustrations. 12mo. Philadelphia, 1856.

Nothing to Say: a Slight Slap at Mobocratic Snobbery. Illustrations. 12mo. New York, 1857.

The Witches of New York. 12mo. New York, 1859.

[Anonymous.] Great Auction Sale of Slaves at Savannah, Ga., March 2, 3, 1859. 24mo. New York [1859].

THOMSON, CHARLES WEST. 1798-1879.

The Limner. 12mo. Philadelphia, 1822.

The Phantom Barge, and other Poems. 12mo. Philadelphia, 1822.

Elliner, and other Poems. 12mo. Philadelphia, 1826.

The Sylph and other Poems. 18mo. Philadelphia, 1828.

The Uncertainty of Literary Fame. With Brooks' Address at Pennsylvania College, Gettysburg, Pa., Feb. 14, 1840. 8vo. Baltimore, 1840.

The Love of Home and other Poems. 12mo. Philadelphia, 1845.

THOREAU, HENRY DAVID. 1817-1862.

A Week on the Concord and Merrimack Rivers. 12mo. Boston, 1848.
*₊*Of the original edition of one thousand copies, published at the author's expense, all except about two hundred copies were, in 1853, returned to him as unsalable, and remained in his possession during his life, but after his death were purchased by Ticknor and Fields, who removed the original title page, and substituted one with their imprint, which designated this issue "second edition," and was dated 1862.
*₊*The same. New and Revised Edition. 12mo. Boston, 1868.

Walden; or, Life in the Woods. Vignette. 12mo. Boston, 1854.

Echoes of Harper's Ferry. [Edited by] James Redpath. 12mo. Boston, 1860.
*₊*Lecture, A Plea for Capt. John Brown, pp. 17-42, and address at Concord, December 2, 1859, pp. 439-445, by Thoreau; speeches by Emerson, at Tremont Temple, pp. 67-71, and at Salem, pp. 119-122; poem by Whittier, and his controversy thereon with William Lloyd Garrison, pp. 303-315; and memorial tributes by Howells, M. D. Conway, Louisa M. Alcott and others.

Excursions. [Edited, with biographical sketch, by R. W. Emerson.] 12mo. Boston, 1863.

The Maine Woods. 12mo. Boston, 1863.

Cape Cod. [Edited by Sophia Thoreau and W. E. Channing.] 12mo. Boston, 1865.

Letters to Various Persons [also poems]. [With prefatory note by R. W. Emerson.] 12mo. Boston, 1865.

A Yankee in Canada, with Anti-Slavery and Reform Papers. [Edited by Sophia Thoreau and W. E. Channing.] 12mo. Boston, 1866.

Early Spring in Massachusetts; from the Journal of Henry D. Thoreau. [Edited, with introductory chapter, by H. G. O. Blake.] 12mo. Boston, 1881.

Summer: from the Journal of H. D. Thoreau. Edited by H. G. O. Blake. Map. 12mo. Boston, 1884.

Winter: from the Journal of H. D. Thoreau. Edited by H. G. O. Blake. 12mo. Boston, 1888.

Thoreau's Thoughts. Selections from the Writings. . . . Edited by H. G. O. Blake. With Bibliography. 16mo. Boston, 1890.

Autumn: from the Journal of H. D. Thoreau. Edited by H. G. O. Blake. 12mo. Boston, 1892.

Miscellanies. With a Biographical Sketch by R. W. Emerson. 12mo. Boston, 1894.

Works. Riverside Edition. Portraits. 10 volumes, 12mo. Boston, 1894.
*.*The same. Large paper. (150 copies.) 10 volumes, 8vo. Cambridge, 1894.
*.*i., A Week on the Concord and Merrimack Rivers; ii., Walden; iii., The Maine Woods; iv., Cape Cod; v., Early Spring; vi., Summer; vii., Autumn; viii., Winter; ix., Excursions; x., Miscellanies (with index to the ten volumes).

Familiar Letters of H. D. Thoreau. Edited with an Introduction and Notes by Frank B. Sanborn; with a Full Index [to Riverside edition of Works, including Letters]. Portrait. 12mo. Boston, 1894.
*.*The same. Large paper. (150 copies.) 8vo. Cambridge, 1894.

Poems of Nature. Selected and edited by H. S. Salt and F. B. Sanborn. 16mo. London, 1895.
*.*See also HAWTHORNE, NATHANIEL.

THORPE, THOMAS BANGS. 1815-1878.

(With others.) The Big Bear of Arkansaw, and other Tales, by Various Authors. Edited by W. T. Porter. 12mo. Philadelphia, 1835.

Legends of a Log Cabin. By A Western Man. 12mo. New York, 1836.

[Anonymous.] Life on the Lakes, being Tales and Sketches collected during a Trip to the Pictured Rocks of Lake Superior. Illustrations. 2 volumes, 12mo. New York, 1839.

The Mysteries of the Backwoods; or, Sketches of the Southwest. Illustrations by Darley. 12mo. Philadelphia, 1846.

Our Army on the Rio Grande. With Descriptions of the Battles of Palo Alto and Resaca de la Palma. . . . Illustrations. 12mo. Philadelphia, 1846.

Our Army at Monterey. . . . 12mo. Philadelphia, 1847.

The Hive of the Beehunter. .A Repository of Sketches including Peculiar American Character, Scenery and Rural Sports. Illustrations. 12mo. New York, 1854.

Lynde Weiss: an Autobiography. 12mo. Philadelphia, 1854.

A Voice to America, the Model Republic; its Glory or its Fall. 8vo. New York, 1855.

Scenes in Arkansaw . . . . with J. M. Field's Night in a Swamp and other Stories. 12mo. New York, 1859.

Reminiscences of Charles L. Elliott, Artist. 8vo. [New York, 1868.]

TICKNOR, GEORGE. 1791-1871.

Syllabus of Lectures on the History and Criticism of Spanish Literature. 8vo. Cambridge, 1823.

[Anonymous.] Outlines of the Principal Events in the Life of General Lafayette. From The North American Review [with alterations and additions]. 8vo. Boston, 1825.

Remarks on Changes lately proposed or adopted, in Harvard University. 8vo. [Boston] 1825.

Report on the United States Military Academy at West-Point, for 1826. 8vo. [Boston, 1826.]

The Remains of Nathaniel Appleton Haven. With a Memoir of his Life. (Privately printed.) 8vo. [Cambridge] 1827.

Remarks on the Life and Writings of Daniel Webster. 8vo. Philadelphia, 1831.

A Lecture on the Best Methods of teaching the Living Languages. Delivered before the American Institute of Education, Aug. 24, 1832. 8vo. Boston, 1833.

Review [signed G. T.] of Memoirs of the Rev. Joseph Buckminister and the Rev. Joseph Stevens Buckminister [by Eliza S. Lee]. 8vo. Cambridge, 1849.

History of Spanish Literature. 3 volumes, 8vo. New York, 1849.

[Anonymous.] Union of the Boston Athenæum and the Public Library. Republished from Boston Advertiser, March 14, 1853. 8vo. [Boston, 1853.]

History of Spanish Literature. Third American Edition, corrected and enlarged. 3 volumes, 12mo. Boston, 1863.
  *.*The same. Large paper. (100 copies.) 3 volumes, 8vo. Boston, 1866.

Life of William Hickling Prescott. Illustrations, including 2 portraits. Square 8vo. Boston, 1864.
  *.*The same. Large paper. (100 numbered copies.) 4to. Boston, 1864.
  *.*Issued also 12mo. and 8vo. Boston, 1864.

Remarks on the Character of Edward Everett, made at a Meeting of the Massachusetts Historical Society, Jan. 30, 1865. 8vo. Boston, 1865.

Life, Letters and Journals of George Ticknor. [Prepared by G. S. Hillard, with Mrs. and Miss Ticknor.] Portrait and plate. 2 volumes, 8vo. Boston, 1876.

TIMROD, HENRY. 1829-1867.

Poems. 12mo. Boston, 1860.

Poems. Edited, with Memoir, by Paul Hamilton Hayne. 12mo. New York, 1873.

TORREY, BRADFORD. 1843—

Birds in the Bush. 16mo. Boston, 1885.

A Rambler's Lease. 16mo. Boston, 1889.

The Foot-Path Way. 16mo. Boston, 1892.
  *.*In a few of the first copies issued the title of the book is given on page 1, as "June and December."

A Florida Sketch-Book. 16mo. Boston, 1894.

TUCKERMAN, HENRY THEODORE. 1813-1871.

    The Italian Sketch Book. By An American. 12mo. Philadelphia, 1835.

    (Edited, anonymously.) The Boston Book. Being Specimens of Metropolitan Literature. 12mo. Boston, 1836.

    (Edited.) The Philadelphia Book, or Specimens of Metropolitan Literature. 12mo. Philadelphia, 1836.

    Isabel; or Sicily: a Pilgrimage. 12mo. Philadelphia, 1839. ***Republished as Sicily and Pilgrimage. 12mo. New York, 1852.

    Rambles and Reveries. 12mo. New York, 1841.

    Thoughts on the Poets. 16mo. New York, 1846.

    Artist Life; or, Sketches of American Painters. 12mo. New York, 1847.

    The Italian Sketch-Book. Second Edition, with Additions. 12mo. New York, 1848.

    Characteristics of Literature. Illustrated by the Genius of Distinguished Men. 12mo. Philadelphia, 1849.

    The Optimist. 12mo. New York, 1850.

    The Life of Silas Talbot, a Commodore in the Navy of the United States. 12mo. New York, 1850.

    Characteristics of Literature. Second Series. 12mo. Philadelphia, 1851.

    Poems. 12mo. Boston, 1851.

    Outlines of English Literature by Thomas B. Shaw. With a Sketch of American Literature by Henry T. Tuckerman. 12mo. Philadelphia, 1852.

    A Memorial of Horatio Greenough; consisting of a Memoir, Selections from his Writings, and Tributes to his Genius. 12mo. New York, 1853.

    [Anonymous.] Leaves from the Diary of a Dreamer. 16mo. London, 1853.

    Mental Portraits; or, Studies of Character. 12mo. London, 1853.

A Month in England. 12mo. New York, 1853.

[Anonymous.] A Memorial of the Life and Character of John W. Francis, Jr. Portrait. (Privately printed.) 8vo. New York, 1855.
   ***In the reprint of this work, also dated 1855, the author's name appears on title page.

Essays, Biographical and Critical; or, Studies of Character. 8vo. Boston, 1857.

Art in America. Its History, Condition and Prospects. Reprinted from the Cosmopolitan Art Journal. 8vo. Macao, 1858.

The Character and Portraits of Washington, illustrated with all the Prominent Portraits [12]; Proofs on India Paper. (150 copies.) 4to. New York, 1859.

The Rebellion: its Latent Causes, and True Significance; in Letters to a Friend Abroad. 12mo. New York, 1861.

A Sheaf of Verse, bound for the [Sanitary Commission] Fair. 16mo. New York, 1864.

America and her Commentators; with a Critical Sketch of Travel in the United States. 12mo. New York, 1864.

Old New York; or Reminiscences of the Past Sixty Years, by the Late John W. Francis, M.D., LL.D. With a Memoir of the Author by H. T. Tuckerman. Portrait. (100 copies.) 4to. New York, 1865.
   ***Reissued, 8vo. New York, 1866.

The Criterion; or, the Test of Talk about Familiar Things. 16mo. New York, 1866.

The Book of the Artists. American Artist Life, comprising Biographical and Critical Sketches of American Artists: preceded by an Historical Account of the Rise and Progress of Art in America. With an Appendix containing an Account of Notable Pictures and Private Collections. Portrait. 8vo. New York, 1867.
   ***The same. Large paper. (150 copies.) India proof portrait. Royal 8vo. New York, 1867.
   ***The same, with 30 photographic portraits. Largest paper. (25 copies.) 4to. New York, 1867.

Maga Papers about Paris; with an Appendix containing a Report on the Great Exposition of 1867. 16mo. New York, 1867.

The Collector: Essays on Books, Authors, Newspapers, Pictures, Inns, Doctors and Holidays. With an Introduction by Dr. Doran. 12mo. London [1868].

(Edited, with William Smith.) A Smaller History of English and American Literature for the Use of Schools. 12mo. New York, 1870.

The Life of John Pendleton Kennedy. Portrait. 12mo. New York, 1871.

TUDOR, WILLIAM. 1779-1830.

An Oration pronounced July 4, 1809. 8vo. Boston, 1809.

Address before the Phi Beta Kappa Society of Harvard University. 8vo. Boston, 1810.

Address before the Phi Beta Kappa Society of Harvard University. 8vo. Boston, 1815.

Discourse before the Humane Society. 8vo. Boston, 1817.

[Anonymous.] Letters on the Eastern States. 12mo. New York, 1820.

Miscellanies. 12mo. Boston, 1821.

Life of James Otis, of Massachusetts, containing also, Notices of some Contemporary Characters and Events from 1760 to 1775. Portrait and plate. 8vo. Boston, 1823.

[Anonymous.] Gebel Teir. 12mo. Boston, 1829.

VERY, JONES. 1813-1880.

Essays and Poems. [Edited by Ralph W. Emerson.] 16mo. Boston, 1839.

Poems [including 73 now first collected]. With an Introductory Memoir by W. P. Andrews. 16mo. Boston, 1883.

Poems and Essays. Complete and Revised Edition [including 438 poems now first collected]. With a Biographical Sketch by James Freeman Clarke and a Preface by C. A. Bartol. Portrait. 12mo. Boston, 1886.

WALLACE, LEW[IS]. 1827—

    The Fair God ; or, the Last of the 'Tzins : a Tale of the Conquest of Mexico. 12mo. Boston, 1873.

    Ben-Hur. A Tale of the Christ. 12mo. New York, 1880.

    Life of General Ben. Harrison. [With Life of Levi P. Morton, by George A. Townsend.] Portraits. 12mo. Philadelphia [1888].

    The Boyhood of Christ. Illustrations. Square 8vo. New York, 1889.

    Ben-Hur. Garfield Edition. Illustrations. 2 volumes, 8vo. New York, 1893.
        *.*The same. Edition de Luxe. (350 copies.) 2 volumes, 8vo. New York, 1893.

    The Prince of India ; or, why Constantinople fell. 2 volumes, 16mo. New York, 1893.

    Constantinople, by Edwin A. Grosvenor ; with an Introduction by Lew Wallace. 8vo. London, 1895.

WALLACE, WILLIAM ROSS. 1819-1881.

    The Battle of Tippecanoe . . . . 12mo. Cincinnati, 1837.

    Wordsworth. 12mo. New York, 1846.

    Alban, the Pirate. A Poetical Romance. 12mo. New York, 1848.

    Meditations in America, and other Poems. 12mo New York, 1851.

    (Edited.) Beadle's Dime Military Song-Book. 12mo. New York, 1861.

    Keep Step with the Music of the Union. With Music by George F..Bristow. 4to. New York, 1861.

    The Liberty Bell. Illustrations. 4to. New York, 1862.

WARD, THOMAS. 1807-1873.

    A Month of Freedom. 12mo. New York, 1837.

    Passaic, a Group of Poems touching that River : with other Musings, by Flaccus. 12mo. New York, 1842.

Flora, or the Gipsy's Frolic; a Pastoral Poem in Three Acts. 8vo. New York, 1858.

War Lyrics. (Privately printed.) 12mo. New York, 1865.

Proceedings Commemorative of the Settlement of Newark, N. J., on its 200th Anniversary, May 17th, 1866 [including poem for the occasion, by Ward]. Plate. 8vo. Newark, 1866.

Address before the New York Society Library on the 100th Anniversary of its Incorporation, November 9th, 1872. 8vo. New York, 1872.

WARE, WILLIAM. 1797-1852.

Sermon on the Communion. 8vo. New York, 1825.

Sermons Illustrative of Unitarian Christianity. 8vo. Utica, 1828.

[Anonymous.] Zenobia: or the Fall of Palmyra. An Historical Romance. In Letters of Lucius M. Piso from Palmyra, to his Friend Marcus Curtius at Rome. 2 volumes, 12mo. New York, 1837.
  . Also. 2 volumes, 12mo. London, 1838.

[Anonymous.] Probus: or Rome in the Third Century. In Letters from Lucius M. Piso from Rome, to Fausta, the Daughter of Gracchus at Palmyra. 2 volumes, 12mo. New York, 1838.
  . In later editions the title of this work reads "Aurelian; or, Rome in the Third Century." .

Julian; or Scenes in Judea. 2 volumes, 12mo. New York, 1841.

(Edited.) American Unitarian Biography. Memoirs of Individuals who have been distinguished by their Writings, Character and Efforts in the Cause of Liberal Christianity. Portraits. 2 volumes, 12mo. Boston, 1850-51.

Sketches of European Capitals. 12mo. Boston, 1851.

Lectures on the Works and Genius of Washington Allston. 12mo. Boston, 1852.

Unitarianism the Doctrine of Matthew's Gospel. 12mo. Boston, 1855.

WARFIELD, CATHERINE ANNE. 1816-1877.

The Household of Bouverie; or the Elixir of Gold: a Romance. By A Southern Lady. 2 volumes, 12mo. New York, 1860.

The Romance of the Great Seal. 8vo. New York, 1867.

Miriam Monfort; or Monfort Hall. 12mo. Philadelphia, 1873.

The Romance of Beauseincourt. 12mo. New York, 1874.

Hester Howard's Temptation. 12mo. Philadelphia, 1875.

Lady Ernestine. 12mo. Philadelphia, 1876.

Sea and Shore. 12mo. Philadelphia, 1876.

Ferne Fleming. 12mo. Philadelphia, 1877.

The Cardinal's Daughter: a Sequel to Ferne Fleming. 12mo. Philadelphia, 1877.

WARNER, CHARLES DUDLEY. 1829 —

(Edited.) The Book of Eloquence. 12mo. Cazenovia, N. Y., 1851.

My Summer in a Garden. 16mo. Boston, 1871.
 *.*The same, with illustrations by Darley. Square 16mo. Boston, 1872.

Saunterings. 16mo. Boston, 1872.
 *.*Also issued 18mo. Boston, 1872.

Backlog Studies. 21 illustrations. Square 16mo. Boston, 1873.

Baddeck, and that Sort of Thing. 18mo. Boston, 1874.

Mummies and Moslems. Frontispiece. 8vo. Hartford, 1876.
 *.*Republished as My Winter on the Nile. Illustrations. 8vo. Boston, 1876.

In the Levant. 12mo. Boston, 1877.

Being a Boy. Illustrations. Square 16mo. Boston, 1878.

In the Wilderness. 18mo. Boston, 1878.

(With W. C. Bryant and Geo. P. Putnam.) Studies of Irving. Square 8vo. New York, 1880.

The American Newspaper. An Essay. 32mo. Boston, 1881.

Washington Irving. Portrait. 12mo. Boston, 1881.

(Edited.) American Men of Letters. Portraits. 12mo. Boston, 1881.
. Of this series Washington Irving was the initial volume; the thirteenth volume, George William Curtis, by Edward Cary, appeared in 1894.

Captain John Smith, sometime Governor of Virginia, and Admiral of New England. A Study of his Life and Writings. 16mo. New York, 1881.

The Work laid upon the Southern College. An Address before the Literary Societies of Roanoke College, Salem, Va., June 12, 1883. 8vo. [Salem, 1883.]

A Roundabout Journey. 12mo. Boston, 1884.

(With others.) Papers on Penology. 16mo. [Reformatory Press, Elmira, N.Y., 1886.]

Their Pilgrimage. Illustrations. 12mo. New York, 1887.

On Horseback. A Tour in Virginia, North Carolina and Tennessee. With Notes of Travel in Mexico and California. 16mo. Boston, 1888.

Studies in the South and West with Comments on Canada. 12mo. New York, 1889.

A Little Journey in the World. A Novel. 12mo. New York, 1889.

Looking forward. The Dual Government realized. 8vo. [New York, 1890.]

Our Italy. Illustrations. 8vo. New York, 1891.

As we were saying. Portrait and illustrations. 16mo. New York, 1891.

Washington Irving. Illustrations. 32mo. New York, 1892.

The Work of Washington Irving. 4 portraits. 32mo. New York, 1893.

As we go. Portrait and illustrations. 16mo. New York, 1894.

Bryant Centennial, Cummington, August 16, 1894. [Address by Warner, pp. 56-58, letter from O. W. Holmes and poem by Julia Ward Howe.] Portraits. 8vo. [Springfield, 1894.]

The Golden House. A Novel. Illustrations. 12mo. New York, 1895.
  *_{*}*See also CLEMENS, S. L.

WARNER, SUSAN (ELIZABETH WETHERELL.). 1819-1885.

The Wide, Wide World. 2 volumes, 12mo. New York, 1850.

Queechy. 2 volumes, 12mo. New York, 1852.

American Female Patriotism. 32mo. New York, 1852.

The Law and the Testimony. 8vo. New York, 1853.

The Hills of the Shatemuc. 12mo. New York, 1856.

The Old Helmet. 2 volumes, 12mo. London, 1863.

Melbourne House. 12mo. New York, 1864.
  *_{*}*Miss Warner was also author of numerous devotional and juvenile publications.

WENDELL, BARRETT. 1855—

The Duchess Emilia, a Romance. 12mo. Boston, 1885.

Rankell's Remains. An American Novel. 12mo. Boston, 1886.

English Composition. Eight Lectures given at the Lowell Institute. 12mo. New York, 1891.

Cotton Mather: the Puritan Priest. Portrait. 12mo. New York [1891].

Were the Salem Witches Guiltless? An Address delivered before the Essex Institute, Feb. 19, 1892. 8vo. Salem, 1892.

Stelligeri and other Essays concerning America. 16mo. New York, 1893.

William Shakspere. A Study in Elizabethan Literature. 12mo. New York, 1894.

WHIPPLE, EDWIN PERCY. 1819-1886.

    Essays and Reviews. 2 volumes, 12mo. Boston, 1848-49.

    Lectures on Subjects connected with Literature and Life. 12mo. Boston, 1849.

    Washington and the Principles of the Revolution. An Oration . . . . Boston, July 4, 1850. 8vo. Boston, 1850.

    Character and Characteristic Men. 16mo. Boston, 1866.

    Eulogy on John Albion Andrew. With an Appendix containing the Proceedings of the City Council . . . . [etc.]. 8vo. Boston, 1867.

    The Literature of the Age of Elizabeth. 16mo. Boston, 1869.

    Success and its Conditions. 12mo. Boston, 1871.

    (Edited, with memoir.) Christianity and Humanity. Sermons by Thomas Starr King. Portrait. 12mo. Boston, 1877.

    (Edited, with introduction.) Substance and Shadow and other Papers, by Thomas Starr King. 12mo. Boston, 1877.

    [Anonymous.] The Character and Genius of Thomas Starr King. 8vo. [Boston, 1878.]

    Some Recollections of Rufus Choate. 32mo. New York, 1879.

    (Edited.) The Great Speeches and Orations of Daniel Webster, with an Essay on Webster as a Master of English Style. Portraits. 8vo. Boston, 1880.

    A Memorial of Elliot C. Cowdin. Portrait. (Privately printed.) Small 4to. [Boston, 1881.]
        *⁎*Consisting of memoir by Whipple; address of Dr. Bellows, and tributes.

    Memorial of Mr. and Mrs. Charles Russell, of Princeton, Mass. (Privately printed.) 8vo. [Boston] 1886.

    Recollections of Eminent Men: with other Papers. With Introduction by C. A. Bartol. Portrait. 12mo. Boston, 1887.

American Literature, and other Papers. With Introductory Note by J. G. Whittier. Small 8vo. Boston, 1887.

Outlooks on Society, Literature and Politics. 12mo. Boston, 1888.

*_{*}*See also ALDRICH, T. B.; and FIELDS, J. T.

WHITE, RICHARD GRANT. 1821–1885.

A Tale of the Hospital. 8vo. New York, 1840.

(Edited.) The Alleghanian: a Weekly Publication. Nos. 5–9, inclusive. 5 numbers, 4to. New York, 1845.

Appeal from the Bishop of New York. 8vo. New York, 1845.

A Companion to the Gallery of Paintings by the Old Masters exhibited at the New York Lyceum. 8vo. New York, 1850.

A Companion to the Bryant Gallery of Christian Art, containing Critical Descriptions of the Pictures and Biographical Sketches of the Painters, with an Introductory Essay and an Index. 8vo. New York, 1853.

*_{*}*The same. Large paper. Royal 8vo. New York, 1853.

Shakespeare's Scholar: being Historical and Critical Studies of his Text, Characters and Commentators, with an Examination of Mr. Collier's Folio of 1632. 8vo. New York, 1854.

(Edited.) The Works of William Shakespeare. The Plays edited from the Folio of 1623, with Various Readings from all the Editions and all the Commentators; Notes, Introductory Remarks, a Historical Sketch of the Text, an Account of the Rise and Progress of the English Drama, a Memoir of the Poet, and an Essay upon his Genius. 12 volumes, 12mo. Boston, 1857–65.

*_{*}*The same. Large paper. 12 volumes, small 8vo. Boston, 1857–65.

*_{*}*The same. Largest paper. (48 copies.) 12 volumes, 8vo. Boston, 1857–65.

*_{*}*Comedies: ii., iii., iv., v., 1857; Histories: vi., vii., viii., 1859; Tragedies: ix., x., xi., xii., 1859; Preface, Notes, Memoirs and Poems: i., 1865.

An Essay on the Authorship of the Three Parts of King Henry the Sixth. (Privately printed; 25 copies.) 8vo. Cambridge, 1859.

Historical Sketches of the Text and Notes, and Comments from Shakespeare's Scholar. Royal 8vo. London, 1859.
***An unauthorised reprint of Shakespeare's Scholar, which was suppressed soon after publication.

National Hymns: how they are written and how they are not written. A Lyric and National Study for the Times. 8vo. New York, 1861.
***The same. With appendix containing a letter to The Saturday Review, and leader from The World, January 5, 1861. (Privately printed, on tinted paper; 30 copies.) 12mo. New York, 1862.

The Book-Hunter, by John Hill Burton. Edited with Additional Notes and Preface by R. G. White. (500 copies.) 12mo. New York, 1863.
***A note by Mr. White, in the sale catalogue of his library, New York, 1870, disclaims all editorial connection with this publication, as well as all responsibility for its index—the additional notes being the only portion of the work which he admits as his. George P. Philes' scathing criticism in The Philobiblion (New York, 1863) may, to some extent, have caused this repudiation of editorial responsibility.

[Anonymous.] The New Gospel of Peace according to St. Benjamin [in four books]. 4 parts, 12mo. New York, 1863–66.
***Book 1st was published July 27th, 1863; book 2nd, Oct. 24th, 1863; book 3rd, July 22, 1864; book 4th, May 19th, 1866.
***The same. Complete edition, with introduction containing two letters by the author. 12mo. New York, 1866.

Revelations: a Companion to The New Gospel of Peace. According to St. Abraham. 2 parts, 12mo. New York, 1863–64.

Memoirs of Shakespeare, an Account of the English Stage, an Essay on Shakespeare's Genius, with an Historical Sketch of his Text. (Privately printed.) 8vo. Cambridge, 1865.
***This work consists of the critical and historical portions of the author's edition of Shakespeare's works, the original pagination of which is retained. Only two copies were issued in this form, one of which was specially prepared for the Shakespearian collection of Thomas P. Barton; the other was retained by the author.

Memoirs of the Life of William Shakespeare, with an Essay towards the Expression of his Genius and an Account of the Rise and Progress of the English Drama to the Time of Shakespeare. 12mo. Boston, 1865.
***The same. Large paper. (100 copies.) 8vo. Boston, 1865.

(Edited.) Poetry; Lyrical, Narrative and Satirical of the Civil War. 12mo. New York, 1866.

[Anonymous.] The Adventures of Sir Lyon Bouse, Bart., in America, during the Civil War. Being Extracts from his Diary. 12mo. New York, 1867.
*₄*The original wrapper bears the inscription "By The Author of the New Gospel of Peace," which is omitted from title page.

Catalogue of a Collection of Books mostly printed in London and on the Continent of Europe, the Greater Part of which are in Fine Condition and a Large Number of which are bound by the Best Binders, forming the Library of Richard Grant White, to be sold at Auction on the 24th of October and following Evenings. [Compiled, with advertisement and numerous characteristic and interesting notes, by R. G. White.] 8vo. New York, 1870.
*₄*The same. Fine paper edition, with altered title. (25 copies.) 8vo. New York, 1870.

Words and their Uses, Past and Present. A Study of the English Language. 12mo. New York, 1870.

The Fall of Man: or, the Loves of the Gorillas. A Popular Lecture upon the Darwinian Theory of Development by Sexual Selection. By A Learned Gorilla. Illustrations. 12mo. New York, 1871.

The Life of Pauline Markham. Written by Herself. Portrait. 18mo. New York, 1871.
*₄*Credited to Mr. White—but without absolute certainty.

The Chronicles of Gotham. 2 volumes, 12mo. New York, 1871–72.

The Confessions of William Henry Ireland containing the Particulars of his Fabrication of the Shakespeare Manuscripts. . . . A New Edition. With an Introduction by R. G. White and Additional Facsimiles. 16mo. New York, 1874.

The American View of the Copyright Question. Reprinted from The Broadway Magazine, May, 1868. With a Postscript. 12mo. New York, 1880.

Every-Day English: a Sequel to Words and their Uses. 12mo. Boston, 1880.

England Without and Within. 12mo. Boston, 1881.

The Dramatic Works of Richard Brinsley Sheridan. With an Introduction by R. G. White. Portraits. (318 copies.) 3 volumes, 8vo. New York [1883].

Selections from the Poetry of Robert Browning. With an Introduction by R. G. White. Portrait. 8vo. New York [1883].
*₀*The same. Printed throughout on Japan paper. (70 copies.) 8vo. New York [1883].

The Fate of Mr. Mansfield Humphreys ; with The Episode of Mr. Washington Adams in England, and An Apology. 12mo. Boston, 1884.

A Grammar of the Grammarless Tongue. [An unauthorized reprint from Words and their Uses.] 8vo. New York, 1884.

Studies in Shakespeare. 12mo. Boston, 1886.

WHITMAN, SARAH HELEN. 1803-1878.

Poem, recited before the Rhode Island Historical Society, ... January 13, 1847 .... 8vo. [Providence, 1847.]

Hours of Life and other Poems. 12mo. Providence, 1853.

Edgar Poe and his Critics. 12mo. New York, 1860.

Poems. [Complete edition.] Portrait. 12mo. Boston, 1879.
*₀*See also LOWELL, J. R.

WHITMAN, WALT[ER]. 1819-1892.

Franklin Evans, or the Inebriate : a Tale of the Times. Royal 8vo. New York, 1842.
*₀*Published as New World Extra Series ; No. 34.

Voices from the Press : a Collection of Sketches, Essays, and Poems, by Practical Printers [Walt Whitman, Woodworth, Willis, Bayard Taylor and others]. 8vo. New York, 1850.

Leaves of Grass. [Prose preface, 10 pp., and 12 poems.] Portrait. 4to. Brooklyn, N. Y., 1855.

Leaves of Grass. [32 poems.] Portrait. 16mo. New York, 1856.
***In this issue the preface of first edition is worked into four poems, By Blue Ontario's Shore, Song of the Answerer, To a foil'd European Revolutionaire, and Song of Prudence. Owing to the storm of criticism which arose against it, the New York publishers withdrew from its publication, and it was issued by the author, with imprint, Brooklyn, N. Y., 1856.

Leaves of Grass. [154 poems.] Portrait, now first published. 12mo. Boston. Year 85 of the States. 1860–61.
***Business conditions, resulting from the Civil War, having caused the failure of the publishers, Thayer & Eldridge, the plates of this edition were sold at auction to an unscrupulous publisher who, for many years, printed from them, retaining the imprint and date of the Thayer edition. The plates were some years since purchased by the author's literary executors.

Drum-Taps. 12mo. New York, 1865.
***Owing to the death of President Lincoln the author delayed the publication of this volume, of which some copies were bound at the time, until a few weeks later, when he added When Lilacs Last in the Door-Yard bloomed; O Captain, my Captain; and a few other poems, which were added (with pagination distinct from that of the original collection) after page 72 as, Sequel to Drum-Taps (since the Preceding came from the Press). When Lilacs Last in the Door-Yard bloomed, and other Pieces. Washington, 1865-6.

Leaves of Grass. 12mo. New York, 1867.
***In this edition the poems are re-arranged, and many are published for the first time. The later issues included Drum-Taps (omitted at first), also Sequel to Drum-Taps, and Songs before Parting.

Selections from Leaves of Grass. Edited by W. M. Rossetti. 12mo. London, 1868.

Leaves of Grass [including poems now first published]. 12mo. Washington, D. C., 1871.

[Anonymous.] Passage to India. 12mo. Washington, D. C., 1871.

Democratic Vistas. 12mo. Washington, D. C., 1871.

After all not to create only. Recited .... New York, September 7, 1871. 12mo. Boston, 1871.

As a Strong Bird on Pinions Free and other Poems. 12mo. Washington, D. C., 1872.

Memoranda during the War. 12mo. Camden, N. J., 1875

Leaves of Grass. [288 poems.] Author's Edition, with Portrait from Life. 12mo. Camden, N. J., 1876.

Two Rivulets, including Democratic Vistas, Centennial Songs, and Passage to India. Author's Edition. 12mo. Camden, N. J., 1876.
*₊*The two preceding volumes were printed from the plates of the 1871 editions, with the addition of Memoranda during the War, Two Rivulets, and other matter.

Leaves of Grass. [293 poems.] 12mo. Boston, 1881.
*₊*On this edition being suppressed by District Attorney Stevens of Massachusetts, the plates were taken over by the author, who printed from them without alteration, except that of publisher's imprint, Leaves of Grass. Author's Edition. 12mo. Camden, N. J. The Philadelphia editions of 1882-83 (Rees, Welsh & Co.), and 1884 (David McKay), were printed from the same plates.

Specimen Days and Collect. 12mo. Philadelphia, 1882-83.
*₊*This edition contains such of the author's prose writings to date, as he desired to retain.

Elegiac Ode, the Words from President Lincoln's Burial Hymn, the Music by C. V. Stanford. Royal 8vo. London, 1884.

Leaves of Grass. Poems .... selected by Ernest Rhys. 18mo. London, 1886.

Specimen Days in America. Newly revised by the Author with Fresh Preface and Additional Notes. 16mo. London, 1887.

November Boughs. 12mo. Philadelphia, 1888.

Complete Poems and Prose. 1855-1888. Portraits and autograph. (600 copies.) Royal 8vo. Philadelphia, 1888.

Democratic Vistas and other Papers. [Published by arrangement with the author.] 16mo. London, 1888.

Leaves of Grass, with Sands at Seventy, and A Backward Glance o'er Travelled Roads. Portraits and autograph. (300 copies.) 8vo. Philadelphia, 1889.

Gems from Whitman. Selected by Elizabeth P. Gould. 12mo. Philadelphia, 1889.

Good-Bye, my Fancy. 2d Annex to Leaves of Grass. 12mo. Philadelphia, 1891.

Leaves of Grass; including Sands at Seventy, First Annex; Good-Bye, my Fancy, Second Annex; A Backward Glance, o'er Travelled Roads; and Portrait from Life. 8vo. Philadelphia, 1891–92.

Complete Prose Works. 8vo. Philadelphia, 1892.

Autobiographia, or the Story of a Life, selected from his Writings. By Arthur Stedman. Frontispiece. 12mo. New York, 1892.

Selected Poems. Edited by Arthur Stedman. 12mo. New York, 1892.

In re Walt Whitman: edited by his Literary Executors, H. L. Traubel, R. M. Bucke, T. B. Harned. (1,000 copies.) Royal 8vo. Philadelphia, 1893.
*₊*Contains original contributions by John Burroughs and others, together with articles by Whitman, including three on his poems published anonymously in 1855–56, and now first published under the author's name.
*₊*Whitman contributed to The New World, The Child's Champion, November 20, 1841. To The Democratic Review he contributed Death in the Schoolroom, August, 1841; Bervance, or, Father and Son, December, 1841; The Tomb Blossoms, January, 1842; The Last of the Sacred Army, March, 1842; The Child's Ghost, a Story of the Last Loyalist, May, 1842; The Angel of Tears, September, 1842; Revenge and Requital, a Tale of a Murder escaped, July, August, 1845; A Dialogue, November, 1845. To The Galaxy, December, 1867, and May, 1868, he contributed Democracy, and Personalism; to The North American Review, June, 1882, Memorandum at a Venture; and to Lippincott's Monthly Magazine, March, 1891, Old-Age Echoes, and Some Personal and Old-Age Memoranda, the latter including a letter from R. W. Emerson, dated 1855.
*₊*See also BURROUGHS, JOHN, and O'CONNOR, W. D.

WHITTIER, JOHN GREENLEAF. 1807–1892.

Incidental Poems, accompanied with Letters . . . . and a Sketch of the Author's Life. [Also a poetical address, J. G. Whittier to the Rustic Bard, not included in any edition of Whittier's poems.] By Robert Dinsmoor, the Rustic Bard 12mo. Haverhill, 1828.

Specimens of American Poetry [including The Sicilian Vespers, by Whittier], with Critical and Biographical Notices. By Samuel Kettell. 3 volumes, 12mo. Boston, 1829.

American Anecdotes, Original and Select [including The Spectre Ship of Salem, by Whittier]. By An American. 2 volumes, 12mo. Boston, 1830.

." An American " is stated by Sabin to have been Freeman Hunt, whilst Cushing credits the work to Lydia Maria Child.

Legends of New England. 12mo. Hartford, 1831.

The American Common-Place Book of Poetry: with occasional Notes, by George B. Cheever. 12mo. Boston, 1831.

. *.*This volume contains many of Whittier's early poems, (including the principal portion of The Minstrel Girl) now first collected, and of which only a few were retained in any edition of his poems.

[Anonymous.] Moll Pitcher, a Poem. 8vo. Boston, 1832.

Justice and Expediency; or Slavery considered with a View to its Rightful and Effectual Remedy, Abolition. (500 copies.) 8vo. Haverhill, 1833.

*.*Also reprinted for gratuitous distribution, by the Anti-Slavery Society of New York, 8vo. New York, 1833.

Mogg Megone, a Poem. 32mo. Boston, 1836.

The Laurel: a Gift for all Seasons. Being a Collection of Poems. By American Authors [Whittier, Holmes, Longfellow, and others]. 18mo. Boston, 1836.

*.*Besides two poems of this collection, bearing Whittier's name, A Love Letter, by J. G. W., is ascribed to him, by Charles A. Dana and others, but bears no trace of his style and cannot be accepted conclusively as his.

A Full Statement of the Reasons which were in Part offered to the Committee of the Legislature of Massachusetts on the Fourth and Eighth of March, showing why there should be no Penal Laws enacted, and no Condemnatory Resolutions passed by the Legislature, respecting Abolitioni[s]ts and Anti-Slavery Societies. 8vo. Boston, 1836.

*.*Containing Stanzas for the Times, pp. 46-48, by Whittier, reprinted from The Boston Courier.

Songs of the Free and Hymns of Christian Freedom [by Whittier, Garrison, Pierpont and others]. 16mo. Boston, 1836.

*.*Whittier's poems, Voice of New England, The Hunting of Men, and Our Countrymen in Chains are here first collected.

Views of Slavery and Emancipation; from Society in America. By Harriet Martineau. [With introduction by Whittier.] 16mo. New York, 1837.

Letters from John Quincy Adams to his Constituents of the Twelfth Congressional District in Massachusetts. To which is added his Last Speech in Congress .... [and two poems, Stanzas for the Times, and Lines written on the Passing of Mr. Pinckney's Resolutions, by Whittier]. 12mo. Boston, 1837.

Poems written during the Progress of the Abolition Question in the United States, between the years 1830 and 1838. 16mo. Boston, 1837.

[Anonymous.] Narrative of James Williams, an American Slave; who was for Several Years a Driver on a Cotton Plantation in Alabama. Portrait. 16mo. New York, 1838.
 *.*A copy of this work has recently been sold by Messrs. Bangs & Co., New York, for $111, and in connection therewith a statement is repeated, which was advanced in 1895, to the effect that Whittier's connection with the Narrative was never made public. This view is not supported by the fact that the Proceedings of the American Anti-Slavery Society, Third Decade, 1864 (which appears in its chronological arrangement in the present list), contains a catalogue of anti-slavery publications, 1750–1863, where the Narrative is described as "drawn up by J. G. Whittier;" and considering Whittier's devotion to, and labors in, the anti-slavery cause, the appearance of his name on the original board cover of the little volume would scarcely seem in keeping with the theory of rigid secrecy.

Address read at the Opening of the Pennsylvania Hall, on the 15th of Fifth Month, 1838. 8vo. Philadelphia, 1838.
 *.*Reprinted in History of Pennsylvania Hall, which was destroyed by a Mob, 17th May, 1838. Plates. 8vo. Philadelphia, 1838.

Poems. 12mo. Philadelphia, 1838.

Freedom's Lyre: or, Psalms, Hymns, and Sacred Songs for the Slave and his Friends. [By Whittier, Garrison, Tappan and others.] Compiled by E. F. Hatfield. 48mo New York, 1840.

Moll Pitcher and The Minstrel Girl. Poems. Revised Edition. 18mo. Philadelphia, 1840.

The North Star: the Poetry of Freedom, by her Friends. 18mo. Philadelphia. 1840.
⁂ Edited, anonymously, by Whittier, who, in addition to the prefatory note and poem, pp. v.-vii., contributed the poems, The Exiles—a Tale of New England, pp. 62-73, and The World's Convention, pp. 108-117, besides which the poem, Granada, pp. 105-107, is almost certainly his. Among the other contributors were his sister, Elizabeth H. Whittier, James T. Fields, John Pierpont, Hannah F. Gould and Elizabeth Lloyd, Jr., (afterwards Mrs. Howell) whose poem, Egypt, an Unfinished Fragment, pp. 86-101, was prepared for publication, with extensive alterations, by Whittier, to whom she was supposed betrothed.

The Anti-Slavery Picknick, or Speeches, Poems, Dialogues and Songs [by Whittier and others] for Use in Schools and Anti-Slavery Meetings. [Edited] By John Collins. 12mo. Boston, 1842.

A Visit to the United States in 1841. By Joseph Sturge. [Containing a historical sketch of the old-school abolitionists, and of the anti-slavery movement, pp. 21-23 and 187-192, also an article, on the destruction of Pennsylvania Hall, by Whittier.] 8vo. London, 1842.
⁂ Reprinted, 12mo. Boston, 1842.

Poetical Remains of the Late Lucy Hooper, collected and arranged; with a Memoir by John Keese [and memorial poem, pp. 31-34, by Whittier]. 12mo. New York, 1842.

Lays of my Home and other Poems. 16mo. Boston, 1843.

The Liberty Minstrel. [Consisting of anti-slavery poems by Whittier, Lowell, Longfellow, and others. Edited, and set to music,] By Geo. W. Clark. 16mo. New York, 1844.

[Anonymous.] The Stranger in Lowell. 12mo. Boston, 1845.

Voices of Freedom. Fourth [fifth, seventh, etc.,] Complete Edition. 12mo. Philadelphia, 1846.
⁂ All copies known bear some such indication of edition as here given, which can be accepted as nothing more than a desire, on the publisher's part, to stimulate a demand for the publication. The dates appended to some of the poems seem sufficient to prove the improbability of any such conclusion as the inscription quoted may suggest.

Memoir of Rev. Charles T. Torrey . . . . by J. C. Lovejoy. [Containing tribute by Whittier, pp. 298–299, reprinted from The Essex Transcript.] Portrait. 12mo. Boston, 1847.

The Supernaturalism of New England. 12mo. New York, 1847.

Sketch of Daniel O'Connell. 8vo. [Boston, 1847.]
  ***Originally published in The Pennsylvania Freeman, April 25, 1839, as a reply to an attack made upon O'Connell, in the United States Senate, by Henry Clay, in a speech on the slavery question.

American Free Soil Almanac for 1849. [Containing Free Soil Pæan, pp. 22–23, by Whittier.] 12mo. Boston [1848].

[Anonymous.] Leaves from Margaret Smith's Journal in the Province of Massachusetts Bay. 1678–9. 12mo. Boston, 1849.

Poems. [First collective edition, including 41 poems now first collected, of which many were not previously published.] Portrait and illustrations. 8vo. Boston, 1849.

Old Portraits and Modern Sketches. 12mo. Boston, 1850.

Songs of Labor, and other Poems. 12mo. Boston, 1850.

Memoir of Richard Dillingham. By A. L. Benedict. With an Introductory Poem by J. G. Whittier. 12mo. Philadelphia, 1852.

Little Eva: Uncle Tom's Guardian Angel. With Music by Emilio. 4to. Boston, 1852.

The Farewell of a Slave Mother to her Daughter. 12mo. Leeds, England, 1852.

Clerical Oppressors. 12mo. Leeds, 1852.
  ***The two preceding titles were issued as Leeds Anti-Slavery Tracts, Nos. 10 and 21.

The Chapel of the Hermits and other Poems. 12mo. Boston, 1853.

A Sabbath Scene. Illustrations. 16mo. Boston, 1853.
  ***Published by Ticknor, Reed & Fields; republished by John P. Jewett & Co., 16mo. Boston, 1854.

Literary Recreations and Miscellanies. 12mo. Boston, 1854.

The Panorama, and other Poems. 12mo. Boston, 1856.

Sound now the Trumpet. [A Frémont campaign song.] Broadside. [1856.]

Poetical Works [including ten Later Poems, 1856-1857, vol. ii., pp. 267-295, now first collected]. Portrait. 2 volumes, 24mo. Boston, 1857.

Proceedings [including poem, Kenoza, by Whittier] at the Dedication of the Kenoza Club House, at Kenoza Lake, (Great Pond) Wednesday Afternoon, August 31, 1859. (Privately printed; 25 copies.) 8vo. Haverhill, 1859.

Home Ballads and Poems. 12mo. Boston, 1860.

Celebration of the Birthday of Robert Burns, in New York [including poem for the occasion, by Whittier]. 4to. New York, 1860.

Celebration of the Hundredth Anniversary of the Birth of Robert Burns, by the Burns Club of Boston, January 25th, 1859. [Poems by Whittier, Lowell and Holmes, and address by Emerson.] 12mo. Boston, 1859.

Oration by Thomas Chase, and Poem by John G. Whittier, delivered before the Alumni Association of the Friends' School at Providence, at their Second Annual Meeting at Newport, 1860. 8vo. Philadelphia, 1860.

A Voice [The Quakers are out]. Broadside. [1860.]

Chimes of Freedom and Union. A Collection of Poems for the Times, by Various Authors [including Whittier, Holmes and others]. 18mo. Boston, 1861.

The Patience of Hope. By the Author of "A Present Heaven" [Dora Greenwell]. With an Introduction [pp. v.-xxxiii.] by John G. Whittier. 16mo. Boston, 1862.

Song of the Negro Boatmen. Broadside. [1862.]

Proceedings of the Alumni Association of Friends' Yearly Meeting School, with the Oration by Moses A. Cartland, and the Poem by J. G. Whittier. Delivered before the Association at their Fifth Annual Meeting at Newport, 1863. 8vo. Providence, 1863.

In War Time and other Poems. 12mo. Boston, 1864.

Proceedings of the American Anti-Slavery Society, at its Third Decade, ... Philadelphia, Dec. 3d and 4th, 1864. [1863.] .... [With an appendix, and a catalogue of anti-slavery publications in America, from 1750 to 1863.] 8vo. New York, 1864.

*₊*Poem, A Northern Song, p. 156, and letters, pp. 6-8, and 153-154, by Whittier. The misprinted date here indicated, appears corrected on wrapper, which contains also additional inscription, including appendix, etc.

Patriotism and other Papers. By Thomas Starr King. With a Biographical Sketch by Hon. Richard Frothingham [and memorial poem by Whittier]. 12mo. Boston, 1864.

National Lyrics [including introductory poem, pp. 5-6, and Laus Deo, pp. 103-104, now first published]. Illustrations. Square 16mo. Boston, 1865.

Snow-Bound. A Winter Idyl. Portrait and vignette. 16mo. Boston, 1866.

Prose Works. Portrait. 2 volumes, 12mo. Boston, 1866.

Poetical Works [including poems now first collected]. 18mo. Boston, 1867.

The Tent on the Beach and other Poems. Vignette. 16mo. Boston, 1867.

Maud Muller. [First separate edition.] Illustrations. 8vo. Boston, 1867.

Among the Hills, and other Poems. Frontispiece and vignette. 16mo. Boston, 1869.

Poetical Works. Complete Edition. [Newly revised, with additions.] Portrait. 2 volumes, 16mo. Boston, 1870.

Ballads of New England. Illustrations. 8vo. Boston, 1870.

Two Letters on the Present Aspect of the Society of Friends. 8vo. London, 1870.

Winter Poems by Favorite American Authors [including The Pageant, pp. 13-20, specially written for this collection, by Whittier]. Illustrations. 8vo. Boston, 1871.

Miriam and other Poems. Frontispiece and vignettes. 16mo. Boston, 1871.

The Journal of John Woolman. With an Introduction [pp. 1-49] by J. G. Whittier. 12mo. Boston, 1871.

The Pennsylvania Pilgrim and other Poems. Illustrations. 16mo. Boston, 1872.

(Edited.) Child Life: a Collection of Poems. Illustrations. Square 12mo. Boston, 1872.

Complete Poetical Works [revised]. Household Edition. 12mo. Boston, 1873.

Child Life in Prose. Edited [with preface, pp. v.-viii., and an original tale, The Fish I did not catch, pp. 137-141] by J. G. Whittier. Illustrations. Square 12mo. Boston, 1874.

Agassiz Memorial; Teachers' and Pupils' Fund. The Prayer of Agassiz, a Poem, by J. G. Whittier; and Agassiz, a Sonnet, by T. W. Parsons. 16mo. Cambridge, 1874.

A Memorial of Charles Sumner [from the Commonwealth of Massachusetts. Poem, Sumner, pp. 97-104, by Whittier, and eulogy, pp. 106-176, by G. W. Curtis]. Portrait. Royal 8vo. Boston, 1874.

Hazel-Blossoms. Frontispiece and vignettes. 16mo. Boston, 1875.
*.*Nine poems by Elizabeth Whittier are included in this volume, pp. 101-133.

Proceedings at the Centennial Celebration of the Battle of Lexington, April 19, 1875 [including poem by Whittier, pp. 37-39]. Illustrations. 8vo. Lexington, 1875.
*.*The poem was also published in Souvenir of Lexington, 1775-1875. Illustrations. Royal 8vo. Boston, 1875.

Mabel Martin. A Harvest Idyl. [First complete edition, with prefatory note by the author.] 58 illustrations. 8vo. Boston, 1876.
*.*The same. 21 illustrations. 16mo. Boston, 1876.

(Edited.) Songs of Three Centuries. 12mo. Boston, 1876.
*.*Also, 8vo. Boston, 1876.

Centennial Hymn. Broadside. [Philadelphia, 1876.]

The Centennial Liberty Bell, Independence Hall; its Traditions and Associations. . . . With an Appendix embracing the Ceremonies, ... July 4th, 1876, by James L. Longshore, and Benjamin L. Knowles. Illustrations. 16mo. Philadelphia, 1876.

*₊*Including Centennial Hymn, first appearance in book form, by Whittier, pp. 140-141; Cantata, by Sidney Lanier, pp. 142-143; Welcome to all Nations, by O. W. Holmes, p. 161; and National Ode, by Bayard Taylor, pp. 163-169. The Centennial Hymn was also issued, with music by J. K. Paine, for the opening ceremonies of the Centennial Exposition, broadside, and with The Star-Spangled Banner and other National Songs, 12mo. Philadelphia, 1876.

Indian Civilization: a Lecture by Stanley Pumphrey. With Introduction by J. G. Whittier. 8vo. Philadelphia, 1877.

The Tent on the Beach. [First separate edition.] Illustrations. 32mo. Boston, 1877.

Favorite Poems. Illustrations. 32mo. Boston, 1877.

Memoir of William Francis Bartlett. By Francis Winthrop Palfrey. [Memorial poem, by Whittier, pp. 302-304.] Portrait and chart. 12mo. Boston, 1878.

The Vision of Echard and other Poems. 16mo. Boston, 1878.

The River Path. [First separate edition.] Illustrations. Square 12mo. Boston, 1878.

Tributes to William Lloyd Garrison, at the Funeral Services, May 28, 1879. [Including poem written for the occasion, by Whittier, pp. 27-28.] Portrait. 8vo. Boston, 1879.

William Lloyd Garrison and his Times. . . . By Oliver Johnson. With an Introduction [pp. ix-xii.] by J. G. Whittier. Portrait. 12mo. Boston, 1879.

Bronze Group commemorating Emancipation. A Gift to the City of Boston from Hon. Moses Kimball. Dedicated December 6, 1879 [with poem for the occasion by Whittier]. Frontispiece. 8vo. Boston, 1879.

The King's Missive and other Poems. Portrait. 16mo. Boston, 1881.

*₊*The King's Missive was first published, with illustrations, in Winsor's Memorial History of Boston, vol. i., pp. xxv.-xxxvii., 1880.

Proceedings of the Massachusetts Historical Society, for
1880-1881. [Containing Whittier's reply to Dr. Ellis'
paper on The King's Missive, pp. 387-394, and Dr. Ellis'
rejoinder to the same, pp. 394-399.] 8vo. Boston, 1881.

Copy of a Letter. [An autobiographical sketch.] Royal
8vo. Amesbury, 5th. Mo. 1882.
    *₊*A three-page leaflet printed for the author, to render easy
    the task of replying to the many enquiries as to his life, works,
    etc., which were daily received by him. The leaflet was re-
    printed in the Amesbury Memorial to Whittier, 1893.

The Bay of Seven Islands and other Poems. Portrait. 16mo.
Boston, 1883.

Jack in the Pulpit. Edited by J. G. Whittier. Small 4to.
[New York, 1884.]
    *₊*Consisting of introductory letter in facsimile of Whittier's
    manuscript, seven pages of text, and eight full-page illustrative
    colored designs, each of which, except the title page, contains a
    selection from the text. A cheaper edition was also issued, con-
    sisting of the illustrated pages and selections only, the pictorial
    boards, introduction and text being omitted.

Re-Union of the Schoolmates of J.G. Whittier. . . . September 10, 1885. With Exercises at Presentation of the Portrait of the Poet to the Haverhill Public Library, December
17, 1885 [including poem and letters by Whittier]. 8vo.
Haverhill, 1886.

Saint Gregory's Guest and Recent Poems. 16mo. Boston,
1886.

Poems of Nature. Portrait and illustrations. Small 4to.
Boston, 1886.

Inauguration of the Statue of Liberty. . . . on Bedlow's
Island, New York, Thursday, October 28, 1886. [Poem,
The Bartholdi Statue, pp. 61-62, by Whittier.] Engraved
facsimile of invitation card. Small 4to. New York, 1887.

One of the Signers. A Poem by John Greenleaf Whittier,
with Autograph Verses. Read at the Unveiling of the
Josiah Bartlett Statue at Amesbury, July 4, 1888. 2 portraits and vignette. Small 4to. [Amesbury, 1888.]

Writings [newly revised]. Portraits. 7 volumes, 12mo.
Boston, 1888-89.
    *₊*The same. Large paper. (400 copies.) 7 volumes, 8vo.
    Cambridge, 1888-89.

The Washington Centenary celebrated in New York, April 29-30 and May 1, 1889. [Poem by Whittier, p. 40; address by Lowell, pp. 71-72; and rhymed toasts by Holmes and Stoddard.] Illustrations. Royal 8vo. New York [1889].

At Sundown. (Privately printed; 50 copies.) 16mo. Cambridge, 1890.

. . . . A Record of the Commemoration, July Second and Third, 1890, of the Two Hundred and Fiftieth Anniversary of the Settlement of Haverhill, Mass. [Ode by Whittier, pp. 121-124, and letters, pp. 3-4, and 355.] Portraits and illustrations. 4to. Boston, 1891.

At Sundown [with prefatory note and seven poems not included in the 1890 edition]. Portrait and illustrations. 16mo. Boston, 1892.
 *₂*The same. Large paper. (250 copies.) 8vo. Cambridge, 1892.

Memorial to J. G. Whittier by the Citizens of Amesbury. Dec. 17, 1892. [Including Autobiographical Sketch, by Whittier, pp. 53-57, address by E. C. Stedman, pp. 64-65, and memorial tributes.] Portraits. Square 8vo. Amesbury, 1893.

Life and Letters, by S. T. Pickard. Portraits. 2 volumes, 12mo. Boston, 1894.
 *₂*The same. Large paper. (400 copies.) 2 volumes, 8vo. Cambridge, 1894.

Complete Poetical Works [including all poems collected since the author's death]. Portrait and vignette. 8vo. Boston, 1895.
 *₂*Many of Whittier's early poems were first published in The Yankee (for which see NEAL, JOHN), The New England Magazine, 1831-35, and The Boston Pearl, 1835-36; to The Democratic Review, 1838-45, he contributed numerous poems and prose sketches, including Supernaturalism of New England, and The Stranger in Lowell; and was editorially connected with The American Manufacturer, Boston, 1829; The Haverhill Gazette, January-June, inclusive, 1830; The New England Review, Hartford, July, 1830-December, 1831, inclusive; The Pennsylvania Freeman, 1838-39; The Anti-Slavery Reporter, N. Y., 1841; and was a frequent contributor, sometimes editorially, to The National Era, 1847-59; for his numerous poems first published in The Atlantic Monthly see index to that journal. The publications named, with a few of the annuals of the time, contained almost his entire contributions to periodical literature.

*** See also BRAINARD, J. G. C.; BRYANT, W. C.; CHILD, L. M.; FIELDS, Annie and J. T.; HOLMES, O. W.; HOWELLS, W. D.; LONGFELLOW, H. W.; LOWELL, J. R.; THOREAU, H. D., and WHIPPLE, E. P.

WILCOX, ELLA WHEELER. 1855 —

    Drops of Water. Temperance Poems. 12mo. New York, 1872.

    Shells. 12mo. Milwaukee, 1873.

    Maurine and other Poems. 12mo. Milwaukee, 1876.

    Poems of Passion. 12mo. Chicago, 1883.

    Mal Moulée. A Tale of Passion. 12mo. New York, 1886.

    Perdita and other Stories. 12mo. New York [1886].

    Poems of Pleasure. 18mo. Chicago, 1887.

    Adventures of Miss Volney. 12mo. New York [1888].

    A Double Life. 12mo. New York, 1890.

    How Salvator won, and other Recitations. 12mo. New York, 1891.

    Was it Suicide? and other Stories. 12mo. Chicago, 1891.

    Song of a Sandwich. Illustrations. 16mo. New York, 1892.

    Sweet Danger. Portrait and illustrations. 12mo. Chicago, 1892.

    The Beautiful Land of Nod. Illustrations. Square 8vo. Chicago, 1892.

    An Erring Woman's Love. Illustrations. Square 8vo. New York [1892].

    Men, Women and Emotions. Portrait. 12mo. Chicago, 1893.

WILKINS, MARY ELEANOR . . . .

    The Adventures of Ann. 12mo. Boston, 1886.

    A Humble Romance and other Stories. 16mo. New York, 1887.

A New England Nun and other Stories. 16mo. New York, 1891.

Young Lucretia and other Stories. Illustrations. 8vo. New York, 1892.

The Pot of Gold and other Stories. Illustrations. 12mo. Boston [1892].

Jane Field. A Novel. Illustrations. 8vo. New York, 1893.

Giles Corey, Yeoman: a Play. Illustrations. 32mo. New York, 1893.

Pembroke: a Novel. Illustrations. 16mo. New York, 1894.

Comfort Pease and her Gold Ring. 16mo. New York, 1895.

WILLIS, NATHANIEL PARKER. 1806–1867.

The Album. [A collection of twelve original, and fifty-two selected poems.] Vignette title. 8vo. New York, 1824.
*⁎*The original poems include Willis' first published poem, which obtained the prize of $50 offered by the publisher of the volume; the selections include some of the earlier poems of Bryant, Halleck and Percival.

Sketches. 8vo. Boston, 1827.

(Edited.) The Legendary: consisting of Original Pieces, principally Illustrative of American History, Scenery and Manners. 2 volumes, 12mo. Boston, 1828.

Fugitive Poetry. 8vo. Boston, 1829.

(Edited.) The Token for 1829. Plates. 16mo. Boston, 1829.

(Edited.) American Monthly Magazine. 2 volumes, 8vo. Boston, 1829–31.

Poem delivered before the Society of United Brothers. . . . September 6, 1831; with other Poems. 8vo. New York, 1831.

Pencillings by the Way. 3 volumes, 8vo. London, 1835.

Melanie and other Poems. Edited by Barry Cornwall. 18mo. London, 1835.
  *₊*Also, 16mo. New York, 1837.

[Anonymous.] Inklings of Adventure. 3 volumes, 12mo. London, 1836.
  *₊*Also, 2 volumes, 12mo. New York, 1836.

American Scenery; or, Land, Lake and River Illustrations of Transatlantic Nature. Portrait and 120 engravings. 2 volumes, or 30 parts, 4to. London, 1838.

Bianca Visconti; or, the Heart overtasked. 12mo. New York, 1839.

Tortesa, the Usurer. A Play. 12mo. New York, 1839.
  *₊*The two preceding volumes were reprinted in London as Two Ways of dying for a Husband, 8vo. 1839.

A l'Abri; or, the Tent pitch'd. 12mo. New York, 1839.

(Edited.) The Corsair: a Gazette of Literature, Art, Dramatic Criticism, Fashion and Novelty. [March 16, 1839–March 7, 1840.] 4to. New York, 1839–40.
  *₊*The numbers of this publication for August, September and October, 1839, contain five original contributions by W. M. Thackeray.

Loiterings of Travel. 3 volumes, 12mo. London, 1840.

Letters from under a Bridge, and Poems. Portrait and 10 engravings. Square 8vo. London, 1840.

(With J. Sterling Coyne.) The Scenery and Antiquities of Ireland. 120 engravings. 2 volumes, or 30 parts, 4to. London, 1840–41.

Canadian Scenery. 120 engravings. 2 volumes, or 30 parts, 4to. London, 1841–42.

Sacred Poems. Royal 8vo. New York, 1843.

Poems of Passion. Royal 8vo. New York, 1843.

Lady Jane, and Humorous Poems. Royal 8vo. New York, 1844.

Letters from under a Bridge. The only Complete Edition. Royal 8vo. New York, 1844.
  *₊*The four preceding titles appeared as numbers of the Mirror Extra series.

Poems Sacred, Passionate and Humorous. Royal 8vo. New York, 1844.

Pencillings by the Way. Written during some Years of Residence and Travel .... First Complete Editions. Royal 8vo. New York, 1844.

Lecture on Fashion, delivered before the New York Lyceum, June, 1844. 8vo. New York [1844].

(Edited.) The Opal. Illustrations. 12mo. New York, 1844.

Dashes at Life with a Free Pencil. 3 parts, 8vo. New York, 1845.
*.*Also, 12mo. New York, 1845.

Complete Prose and Poetical Works. Royal 8vo. New York, 1846.

Poems of Early and After Years [including many now first collected]. Portrait and 16 engravings. 8vo. Philadelphia, 1847.

Rural Letters and other Records of Thought at Leisure, written in the Intervals of more Hurried Literary Labor. 12mo. New York, 1849.

People I have met; or, Pictures of Society and People of Mark, drawn under a Thin Veil of Fiction. 12mo. New York, 1850.

Life here and there; or Sketches of Society and Adventures at Far-Apart Times and Places. 12mo. New York, 1850.

(Edited.) The Gem of the Season, for 1850. 16 engravings. 8vo. New York, 1850.

(Edited.) Trenton Falls, Picturesque and Descriptive. Illustrations. Square 16mo. New York, 1851.

Memoranda of the Life of Jenny Lind. Portrait. 12mo. Philadelphia, 1851.

Hurry-Graphs; or Sketches of Scenery, Celebrities and Society, taken from Life. 12mo. New York, 1851.

Poems by Mary H. Pumpelly. [With a preface by Willis.] 8vo. New York, 1852.

A Summer Cruise in the Mediterranean on Board an American Frigate. 12mo. New York, 1853.

A Health Trip to the Tropics. 12mo. New York, 1853.

Fun Jottings; or, Laughs I have taken a Pen to. 12mo. New York, 1853.

Ephemera. 12mo. New York, 1854.

Famous Persons and Places. 12mo. New York, 1854.

Famous Persons and Famous Places. 12mo. London, 1854.

Out-Doors at Idlewild; or, the Shapings of a Home on the Banks of the Hudson. 12mo. New York, 1855.

The Rag-Bag, a Collection of Ephemera. 12mo. New York, 1855.

Paul Fane; or, Parts of a Life else Untold. 12mo. New York, 1857.

The Convalescent. 12mo. New York, 1859.

Poems, Sacred, Passionate and Humorous. [Newly revised.] 24mo. New York, 1861.

Poems. Complete Edition. 8vo. New York, 1868.
**See also MORRIS, G. P.; PAULDING, J. K.; POE, E. A.; TAYLOR, BAYARD; WHITMAN, W.

WILMER, LAMBERT A. 1805-1863.

The Quacks of Helicon. A Satire. 18mo. Philadelphia, 1841.

Recantation. A Poem. 18mo. Philadelphia, 1843.

Somnia. 12mo. Philadelphia, 1848.

Liberty Triumphant. 12mo. Philadelphia, 1853.

The Life, Travels and Adventures of Ferdinand de Soto the Discoverer of the Mississippi. 8vo. Philadelphia, 1858.

Our Press-Gang; or, a Complete Exposition of the Corruptions and Crimes of the American Newspaper. 12mo. Philadelphia, 1859.

WINSOR, JUSTIN. 1831—

History of the Town of Duxbury, Massachusetts, with Genealogical Registers. Frontispiece. 8vo. Boston, 1849.

(With George H. Hepworth.) Songs of the Unity; a Selection of Lyrics for Public Worship, with Tunes for Congregational Use. 12mo. Boston, 1859.

Celebration of the Centennial Anniversary of the Battle of Bunker Hill. With an Appendix containing a Survey of the Literature of the Battle [by Justin Winsor]. Plates. Royal 8vo. Boston, 1875.

A Bibliography of the Original Quartos and Folios of Shakespeare: with Particular Reference to Copies in America. 68 facsimiles. (200 copies.) 4to. Boston, 1875.

Shakespeare's Poems: a Bibliography of the Earlier Editions. 8vo. Cambridge, 1879.

The Reader's Handbook of the American Revolution. 16mo. Boston, 1880.

(Edited.) Memorial History of Boston, including Suffolk County, Massachusetts, 1630–1880. 4 volumes, 4to. Boston, 1880–81.
 *₊*i., 1880; ii., iii., iv., 1881.
 *₊*Vol. i. contains The King's Missive, pp. xxv.-xxxvii., specially contributed by Whittier; vol. iv., Medicine in Boston, pp. 527–549, by Samuel A. Green, M.D., with Additional Memoranda, pp. 549–570, by O. W. Holmes.

Halliwelliana: a Bibliography of the Publications of James Orchard Halliwell-Phillips. 8vo. Cambridge, 1881.

Governor Bradford's Manuscript History of Plymouth Plantation and its Transmission to our Times. 8vo. Cambridge, 1881.

Massachusetts. [Reprinted from The Encyclopædia Brittannica.] 12mo. Boston, 1882.

(Edited.) Narrative and Critical History of America. With Bibliographical and Critical Essays on its Historical Sources and Authorities . . . . Portraits, facsimiles and illustrations. 8 volumes (issued also in 24 sections, or 72 parts), royal 8vo. Boston, 1884–89.
 *₊*iii., iv., 1884; ii., 1886; v., 1887; vi, vii., 1888; i., viii., 1889.
 *₊*The same. Large paper. (550 copies.) 16 volumes, 4to. Boston, 1884–89.

Elder William Brewster, of the Mayflower: his Books and Autographs, with other Notes. 8vo. Cambridge, 1887.

(Edited.) Was Shakespeare Shapleigh? A Correspondence in Two Entanglements. 16mo. Boston, 1887.

Address delivered at the 250th Anniversary of the Incorporation of the Town of Duxbury, Mass., June 17, 1887. 8vo. Cambridge, 1887.

Charles Deane, LL.D. A Memoir. (Privately printed.) Portrait. 8vo. Cambridge, 1891.

Christopher Columbus, and how he received and imparted the Spirit of Discovery. Portraits and illustrations. 8vo. Boston, 1891.

The Earliest Printed Sources of New England History, 1602–1629. 8vo. Cambridge, 1894.

Cartier to Frontenac: a Study of Geographical History in the Interior of North America, in its Historical Relations, 1534–1700. Illustrations. 8vo. Boston, 1894.

Exploration of the Mississippi Basin. The Struggle in America between England and France, 1697–1763. Illustrations. 8vo. Boston, 1895.
***Mr. Winsor is also author of several bibliographical treatises, commencement addresses, etc.
***See also LOWELL, J. R.

WINTER, WILLIAM. 1836—

Poems. 12mo. Boston, 1855.

The Emotion of Sympathy. 12mo. Boston, 1856.

The Queen's Domain and other Poems. 12mo. Boston, 1859.

My Witness. 16mo. Boston, 1871.

Edwin Booth in Twelve Dramatic Characters [with biographical sketch by Winter]. 12 portraits. Folio. Boston, 1871.

Seventh Annual Re-Union of the Society of the Army of the Potomac at Philadelphia, June 6, 1876. [Poem, pp. 22–26, by Winter.] 8vo. New York, 1877.

Thistle-Down: a Book of Lyrics. 16mo. London, 1878.
***Part of the edition was issued, with the importers' imprint, 16mo. Boston, 1878.

Tenth Annual Re-Union of the Society of the Army of the Potomac at Albany, June 19, 1879. [Poem by Winter, pp. 77-79.] 8vo. New York, 1879.

A Trip to England. 12mo. Boston, 1879.

A Trip to England [with additions]. Illustrations by Joseph Jefferson. 12mo. Boston, 1881.

Poems. Complete Edition. 12mo. Boston, 1881.

(Edited, with memoir.) The Poems and Stories of Fitz-James O'Brien. Portraits and illustrations. 12mo. Boston, 1881.

The Jeffersons. Portraits and illustrations. 12mo. Boston, 1881.
 *₊*The same. Large paper. (100 copies.) 4to. Boston, 1881.

Fiftieth Anniversary of the First Appearance on the Stage of William Warren, Boston's Favorite Comedian. Fifty Years of an Actor's Life. [Address and poem by Winter, pp. 44-48.] Portrait. 18mo. [Boston] 1882.

English Rambles and other Fugitive Pieces in Prose and Verse. 12mo. Boston, 1884.

The Dedication Exercises of the Actors' Monument to Edgar Allan Poe .... at the Metropolitan Museum of Art, N. Y., May 4, 1885. [Speech and poem, pp. 40-45, by Winter.] 8vo. [New York, 1885.]

Henry Irving. 2 portraits. 12mo. New York, 1885.
 *₊*The same. Large paper. (50 copies.) 8vo. New York, 1885.

The Stage Life of Mary Anderson. Portrait. 12mo. New York, 1886.
 *₊*The same. Large paper. (50 copies.) 8vo. New York, 1886.

Shakespeare's England. 24mo. Boston, 1886.

Taming of the Shrew. . . . Arranged by Augustin Daly. . . . With an Introduction by W. Winter. (Privately printed.) 8vo. New York, 1887.

Wanderers: being a Collection of Poems. 16mo. Edinburgh, 1888.
 *₊*Also, 16mo. Boston, 1889.

The Press and the Stage: an Oration. Delivered before the Goethe Society, N. Y., January 28th, 1889. (250 copies.) 8vo. New York, 1889.

In Memory of John McCullough. 8vo. New York, 1889.

Brief Chronicles. Portraits. 3 volumes, 8vo. New York: The Dunlap Society, 1889-90.

John Gilbert. A Sketch of his Life, together with Extracts from his Letters and Souvenirs of his Career. Portrait and illustrations. 8vo. New York: The Dunlap Society, 1890.

The Actor and other Speeches, chiefly on Theatrical Subjects and Occasions. Portrait. 8vo. New York: The Dunlap Society, 1891.

Ada Rehan: a Study. (Privately printed.) Portrait. 8vo. New York, 1891.

Gray Days and Gold. 24mo. Edinburgh and New York, 1891.

Old Shrines and Ivy. 24mo. Edinburgh and New York, 1892.

Shadows of the Stage. Portrait. 24mo. New York, 1892.

Shakespeare's England. New Edition, revised [with additions]. Illustrations. 12mo. New York, 1893.

George William Curtis. A Eulogy delivered before the People of Staten Island, Feb. 24, 1893. Portrait. 24mo. New York, 1893.

Shadows of the Stage. Second Series. 24mo. New York, 1893.

The Life and Art of Edwin Booth. Portraits. 12mo. New York, 1893.
 ***The same. Large paper. (250 copies.) 8vo. New York, 1893.
 ***Also 25 copies, with proofs on Whatman paper, 8vo. New York, 1893.

The Life and Art of Joseph Jefferson, together with some Account of his Ancestry, and of the Jefferson Family of Actors. Portraits and illustrations. 12mo. New York, 1894.
 ***The same. Large paper. (200 copies.) 8vo. New York, 1894.

Shadows of the Stage. Third Series. 24mo. New York, 1895.

*₊*Mr. Winter also edited, with prefaces and notes, the prompt-books of plays produced by Edwin Booth, New York, 1878 *et seq.*

*₊*See also ARNOLD, GEORGE, and BROUGHAM, JOHN.

WINTHROP, THEODORE. 1828–1861.

A Companion to the Heart of the Andes. [A description of the picture, bearing this title, by F. J. Church.] 12mo. New York, 1859.

Cecil Dreeme. [With memoir by George W. Curtis.] 12mo. Boston, 1861.

John Brent. 12mo. Boston, 1862.

Edwin Brothertoft. 12mo. Boston, 1862.

The Canoe and the Saddle. Adventures among the North Western Rivers and Forests; and Isthmiana. 12mo. Boston, 1863.

Life in the Open Air; and other Papers. Portrait. 12mo. Boston, 1863.

Life and Poems. Edited by his Sister. Portrait. 12mo New York, 1884.

WISE, HENRY AUGUSTUS (HARRY GRINGO). 1819–1869.

Los Gringos: or, an Inside View of Mexico and California, with Wanderings in Peru, Chili, and Polynesia. 12mo. New York, 1850.

Tales for the Marines. Illustrations. 12mo. Boston, 1855.

Scampavias from Gibel Tarek to Stamboul. Illusrrations. 12mo. New York, 1857.

Captain Brand of the "Centipede": a Pirate of Eminence in the West Indies; his Loves and Exploits .... 12mo. London, 1860.

*₊*Also, 8vo. New York, 1864.

WOODBERRY, GEORGE EDWARD. 1855—

The Relation of Pallas Athene to Athens. Written for the Harvard Commencement, 1877. (Privately printed.) 12mo. [Abingdon, Mass.,] 1877.

The North Shore Watch: a Threnody. Frontispiece. (Privately printed.) 8vo. [Cambridge] 1883.

A History of Wood Engraving. 8vo. New York, 1883.

Edgar Allan Poe. Portrait. 12mo. Boston, 1885.

My Country. (Privately printed; 50 copies.) 8vo. Cambridge, 1886.

The North Shore Watch and other Poems. 16mo. Boston, 1890.

Studies in Letters and Life. 12mo. Boston, 1890.

(Edited.) The Complete Poetical Works of Percy Bysshe Shelley, the Text newly collated and revised . . . . with Notes and a Memoir. Portrait. 4 volumes, 12mo. Boston, 1892.
  *.*The same. Large paper. (250 copies). 8 volumes, 8vo. Boston, 1892.

(Edited, with memoir.) Lamb's Essays of Elia. Vignettes. 12mo. Boston, 1892.
  *.*The same. Large paper. (100 copies.) 2 volumes, 8vo. Boston, 1892.

The Players' Elegy on the Death of Edwin Booth: read at the Memorial Services . . . . in the Madison Square Garden Concert Hall, Nov. 13, 1893. (Privately printed; 35 copies.) Small 4to. New York, 1893.

(Edited, with introduction.) Select Poems of Aubrey de Vere. 12mo. New York, 1894.

To A. V. W. J. (Privately printed; 20 copies.) Small 4to New York, 1895.

Household Waifs for Many Years, by Known and Unknown Poets: arranged [with an introductory quatrain] by George E. Woodberry. (Privately printed; 20 copies.) Small 4to. New York, Christmas, 1895.
  *.*See also GRANT, ROBERT, and POE, E. A.

WOODWORTH, SAMUEL. 1785-1842.

New Haven: a Poem, Satirical and Sentimental. 12mo. New York, 1809.

Beasts at Law; or, Zoological Jurisprudence; a Poem. Translated from the Arabic of Sampfilius Philoerin. 16mo. New York, 1811.

Quarter-Day; or, the Horrors of the First of May. Poem. 12mo. New York, 1812.

(Edited.) The War. Being a Faithful Record of the Transactions of the War between the United States and Great Britain. 2 volumes, 4to. New York, 1813-14.

Bubble and Squeak .... 12mo. New York, 1814.

La Fayette. 18mo. New York [1815?].

The Champions of Freedom, or the Mysterious Chief. A Romance of the Nineteenth Century founded on the Events of the War between the United States and Great Britain, which terminated in 1815. 2 volumes, 8vo. New York, 1816.

The Complete Coiffeur; or an Essay on the Art of Adorning Natural, and of creating Artificial, Beauty. By J. B. M. D. Lafoy, Ladies' Hair-Dresser. Engraved titles and plates. 16mo. New York, 1817.
*⁎*Arranged in two parts, of which the second is a translation, into French, of the first. The first part of the work is certainly Woodworth's, and whilst the second part cannot with such certainty be credited to him, it is more than probable that both are his.

Poems, Odes, Songs and other Metrical Effusions. Portrait. 8vo. New York, 1818.

(Edited.) The Ladies' Literary Cabinet; being a Repository of Miscellaneous Literary Productions in Prose and Verse. [October, 1819-November, 1820.] 2 volumes, 4to. New York, 1819-20.

The Deed of Gift, a Comic Opera, in Three Acts. 18mo. New York, 1822.

The Forest Rose. A Pastoral Poem. 18mo. New York, 1825.

King's Bridge Cottage, a Revolutionary Incident founded on an Incident which occurred a Few Days previous to the Evacuation of New York by the British. A Drama in Two Acts. 16mo. New York, 1826.

Melodies, Duets, Trios, Songs and Ballads. Frontispiece and engraved title. 16mo. New York, 1826.

Festivals, Games and Amusements; Ancient and Modern, by Horatio Smith. With Additions by S. Woodworth. 18mo. New York, 1831.

Poetical Works. Edited by his Son, with Memoir by George P. Morris. 2 volumes, 24mo. New York, 1861.
 ***See also Morris, G. P.; Paulding, J. K., and Whitman, W.

WOOLSON, CONSTANCE FENIMORE. 1848–1894.

The Old Stone House. By Anne March. Illustrations. 12mo. Boston, 1873.

Castle Nowhere: Lake-Country Sketches. 12mo. Boston, 1875.

Two Women: 1862. A Poem. 12mo. New York, 1877.

Rodman the Keeper: Southern Sketches. 16mo. New York, 1880.

Anne. A Novel. 16mo. New York, 1882.

For the Major: a Novelette. 16mo. New York, 1883.

East Angels. A Novel. 16mo. New York, 1886.

Jupiter Lights. A Novel. 16mo. New York, 1889.

Horace Chase. 12mo. New York, 1894.

The Front Yard and other Italian Stories. Illustrations. 16mo. New York, 1895.

ADDENDA.

ALDRICH, ANNE REEVE.

Nadine and other Poems. (Privately printed.) 16mo. New York, 1893.

APPLETON, THOMAS GOLD.

[Anonymous.] Fresh Leaves. (Privately printed.) Small 4to. [Boston, 1874.]
  *₊*The pagination is continued from that of Faded Leaves, 1872.

EMERSON, RALPH WALDO.

Over-Songs. Small 4to. [Cambridge] 1864.
  *₊*A collection of six poems, by R. W. Emerson, Jean Ingelow, Bayard Taylor, Theodore Tilton, George W. Curtis, and Lucy Larcom; with Dedication, Prelude, and Accompaniment, by the editor, A. M. I[de]. The poems were contributed, as a testimonial of the authors' esteem, on the occasion of the marriage of Henry Morton Lovering and Isabel Francelia Morse, of Taunton, June 28, 1864, and not more than ten copies are believed to have been printed, for presentation to the authors and to family friends.

FISKE, JOHN.

The Beginnings of New England; or, the Puritan Theocracy in its Relations to Civil and Religious Liberty. 12mo. Boston, 1889.

HOLMES, OLIVER WENDELL.

The New England Tour of . . . . the Prince of Wales . . . . containing an Account of the Journey from Albany . . . . to Boston . . . . Reception . . . . [the festival at Music Hall, including International Ode, written for the occasion, by Holmes, p. 15] . . . . and the Sailing of the Fleet. 8vo. Boston, 1860.

A Discourse delivered before the Ancient and Honorable Artillery Company, ... June 3, 1861. By S. K. Lothrop. [With hymn for the occasion, pp. 59–60, by Holmes.] 8vo. Boston, 1861.

The Harvard Book. A Series of Historical, Biographical and Descriptive Sketches. By Various Authors. Collected by F. O. Vaille and H. A. Clark. Illustrations. 2 volumes, royal 4to. Boston, 1878.
*₄*The Medical School, vol. i., pp. 239–251; and The Holmes Estate, vol. ii., pp. 424–426, by O. W. Holmes; Class Day, vol. ii., pp. 157–172, by J. R. Lowell, and contributions by T. W. Higginson, C. E. Norton, C. P. Cranch and others.

Addresses at the Complimentary Dinner to Dr. Benjamin Apthorp Gould. Hotel Vendôme, Boston, May 6, 1885. [Including poem for the occasion by Holmes, pp. 22–24.] 8vo. Lynn, 1885.

Response to the Toast, "The President of the United States" together with the Response of the Guest of the Evening, Dr. Oliver Wendell Holmes, at the Banquet to his Honour by the Liverpool Philomathic Society, August 20th, 1886. Etched wrapper. (Privately printed.) Square 12mo. Liverpool, England, September 1, 1886.

The Story of the Memorial Fountain to Shakspeare at Stratford-upon-Avon. ... Also Accounts of .... [other] Gifts of Geo. W. Childs. Edited by L. Clarke Davis. Portrait and plate. (Privately printed.) 12mo. Cambridge, 1890.
*₄*Poem, written for dedication of the fountain, by Holmes, pp. 41–44, and letter, p. 22; letter of J. R. Lowell, pp. 35–38; and letters of J. G. Whittier, pp. 38, 209.

LONGFELLOW, HENRY WADSWORTH.

Noël. 16mo. Cambridge, 1864.
*₄*The original French text, of which not more than twenty-five copies were privately printed; the author's English version of the poem appears in Flower-de-Luce, 1867.

The Hanging of the Crane. Square 16mo. Boston, 1874.
*₄*A privately printed issue, of not more than fifty copies, for presentation by the author.

QUINCY, JOSIAH PHILLIPS.

The Peckster Professorship. An Episode in the History of Psychological Research. 12mo. Boston, 1888.

INITIALS AND PSEUDONYMS.

A., T. B. Aldrich, T. B.
A., T. G. Appleton, T. G.
Æsop, G. Washington. Lanigan, G. T.
Agapida, Fray Antonio. Irving. W.
Alethitoras. Osborn, L.
Amateur, An. Paulding, J K.
Amateur of Fashion, An. Paulding, J. K.
American, An. Calvert, G. H.
American, An. Child, L. M.
American, An. Cooper, J. F.
American, An. Longfellow, H. W.
American, An. Motley, J. L.
American, An. Palmer, J. W.
American, An. Pickering, H.
American, An. Tuckerman, H. T.
American Gentleman, An. Irving, W.
Apes, William. Snelling, W. J.
Autodycus. Osborn, L.
Asarias, Brother. Mullany, P. F.
B., C. T. Brooks, C. T.
Bachelor Knight, A. Simms, W. G.
Backwoodsman, A. Dunlap, William.
Barnwell. Roosevelt, R. B.
Barrett, Walter. Scoville, J. A.
Bell, Solomon. Snelling, W. J.
Benson, Carl. Bristed, C. A.
Berkeley, Helen. Ritchie, A. C. M.
Billings, Josh. Shaw, H. W.
Boisgilbert, Edmund. Donnelly, Ignatius.
Bonneville, Capt. B. L. E. Irving, W.
Boston Bard, The. Coffin, R. S.
Bostonian, A. Poe, E. A.
Brooke, Wesley. Lunt, G.
Broken-Down Critic, A. Bristed, C. A.
Bull-us, Hector. Paulding, J. K.
Chandler, Ellen Louise. Moulton, L. C.
Citizen of New York, A. Dunlap, W.
City Bachelor, A. Simms, W. G.
Clerke of Oxenforde, The. Kennedy, J. P.
Cooper, Frank. Simms, W. G.
Country Schoolmaster, A. Leggett, W.
Coventry, John. Palmer, J. W.
Crayon, Geoffrey. Irving, W.
Croaker, Croaker & Co. Drake, J. R.
Crowfield, Christopher. Stowe, H. B.
D., H. N. Ireland, J. N.
Doesticks, Q K. Philander. Thompson, M. M.
Doubting Gentleman, A. Paulding, J. K.
Downing, Major Jack. Smith, Seba.
Editor, An. Simms, W. G.
Effingham, C. Cooke, J. E.
"Ellen Louise." Moulton, L. C.
Ex-Pension Agent, An. Morford, Henry.
Fellow, R. Scudder, H. E.
Flaccus. Ward, T.
Franco, Harry. Briggs, C. F.
Free Man, A. Snelling, W. J.
G., L. I. Guiney, L. I.
Gentleman of New York, A. Irving, W.

Gentleman of Portsmouth, A. Sewall, J. M.
Gringo, Harry. Wise, H. A.
H., The Letter. Halpine, C. G.
H., A. S. Hardy, A. S.
H. H. Jackson, H. H.
Hamilton, Gail. Dodge, M. A.
Hartwell, Mary. Catherwood, M. H.
Haywarde, Richard. Cozzens, F. S.
His [M. D. Richardson's] Friend. Simms, W. G.
Huntley, Lydia. Sigourney, L. H.
Instructor, An. Longfellow, H. W.
Isabel. Ritchie, A. C. M.
Johnson, Benj. F. Riley, J. W.
Jones, Cupid. Saltus, F. S.
J. S., of Dale. Stimson, F. J.
Kerr, Orpheus C. Newell, R. H.
Knickerbocker, Diedrich. Irving, W.
Lady, A. Cooper, S. F.
Lady, A. Moulton, L. C.
Lady of Massachusetts, A. Child, L. M.
Lafoy, J. B. D. Woodworth, S.
Langstaffe, Launcelot. Irving, Washington.
Learned Gorilla, A. White, R. G.
Lover of the Fine Arts, A. Brooks, M.
Lynn Bard, The. Lewis, A.
M., B. A. Mullany, P. F.
M., L. C. Moulton, L. C.
Manhattan. Scoville, J. A.
Manners, Motley. Duganne, A. J. H.
March, Anne. Woolson, C. F.
Marvel, Ik. Mitchell, D. G.
Member of the Vermont Bar, A. Thompson, D. P.
Midshipman of the United States Navy, A. Leggett, W.
Miller, Joaquin. Miller, C. H.
Murray, Lieut. Ballou, M. M.
Nasby, Petroleum V. Locke, D. R.
Native of Virginia, A. Conway, M. D.
New Englander Over-Sea, A. Neal, J.

New-England Man, A. Paulding, J. K.
New Yorker, A. Bristed, C. A.
New Yorker, A. Hoffman, C. F.
Nil Admirari, Esq. Shelton, F. W.
Northern Man, A. Paulding, J. K.
O'Cataract, Jehu. Neal, J.
Occidente, Maria del. Brooks, Maria.
Old Man, An. Johnston, R. M.
One of her [Fanchette's] Admirers. Cooke, J. E.
One of his [H. W. Beecher's] Congregation. Proctor, E. D.
One of the Editors of The N. Y. Mirror. Fay, T. S.
One of the Types. Shillaber, B. P.
Opera Goer, An. Mitchell, D. G.
O'Reilly, Private Miles. Halpine, C. G.
Oudenarde, Dominie Nicholas Ægidus. Paulding, J. K.
P., M. L. Putnam, M. L.
Page, Stanton. Fuller, H. B.
Partington, Mrs. Shillaber, B. P.
Penn, Arthur. Matthews, J. B.
Perch, Philemon. Johnston, R. M.
Percy, Florence. Akers, E. C.
Phlogobombos, Terentius. Judah, S. B. H.
Phœnix, John. Derby, G. H.
Pindar, Jonathan. Freneau, P.
Reverie, Reginald. Mellen, G.
S., L. H. Sigourney, L. H.
Secondthoughts, Solomon. Kennedy, J. P.
Several American Authors. Bryant, W. C.
Sexton of the Old School, A. Sargent, L. M.
Sigma. Sargent, L. M.
Slender, Robert. Freneau, P.
Smith, Ben. Mathews, C.
South Carolinian, A. Simms. W. G.
Southern Lady, A. Warfield, C. A.
Southron, A. Simms, W. G.
Squatter, A. Jones, J. B.
Stella. Lewis, E. S.
Sterne, Stuart. Bloede, G.
T., G. Ticknor, G.

Terry, Rose. Cooke, R. T.
Thanet, Octave. French, A.
Titcomb, Timothy. Holland, J. G.
Travelling Bachelor, A. Cooper, J. F.
Twain, Mark. Clemens, S. L.
Two Friends. Howells, W. D.
Two in one House. Piatt, J. J.
Two Wags. Bangs, J. K.
Uncle Remus. Harris, J. C.
Van Tromp. Sargent, L. M.
Various Contributors. Bryant, W. C.

Virginian, A. Carruthers, W. A.
Virginian, A. Cooke, J. E.
Volunteer in the U. S. Service, A. Brownell, H. H.
W. Prime, W. C.
Ward, Artemus. Browne, C. F.
Western Man, A. Thorpe, T. B.
Wetherell, Elizabeth. Warner, Susan.
Wilbur, Homer. Lowell, J. R.
Youth of Thirteen, A. Bryant, W. C.

ANONYMS.

Adams, J. Q. Letters to his Constituents. . . . Boston, 1837. J. G. Whittier.
Adams, J. Q. The Jubilee of the Constitution. New York, 1839. W. C. Bryant.
Address to. . . . Congress. . . . on Restriction on Foreign Trade. . . . . Philadelphia, 1809. C. B. Brown.
Address to the Government on the Cession of Louisiana, 1803. C. B. Brown.
Advice of a Father to his Son. Albany, 1871. S. G. W. Benjamin.
Africans, The. Philadelphia, 1811. W. Dunlap.
Afterglow. Boston, 1877. G. P. Lathrop.
Agassiz, Louis. Address on A. von Humboldt. Boston, 1869. O. W. Holmes.
Alnwick Castle. . . . New York, 1827. Fitz-Greene Halleck.
Alpha Delta Chi. Proceedings. . . . 25th Anniversary. . . . New York, 1858. D. G. Mitchell.
Amateur, The. Boston, 1830-31. O. W. Holmes.
American Academy of Arts and Sciences. Memoirs, vols. viii., ix. Cambridge, 1862-64. F. G. Child.
American Academy of Arts and Sciences. Proceedings, vol. ii. Cambridge, 1852. O. W. Holmes.
American Adventures by Land and Sea. New York, 1841. E. Sargent.
American Anecdotes. Boston, 1830. J. G. Whittier.
American Anti-Slavery Society. Proceedings. . . . Dec., 1863. New York, 1864. J. G. Whittier.
American Authors, Homes of. New York, 1853. C. F. Briggs.
American Free Soil Almanac, for 1849. Boston. J. G. Whittier.
American Landscape, The. New York, 1830. W. C. Bryant.
American Magazine of Useful Instruction, vol. ii. Boston, 1836. N. Hawthorne.
American Medical Society. Report . . . . on Medical Literature. Philadelphia, 1848. O. W. Holmes.
American Monthly Magazine. New York, 1838. C. F. Hoffman.
American Travel, Some Highways and Byways of. Philadelphia, 1878. S. Lanier.
Analectic Magazine, The. Philadelphia, 1813-15. W. Irving.
Anglomaniacs, The. New York. C. C. Harrison.
Arthur Clenning. Philadelphia, 1828. T. Flint.
Arthur Mervyn. Philadelphia, 1799. C. B. Brown.
Atalantis. New York, 1832. W. G. Simms.
Atlantic Almanac. Boston, 1870. J. R. Lowell.

Atlantic Club-Book, The. New York, 1834. J. K. Paulding.
Atlantic Magazine, The. New York, 1824. W. C. Bryant.
Attucks, Crispus. Memorial. Boston, 1889. J. Fiske.
Autocrat of the Breakfast Table, The. Boston, 1858. O. W. Holmes.
Autograph Leaves of our Country's Authors. Baltimore, 1864. J. P. Kennedy.
Bacon, Delia. London, 1888. N. Hawthorne.
Ballad of the Abolition Blunder-buss, The. Boston, 1861. L. M. Sargent.
Balloon Post. Boston, 1871. H. James.
Bartlett, W. F. Memoir by F. W. Palfrey. Boston, 1878. J. G. Whittier.
Batchelder, S. Poetry of the Bells. Cambridge, 1858. J. R. Lowell.
Behemoth. New York, 1839. C. Mathews.
Berkshire Jubilee, The. . . . Albany, 1845. O. W. Holmes.
Book of Jasher, The. New York, 1840. M. M. Noah.
Book of Rubies, The. New York, 1866. T. D. English.
Border Beagles. Philadelphia, 1840. W. G. Simms.
Boston Athenæum and Public Library, Union of. 1853. G. Ticknor.
Boston Book, The. Boston, 1836. H. T. Tuckerman.
Boston Book, The. Boston, 1850. J. T. Fields.
Boston Miscellany of Literature and Fashion, The. Boston, 1842. J. R. Lowell.
Boston Museum of the Fine Arts. A Companion to the Catalogue. Boston, 1877. T. G. Appleton.
Boston Pier, The. Centennial. Boston, 1873. O. W. Holmes.
Bouse, Sir Lyon. The Adventures of. New York, 1867. R. G. White.
Bridal of Vaumond, The. New York, 1817. R. C. Sands.
Bridgewater, Mass. 200th Anniversary. Boston, 1856. W. C. Bryant.
British Prison-Ship, The. Philadelphia, 1781. P. Freneau.
Bronze Group Commemorating Emancipation. Boston, 1879. J. G. Whittier.
Brother Jonathan. Edinburgh, 1825. John Neal.
Brown, John. Invasion . . . . Boston, 1860. R. W. Emerson.
Browne, Sir Thomas. Religio Medici . . . . Boston, 1862. J. T. Fields.
Browning, Robert. Memorial. Cambridge. C. P. Cranch.
Bryant Memorial Meeting. New York. E. C. Stedman.
Buckwheat Cake, The. Boston, 1831. H. Pickering.
Bunker Hill. Centennial Anniversary. Boston, 1875. J. Winsor.
Bunker Hill. Memorial. Boston, 1875. O. W. Holmes.
Bunker Hill. Memorial of the American Patriots who fell at the Battle, June 17, 1775 . . . . Boston, 1889. T. W. Parsons.
Buntling Ball, The. New York, 1884. E. Fawcett.
Burns, Robert. Celebration of 100th Anniversary. Boston, 1859. J. G. Whittier.
Burns, Robert. Celebration of 100th Anniversary. New York, 1859. J. G. Whittier.
Burns, Robert. Celebration of 110th Anniversary. Jersey City, 1869. W. C. Bryant.

Burns, Robert. Celebration of 111th Anniversary. New York, 1870. O. W. Holmes.
Calavar. Philadelphia, 1834. R. M. Bird.
Call to my Countrymen, A. New York, 1863. M. A. Dodge.
Cambridge in the Centennial. Cambridge, 1875. J. R. Lowell.
Cambridge of 1776, The. Cambridge, 1876. W. D. Howells.
Cambridge. 250th Anniversary .... Cambridge, 1881. O. W. Holmes.
Cambridge. 250th Anniversary of First Church. Cambridge, 1886. O. W. Holmes.
Carlyle, Thomas. Critical and Miscellaneous Essays. Boston, 1838. R. W. Emerson.
Carlyle, Thomas. Past and Present. Boston, 1843. R. W. Emerson.
Carlyle, Thomas. Sartor Resartus. Boston, 1836. R. W. Emerson.
Celebration of the Introduction of the Water of Cochituate Lake, ... Oct. 25, 1848. Boston. J. R. Lowell.
Chanticleer. New York, 1850. C. Mathews.
Charleston Book, The. Charleston, 1845. W. G. Simms.
Child of Bristowe, The. Cambridge. 1886. F. J. Child.
Chimes of Freedom and Union. Boston, 1861. J. G. Whittier.
Choice Thoughts from Shakespeare. London, 1886. J. Bartlett.
Christmas Gift from Fairyland, A. New York. J. K. Paulding.
Chronicles of Cooperstown, The. Cooperstown, 1838. J. F. Cooper.
City and the Sea, The. Cambridge, 1881. H. W. Longfellow.
Clark, Geo. H. The Liberty Minstrel. New York, 1844. J. G. Whittier.
Clarke, James Freeman. Commemoration of 50th Birthday. Boston, 1860. O. W. Holmes.
Clarke, James Freeman. Commemoration of 70th Birthday. Boston, 1880. O. W. Holmes.
Class of 1829. Songs and Poems. Boston, 1854, 1868, 1881, 1889. O. W. Holmes.
Class Poem. 1838. J. R. Lowell.
Club-Room, The. Boston, 1820. W. H. Prescott.
Coggeshall, W. T. The Poets and Poetry of the West. Columbus, 1860. W. D. Howells.
Collegian, The. Cambridge, 1830. O. W. Holmes.
Collins, John. The Anti-Slavery Picknick. Boston, 1840. J. G. Whittier.
Columbus, Christopher. Memorial. Boston, 1893. J. Fiske.
Concord. Celebration .... 250th Anniversary. Concord, 1885. J. R. Lowell.
Concord Fight. Centennial Celebration. ... Concord, 1876. J. R. Lowell.
Concord. Free Public Library. Dedication. ... Concord, 1873. R. W. Emerson.
Concord. Social Circle. Centennial .... Cambridge, 1882. R. W. Emerson.
Concord. Soldiers' Monument. Dedication .... Concord, 1867. R. W. Emerson.
Confessions of a Poet, The. Philadelphia, 1835. L. Osborn.

Connecticut, Sketch of. Hartford, 1814. L. H. Sigourney.
Considerations on some Recent Social Theories. Boston, 1853. C. E. Norton.
Controversy touching the Old Stone Mill. Newport, 1851. C. T. Brooks.
Cooper, J. F. Memorial. New York, 1852. W. C. Bryant.
Copperheads, Ye Book of. Philadelphia, 1863. C. G. Leland.
Crayon, The. New York, 1855-61. W. J. Stillman.
Damon's Ghost. Boston, 1881. E. L. Bynner.
Daughter of the Philistines, A. Boston, 1883. H. H. Boyesen.
Desmond Hundred, The. Boston, 1882. J. G. Austin.
Dial, The. Boston, 1840-44. R. W. Emerson.
Dickens, Charles. Mystery of Edwin Drood .... Boston, 1870. J. T. Fields.
Dickens, Charles. Report of the Dinner to. Boston, 1842. O. W. Holmes.
Dinsmoor, Robert. Incidental Poems. . . . Haverhill, 1828. J. G. Whittier.
Dobson, Austin. Vignettes in Rhyme. New York, 1880. E. C. Stedman.
Dora Darling. Boston, 1865. J. G. Austin.
Dove and the Eagle, The. Boston, 1851. G. Lunt.
Dusenbury, B. M. Monument to .... Andrew Jackson. Nashua, 1846. G. Bancroft.
Duyckinck, E. A. Fitz-Greene Halleck Memorial. New York, 1871. B. Taylor.
East and West. Philadelphia, 1836. F. W. Thomas.
Elegy on the Late Titus Hosmer, An. Hartford, 1780. J. Barlow.
Emerson. Cambridge. 1865. A. B. Alcott.
Ephemera. Boston, 1852. G. E. Rice.
Estray, The. Boston, 1847. H. W. Longfellow.
Fable for Critics, A. New York, 1848. J. R. Lowell.
Fair Play. Waltham. O. W. Holmes.
Fanny. New York, 1819. Fitz-Greene Halleck.
Fanshawe. Boston, 1828. N. Hawthorne.
Farmer and Soldier, The. Hartford, 1833. L. H. Sigourney.
Felton, Cornelius C. Addresses at Inauguration .... Cambridge, 1860. O. W. Holmes.
Few Verses for a Few Friends, A. J. T. Fields.
Fields, James T. Boston, 1881. A. Fields.
Fifteen Days. Boston, 1866. M. L. Putnam.
First of the Knickerbockers, The. New York, 1848. P. H Myers.
First Ten Cantos of the Inferno, The. Boston, 1843. T. W. Parsons.
Forest and Stream Fables. New York, 1886. R. E. Robinson.
Forsaken, The. Philadelphia, 1831. R. P. Smith.
Four Old Plays. Cambridge, 1848. F. J. Child.
Fox, C. J. History of Dunstable. . . . Nashua, 1846. O. W. Holmes.
Francis Berrian. Boston, 1826. T. Flint.
Francis, J. W., Jr. Memorial. New York, 1855. H. T. Tuckerman.
Fresh Leaves. T. G. Appleton.
Frothingham, O. B. Reception. . . . April 22, 1879. New York, 1879. E. C. Stedman.
Full Statement .... respecting Abolitionists and Anti-Slavery Societies. Boston, 1836. J. G. Whittier.

Fuller, George. Life and Works. Boston, 1886. W. D. Howells.
Furbish, Julia A. M. The Flower of Liberty. Boston, 1866. O. W. Holmes.
Fuz-Buz, The Wonderful Story of. Philadelphia, 1867. S. W. Mitchell.
Garfield. [Memorial] Meeting. . . . Exter Hall. . . . London, 1881. J. R. Lowell.
Garfield. The Poets' Tribute. Cambridge, 1881. O. W. Holmes.
Garrison, William Lloyd. Selections from. . . . Writings. Boston, 1852. J. R. Lowell.
Garrison, W. L. Tributes at the Funeral Services. Boston, 1879. J. G. Whittier.
Glory of Columbia, The. New York, 1803. W. Dunlap.
Golden-Rod. New York, 1880. C. C. Harrison.
Good Gray Poet, The. New York, 1866. W. D. O'Connor.
Gotham and the Gothamites. New York, 1823. S. M. B. Judah.
Great Auction Sale of Slaves at Savannah, March, 1859. New York. M. M. Thompson.
Gunderode. Boston, 1842. S. M. Fuller.
Hadley, Mass. 200th Anniversary. Northampton, 1859. W. C. Bryant.
Harbinger, The. Boston, 1833. O. W. Holmes.
Harrington. Boston, 1860. W. D. O'Connor.
Harvard Advocate, Verses from. New York, 1876. R. Grant.
Harvard Book, The. Boston, 1878. O. W. Holmes.
Harvard Club, N. Y. Celebration. . . . Feb., 1878. New York, 1878. O. W. Holmes.
Harvard College. Record of Commemoration. . . . Nov., 1886. Cambridge, 1887. J. R. Lowell.
Harvard College. Services. . . . Oct. 6, 1870. O. W. Holmes.
Harvardiana. Cambridge, 1838. J. R. Lowell.
Harvard Medical School. The New Century and the New Building. Cambridge, 1884. O. W. Holmes.
Harvard Memorial Biographies. Cambridge, 1865. T. W. Higginson.
Harvard Register. Cambridge, 1827-28. O. W. Holmes.
Hasheesh Eater, The. New York, 1857. F. H. Ludlow.
Hatfield, E. F. Freedom's Lyre. New York, 1840. J. G. Whittier.
Haverhill, Mass. . . . Commemoration. . . . 250th Anniversary. Boston, 1891. J. G. Whittier.
Hawks of Hawk Hollow, The. Philadelphia, 1835. R. M. Bird.
Hetty's Strange History. Boston, 1877. H. H. Jackson.
His Second Campaign. Boston, 1883. M. Thompson.
Hooper, Lucy. Poetical Remains. New York, 1842. J. G. Whittier.
Humboldt, Alexander von. Life, Travels and Books. New York, 1860. R. H. Stoddard.
Idle Man, The. New York, 1821-22. R. H. Dana.
Il Pesceballo. J. R. Lowell.
Inauguration of the Statue of Liberty. New York, 1887. J. G. Whittier.
Indian Fairy Book, The. C. Mathews.
Inklings of Adventure. London, 1836. N. P. Willis.
Irving, Washington. Commemoration. . . . 100th Anniversary. New York, 1884. D. G. Mitchell.

Jefferson, The Youth of. New York, 1854. J. E. Cooke.
Joan of Arc. 1860. G. H. Calvert.
Jokeby. New York, 1813. J. K. Paulding.
Jubilee Days. Boston, 1872. T. B. Aldrich.
Katherine Walton. Philadelphia, 1851. W. G. Simms.
Keats, John. Poetical Works. Boston, 1854. J. R. Lowell.
Kendall, James. Sermon at the Ordination of Hersey B. Goodwin. . . . . Concord, 1830. R. W. Emerson.
Kenoza Club House. . . . Dedication. . . . Haverhill, 1859. J. G. Whittier.
Kettell, Samuel. Specimens of American Poetry. Boston, 1829. J. G. Whittier.
King, Thomas Starr. Character and Genius of. E. P. Whipple.
King, Thomas Starr. Patriotism and other Papers. Boston, 1864. J. G. Whittier.
King's Chapel, Boston. Commemoration. . . . 200th Anniversary. Boston, 1887. O. W. Holmes.
King's Chapel, Boston. Commemorative Services. . . . Dec. 15, 1886. O. W. Holmes.
Koningsmarke. New York, 1823. J. K. Paulding.
Kossuth in New England. Boston, 1852. R. W. Emerson.
Lafayette, General. Outlines of Principal Events in Life of. Boston, 1825. G. Ticknor.
Lambs, The. Boston, 1883. R. Grant.
Lanier, J. F. D. Sketch of the Life of. New York. S. Lanier.
Laurel, The. Boston, 1836. J. G. Whittier.
Lay of the Scottish Fiddle, The. New York, 1813. J. K. Paulding.
Leaves from Margaret Smith's Journal. Boston, 1849. J. G. Whittier.
Leaves from the Diary of a Dreamer. London, 1853. H. T. Tuckerman.
Le Ministre de Wakefield. Boston, 1831. H. W. Longfellow.
Lessing, G. E. Nathan the Wise. New York, 1868. H. H. Jackson.
Letheon, Some Account of the. . . . Boston, 1847. O. W. Holmes.
Letters from the South. New York, 1817. J. K. Paulding.
Letters from Virginia. Baltimore, 1816. J. K. Paulding.
Letters on the Eastern States. New York, 1825. W. Tudor.
Letter to the President of the Archæological Institute. Boston, 1884. C. E. Norton.
Lexington, A Tale of. New York, 1823. S. M. B. Judah.
Lexington. Centennial Celebration. Lexington, 1875. J. G. Whittier.
Lexington. Souvenir. Boston, 1875. J. G. Whittier.
Liberty Chimes. Providence, 1845. J. R. Lowell.
Life on the Lakes. New York, 1839. T. B. Thorpe.
Light, Geo. W. The Young American's Magazine. Boston, 1847. J. R. Lowell.
Lincoln, Abraham. Memorial. Boston, 1865. O. W. Holmes.
Linn, John Blair. Valerian. Philadelphia, 1805. C. B. Brown.
Logan. Philadelphia, 1822. J. Neal.
Lothrop, S. K. Discourse before the Ancient and Honorable Artillery Company. Boston, 1861. O. W. Holmes.
Loud, Mrs. M. St. Leon. Wayside Flowers. Boston, 1851. P. Benjamin.

Lovejoy, J. C. Memoir of C. T. Torrey. Boston, 1847. J. G. Whittier.
Lowell Offering, The. Lowell, 1840-45. Lucy Larcom.
Lowell Putnam. Cambridge, 1863. M. L. Putnam.
Lyteria. Boston, 1854. J. P. Quincy.
Macdonough, A. R. The Lovers of Provence. New York. E. C. Stedman.
Manuel de Proverbes Dramatiques. Portland, 1830. H. W. Longfellow.
Manuscript Corrections from . . . . Shakespeare's Plays. Boston, 1854. J. P. Quincy.
Markham, Pauline. Life . . . . New York, 1871. R. G. White.
Marshall, Charles H. Memorial. New York, 1867. W. A. Butler.
Martineau, Harriet. Views of Slavery and Emancipation. New York, 1837. J. G. Whittier.
Martin Faber. New York, 1833. W. G. Simms.
Mason and Slidell. J. R. Lowell.
Masque of Poets, A. Boston, 1878. G. P. Lathrop.
Massachusetts Historical Society. Lectures by Members of . . . Boston, 1869. O. W. Holmes.
Massachusetts Historical Society. Proceedings, 1870, 1887, J. R. Lowell; 1871, 1874, 1878, 1879, 1882, 1888, 1889, O. W. Holmes; 1881, J. G. Whittier; and 1893, F. Parkman.
Massachusetts Historical Society. Special Meetings, Dec. 1859, H. W. Longfellow; Dec. 1873, O. W. Holmes.
Massachusetts Historical Society. Tributes, Edward Everett, 1865 and George Livermore, 1866, O. W. Holmes; Edmund Quincy and J. L. Motley, 1877, J. R. Lowell; W. C. Bryant, 1878, W. C. Bryant; and Longfellow and Emerson, 1882, R. W. Emerson.
Massachusetts Quarterly Review. Boston, 1847-50. R. W. Emerson.
McLellan. How McLellan took Manassas. New York, 1865. G. H. Boker.
McLellan's Own Story. New York, 1887. W. C. Prime.
Memorial: R. G. S. Cambridge, 1864. J. R. Lowell.
Mercy Philbrick's Choice. Boston, 1876. H. H. Jackson.
Merry Mount. Boston, 1849. J. L. Motley.
Modern Mephistopheles, A. Boston, 1877. L. M. Alcott.
Moll Pitcher. Boston, 1832. J. G. Whittier.
Monaldi. Boston, 1841. W. Allston.
Morton of Morton's Hope. London, 1839. J. L. Motley.
Mount Vernon: a Letter. New York, 1859. S. F. Cooper.
Mr. Jacobs. Boston, 1883. A. Bates.
Mrs. Beauchamp Brown. Boston, 1880. J. G. Austin.
Mrs. Limber's Raffle. New York, 1877. W. A. Butler.
My Mother's Gold Ring. Boston, 1833. L. M. Sargent.
Nameless Nobleman, A. Boston, 1881. J. G. Austin.
Narrative of Arthur Gordon Pym. New York, 1838. E. A. Poe.
Narrative of James Williams. New York, 1838. J. G. Whittier.
Nature. Boston, 1836. R. W. Emerson.
Nautilus. O. W. Holmes.
Near Home. Boston, 1858. W. E. Channing.
Newark, N. J. Proceedings. . . . 200th Anniversary. Newark, 1866. T. Ward.

New Gospel of Peace, The. New York, 1863-66. R. G. White.
New King Arthur, The. New York, 1885. E. Fawcett.
New Priest in Conception Bay, The. Boston, 1858. R. T. S. Lowell.
New Travels through North America. Boston, 1784. P. Freneau.
New York Book of Poetry, The. New York, 1837. C. F. Hoffman.
New York Historical Society. Report on a National Name. 1845. C F. Hoffman.
New York Historical Society. Proceedings.... 1843. C. F. Hoffman.
New York Historical Society. Semi-Centennial Celebration. New York, 1854. G. Bancroft.
New York Medical Journal. April, 1871. O. W. Holmes.
New York Review and Athenæum. 1825-26. W. C. Bryant.
Nile Notes of a Howadji. New York, 1851. G. W. Curtis.
Nimport, Boston, 1877. E. L. Bynner.
North American Review. April, 1840; July, 1857. O. W. Holmes.
North Star, The. Philadelphia, 1840. J. G. Whittier.
Nothing to Wear. New York, 1857. W. A. Butler.
Novelas Españolas. Brunswick, 1830. H. W. Longfellow.
Oasis, The. Boston, 1834. J. G. Whittier.
Official Monthly Bulletin. . . . Musical Festival. Boston, 1869. O. W. Holmes.
Old House by the River, The. New York, 1853. W. C. Prime.
One Summer. Boston, 1875. B. W. Howard.
Only Once. New York. W. C. Bryant.
Osgood, Mrs. Memorial. New York, 1851. N. Hawthorne.
Ossoli, Margaret Fuller. Memoirs. Boston, 1852. R. W. Emerson.
Our Chronicle of '26. Boston, 1827. G. Mellen.
Our Pastor's Offering. Boston, 1845. R. W. Emerson.
Outcroppings. San Francisco, 1866. Bret Harte.
Outre Mer Boston 1833-34. H. W. Longfellow.
Parker, Theodore. Tributes. . . . Boston. 1860. R. W. Emerson.
Passage to India. Washington, 1871. W. Whitman.
Passion Flowers. Boston, 1854. J. W. Howe.
Patty's Perversities. Boston, 1881. A. Bates.
Peabody, Elizabeth P. Æsthetic Papers. Boston, 1849. N. Hawthorne.
Peirce, Benjamin. Cambridge, 1881. O. W. Holmes.
Percy's Masque. New York, 1820. J. A. Hillhouse.
Peter Parley's Universal History. Boston, 1837. N. Hawthorne.
Peter Pilgrim. Philadelphia. 1838. R. M. Bird.
Philadelphia Book, The. Philadelphia, 1836. H. T. Tuckerman.
Phillips Academy Alumni . . . . Speeches at First Dinner. Boston, 1886. O. W. Holmes.
Phillips, Wendell. Memorial. Boston, 1884. G. W. Curtis.
Pilgrims, National Monument to the. Proceedings on Completion. . . . Plymouth, 1889. J. B. O'Reilly.
Planchette. Boston, 1869. E. Sargent.
Poe, E. A. Dedication of the Actors' Monument, May 4, 1885. W. Winter.
Poem and Valedictory Oration. New Haven, 1861. E. R. Sill.
Poem on the Rising Glory of America. Philadelphia, 1772. P. Freneau.
Poems. New York, 1841. R. W. Griswold.

Poems of Religious Sorrow. New York, 1863. F. J. Child.
Poem spoken at . . . . Yale, Sept. 17, 1781. Hartford. J. Barlow.
Potiphar Papers, The. New York, 1853. G. W. Curtis.
Power of Cotton, The. New York, 1856. . G. WSimms.
Precaution. New York, 1820. J. F. Cooper.
Prince of Wales . . . . New England Tour . . . . Reception, etc. Boston, 1860. O. W. Holmes.
Prince Oscar at the National Celebration . . . . Boston, 1876. O. W. Holmes.
Probus. New York, 1838. W. Ware.
Proctor, Adelaide A. The Victoria Regia. London, 1861. J. R. Lowell.
Prospectus of a National Institution . . . . Washington, 1806. J. Barlow.
Prospectus of a New Periodical. New York, 1833. J. H. Payne.
Pumpelly, Mary H. Poems. New York, 1852. N. P. Willis.
Pym, Arthur Gordon, Narrative of. New York, 1838. E. A. Poe.
Quest of the Holy Grail, The. London, 1895. H. James.
Radicalism in Religion, Philosophy and Social Life. Boston, 1858. G. Lunt.
Reconstruction Letter, A. New York, 1866. E. C. Stedman.
Record, Literary and Political, ... 1813. New York. W. Dunlap.
Record of an Obscure Man. Boston, 1861. M. L. Putnam.
Redpath, James. Echoes of Harper's Ferry. Boston, 1860. H. D. Thoreau.
Report of the Proceedings of Professed Spiritual Agents. Boston, 1859. G. Lunt.
Requiem to the . . . . Slain in Battle. G. Lunt.
Richard Edney and the Governor's Family. Boston, 1850. S. Judd.
Rill from the Town Pump, A. London, 1857. N. Hawthorne.
Rob of the Bowl. Philadelphia, 1838. J. P. Kennedy.
Rodolph. Baltimore, 1823. E. C. Pinkney.
Roger Camerden. New York, 1886. J. K. Bangs.
Rollo's Journey to Cambridge. Boston, 1880. F. J. Stimson.
Romero, Señor Matias. Dinner . . . . New York, 1866. W. C. Bryant.
Ruins of Pœstum, The. Salem, 1822. H. Pickering.
Sack and Destruction of Columbia, S. C. Columbia, 1865. W. G. Simms.
Sargent, Mrs. J. T. Sketches . . . . . of the Radical Club. Boston, 1880. R. W. Emerson.
Scenery of the Pacific Railways. New York. W. H. Rideing.
Seaweeds from the Shores of Nantucket. Boston, 1853. C. F. Briggs.
Sedgwick, Major-General. Dedication of Statue. New York, 1869. G. W. Curtis.
Sergeant Von. New York, 1889. W. H. Bishop.
Seven Little People and their Friends. New York, 1862. H. E. Scudder.
Seventeen Cantos of the Inferno. Boston, 1865. T. W. Parsons.
Seventy-six. Baltimore, 1823. J. Neal.
Sewall, Samuel. Diary of. Boston, 1878-82. J. R. Lowell.

Shea, John Gilmary. The Lincoln Memorial. New York, 1865. R. W. Emerson.
Shepard Lee. Philadelphia, 1836. R. M. Bird.
Sir Rohan's Ghost. Boston, 1860. H. P. Spofford.
Sixty Years of the Life of Jeremy Levis. New York, 1831. L. Osborn.
Smith, Margaret . . . . Journal in Massachusetts Bay. Boston, 1849. J. G. Whittier.
Smith, Roswell. A Memory of. New York. G. W. Cable.
Society of the Army of the Potomac. Reports of Annual Re-Unions: 1872, B. Harte; 1873, E. C. Stedman; 1877, W. Winter; 1878, R. H. Stoddard; 1888, G. W. Curtis.
Songs of '71. New York, 1871. B. Matthews.
Songs of the Free. Boston, 1836. J. G. Whittier.
Songs of the Unity. Boston, 1859. J. Winsor.
Spenser, Edmund. Poetical Works. Boston, 1855. F. J. Child.
Spirit of the Fair. New York, 1864. J. R. Lowell.
Stories from the Persian. Cambridge, 1887. F. J. Child.
Stranger in Lowell, The. Boston, 1845. J. G. Whittier.
Sturge, Joseph. A Visit to the United States. London, 1842. J. G. Whittier.
Sumner, Charles. A Memorial. Boston, 1874. J. G. Whittier.
Swallow Barn. Philadelphia, 1832. J. P. Kennedy.
Sydney Clifton. New York, 1839. T. S. Fay.
Tales of an Indian Camp. London, 1830. J. A. Jones.
Tales of the North West. Boston, 1830. W. J. Snelling.
Talisman, The. New York, 1827-28-29. W. C. Bryant.
Tallahassee Girl, A. New York, 1882. M. Thompson.
Tardy George. New York, 1865. G. H. Boker.
Thackeray, W. M. Early and Late Papers. Boston, 1867. J. T. Fields.
Thalatta. Boston, 1853. T. W. Higginson.
That Girl of Mine. Philadelphia, 1877. M. F. Egan.
That Lover of Mine. Philadelphia, 1877. M. F. Egan.
Thirty Years Ago. New York, 1836. W. Dunlap.
Tragedy of Errors. Boston, 1862. M. L. Putnam.
Tragedy of Success. Boston, 1862. M. L. Putnam.
Traits of the Aborigines of America. Cambridge, 1822. L. H. Sigourney.
Transplanted Daisy, The. New York, 1865. L. H. Sigourney.
Triangular Society, The. Portland, 1886. E. C. Akers.
Troubled Heart, A. Notre Dame, 1885. C. W. Stoddard.
Truth. Boston, 1831. W. J. Snelling.
Two Years before the Mast. New York, 1840. R. H. Dana, Jr.
Union, The. Boston, 1860. G. Lunt.
United States and England, The. New York, 1815. J. K. Paulding.
United States Literary Gazette. Boston, 1825-26. H. W. Longfellow.
United States Literary Gazette. Miscellaneous Poems selected from. Boston, 1826. W. C. Bryant.
United States Review and Literary Gazette. Boston, 1826-27. W. C. Bryant.
Valentine, D. Obsequies of Abraham Lincoln. New York, 1866. W. C. Bryant.

Variegated Leaves. Boston, 1873. J. T. Fields.
Verses occasioned by .... Answer of the President .... Boston, 1797. J. M. Sewall.
Village Merchant, The. Philadelphia, 1794. P. Freneau.
Vision of Rubeta, The. Boston, 1838. L. Osborn.
Visit to the Celestial City, A. Philadelphia. N. Hawthorne.
Voices from the Press. New York, 1850. W. Whitman.
Waif, The. Boston, 1845. H. W. Longfellow.
Wandering Boys, The. Boston, 1821. M. M. Noah.
Ward's Statue of Shakespeare. ... Inauguration. New York, 1873. W. C. Bryant.
Ware, Rev. Henry. Sermon at Ordination of Rev. Chandler Robbins. Boston, 1833. R. W. Emerson.
Warren, William. 50th Anniversary. 1882. W. Winter.
War-Songs for Freemen. Boston, 1862. F. J. Child.
Washington Centenary, The. April-May, 1889. New York. J. G. Whittier.
Waterston, Helen Ruthven. Boston, 1860. H. B. Stowe.
Weal-Reaf, The. Salem, 1860. N. Hawthorne.
Webster, Daniel. 74th Anniversary. Boston, 1856. O. W. Holmes.
Week Away from Time, A. Boston, 1887. A. Fields.
Wensley. Boston, 1854. E. Quincy.
Weston, E. P. The Bowdoin Poets. Brunswick, 1840. H. W. Longfellow.
Where will it end? Providence, 1863. E. Quincy.
Wieland. New York, 1798. C. B. Brown.
Wild-Goose-Chace, The. New York, 1800. W. Dunlap.
Williams, James. Narrative of. New York, 1838. J. G. Whittier.
Winter Poems. Boston, 1871. J. G. Whittier.
Woman's Poems, A. Boston, 1871. S. M. B. Piatt.
Wordsworth, William. Poetical Works. Boston, 1854. J. R. Lowell.
Zenobia. New York, 1837. W. Ware.

www.ingramcontent.com/pod-product-compliance
Lightning Source LLC
Chambersburg PA
CBHW020230240426
43672CB00006B/479